AF483178

R. Gupta's®

Joint CSIR-UGC NET

Junior Research Fellowship & Eligibility for Lectureship

Physical Sciences

Practice Test Papers

(Solved)

By
RPH Editorial Board

RAMESH PUBLISHING HOUSE, New Delhi

Published by
O.P. Gupta *for* Ramesh Publishing House

Admin. Office
12-H, New Daryaganj Road, Opp. Officers' Mess,
New Delhi-110002 ✆ 23261567, 23275224, 23275124

E-mail: info@rameshpublishinghouse.com
Website: www.rameshpublishinghouse.com

Showroom
- Balaji Market, Nai Sarak, Delhi-6 ✆ 23253720, 23282525
- 4457, Nai Sarak, Delhi-6, ✆ 23918938

© Reserved with the Publisher

No Part of this book may be reproduced or transmitted in any form or by any means, electronic or mechanical including photocopying, recording or by any transformation storage and retrieval system without written permission from the Publisher.

Indemnification Clause: ***This book is being sold/distributed subject to the exclusive condition that neither the author nor the publishers, individually or collectively, shall be responsible to indemnify the buyer/user/possessor of this book beyond the selling price of this book for any reason under any circumstances. If you do not agree to it, please do not buy/accept/use/possess this book.***

Book Code: R-1879

ISBN: 978-93-86298-64-5

HSN Code: 49011010

PHYSICAL SCIENCES

SCHEME OF EXAM

CSIR-UGC (NET) Exam for Award of Junior Research Fellowship and Eligibility for Lecturership shall be a Single paper Test having Multiple Choice Question (MCQs). The question paper is divided into three parts:

Part 'A': This part shall carry 20 questions pertaining to General Science, Quantitative Reasoning & Analysis and Research Aptitude. The candidates shall be required to answer any 15 questions. Each question shall be of two marks. The total marks allocated to this section shall be 30 out of 200.

Part 'B': This part shall contain 25 Multiple Choice Questions (MCQs) generally covering the topics given in the Part 'A' of syllabus. Each question shall be of 3.5 Marks. The total marks allocated to this section shall be 70 out of 200. Candidates are required to answer any 20 questions.

Part 'C': This part shall contain 30 questions from Part 'B' and Part 'A' that are designed to test a candidate's knowledge of scientific concepts and/or application of the scientific concepts. The questions shall be of analytical nature where a candidate is expected to apply the scientific knowledge to arrive at the solution to the given scientific problem. A candidate shall be required to answer any 20. Each question shall be of 5 marks. The total marks allocated to this section shall be 100 out of 200.

➤ There will be negative marking @25% for each wrong answer.

CONTENTS

10 PRACTICE SETS (Solved)

Set–1 3-22

Set–2 23-42

Set–3 43-61

Set–4 62-80

Set–5 81-99

Set–6 100-119

Set–7 120-137

Set–8 138-155

Set–9 156-174

Set–10 175-196

CSIR-UGC TEST FOR JRF & NET EXAM

PHYSICAL SCIENCES

10 Practice Sets

SET–1

CSIR–UGC (NET) PHYSICAL SCIENCES

PART-A

1. A large tank filled with water is to be emptied by removing half of water present in it everyday. After how many days will there be closest to 10% water left in the tank?

A. Three B. One
C. Five D. Two

2. For a particle moving along a straight line, the displacement x depends on time t as $x = \alpha t^3 + \beta t^2 + \gamma t + 8$. The ratio of its initial acceleration to its initial velocity depends.

A. Only on α and β B. Only on β and γ
C. Only on α and γ D. Only on α

3. In a certain code 'ni ra ge' stands for 'who are you', 'bio wo dur' stands for 'going far away' and 'wo ge chi' stands for 'you went away'. Which of the following in the code for 'went'?

A. chi B. ra
C. boi D. wo

4. Which one number can be placed at the sign (?) of interrogation?

15	6	5
13	3	9
8	2	?
20	7	13

A. 0 B. 1
C. 2 D. 3

5. If FACE is coded as GBDF, the BADE will be coded as

A. CBFE B. CEBF
C. CBEF D. CEFB

6. Sony remembers that her mother's birthday is after seventeenth April but before twenty-first April, whereas her sister Mini remembers that their mother's brother is after nineteenth but before twenty-fourth April. Which of the following days in April is definitely their mother's birthday?

A. Twenty-second B. Twenty-first
C. Twentieth D. Nineteenth

7. If Δ means square the first number and then multiply it by the next number and $\square$ means multiply the product with the second number and subtract the second number from the product of the two numbers then find the value of $2 \; \Delta \; 3 \; \square \; 5$?

A. 60 B. 55
C. 45 D. 40

8. The ratio between two numbers is 3 : 4. If each number be increased by 2, the ratio becomes 7 : 9. Find the numbers.

A. 15, 18 B. 12, 16
C. 18, 21 D. 23, 24

9. If three cubes of iron, each with an edge of 6 cm, 8 cm and 10 cm respectively, are melted to form a single cube, then find the diagonal of the new cube.

A. 15.3 cm B. 16.7 cm
C. 20.8 cm D. 29.6 cm

10. An ant is crawling along the x-axis such that the graph of its position in the x-axis versus time is a semicircle (fig.) The total distance covered in the 4s is

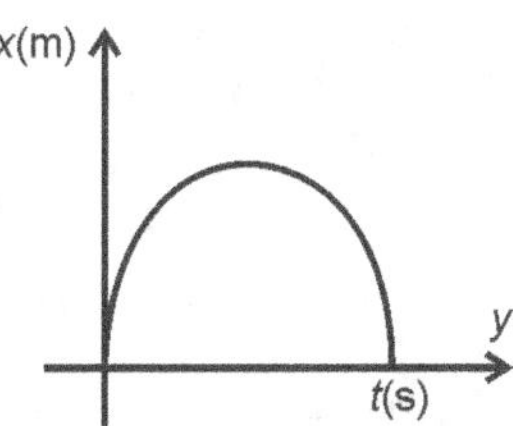

A. 2 m B. 2π m
C. 4π m D. 4 m

11. Which one number can be place at the sign of interrogation?

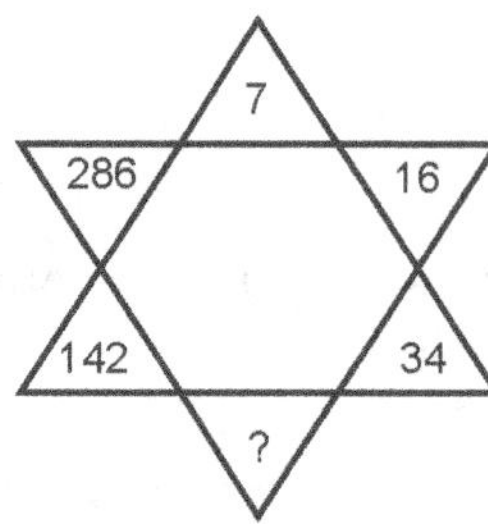

A. 68 B. 70
C. 92 D. 56

12. A sphere of metal of radius $\frac{R}{2}$ fixed to one end of a string was lowered into water in a cylindrical container of base radius R to keep exactly half the sphere dipped. The rise in the level of water in the container will be

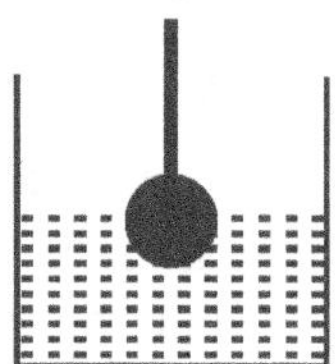

A. $\frac{R}{12}$ B. $\frac{R}{9}$

C. $\frac{R}{5}$ D. $\frac{R}{7}$

13. Which of the following numbers is the largest:

$2^{3^4}, 2^{4^3}, 3^{2^4}, 3^{4^2}, 4^{2^3}, 4^{3^2}$

A. 3^{4^2} B. 2^{3^4}

C. 4^{3^2} D. 2^{4^3}

14. What is the number of rectangles in the figure given below?

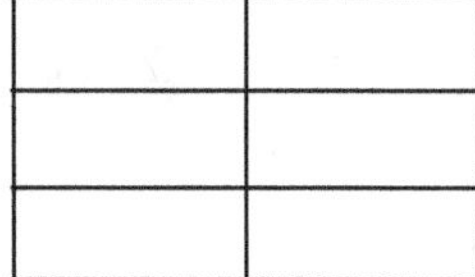

A. 14 B. 11
C. 16 D. 10

15. The diameter of a coin is 1 cm. If four of these coins be placed on a table so that the rim of each touches that of the other two, find the area of the unoccupied space between them. [Take π = 3.1416]

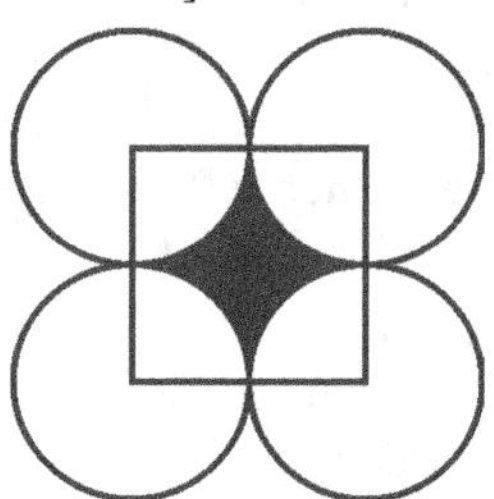

A. 0.235 sq cm B. 0.215 sq cm
C. 0.125 sq cm D. 0.199 sq cm

16. If 15 apples and 20 oranges cost as much as 20 apples and 15 oranges which of the following conclusions is correct.

A. Orange and apple have identical prices
B. Orange's price is double that of apple
C. No conclusion can be drawn
D. Apple is cheaper than orange

17. The sides AB, BC, CA of a triangle ABC have 3, 5 and 6 interior points respectively on them. The number of triangles that can be constructed using these points as vertices is given by

A. 333 B. 340
C. 351 D. 365

18. There is a road beside a river. Two friends started from a place A, moved to a temple situated at another place B and then returned to A again. One of them moves on a cycle at a speed of 12 km/hr, while other sails on a boat at the speed of 10 km/hr. If the river flows at the speed of 4 km/hr, then which of the two friends will return to place A first?

A. Cyclist
B. Boat sailor
C. Both in same time
D. None of these

19. Vinod, Virendra and Rohilla are three friends, one of whom is a player, another is dancer and third is a singer. Vinod is the shortest, the tallest person is player. One dancer's height is the geometric mean of the heights of the other two. Then which of the following is true?

A. Vinod is a player and he is the tallest
B. Virendra is singer and he is the tallest
C. Rohilla is dancer and he is the shortest
D. Rohilla is player and he is the tallest

20. Three particles A, B and C are thrown from the top of a tower with the same speed. A is thrown straight up, B is thrown straight down and C is thrown horizontally. They hit the grand with speeds v_A, v_B and v_C respectively.

A. $v_A = v_B = v_C$ B. $v_B > v_C > v_A$
C. $v_A = v_B > v_C$ D. $v_A > v_B = v_C$

PART-B

21. A cannon shell lands 2 km away from the cannon. A second shell, fired identically, breaks into two equal parts at the highest point. One part falls vertically. How far from the cannon will the other land?

A. 2 km B. 3 km
C. 4 km D. 5 km

22. In the op-amp circuit shown in Fig. the input voltage V_i is 1V. The value of the output V_o is

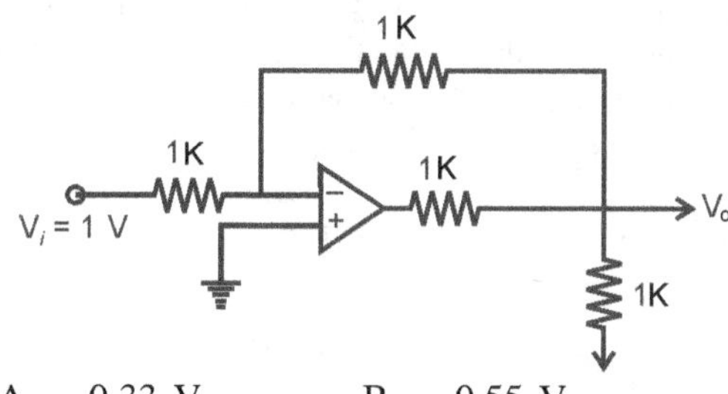

A. – 0.33 V B. – 0.55 V
C. – 1.00 V D. – 0.25 V

23.

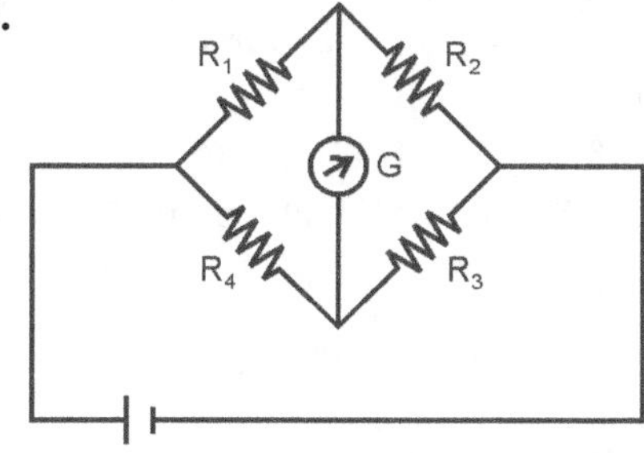

The Wheatstone bridge shown in the above figure is balanced. If the positions of the cell C and the galvanometer G are now interchanged, G will show zero deflection

A. in all cases
B. only if all the resistances are equal
C. only if $R_1 = R_3$ and $R_2 = R_4$
D. only if $R_1/R_3 = R_2/R_4$

24. The matrix A is defined as

$$A = \begin{bmatrix} 1 & 2 & -3 \\ 0 & 3 & 2 \\ 0 & 0 & -2 \end{bmatrix}$$

Find the eigen values of $3A^3 + 5A^2 - 6A + 2I$.

A. 2, 105, 5 B. 4, 110, 10
C. 5, 84, 52 D. 3, 90, 7

25. The mean free path of nitrogen molecules at 0°C and one atmospheric pressure is 8 μm. Concentration at this temperature and pressure is 2.7×10^{25}. The molecular diameter is

A. 3.2×10^{-11} m B. 1.6×10^{-11} m
C. 1.1×10^{-10} m D. 0.9×10^{-12} m

26. The frequency of oscillation of a hydrogen molecule, if its force constant is 4.8×10^2 Nm^{-1} and mass of hydrogen atom = 1.67×10^{-27} kg is

A. 1.5×10^{23} Hz B. 1.2×10^{24} Hz
C. 1.9×10^{24} Hz D. 2.3×10^{23} Hz

27. A half wave rectifier is used to supply 50 V DC to a resistive load of 800 Ω. The diode has a resistance of 250 Ω. AC voltage required is

A. 110 V B. 139 V
C. 162 V D. 180 V

28. In an amplifier, the output power 1.5 watts at 2 kHz and 0.3 watt at 20 Hz, while the input power is constant at 10 mW. Calculate by how many decibels gain at 20 kHz is below that at 2 kHz?

A. 6.99 dB B. 2.45 dB
C. 3.49 dB D. 4.05 dB

29. For the circuit shown in Fig., find the current flowing through the 1 Ω resistor. Assume that the two diodes, D_1 and D_2 are ideal diodes.

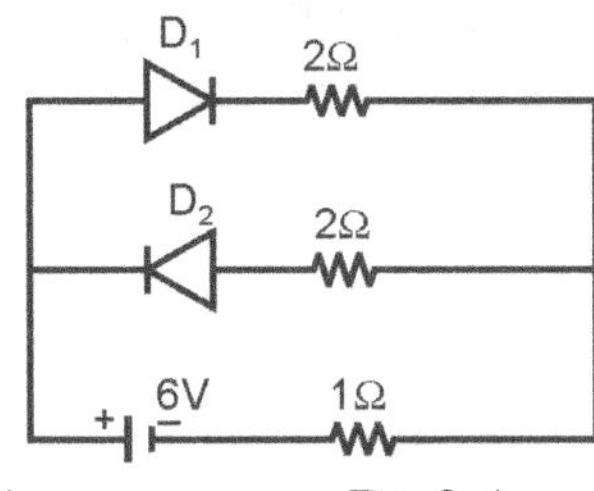

A. 5 A B. 2 A
C. 4 A D. 1 A

30. For a gas the critical pressure is 12.8 atm and the critical volume for the mole 70×10^{-6} m³. The vander Waal's constants of the gas and its critical temperature: 1 atm = 10^{-5} Nm^{-2} is

A. 18.8 K B. 28.8 K
C. 31.2 K D. 39.6 K

31. The emitted radiant energy from a piece of metal is measured and the temperature is found to be 1065° assuming a surface emissivity of 0.82. It was later found out that the true emissivity is 0.75. The error in temperature measurement is

A. –10°C B. –15°C
C. –30°C D. –40°C

32. The radiations given off by the Hg atoms returning to their normal states were studied by Frank and Hertz and a line was observed at 2537 Å. The excitation potential for Hg is

A. 3.5 V B. 4.9 V
C. 1.2 V D. 2.4 V

33. Using Green's theorem evaluate $\int_c (x^2 y dx + x^2 dy)$, where c is the boundary described counter clockwise of the triangle with vertices (0, 0), (1, 0) (1, 1).

A. $\frac{5}{12}$ B. $\frac{3}{4}$
C. $\frac{1}{12}$ D. $\frac{4}{21}$

34. Two electrons moved towards each other, the speed of each being 0.9 c in a Galilean frame of reference. What is their speed relative to each other?

A. – 0.995 c B. – 0.543 c
C. – 0.764 c D. – 0.154 c

35. When light of a given wavelength is incident on a metallic surface, the stopping potential for the photoelectrons is 3.2 V. If a second light source whose wavelength is double that of the first is used, the stopping potential drops to 0.8 V. From this data, the wavelength of the first radiation is

A. 2.6×10^{-6} m B. 1.2×10^{-5} m
C. 0.5×10^{-6} m D. 5.2×10^{-6} m

36. Given that the grand state energy of the hydrogen atom is –13.6 eV, the grand state energy of postronium (which is a bound state of an electron and a positron) is

A. + 6.8 eV B. – 6.8 eV
C. – 3.6 eV D. – 27.2 eV

37. In a series of five cricket matches, one of the captains calls 'Heads' every time, when the toss is taken. The probability that he will win 3 times and loss 2 times is

A. $\frac{1}{8}$ B. $\frac{5}{8}$
C. $\frac{3}{16}$ D. $\frac{5}{16}$

38. For a transistor working as common base amplifier, current gain is 0.96. If the emitter current is 7.2 mA, the base current is

A. 0.29 mA B. 0.59 mA
C. 0.11 mA D. 0.09 mA

39. The output V_o of the ideal op-amp circuit shown in the fig. is

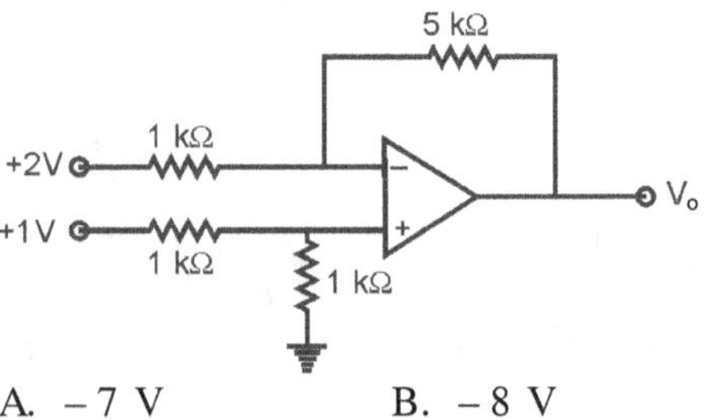

A. – 7 V B. – 8 V
C. – 5 V D. – 4 V

40. The phase velocity (v_p) and the group velocity (v_g) of a de-Broglie wave in free space (speed of light = c) are related as

A. $v_p v_g = c^2$ B. $\frac{v_p}{v_g} = c^2$

C. $\frac{v_p}{v_g} = \sqrt{2}$ D. $v_p v_g = \sqrt{2}\, c^2$

41. The wave function of a particle is given by $\psi = \left(\frac{1}{\sqrt{2}}\phi_0 + i\phi_1\right)$, where ϕ_0 and ϕ_1 are the normalized eigen functions with energies E_0 and E_1 corresponding to the grand state and first excited state, respectively. The expectation value of the Hamiltonian in the state ψ is

A. $\frac{1}{3}(E_0 + E_1)$ B. $\frac{1}{3}(E_0 + 2E_1)$

C. $\frac{1}{2}(E_0 - 2E_1)$ D. $E_0 - 2E_1$

42. For a charged particle in an electromagnetic field, the canonical momenta are:

A. $\frac{1}{2}mv^2 + \frac{q}{c}\bar{A}$ B. $mv^2 + \frac{q^-}{2c}A$

C. $m\bar{v} + \frac{q^-}{c}A$ D. $m\bar{v} - \frac{q^-}{c}A$

43. The electric flux passing through a hemispherical surface of radius R placed in an electric field $\vec{E}$ with the axis parallel to the field is

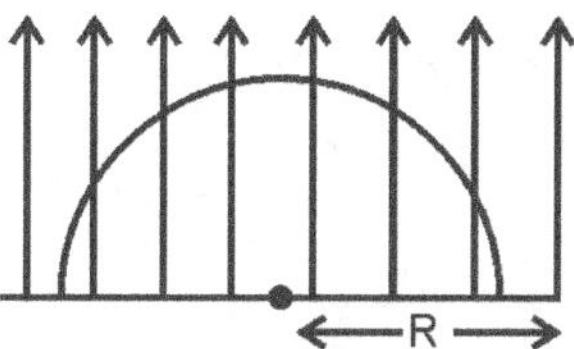

A. $2\pi R^2 E$ B. $2\pi RE$

C. $\pi R^2 E$ D. $\pi R^3 E$

44. A thermo bottle containing tea is vigorously shaken and thereby the temperature of tea rises. Regard the tea as the system

A. $\Delta Q = 0$; $\Delta W = +ve$; $\Delta U = -ve$

B. $\Delta Q = 0$; $\Delta W = -ve$; $\Delta U = +ve$

C. $\Delta Q = 0$; $\Delta W = +ve$; $\Delta U = +ve$

D. $\Delta Q = 0$; $\Delta W = -ve$; $\Delta U = -ve$

45. Mass m_p are accelerated through the same potential difference, the ratio of the wavelengths associated with an electrons to that associated with proton is

A. $\frac{m_e}{m_p}$ B. $m_e \cdot m_p$

C. $\sqrt{\frac{m_p}{m_e}}$ D. $\frac{m_p}{m_e}$

PART-C

46. The output of the circuit shown in fig. is equal to

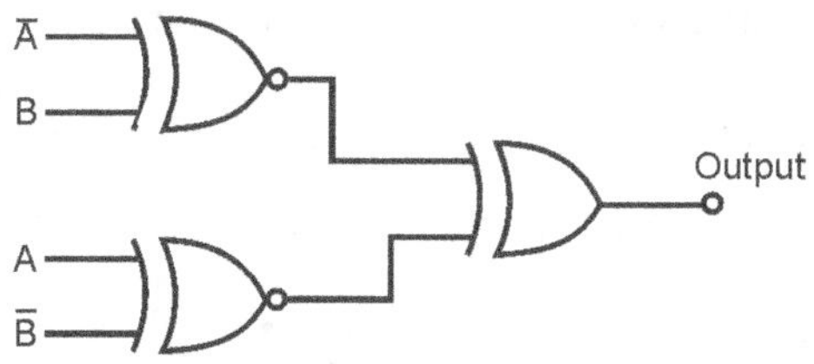

A. 0 B. $\bar{A}B \rightarrow A\bar{B}$

C. $\overline{(\bar{A} * B)} * \overline{(A * \bar{B})}$ D. 1

47. By capturing an electron, $^{54}_{25}Mn_{29}$ transforms into $^{54}_{24}Cr_{30}$ releasing:

A. A neutrino B. An antineutrino

C. An α-particle D. A positron

48. An astronaut moves in a super spaceship travelling at a speed of 0.8 c. The astronaut observes a photon approaching him from space. The speed of photon with respect to the astronaut is

A. 0.1 c B. 0.2 c

C. c D. 0.6 c

49. A uniform current I is flowing along the surface of a hollow conducting cylinder of radius a parallel to its axis. The magnetic induction inside the cylinder is

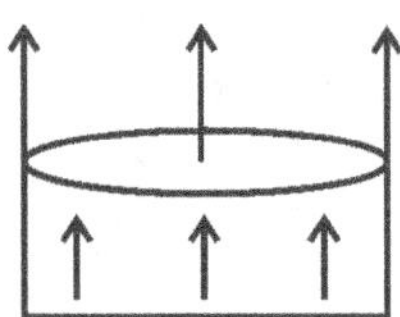

A. $\frac{\mu_0 I}{2\pi a}$ B. $\frac{I}{a}$

C. 0   D. $\frac{I}{\pi a^2}$

50. The work done W during an isothermal process in which the gas expands from an initial volume V_1 to a final volume V_2 is given by (R-Gas constant, T = temperature)

A. $RT \log_e \left(\frac{V_1}{V_2}\right)$

B. $RT \log_e \left(\frac{V_2}{V_1}\right)$

C. $R(T_2 - T_1) \log_e \left(\frac{T_1}{T_2}\right)$

D. $R(V_2 - V_1) \log_e \left(\frac{V_2}{V_1}\right)$

51. The resistance of a thermometer is 5Ω at 30°C and 6.5 Ω at 60°C. Using linear approximation, the value of resistance temperature coefficient at 45°C

A. 0.0087/°C
B. 0.0023/°C
C. 0.0187/°C
D. 0.1045/°C

52. Two dielectric materials A and B exhibit both ionic and orientational polarizabilities. The variation of their susceptibilities X (= $\epsilon_r - 1$) with temperature T is shown in the fig., where ϵ_r is the relative dielectric constant. It can be inferred from the figure that

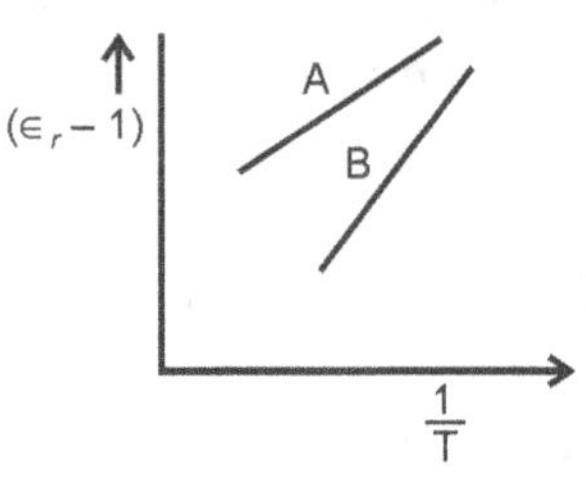

A. A is more polar and it has higher value of ionic polarizability than that of B
B. B is more polar and it has a higher value of ionic polarizability than that of A
C. B is more polar and it has a smaller value of ionic polarizability than that of A
D. None of these

53. What should be the values of the components R_1, R_2 which that the frequency of the Wein Bridge oscillator is 300 Hz?

(Given: C = 0.01 μF and R_1 12 kΩ)

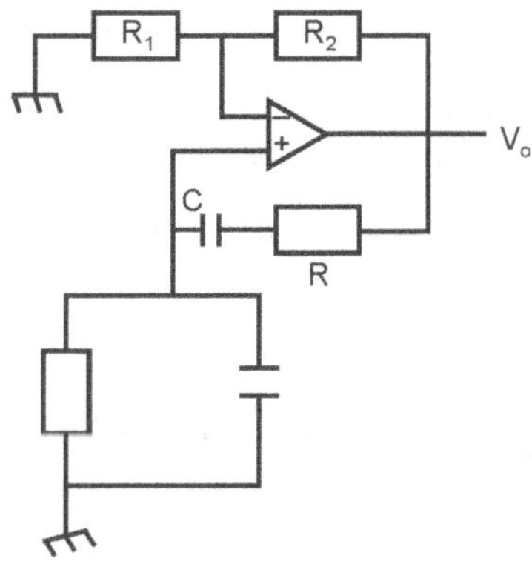

A. R_1 = 53 kΩ and R_2 = 24 kΩ
B. R_1 = 430 Ω and R_2 = 1 mΩ
C. R_1 = 57 Ω and R_2 = 15 kΩ
D. R_1 = 32 Ω and R_2 = 2 kΩ

54. The probability of solving a problem by three students A, B, C independently are $\frac{1}{3}, \frac{1}{4}, \frac{1}{5}$. The probability that the problem will be solved as

A. $\frac{12}{60}$ B. $\frac{31}{60}$

C. $\frac{36}{60}$ D. $\frac{53}{60}$

55. If the two sub-system 1 and 2 are in thermal equilibrium and the entropy σ of the total system must have maximum value with respect to sm all transfer of energy from one subsystem to the other then the statistical tem perature x is defined as

A. $\frac{1}{T}=\left(\frac{\partial\sigma}{\partial U}\right)$ B. $\frac{1}{T}=-\left(\frac{\partial\sigma}{\partial U}\right)$

C. $T=\left(\frac{\partial\sigma}{\partial U}\right)$ D. $T=-\left(\frac{\partial\sigma}{\partial U}\right)$

56. If the input signal e, applied to the op-amp of the circuit shown in the given fig. is sinusoidal at maximum value 1 mV and of 1 kHz frequency, then the magnitude of the peak value of the output voltage waveform would be

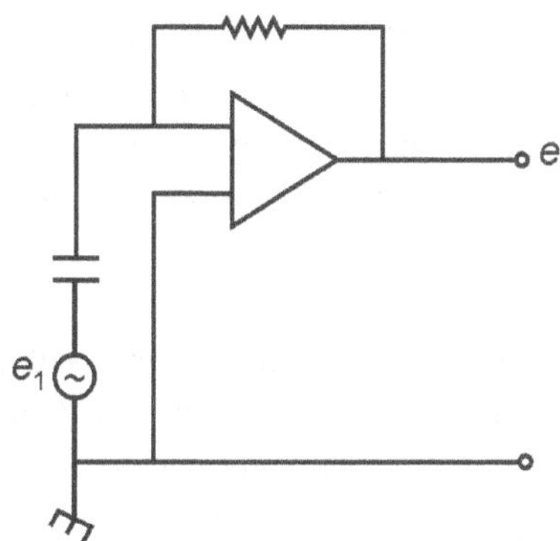

A. 628 mV B. 6.2 mV
C. 2.59 mV D. 1.59 mV

57. The motor of a refrigerator has a power output of 200 watts. If the freezing compartment is at 270 K and the outside air is at 300 K, what is the maximum amount of heat that can be extracted from the freezing compartment in 10 minutes?

A. 25.7×10^4 calories
B. 32.9×10^4 calories
C. 48.5×10^4 calories
D. 11.2×10^4 calories

58. The gain and distortion of an amplifier are 150 and 5% respectively without feedback. If the stage has 10% of its output voltage applied as negative feedback, find the distortion of the amplifier with feedback

A. 0.131% B. 0.031%
C. 0.313% D. 0.512%

59. It is desired to set the operating point at 2V, 1mA by biasing a silicon transistor with feedback resistor R_B. If $\beta = 100$, find the value of R_B.

A. 110 kΩ B. 101 kΩ
C. 190 kΩ D. 130 kΩ

60. The emitted radiant energy from a piece of metal is measured and the temperature is found to be 1065°C assuming a surface emissivity of 0.82. It was later found out that the true emissivity is 0.75. The error in temperature measurement is

A. – 30°C B. – 20°C
C. 50°C D. – 40°C

61. The number of photons emitted per second from a 1 W Ar-ion laser operating at 488.0 nm is approximately

A. 10.23×10^{19} B. 2.46×10^{18}
C. 10.23×10^{17} D. 2.46×10^{15}

62. The angle of reflection of neutron beam from a crystal of interplanar spacing 3.84Å is 30°, the speed of neutrons will be

A. 1.03×10^6 cm/s B. 1.03×10^5 cm/s
C. 1.03×10^4 cm/s D. 1.03×10^3 cm/s

63. Atomic mass number of an element is 232 and its atomic number is 90. The end product of this radioactive element is an isotope of lead (atomic mass 208 and atomic number 82). The number of α- and β-particles emitted are

A. $\alpha = 6$ and $\beta = 0$ B. $\alpha = 6$ and $\beta = 4$
C. $\alpha = 4$ and $\beta = 6$ D. $\alpha = 3$ and $\beta = 3$

64. A particle acted on by two forces $4\hat{i}+\hat{j}-3\hat{k}$ and $3\hat{i}+\hat{j}-\hat{k}$, is displaced from the point $\hat{i}+2\hat{j}+\hat{k}$ to the point $5\hat{i}+4\hat{j}+\hat{k}$, then work done by the force

A. 28 B. 30
C. 32 D. 34

65. Laser are light source which given almost perfectly parallel beam of high intensity. If a 2 kW laser beam is concentrated by a lens into cross-sectional area about 10^{-6} cm^2, then the value of poynting vector is

A. 2×10^{11} W/m^2 B. 2×10^{12} W/m^2
C. 2×10^{13} W/m^2 D. 2×10^{14} W/m^2

66. A system of N particles enclosed in a volume V at a temperature T. The logarithmic of the partition function is given by $\ln Z = N \ln [(V - bN)(k_B T)^{3/2}]$ where b is a constant with approximate dimensions. If P is the pressure of the gas, the equation of the state is given by

A. $P(V - bN) = Nk_B T$
B. $P(V - bN) = k_B T$
C. $P(V - b) = Nk_B T$
D. $P(V - b) = k_B T$

67. A planet of mass m moves in the gravitational field of the Sun (mass M). If the semi-major and semi-minor axes of the orbit are a and b respectively, the angular momentum of the planet is:

A. $\sqrt{2GMm^2(a+b)}$ B. $\sqrt{2GMm^2(a-b)}$

C. $\sqrt{\dfrac{2GMm^2ab}{a-b}}$ D. $\sqrt{\dfrac{2GMm^2ab}{a+b}}$

68. For a certain p-channel JFET/$V_{GS(off)} = 8$ V. The value of V_{GS} for an approximate mid-point bias is

A. 4 V B. 0 V
C. 1.25 V D. 2.34 V

69. The eigenvalues of the antisymmetric matrix,

$$A = \begin{pmatrix} 0 & -n_3 & n_2 \\ n_3 & 0 & -n_1 \\ -n_2 & n_1 & 0 \end{pmatrix}$$ where n_1, n_2 and n_3 are the components of a unit vector, are

A. 0, i, $-i$
B. 0, 1, -1
C. 0, $1 + i$, $-1 - i$
D. 0, 0, 0

70. An X-Y flip-flop, whose characteristic table is given below is to be implemented using a JK flip-flop. This can be done by making:

X	Y	Q_{n+1}
0	0	1
0	1	Q_n
1	0	$\bar{Q}_n$
1	1	0

A. $J = X, K = \bar{Y}$
B. $J = \bar{X}, K = Y$
C. $J = Y, K = \bar{X}$
D. $J = \bar{Y}, K = X$

71. A signal contains sinusoidal frequencies of 2, 4, 6 and 10 kHz. The respective peak values are 10, 5, 7, 2 and 3 volts. The harmonic distortion is

A. 93.27% B. 52.52%
C. 72.11% D. 29.13%

72. If n_ϕ and n for an electron iron elliptical orbit are 1 and 2 respectively, then the ratio of semimajor axis and semiminor axis is

A. 0.25 B. 0.5
C. 2 D. 1

73. In amplitude modulated system, if the total power is 600 W and the power in carrier is 400 W, then the modulation index is

A. 0.5 B. 0.75
C. 0.9 D. 1

74. In hydrogen atom, the electron is replaced by a neon whose mass is 200 times that of an electron and charge is same as that of electrons, the ionization potential on the basis of Bohr's theory is

A. 2.72×10^3 eV
B. 3.51×10^3 eV
C. 1.21×10^4 eV
D. 2.27×10^4 eV

75. The maximum energy of deuteron coming out of a cyclotrons accelerator is 20 MeV. The maximum energy of protons that can be obtained from this acceleration is

A. 10 MeV B. 20 MeV
C. 30 MeV D. 40 MeV

ANSWERS

1	2	3	4	5	6	7	8	9	10
A	B	A	B	C	C	B	B	C	B
11	**12**	**13**	**14**	**15**	**16**	**17**	**18**	**19**	**20**
B	A	B	A	B	A	A	A	A	A
21	**22**	**23**	**24**	**25**	**26**	**27**	**28**	**29**	**30**
A	C	D	B	A	B	C	A	B	B
31	**32**	**33**	**34**	**35**	**36**	**37**	**38**	**39**	**40**
C	B	A	A	A	B	D	A	A	A
41	**42**	**43**	**44**	**45**	**46**	**47**	**48**	**49**	**50**
B	C	C	B	C	A	A	C	C	B
51	**52**	**53**	**54**	**55**	**56**	**57**	**58**	**59**	**60**
A	B	A	C	A	A	A	C	D	A
61	**62**	**63**	**64**	**65**	**66**	**67**	**68**	**69**	**70**
B	B	B	C	C	A	D	D	A	D
71	**72**	**73**	**74**	**75**					
A	C	D	A	A					

EXPLANATORY ANSWERS

1. Clearly, 10% of water left = 0.1 V of water left here, V = total volume of water in tank.

Now, water left out in tank on the first day

= 0.5 V

Water left in the tank on 2nd day = 0.25 V again, water left in the tank on the 3rd day

= 0.125 V

It is nearest to 0.1 V

Hence, option (A) is correct.

2. As $x = \alpha t^3 + \beta t^2 + \gamma t + 8$

$\dot{x} = v = 3\alpha t^2 + 2\beta t + \gamma$

for $t = 0,\ v_i = \gamma,\ \ \ddot{x} = a = 6\alpha t + 2\beta$

for $t = 0,\ a_i = 2\beta,\ \ \therefore$ for $t = 0$

$\Rightarrow \quad \dfrac{a_i}{v_i} = \dfrac{2\beta}{\gamma}.$

3. The given information is:

	Code	**Sentence**
1.	ni ra ge	who are you
2.	boi wo dur	going far away
3.	wo ge chi	you went away

The word went is in third sentence only. The word you is common in first and third sentence and so is the code 'ge'. The word away is common in second and third sentence and so is the code 'wo'. The only code—remaining is 'chi' which stands for 'went'.

4. The pattern of logic is column-wise. The sum of numbers is first and second column equals the sum of numbers in third and fourth column—

i.e., 15 + 13 = 28 = 8 + 20

Therefore, 5 + 9 = 14 and

13 + 1 = 14 or 14 − 13 = 1

Hence, 1 completes the matrix.

5. The word is coded by moving the letters one step forward.

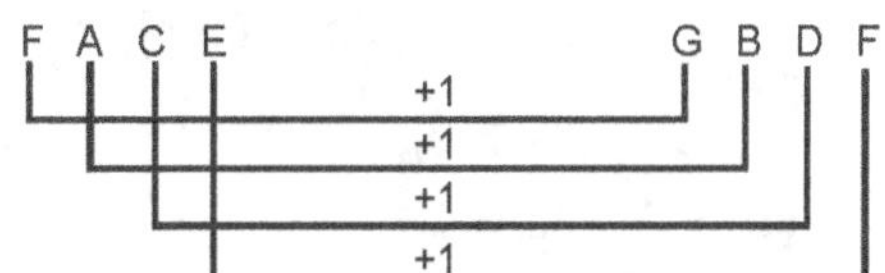

Similarly,

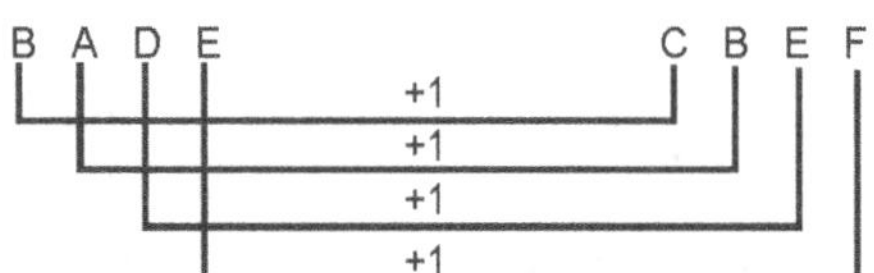

6. According to Sony is from 17th ⊢—⊣ 21st

According to Mini is from 19th ⊢——⊣ 24th

Mother's birthday in the month of April. It is clear that the mother's brother birthday is between 19th and 21st April and so the define date is 20th April.

7.
$$2 \,\Delta\, 3 \,\square\, 5$$
$$2 \times 2 \times 3 \,\square\, 5$$
$$12 \,\square\, 5 = 12 \times 5 - 5$$
$$= 60 - 5 = 55.$$

8. Let the numbers are $3x$ and $4x$.
According to question,

$$\frac{3x+2}{4x+2} = \frac{7}{9}$$
$$9(3x + 2) = 7(4x + 2)$$
$$\Rightarrow \quad 27x + 18 = 28x + 14$$
$$\Rightarrow \quad x = 4$$

∴ Hence, number are 12 and 16.

9. Here, the side of new cube

$$= (6^3 + 8^3 + 10^3)^{1/3} = (1728)^{1/3}$$
$$= 12 \text{ cm}$$

Then, the diagonal of the new cube

$$= 12\sqrt{3} = 12 \times 1.73$$
$$= 20.8 \text{ cm.}$$

10. Total distance covered in 4 seconds

$$= \frac{1}{2}(2\pi r)$$
$$= \frac{1}{2} \times 2 \times \frac{22}{7} \times 2 = 2\pi \text{ m.}$$

11. Clockwise starting from 7, the next number is obtained by doubling the number and adding 2, *i.e.*,

$$(7 \times 2) + 2 = 16$$
$$(16 \times 2) + 2 = 34$$
$$(34 \times 2) + 2 = 70$$
$$(70 \times 2) + 2 = 142$$
$$(142 \times 2) + 2 = 286.$$

12. The weight of the cube is balanced by the buoyant force. The buoyant force is equal to the weight of water displaced.

Volume of sphere dipped inside water

$$= \frac{2}{3}\pi\left(\frac{R}{2}\right)^3$$

Let rise in water level is h

hence, $$\frac{2}{3}\pi\left(\frac{R}{2}\right)^3 = \pi R^2.h$$

$$\Rightarrow \quad h = \frac{R}{12}.$$

13. We have, $2^{3^4} = 67108864 \times 2^{55} = 2^{81}$

$$3^{4^2} = 3^{16} = 4{,}30{,}46{,}721$$
$$4^{3^2} = 4^9 = 2{,}62{,}144$$

and $4^{2^3} = 4^8 = 65536$

Hence, $2^{81} > 3^{16} > 2^{18} > 2^{16}$.

14. From rectangle ABCD, *i.e.*, rectangle, the simplest rectangles, are AEKG, GKLH, HLFB, EDIK, KIJL and LJCF, *i.e.*, 6 rectangles.

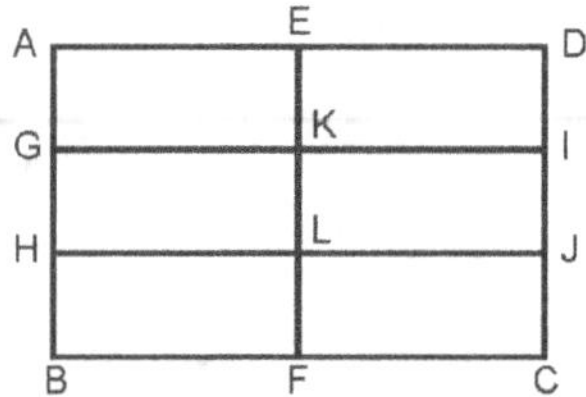

Other horizontal rectangles are: ADIG, GIJH, HJCB, ADJH and GICB are: 5 rectangles.
Now, we have vertical rectangles, AEFB and EDCF are : 2 rectangles

∴ Total number of rectangles are:

$$1 + 6 + 5 + 2 = 14.$$

15. Given, diameter of circle = 1 cm

∴ Radius of circle = 0.5 cm

Area of square = 1 cm^2

Now, Area of each sector $= \frac{\pi r^2}{4} = \frac{3.14 \times (0.5)^2}{4}$

$$= 0.19625 \text{ sq cm}$$

$\therefore$ Area of 4 sectors = 4 × 0.19625 sq cm
= 0.785 sq cm

$\therefore$ Area of unoccupied space
= (1 – 0.785) sq cm
= 0.215 sq cm.

16. 15 apples + 20 oranges
= 20 apples + 15 oranges

20 oranges – 15 oranges
= 20 apples – 15 apples

5 oranges = 5 apples

$\therefore$ orange = apple.

17. Here, 3 points from given 14 points can be made

$$^{14}C_3 = \frac{14 \times 13 \times 12}{3 \times 2 \times 1} = 364$$

Now, the selection of 3 points from the points on one line cannot give any triangle. So that the selection are

$^3C_3 + {^5C_3} + {^6C_3} = 1 + 10 + 20 = 31$

Therefore, the total triangles that can be termed
= 364 – 31 = 333.

18. Downstream speed = 10 + 4 = 14 km/hr.

Upstream speed = 10 – 4 = 6 km/hr.

Hence, their average speed

$$= \frac{x+x}{\frac{x}{14}+\frac{x}{6}} = \frac{2x}{5x/21} = \frac{42}{5} = 8.4 \text{ km/hr.}$$

Since, average speed of cyclist (12 km/hr) > average speed of boat sailor (8.4 km/hr).

Therefore, the cyclist will return to A first.

19. According to the given information, we have:

Person	Profession	Height
Vinod	Player	Tallest
Virendra	Dance	Shortest
Rohilla	Singer	GM height

20. The increase in kinetic energy = the loss in potential energy.

This is same for all three particles.

21. Let v = horizontal component of the velocity of shell, and

T = Total time of flight

$\therefore$ vT = 2 km

When the shell breaks, the part which falls vertically does not have any horizontal velocity and hence the other part acquires horizontal velocity $2v$, by conservation of momentum.

Also, its remaining time of flight will be $\frac{T}{2}$. It will travel a further distance.

$$2v\left(\frac{T}{2}\right) = vT = 2 \text{ km}$$

Hence, it will land 2 km away from the cannon.

22. From the fig., this circuit refers to inverting constant gain multiplier.

Output voltage

$$V_o = \frac{-R_f}{R_L} V_i$$

$$\Rightarrow \quad V_o = -\frac{1}{1}(1) = -1.00 \text{ V.}$$

23. In a Wheatstone bridge, the deflection in the galvanometer does not change, if the battery and galvanometer are interchanged.

24. We have $|A - \lambda I| = 0$

$$\begin{vmatrix} 1-\lambda & 2 & -3 \\ 0 & 3-\lambda & 2 \\ 0 & 0 & -2-\lambda \end{vmatrix} = 0$$

or $(1 - \lambda)(3 - \lambda)(-2 - \lambda) = 0$ or $\lambda = 1, 3, -2$

Eigen values of A^3 = 1, 27, –8

Eigen values of A^2 = 1, 9, 4

Eigen values of A = 1, 3, –2

Eigen values of I = 1, 1, 1

$\therefore$ Eigen values of $3A^3 + 5A^2 - 6A + 2I = 0$

$3(1)^3 + 5(1)^2 - 6(1) + 2(1)$

$\Rightarrow$ 3 + 5 – 6 + 2 = 4

$\Rightarrow$ $3(3)^3 + 5(3)^2 - 6(3) + 2(1)$

$\Rightarrow$ 3(27) + 5(9) – 18 + 2

$\Rightarrow$ 81 + 45 – 16 = 110

and $3(-2)^3 + 5(-2)^2 - 6(-2) + 2(1)$

$\Rightarrow$ –24 + 20 + 12 + 2

$\Rightarrow$ –24 + 34 = 10

Hence, eigen values are: 4, 110, 10.

25. The correct value of mean free path is given by

$$\lambda = \frac{1}{\sqrt{2n\pi\sigma^2}}$$

or $$\sigma^2 = \frac{1}{\sqrt{2n\pi\lambda}}$$

$$= \frac{1}{\sqrt{2 \times 2.7 \times 10^{25} \times \pi \times 8 \times 10^{-6}}}$$

$$= 1.042 \times 10^{-21}$$

$\therefore$ $\sigma = 3.2 \times 10^{-11}$ m.

26. As, $$\nu = \frac{1}{2\pi}\sqrt{\frac{k}{\mu}}$$

For reduced mass

$$\mu = \frac{m_1 m_2}{m_1 + m_2} = \frac{m}{2}$$

$k = 4.8 \times 10^2$ Nm^{-1},

$$\mu = \frac{1.6 \times 10^{-27}}{2} = 0.835 \times 10^{-27} \text{ kg}$$

$\therefore$ $$\nu = \frac{1}{2\pi} \cdot \sqrt{\frac{4.8 \times 10^2}{0.835 \times 10^{-27}}}$$

$\therefore$ $\nu = 1.2 \times 10^{24}$ Hz.

27. Output DC voltage > $V_{DC} = 50$ V

Diode resistance, $r_f = 25\Omega$

Load resistance, $R_L = 800\Omega$

Let V_m be the maximum value of AC voltage required

$\therefore$ $$V_{DC} = I_{DC} \times R_L$$

$$= \frac{I_m}{\pi} \times R_L = \frac{V_m}{\pi(r_f + R_L)} \times R_L$$

$$\left[\because I_m = \frac{V_m}{r_f + R_L}\right]$$

or $$50 = \frac{V_m}{\pi(25 + 800)} \times 800$$

$\therefore$ $$V_m = \frac{\pi \times 825 \times 50}{800} = 162 \text{ V.}$$

28. dB power gain at 2 KHz

At 2 KHz, the output power is 1.5 W and input power 10 mW.

$\therefore$ Power gain at 20 Hz.

At 20 Hz, the output power is 0.3 W and input power is 10 mW.

$\therefore$ Power gain dB $= 10 \log_{10} \dfrac{0.3 \text{ W}}{10 \text{ mW}}$

$= 14.77$

Fall in gain from 2 KHz to 20 Hz

$= 21.76 - 14.77 = 6.99$ dB.

29. Diode D_1 is forward biased and offers zero resistance.

2Ω

1Ω

6V

Diode D_2 is reverse biased and offers infinite current.

The given circuit reduces to the equivalent circuit as shown in fig.

According to Ohm's law, the current through the 1Ω resistance is

$$I = \frac{6}{2+1} \text{ A} = 2 \text{ A.}$$

30. Since $V_c = 3b$,

$\therefore$ $$b = \frac{V_c}{3} = \frac{70 \times 10^{-6}}{3}$$

$$= 23.3 \times 10^{-6} \text{ m}^3$$

As, $$P_c = \frac{a}{27b^2}$$

or $$a = 27b^2$$

$$P_c = 27 \times (23.3 \times 10^{-6})^2 \times (12.8 \times 10^5)$$

$$= 0.0188 \text{ Nm}^4$$

$$T_c = \frac{8a}{27Rb} = \frac{8 \times 0.0188}{27 \times 8.3 \times 2.3 \times 10^{-6}}$$

$$= 28.8 \text{ K.}$$

31. Absolute temperature with emissivity of 0.82 is $= 1065 + 273 = 1338$ K

$\therefore$ Apparent absolute temperature is

$$T_a = (0.82)^{-1/4} (1338) = 1273 \text{ K}$$

Actual absolute temperature, when the emissivity is 0.75

$$= (0.75)^{-1/4} (1273) = 1368 \text{ K}$$

Actual temperature $= 1368 - 273 = 1095$°C

Therefore, error in temperature measure

$$= 1065 - 1095 = -30°\text{C.}$$

32. Given, λ = 2537Å = 2537 × 10^{-10} m

Let the excitation potential be V

$$\therefore \quad eV = h\nu = \frac{hc}{\lambda}$$

or $$V = \frac{hc}{e\lambda}$$

$$\Rightarrow \quad V = \frac{6.6\times10^{-34}\times3\times10^{8}}{1.6\times10^{-19}\times2537\times10^{-10}}$$

= 4.9 V.

33. According to Green's theorem,

$$\int_c (\phi dx + \psi dy) = \iint_R \left(\frac{\partial\psi}{\partial x} - \frac{\partial\phi}{\partial y}\right) dx\, dy$$

$$\int_c (x^2 y\, dx + x^2 dy) = \iint_R (2x - x^2)\, dx\, dy$$

$$= \int_0^1 (2x - x^2)\, dx \int_0^x dy = \int_0^1 (2x - x^2)\, dx [y]_0^x$$

$$= \int_0^1 (2x - x^2)(x) dx = \int_0^1 (2x^2 - x^3) dx$$

$$= \left(\frac{2x^3}{3} - \frac{x^4}{4}\right)_0^1 = \left(\frac{2}{3} - \frac{1}{4}\right) = \frac{5}{12}.$$

34. S is Galilean frame, S′ is attached with one particle moving with relative speed + 0.9 c (= v_1) wrt S. S″ is attached with second particle moving with relative speed – 0.9 c (= v) wrt S. Now, calculating the relative speed of S″ with S′ *i.e.*, v_2.

Therefore, $v = 0.9\,c$

$v_1 = +\,0.9\,c,\quad v_2 = ?$

Relation is, $$v = \frac{v_1 + v_2}{1 + \frac{v_1 v_2}{c^2}}$$

$$= \frac{0.9c + v_2}{1 + \frac{0.9c\, v_2}{c^2}}$$

$$W - 0.9c = \frac{0.9c + v_2}{1 + \frac{0.9c\, v_2}{c^2}}$$

$-0.9c - (0.9)^2 v_2 = 0.9c + v_2$

$\Rightarrow \quad -1.8c = 1.81 v_2$

$\Rightarrow \quad v_2 = -0.995c.$

35. The wavelength of the second radiation is double that of the first one $\lambda_2 = 2\lambda_1$, we can write:

$$V_{s_1} = \frac{hc}{e\lambda_1} - \frac{W}{e} \quad ...(i)$$

where W is the work function of the metal, V_{s_1} is the stopping potential of the metal

$$V_{s_2} = \frac{hc}{e\lambda_2} - \frac{W}{e} = \frac{hc}{2e\lambda_1} - \frac{W}{e} \quad ...(ii)$$

To obtain λ_1, we have to subtract (*i*) from (*ii*), we get

$$V_{s_1} - V_{s_2} = \frac{hc}{e\lambda_1}\left(1 - \frac{1}{2}\right) = \frac{hc}{2e\lambda_1}$$

Hence, wavelength,

$$\lambda_1 = \frac{hc}{2e\left(V_{s_1} - V_{s_2}\right)} = 6.6 \times 10^{-34}\ \text{Js}$$

$$= \frac{6.6\times10^{-3}\,\text{Js}\times3\times10^{8}\,\text{ms}^{-1}}{2\times1.6\times10^{-19}c\times(3.2\text{V}-0.8\text{V})}$$

= 2.6 × 10^{-6} m.

36. The grand state binding energy of positronium is half of that of hydrogen. This is so because the energy is proportional to the reduced mass and that of the positronium has a reduced mass of half that of hydrogen.

37. Probability for heads

$$P(x) = \frac{1}{2}$$

Probability for tail $P(y) = \frac{1}{2}$

No. of tosses (n) = 5

Therefore, required probability for 3 heads and 2 tails,

$${}^5C_3 (x)^3 . (y)^2$$

$$= \frac{5!}{3!2!}\left(\frac{1}{2}\right)^3\left(\frac{1}{2}\right)^2$$

$$= \frac{5\times4\times3\times2\times1}{3\times2\times1\times2\times1} = 5\times2\left(\frac{1}{2}\right)^5$$

$$= \frac{5}{16}.$$

38. Given, $\alpha = 0.96$, $I_e = 7.2$ mA

As, $\alpha = \frac{I_c}{I_e}$ or $I_c = \alpha I_e$

$\Rightarrow$ $I_c = 0.96 \times 7.2$

$= 6.91$ mA

Also, $I_e = I_c + I_b$ or $I_b = I_e - I_c$

$= 7.2 - 6.91 = 0.29$ mA.

39.

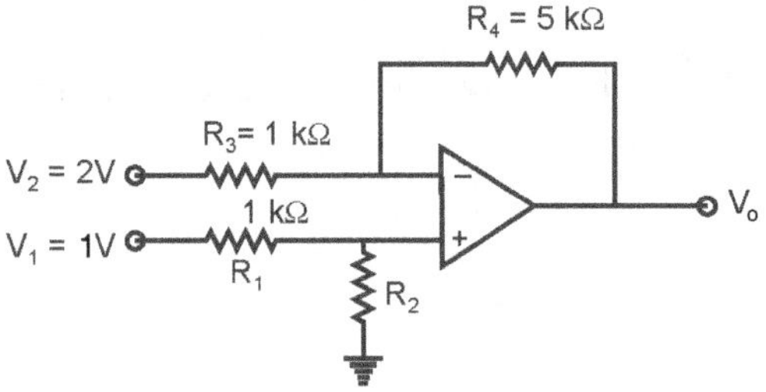

$R_4 = 5\ k\Omega$, $R_3 = 1\ k\Omega$, $V_2 = 2V$, $1\ k\Omega$, $V_1 = 1V$, R_1, R_2, V_o

Given, $R_1 = 1\ k\Omega$, $R_2 = 1\ k\Omega$,

$R_3 = 1\ k\Omega$, $R_4 = 5\ k\Omega$,

$V_1 = 1$ V, $V_2 = 2$ V

$$V_o = \left(\frac{R_3 + R_4}{R_3}\right) \cdot \left(\frac{R_2}{R_1 + R_3}\right) - \frac{R_4}{R_3} V_2$$

$$= \left(\frac{1+5}{1}\right)\left(\frac{1}{1+1}\right) - \frac{5}{1} \times 2$$

$$= 6 \times \frac{1}{2} - 10 \Rightarrow (3 - 10)\text{V}$$

$\Rightarrow$ $= -7$ V

40. As, $E = h\nu = mc^2$

$$\Rightarrow \quad \omega = \frac{2\pi mc^2}{h} \qquad ...(i)$$

We know that, $m = \frac{m_o}{\sqrt{1 - \frac{v^2}{c^2}}}$

and $$k = \frac{2\pi}{\lambda} = \frac{2\pi m\nu}{h} \qquad ...(ii)$$

$$= \frac{2\pi mc^2}{h} = \frac{2\pi}{h}\left(\frac{m_o}{\sqrt{1 - \frac{v^2}{c^2}}}\right)c^2$$

and $$k = \frac{2\pi m_o \nu^2}{h\sqrt{1 - \frac{v^2}{c^2}}}$$

$$\frac{d\omega}{d\nu} = \frac{2\pi m_o \nu^2}{h\left(1 - \frac{v^2}{c^2}\right)^{\frac{3}{2}}}$$

and $$\frac{dk}{d\nu} = \frac{2\pi m_o \nu}{h\left(1 - \frac{v^2}{c^2}\right)^{\frac{3}{2}}}$$

Now, $$\nu_p = \frac{\omega}{k} = \frac{2\pi mc^2}{h} \times \frac{h}{2\pi m\nu}$$

or $$\nu_p = \frac{c^2}{\nu}.$$

$$\nu_p = \frac{c^2}{\nu_g}$$

or $$\nu_p \nu_g = c^2.$$

41. Given, $\psi = \frac{1}{\sqrt{2}}\phi_0 + i\phi_1$

The expectation value for H,

$$<H> = \frac{<\psi H \psi>}{<\psi / \psi>}$$

$$<\psi/\psi> = <\frac{1}{\sqrt{2}}\phi_0 - i\phi_1 \Big/ \frac{1}{\sqrt{2}}\phi_0 - i\phi_1>$$

$$= \frac{1}{2} + 1 = \frac{3}{2}$$

$$<\psi | H | \psi> = <\frac{1}{\sqrt{2}}\phi_0 - i\phi_1 | H | \frac{1}{\sqrt{2}}\phi_0 - i\phi_1>$$

$$= \frac{1}{2}E_0 - i \times iE_1$$

So $$<H> = \frac{\frac{1}{2}E_0 + E_1}{\frac{3}{2}} = \frac{E_0 + 2E_1}{3}$$

42. We know that Langrangian for a charged particle in an electromagnetic field

$$L = \frac{1}{2}mv^2 - q\phi + q\frac{\bar{v}\cdot\bar{A}}{c}$$

The canonical momenta are

$$P = \frac{\partial L}{\partial v} = m\bar{v} + \frac{q}{c}\bar{A}.$$

43. Electric flux, $\phi = \int \vec{E}\cdot\vec{ds}$

where $\int ds = \pi r^2 \rightarrow$ surface area of hemispherical surface of radius r.

$\therefore \quad \phi = \pi R^2 E.$

44. The heat has not been transferred to tea which is thermally insulated. By shaking work has been done on tea (system) against the viscous forces in it.

According to first law,

$$\Delta U = \Delta Q - \Delta W$$

Here, ΔQ is zero, because system is isothermal.

and $\quad \Delta W = -ve$

Hence, ΔU is +ve *i.e.*, the internal energy of the system has decreased

$$\Delta W = -ve; \quad \Delta Q = 0; \quad \Delta U = +ve.$$

45. Wavelength associated with an electron,

$$\lambda_e = \frac{h}{\sqrt{2m_e E}}$$

and $$\lambda_p = \frac{h}{\sqrt{2m_p E}}$$

$$E = eV$$

or $$\lambda_e = \frac{h}{\sqrt{2m_e \cdot eV}} \quad ...(i)$$

and $$\lambda_p = \frac{h}{\sqrt{2m_p eV}} \quad ...(ii)$$

Dividing equation (*i*) by (*ii*), we get

$$\frac{\lambda_e}{\lambda_p} = \sqrt{\frac{2m_p eV}{2m_e eV}}$$

$$\Rightarrow \quad \frac{\lambda_e}{\lambda_p} = \sqrt{\frac{m_p}{m_e}}.$$

46. $\overline{(A\oplus\bar{B})}+\overline{(\bar{A}\oplus B)}$

$= \overline{(A\bar{B}+\bar{A}\bar{B}+\bar{A}B+\bar{A}\bar{B})}$

$= \overline{(A\bar{B}+\bar{A}B+\bar{A}B+A\bar{B})} = 0.$

47. By capturing an electron, *a* neutrino is released while emission of electron accompanied by an antineutrino.

48. Speed of photon = c

Speed of astronaut = $0.8c$

Let the photon and astronauts super spaceship moving along positive and negative directions of x-axis respectively.

Let the electron moving with velocity $-0.8c$.

So, $$u_n = \frac{u+v}{1+\frac{uv}{c^2}} = \frac{c+0.8c}{1+\frac{0.8c\cdot(c)}{c^2}}$$

$$= \frac{1.8c}{1.8} = c$$

$\therefore \quad u_n = c.$

49. Outside the cylinder

$$\oint B\cdot dl = \mu_0 I$$

$$B.2\pi r = \mu_0 I$$

$$\Rightarrow \quad B = \frac{\mu_0 I}{2\pi r}$$

Inside the cylinder,

$$\oint \vec{B}\cdot\vec{dl} = 0$$

Which gives us

$$\vec{B} = 0.$$

50. Work done W is given by

$$W = \int_{W_1}^{W_2} PdV$$

Since the expansion is isothermal

$$PV = RT$$

or $$P = \frac{RT}{V}$$

$\therefore \quad W = \int_{V_1}^{V_2} \frac{RT}{V} dV$

$W = RT |\log_e V|_{V_1}^{V_2}.$

$\therefore \quad W = RT \log_e \frac{V_2}{V_1}$

51. Given, $\theta_1 = 30°, \quad \theta_2 = 60°$

$\theta_0 = 45°C$

$R_1 = 5\Omega, \quad R_2 = 6.5\Omega$

$\therefore \quad R_0 = \frac{5+6.5}{2} = \frac{11.5}{2}$

$= 5.75\ \Omega$

Now, linear expansion,

$$\alpha_{\theta_0} = \frac{1}{R_0}\left[\frac{R_{\theta_2} - R_{\theta_1}}{\theta_2 - \theta_1}\right]$$

$$= \frac{1}{5.75}\left[\frac{6.5-5}{60-30}\right]$$

$$= \frac{1}{5.75} \cdot \frac{1.5}{30} = 0.0087°C.$$

52. Higher the slope means more polar, since B more steeper than A, hence B is more polar than A.

But A $= N (a_e + a_i)$ is more for A than B, so A has higher value of ionic polarizability than B.

53. Given, $c = 0.01\ \mu F$

$f = 300$ Hz and R = 12 kΩ

and for zero phase shift in Wein Bridge oscillator

$$f = \frac{1}{2\pi RC}$$

or $\quad R = \frac{1}{2\pi Cf} = \frac{1}{2\pi \times 0.01 \times 10^{-6} \times 300}$

$= 53\ k\Omega$

Since $\frac{R_2}{R_1} = 2$

or $\quad R_2 = 2R_1 = 2 \times 12\ k\Omega = 24\ k\Omega$

$\therefore \quad R_2 = 24\ k\Omega$

$R_L = 53\ k\Omega.$

54. The probability that A can solve the problem $= \frac{1}{3}$

The probability that A cannot solve the problem $= 1 - \frac{1}{3} = \frac{2}{3}$

Similarly, the probability that B and C cannot solve that problem is $\frac{3}{4}$ and $\frac{4}{5}$ respectively. Hence, the probability that the problem will be solved, *i.e.*, at least one student will solve it

$$= 1 - \frac{2}{3} \times \frac{3}{4} \times \frac{4}{5} = 1 - \frac{2}{5} = \frac{3}{5}$$

$$= \frac{3}{5} \times \frac{12}{12} = \frac{36}{60}.$$

55. If σ_1 and $\sigma_2 \rightarrow$ entropies of the subsystems 1 and 2, then additive property of entropy

$\sigma = \sigma_1 + \sigma_2 \quad ...(i)$

Also, $\quad \sigma = \sigma(U_1, U_2)$

and $\quad U = U_1 + U_2 \quad ...(ii)$

Then, $\quad \delta\sigma = \delta\sigma_1 + \delta\sigma_2 \quad ...(iii)$

Then, $\quad \delta\sigma = \delta\sigma_1 + \delta\sigma_2$

$$= \left(\frac{\partial \sigma_1}{\partial U_1}\right)\delta U_1 + \left(\frac{\partial \sigma_2}{\partial U_2}\right)\delta U_2 \quad ...(iv)$$

and $\quad \delta U = \delta U_1 + \delta U_2 \quad ...(v)$

For thermal equilibrium,

$\delta U = \delta U_1 + \delta U_2 = 0$

or $\quad \delta U_1 = -\delta U_2 \quad ...(vi)$

and $\quad \delta\sigma = \left(\frac{\partial \sigma_1}{\partial U_1}\right)\delta U_1 + \left(\frac{\partial \sigma_2}{\partial U_2}\right)\delta U_2 = 0 \quad ...(vii)$

From equations (*vi*) and (*vii*), we get

$$\delta\sigma = \left[\frac{\partial \sigma_1}{\partial U_1} - \frac{\partial \sigma_2}{\partial U_2}\right]\delta U_1 = 0$$

δU_1 is arbitrary variation

hence, $\delta U_1 \neq 0$

$$\therefore \quad \frac{\partial \sigma_1}{\partial U_1} = \frac{\partial \sigma_2}{\partial U_2}$$

or, we can define quantity T by

$$\frac{1}{T} = \left(\frac{\partial \sigma}{\partial U}\right).$$

56. Given, $$\frac{0 - e_i}{1/j\omega C} = \frac{e_0 - 0}{R}$$

$$\therefore \quad e_0 = -j\omega RCe_i$$

$$= -RC\frac{de_i}{di}$$

Input voltage, $e_i = 10^{-3}\omega \cos \omega t$

$$e_o = -RC \times 10^{-3} \omega \cos \omega t$$

For maximum value of output voltage

$= RC \times 10^{-3} \times \omega$

$= 100 \times 10^3 \times 1 \times 10^{-3} \times (2\pi \times 10^3) \times 10^{-3}$

$= 628$ mV.

57. e (refrigerating efficiency)

$$= \frac{1}{\frac{T_1}{T_2} - 1} = \frac{1}{\frac{300}{270} - 1} = 9.$$

Also, $e = \frac{Q_2}{W}$; $\therefore \quad 9 = \frac{Q_2}{200}$

or $Q_2 = 1800$ watt.

$\therefore \quad Q_2 = 1800$ joule per sec.

$\therefore$ Heat extracted in 10 minutes

$= 1800 \times 10 \times 60$ J

$$= \frac{1800 \times 10 \times 60}{4.2} \text{ cal}$$

$= 25.7 \times 10^4$ calories.

58. Gain without feedback, $A = 150$
Distortion without feedback, $D = 5\% = 0.05$
Feedback fraction, $m = 10\% = 0.1$
If D′ is the distortion with negative feedback, then

$$D' = \frac{D}{1 + Am} = \frac{0.05}{1 + 150 \times 0.1}$$

$= 0.00313 = 0.313\%$

It may be seen that by the application of negative feedback, the amplifier distortion is reduced from 5% to 0.313%.

59. For a silicon transistor,

$$V_{BE} = 0.7 \text{ V}$$

$$I_B = \frac{I_C}{\beta} = 1/100 = 0.01 \text{mA}$$

Now, $V_{CE} = V_{BE} + V_{CB}$

or $2 = 0.7 + V_{CB}$

$\therefore \quad V_{CB} = 2 - 0.7 = 1.3$ V

$$R_B = \frac{V_{CB}}{I_B} = \frac{1.3\text{V}}{0.01\text{mA}} = 130\text{ k}\Omega$$

60. Absolute temperature with emissivity of 0.82 is = 1065 + 273 = 1338 K

$\therefore$ Apparent absolute temperature is

$$T_a = (0.82)^{-1/4}(1338) = 1273 \text{ K}$$

Actual absolute temperature, when the emissivity is 0.75

$= (0.75)^{-1/4} (1273) = 1368$ K

$\therefore$ Actual temperature

$= 1368 - 273 = 1095$°C

Hence, error in temperature measure

$= 1065 - 1095 = -30$°C.

61. Number of photon emitted $= \frac{E_1}{E_2}$

$$E_2 = \frac{hc}{\lambda}$$

$$= \frac{6.6 \times 10^{-34} \times 3 \times 10^8}{488 \times 10^{-9}}$$

$$= \frac{66 \times 3}{488} \times 10^{-18}$$

or No. of photons $= \dfrac{1}{\frac{198}{488} \times 10^{-18}}$

$$= \frac{488}{198} \times 10^{18}$$

$= 2.46 \times 10^{18}$.

62. Bragg's condition,

$$2dm\theta = n\lambda$$

$$d = 3.84 \text{ Å} \Rightarrow \theta = 30°$$

$$2 \times 3.84 \sin 30° = \lambda \Rightarrow \lambda = 3.84\text{Å}$$

then the speed of neutron will be

$$\lambda = \frac{h}{p} = \frac{h}{mv} \quad \text{or} \quad v = \frac{h}{m\lambda}$$

$$= \frac{6.6 \times 10^{-34} \text{ Js}}{1.6 \times 10^{-27} \times 3.84 \times 10^{-8}}$$

$$= 1.03 \times 10^5 \text{ cm/s}$$

63. Let a and b be the number of α and β particles are emitted when an element $^{232}_{90}\text{X}$ decays to $^{208}_{82}\text{Y}$, we know.

(*i*) The emission of α-particle $_2\text{He}^4$ decrease the atomic number by 2 and mass number by 4.

$\therefore$ Emission of a α-particle reduces the atomic number by $2a$ and mass number by $4a$.

(*ii*) Emission of $b\beta$ particles increase the atomic number by $b \times 1 = b$

Then $^{232}_{90}\text{X} \rightarrow {}^{208}_{82}\text{Y} \rightarrow a(_2\text{He}^4) + b\,(_{-1}\beta^0)$

Applying the law of conservation,

$$90 = 82 + 2a - b$$

and $232 = 208 + 4a$

$\Rightarrow \quad 4a = 24$

$\therefore \quad a = 6$

Now, we have

$$90 = 82 + 12 - b$$

$\Rightarrow \quad 90 - 94 = -b$

$\Rightarrow \quad b = 4$

$\therefore$ Number of emitted α-particle = 6 and no. of emitted β-particle = 4.

64. Total force, $f = (4\hat{i} + \hat{j} - 3\hat{k}) + (3\hat{i} + \hat{j} - \hat{k})$

$$= (7\hat{i} + 2\hat{j} - 4\hat{k})$$

Net displacement,

$$= (5\hat{i} + 4\hat{j} + \hat{k}) - (\hat{i} + 2\hat{j} + \hat{k})$$

$$= 4\hat{i} + 2\hat{j}$$

$\therefore$ Work done $=$ F.d cos θ

$$= (7\hat{i} + 2\hat{j} - 4\hat{k})(4\hat{i} + 2\hat{j})$$

$$= 28 + 4 = 32.$$

65. Power $= 2$ KW $= 2 \times 10^3$ W

Cross-sectional area $= 10^{-6}$ cm^2

Poynting vector, $S = \dfrac{P}{A}$

$$= \frac{2 \times 10^3 \text{ W}}{10^{-6} \times (10^{-2} \text{ m})^2}$$

$$= 2 \times 10^{3+10} \text{ W/m}^2$$

$$S = 2 \times 10^{13} \text{ W/m}^2.$$

66. We have,

$$\ln Z = N \ln \{(V - bN)(k_{BT})^{3/2}\}$$

and $\quad P = k_{BT}\left(\dfrac{\partial \ln z}{\partial V}\right)_{T,N}$

$$= k_B\, T \frac{\partial}{\partial N}[N \ln\{(V - bN)(k_B T)^{-3/2}\}]$$

$$\therefore\ P_2 k_B T\left[N \cdot \frac{(k_B T)^{3/2}}{(V - bN)(k_B T)^{3/2}}\right]$$

$\therefore$ $P(V - bN) = Nk_B T$.

67. Angular momentum of the planet of mass (m), moving in the gravitational field of the sum

$$L = V.r = mr \cdot \sqrt{\frac{GM}{r}}$$

here distance r is

$$\frac{2}{r} = \frac{1}{a} + \frac{1}{b}$$

or, $$\frac{2}{r} = \frac{a+b}{ab}$$

or, $$r = \frac{2ab}{a+b}$$

Hence, angular momentum

$$L = \sqrt{GMm^2\left(\frac{2ab}{a+b}\right)}$$

$$= \sqrt{2GMm^2 \frac{ab}{(a+b)}}.$$

68. Mid-point Bias is usually desirable to bias a JFET near the mid-point of its transfer characteristic curve where,

$$I_D = \frac{F_{DSS}}{2}$$

Under signal condition, mid-point bias allows the maximum amount of drain current swing between I_{DSS} and 0

Since, $I_D = I_{DSS}\left(1 - \frac{V_{GS}}{V_{GS(off)}}\right)^2$

Since, $I_D = 0.5\ I_{DSS}$

$\therefore \quad 0.5\ I_{DSS} = I_{DSS}\left(1 - \frac{V_{GS}}{V_{GS(off)}}\right)^2$

If $V_{GS} = \frac{V_{GS(off)}}{3.4}$

Here, $V_{GS(off)} = 8$ V

$$V_{GS} = \frac{8}{3.4}$$

$$V_{GS} = 2.34 \text{ V}.$$

69.

$$A = \begin{vmatrix} 0 & -n_3 & n_2 \\ n_3 & 0 & -n_1 \\ -n_2 & n_1 & 0 \end{vmatrix}$$

Characteristics equation

$$|A - \lambda I| = \begin{vmatrix} -\lambda & -n_3 & n_2 \\ n_3 & -\lambda & -n_1 \\ -n_2 & n_1 & -\lambda \end{vmatrix}$$

$$-\lambda(\lambda^2 + n_1^2) - n_3(n_1 n_2 + \lambda n_3)$$

$$+ n_2(n_1 n_3 - \lambda n_2) - \lambda^3 - \lambda(n_1^2 + n_2^2 + n_3^2)$$

As n_1, n_2 and n_3 are components of a unit vector

so, $n_1^2 + n_2^2 + n_3^2 = 1$

so, $|A - \lambda I| = -\lambda^3 - \lambda$

when $|A - \lambda I| = 0$

$$\lambda^3 + \lambda = 0$$

$$\lambda(\lambda^2 + 1) = 0$$

$$\lambda = 0, -i, i$$

70. JK FF

J	K	Q_n	Q_{n+1}
0	0	0	0
0	0	1	1
0	1	0	0
0	1	1	0
1	0	0	1
1	0	1	1
1	1	0	1
1	1	1	0

X-Y FF Excitation

X	Y	Q_n	Q_{n+1}
×	1	0	0
×	0	0	1
1	×	1	0
0	×	1	0

Kmap

J	K	Q_n	1
0	0	×	0
0	1	×	1
1	1	×	0
1	0	×	0

$X = k$

J	K	Q_n	1
0	0	1	×
0	1	1	×
1	1	0	×
1	0	0	×

$Y = \overline{J}$

So, $J = \overline{Y}$, $k = X$

71. As the individual components are pure sinusoidal their rms values are given by

$$HD = \frac{\sqrt{V_2^2 + V_3^2 + V_4^2 + \ldots}}{V_1}$$

$$\therefore \quad V_{rms} = \frac{V_{peak}}{\sqrt{2}}.$$

72. For an ellipse $(1 - \epsilon^2) = \frac{b^2}{a^2}$

where a and b are the semimajor and semiminor axis respectively.

Therefore, $\frac{b^2}{a^2} = \frac{n_\phi^2}{n^2}$

or $\frac{b}{a} = \frac{n_\phi}{n}$

$n\phi = n; \quad n = 2$

Ratio of semimajor axis a and semiminor axis b is

$$\frac{a}{b} = \frac{n}{n_\phi} = \frac{2}{1}.$$

73. Total power

$$P_t = P_c + P_s$$

$$= \frac{A_c^2}{2} + \frac{A_c^2}{4}\mu^2$$

$$= \frac{A_c^2}{2}\left(1 + \frac{\mu^2}{2}\right) = 600 \text{ W}$$

$$P_c = \frac{A_c^2}{2} = 400 \text{ W}$$

$$\therefore \quad \frac{600}{400} = 1 + \frac{\mu^2}{2}$$

$$\Rightarrow \quad \frac{\mu^2}{2} = \frac{1}{2}$$

$\therefore$ Modulation index $\mu = 1$.

74. In case of hydrogen atom, having an electrons, the ionisation of potential

$$\phi = \frac{me^2}{8 \epsilon_0^2 h^2}$$

When electron is replaced by muon,

$$m_1 = 200 \text{ m}$$

$$\phi_1 = \frac{m_1 e^4}{8 \epsilon_0^2 h^2} = \frac{(200m)e^4}{8 \epsilon_0^2 h^2}$$

$$\text{or} \quad \frac{\phi_1}{\phi} = 200 \Rightarrow \phi_1 = 200\ \phi$$

$$\phi = 13.6 \text{ eV}$$

$$\therefore \quad \phi_1 = 200 \times 13.6 \text{ eV}$$

$$= 2.72 \times 10^3 \text{ eV}$$

75. As deuteron consists of equal number of neutron and proton, the reduced mass of system.

$$\mu = \frac{M_n M_p}{M_n + M_p} = \frac{M}{2}$$

Maximum energy, $E = \dfrac{e^2B^2r^2}{2M}$

For deuteron, $E_1 = \dfrac{e^2B^2r^2}{2\left(\dfrac{M}{2}\right)} = 20$

$$\text{or} \quad \frac{e^2B^2r^2}{2M} = \frac{20}{2} = 10 \text{ MeV}$$

Maximum energy of proton

$$= \frac{e^2B^2r^2}{2M} = 10 \text{ MeV}.$$

SET–2

CSIR–UGC (NET) PHYSICAL SCIENCES

PART-A

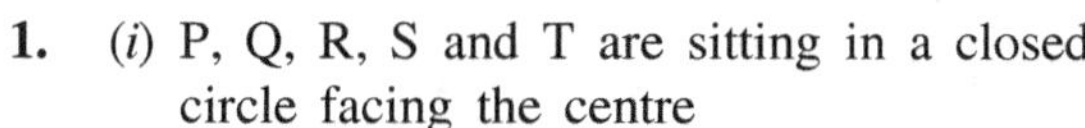

1. (*i*) P, Q, R, S and T are sitting in a closed circle facing the centre

(*ii*) R is just left of T

(*iii*) P is between S and T, then who is just left of R?

A. Q B. P
C. S D. R

2. Three groups of letters out of the following four groups are same in any way but the rest one is different from the three. Find out the different group:

A. LND B. VXZ
C. SUW D. BDG

3. A club has 108 members. Two-thirds of them are men and the rest are women. All the members are married except for 9 women members. How many married women are there in the club?

A. 20 B. 24
C. 27 D. 30

4. A lady is making 'Rangoli' to decorate the door step of her house. To start with she puts 13 dots as shown in fig. below in symmetrical placement. Before colouring the figure, she joins with straight lines, the points 1 to 9, 9 to 5, 5 to 13 and 1 to 13. Now, state how many triangles would she have in the figure to fill with coloured dust for completing her 'Rangoli'?

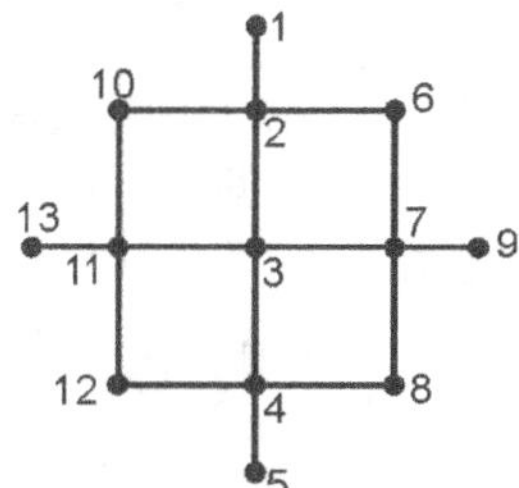

A. 8 B. 12
C. 16 D. 20

5. Two right angles having a common hypothenuse, lie on mutually perpendicular planes. Find the distance between the vertices of the right angles of the triangle, if the legs of the triangles are 4 cm and 3 cm in length:

A. $\frac{12\sqrt{2}}{5}$ B. $\frac{6\sqrt{2}}{3}$
C. $\frac{4\sqrt{3}}{5}$ D. 2

6. The circle of radius 5 units in the *xy* plane has its centre in the first quadrant, touches the *x*-axis and has a chord of length 6 units on the *y*-axis. The coordinates of its centre are

A. (2, 6) B. (3, 7)
C. (4, 5) D. (3, 5)

7. A doctor said to his compounder, "I go to see the patients at their resistance after every 3:30 hours. I have already gone to the patient 1:20 hours ago and next time I shall go at 1:40 pm." At what time this information was given to the compounder by the doctor?

A. 10:10 B. 11:30
C. 8:50 D. 11:20

8. Problem figures

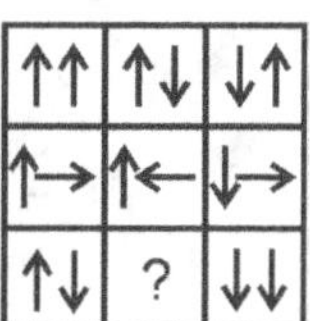

Answer Figures

A. ↑↑ B. ↓↑
C. ↑↓ D. ↑→

9. The age of A is 3 times the age of B, four years ago the age of C was 2 times the age of A. If the age of A will be 31 years after 4 years, what is the present age of C?

A. 50 yrs B. 25 yrs
C. 40 yrs D. 30 yrs

10. A conical vessel with semi-vertical angle 30° and height 10.5 cm has a thin lid. A sphere kept inside it touches the lid. The radius of the sphere in cm is

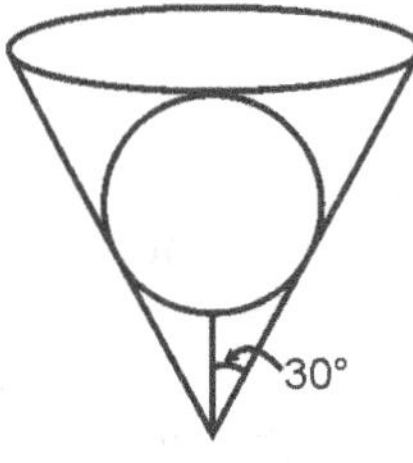

A. 3.5 B. 2.4
C. 4.5 D. 6.0

11. There are three pillars A, B and C of different heights. Three spiders x, y and z start to climb on these pillars simultaneously. In one chance X climbs on A by 5 cm, but slips down 1 cm. Y climbs on B 6 cm but slips down 3 cm. Z climbs 7 cm but slips down 2 cm. If they each requires 50 chances to reach the top of the pillar. The height of the shortest pillar is

A. 153 cm B. 122 cm
C. 141 cm D. 162 cm

12. There are four equilateral triangles. Three of them are inscribed in respective outer triangle as shown in fig. If the area of the smallest triangle be 100 cm^2, then area of the largest triangle will be

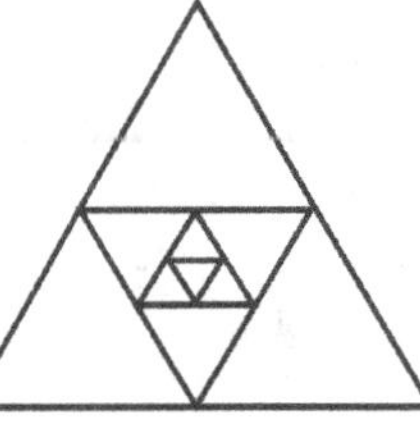

A. 0.32 m^2 B. $0.32\sqrt{3}$ m^2

C. 0.64 m^2 D. $\frac{0.64}{\sqrt{3}}$ m^2

13. In a row of ladies Lazy is 20th from the right and Savita is 10th from the left. When they interchange their positions Lazy becomes 25th from the right. What is the total number of ladies in the row?

A. 34 B. 41
C. 24 D. 54

14. Aman remembers that his elder brother was born between 13th and 16th April while his mother remembers that he was born after 14th April and before 17th April. If the statements of both are considered correct, then on which date of April he was born?

A. 13 B. 15
C. 16 D. 14

15. The value of the surface integral $\iint_S \vec{F}\cdot\vec{n}\, ds$, where s is the surface of the sphere $x^2 + y^2 + z^2 = 4$, n is the unit outward normal and $\vec{F} = x\hat{i} + y\hat{j} + z\hat{k}$

A. 6π B. 8π
C. 32π D. 16π

16. A man starts walking from a particular point, towards the north. After walking a distance of 200 m, he turns right and walks a distance of 800 m, then he again turns right and walks a further distance of 800 metres. How far is he from the starting point and in which direction?

A. 1000 m in south-east direction
B. 800 m east
C. 1000 m in south-west direction
D. 600 m south

17. Which one number when placed at the sign of interrogation?

4	5	6
2	3	7
1	8	3
21	98	?

A. 16 B. 73
C. 76 D. 94

18. A complete cycle of a traffic light takes 60 seconds. During each cycle, the light is green for 25 seconds, yellow for 5 seconds and red for 30 seconds. At a randomly chosen time, the probability that the light will not be green, is

A. $\frac{1}{12}$ B. $\frac{3}{4}$

C. $\frac{7}{12}$ D. $\frac{1}{3}$

19. A circle is circumscribed around a square. The area of one of the four shaded portions is equal to 4/7. The radius of the circle is

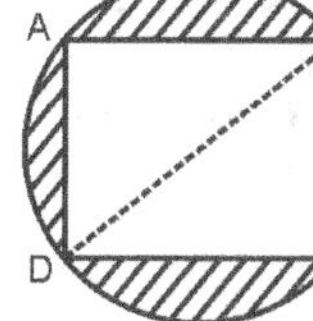

A. 3 B. 2

C. $\sqrt{2}$ D. $\frac{1}{\sqrt{2}}$

20. The Cartesian co-ordinates of four points QRSP are (2, 4), (4, 4), (4, 1) and (0, 0) respectively. Area of the quadrilateral PQRS is

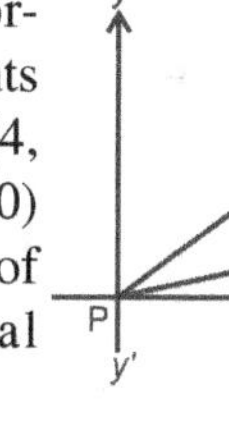

A. 9 B. 10
C. 11 D. 12

PART-B

21. The electric field due to a point charge Q is expressed $\vec{E} = \frac{Q\hat{r}}{4\pi \epsilon_0 r^2}$, then the divergence of electric field due to that point charge is

A. $\frac{3Q}{4\pi \epsilon_0 r^2}$ B. $\frac{2Q}{4\pi \epsilon_0 r}$

C. 0 D. $\frac{3Q}{4\pi \epsilon_0 r}$

22. An artificial satellite revolves about the earth at height H above the surface, the orbital period so that a man in the satellite will be in the slate of weightlessness is

A. $2\pi\sqrt{\frac{g}{R}}$ B. $2\pi\sqrt{\frac{R}{g}}$

C. $\frac{1}{2\pi}\sqrt{\frac{g}{R}}$ D. $\frac{1}{2\pi}\sqrt{\frac{R}{g}}$

23. The magnetic field due to a long straight current carrying conductor of radius R, when $r > R$ [$r \rightarrow$ distance between the point and the axis of wire] proportional to:

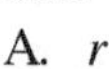

A. r B. r^{-1}
C. r^2 D. r^{-2}

24. The value of entropy at absolute zero of temperature would be

A. zero for all the materials
B. finite for all the materials
C. zero for some materials and non-zero for others
D. unpredictable for any material

25. Efficiency for engine, following the given curve, if in an isothermal expansion the gas volume increases in the same proportion

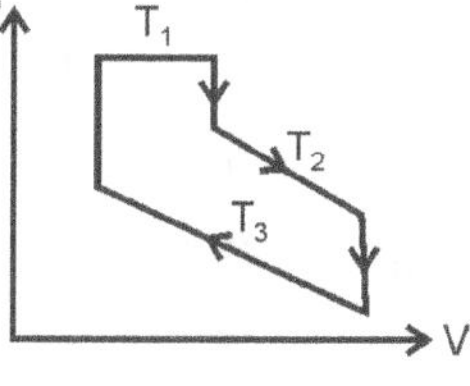

A. $1 - \frac{T_3}{T_1 + T_2}$ B. $1 - \frac{2T_3}{T_1 + T_2}$

C. $\frac{T_3}{T_1 + T_2}$ D. $\frac{2T_3}{T_1 + T_2}$

26. Current I_1 and I_2 flow when large forward voltage V_1 and V_2 are applied to a semiconductor diode. If $V_1 = 2V_2$, then the value of the reverse saturation current is

A. $\frac{I_1 I_2}{I_1 + I_2}$ B. $\frac{I_1^2}{I_2}$

C. $\frac{I_2^2}{I_1}$ D. $\frac{I_1^2 + I_2^2}{I_1 + I_2}$

27. An 0 – 10 A ammeter has a guaranteed accuracy of 1 per cent of full scale deflection. The limiting error while reading 2.5 A is

A. 1% B. 2%
C. 4% D. 5%

28. To go through the ionosphere an electromagnetic wave should have a frequency of at least (H_2)

A. 10 B. 10^4
C. 10^8 D. 10^9

29. The matrix A = $\begin{bmatrix} 1 & 0 \\ 2 & 4 \end{bmatrix}$ is given. The eigen values of $4A^{-1} + 3A + 2I$ are:

A. 6, 15 B. 9, 12
C. 9, 15 D. 7, 15

30. The Symmetric part of P = $\begin{pmatrix} a \\ b \end{pmatrix}(a-2b)$ is

A. $\begin{pmatrix} a^2-2 & ba-1 \\ ba-1 & b^2-2 \end{pmatrix}$

B. $\begin{pmatrix} a(-2) & b \\ b & b^2 \end{pmatrix}$

C. $\begin{pmatrix} a(a-1) & b(a-1) \\ b(a-1) & b^2 \end{pmatrix}$

D. $\begin{pmatrix} a(a-2) & b(a-1) \\ b(a-1) & b^2 \end{pmatrix}$

31. The momentum of an electron (mass m) which has the same kinetic energy as its rest mass energy is

A. $\sqrt{3}\, mc$ B. $\sqrt{2}\, mc$
C. mc D. $\frac{mc}{\sqrt{2}}$

32. The ratio of electric field $\vec{E}$ and magnetic field vector $\vec{H}\left(\frac{E}{H}\right)$ has the dimensions of

A. Impedance B. Resistance
C. Capacitance D. Inductance

33. What is the entropy change of water when 1000 gm of water are heated from 20°C to 80°C. Given that specific heat of water has a constant value 4.2 J gm °C.

A. 682 Jk^{-1} B. 782 Jk^{-1}
C. 385 Jk^{-1} D. 437 Jk^{-1}

34. A change of 200 mV in base-emitter voltage causes a change of 100 mA in the basecurrent. The input resistance of the transistor is

A. 5 kΩ B. 3 kΩ
C. 2 kΩ D. 4 kΩ

35. A signal contains sinusoidal frequencies of 2, 4, 6, 8 and 10 kHz. The respective peak values are 10, 5, 7, 2 and 3 volts. The harmonic distortion is

A. 93.27% B. 89.11%
C. 101.04% D. 72.08%

36. An atom (with l = 2) is placed in a magnetic field of 1.0 Wb/m^2. The rate of precession is

A. 8.8×10^{10} rev/sec
B. 3.5×10^{10} rev/sec
C. 4.5×10^{10} rev/sec
D. 6.9×10^{10} rev/sec

37. The spacing between successive (100) planes in NaCl is 2.820 Å. X-ray incident upon the surface of this crystal, is found to give rise to first order Bragg reflection at a grazing angle of 8°35′. The wavelength of the X-ray is

A. 0.542 Å B. 0.734 Å
C. 0.842 Å D. 0.425 Å

38. Find the energy release, if two ${}_1H^2$ nuclei can fuse together to form ${}_2He^4$ nucleus. The binding energy per nucleon of H^2 and He^4 is 1.1 MeV and 7.0 MeV respectively.

A. 23.6 MeV B. 25.8 MeV
C. 14.7 MeV D. 19.7 MeV

39. A thermometer is calibrated 150°C to 200°C. The accuracy is specified within ±0.25% of instrument span. What is the maximum static error.

A. ± 0.125°C B. ± 0.223°C
C. ± 0.101°C D. ± 325°C

40. A certain amplifier has voltage gain of 15 dB. If the input signal voltage is 0.8 V, what is the output voltage?

A. 3.5 V B. 4.5 V
C. 1.5 V D. 2.5 V

41. A half-wave rectifier is used to supply 50 V d.c. to a resistive load of 800Ω. The diode has a resistance of 25Ω. Calculate a.c. voltage required.

A. 150 V B. 162 V
C. 225 V D. 350 V

42. In a system in thermal equilibrium at absolute temperature T, two states with energy difference 4.83×10^{-21} occur with relative probability e^2. Deduce the temperature.

($k = 1.38 \times 10^{-23}$ joule/K)

A. 198 K B. 102 K
C. 175 K D. 325 K

43. A particle of mass m, moves under the action of a central force whose potential is $v(r^1) = kmr^3$ $(k > 0)$, then energy for which the orbit will be a circle of radius a, about the origin is

A. $\frac{3}{2}mka^3$ B. $\frac{3}{2}mka^2$

C. $\frac{1}{2}mka$ D. $\frac{1}{2}mka^2$

44. A 45 kW broadcasting antenna emits radio waves at a frequency of 4 MHz. How many photons are emitted per second?

A. 1.7×10^{31} B. 2.7×10^{31}
C. 3.7×10^{31} D. 0.7×10^{31}

45. A particle under Brownian motion at 27°C has a r.m.s. speed of 1 metre/sec. The mass of the particle is
(Boltzmann constant $k = 1.38 \times 10^{-23}$ J/K.)

A. 3.12×10^{-20} kg B. 1.24×10^{-20} kg
C. 6.25×10^{-20} kg D. 1.25×10^{-19} kg

PART-C

46. The radiations given off by the Hg atoms returning to their normal states were studied by Frank and Hertz and a line was observed at 2537Å. The excitation potential for Hg is

A. 2.4 V B. 4.9 V
C. 6.5 V D. 7.2 V

47. The diamond crystal structure has the cube edge of 356 Å. Calculate the distance between the nearest neighbours

A. 2.45 Å B. 3.25 Å
C. 1.54 Å D. 1.03 Å

48. In an n-type semiconductor $N_d = 10^{15}$/cc, $m_n = m$ and the donor levels lie below the conduction band by 0.05 eV. Find the temperature at which $n = \frac{1}{2}N_d$.

A. 53.8 K B. 25.7 K
C. 48.2 K D. 61.7 K

49. A nucleus with A = 235, splits into two nuclei whose mass numbers are in the ratio 2 : 1. Find the radii of the new nuclei.

A. 5.99 fm, 7.55 fm B. 3.54 fm, 6.54 fm
C. 1.24 fm, 4.12 fm D. 0.35 fm, 1.35 fm

50. Consider a system of 2 identical particles each of which can be in any one of 3 single particle states. The number of states of the systems are possible in BE statics

A. 9 B. 3
C. 6 D. 1

51. An amplifier whose bandwidth is 100 kHz has a noise power spectrum density input of 7×10^{-21} J. If the input resistance is 50 kΩ and amplifier gain 100. What is the noise output voltage?

A. 1.183 mV B. 11.83 mV
C. 0.83 mV D. 0.35 mV

52. The ratio of frequencies of the first line of the Lyman series and the first line of Balmer series is

A. $\frac{27}{5}$ B. $\frac{27}{8}$

C. $\frac{8}{27}$ D. $\frac{4}{27}$

53. In an experiment with benzene the wavelengths of a pair of stokes and antistokes lines were measured to be 4554 Å and 4178Å respectively. The wavelength of the corresponding infrared absorption line is:

A. 1.012×10^5 Å
B. 2.012×10^5 Å
C. 3.012×10^5 Å
D. 0.125×10^5 Å

54. If maximum and minimum amplitudes of an amplitude modulated waves are 10 V and 5 V respectively, the modulation index is

A. 2 B. 0.5
C. 3.3 D. 0.33

55. The doublet spilting of the first excited state $^2P_{\frac{3}{2}} - {}^2P_{\frac{1}{2}}$ of H is 0.365 cm^{-1}. Calculate the corresponding separation for Li^{++}.

A. 29.6 cm^{-1} B. 38.5 cm^{-1}
C. 41.7 cm^{-1} D. 59.6 cm^{-1}

56. The black body spectrum of an object O_1 is such that its radiant intensity (i.e., intensity per unit wavelength interval) is maximum at a wavelength of 200 nm. Another object O_2 has the maximum radiant intensity at 600 nm. The ratio of power emitted per unit area by O_1 to that of O_2 is

A. $\frac{1}{81}$ B. $\frac{1}{9}$
C. 9 D. 81

57. A metal has a static conductivity of 4 × 10^7 mho/m. Assuming that the true charge carriers are free electrons and they are 2 × 10^{28} per m^3, calculate the relaxation time.

A. 7.1 × 10^{-14} s B. 5.1 × 10^{-12} s
C. 6.2 × 10^{-13} s D. 1.2 × 10^{-14} s

58. Chlorine-33 decays by positron emission with a maximum energy of 4.3 MeV. Calculate the radius of the nucleus from this is

A. 1.25 × 10^{-15} m B. 3.16 × 10^{-14} m
C. 4.54 × 10^{-15} m D. 9.76 × 10^{-15} m

59. The region between a pair of parallel perfectly conducting planes of infinite extent in the *y*- and *z*-directions is partially filled with a dielectric as shown in figure. A 30 GHz TE_{10} wave is incident on the air dielectric interface as shown. Find the VSWR at the interface.

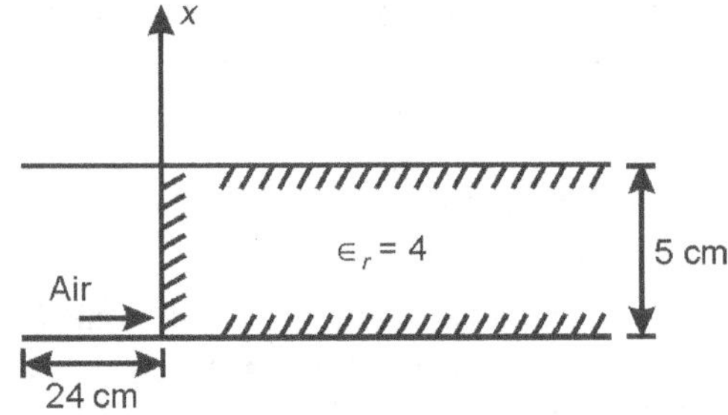

A. 3 B. 2
C. 1 D. 0

60. A 555 timer configured to run in the astable mode oscillation is shown in figure given below. The frequency of the output and the duty cycle is

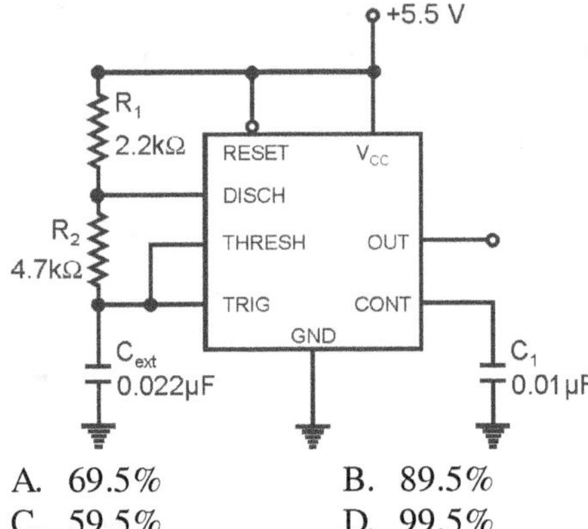

A. 69.5% B. 89.5%
C. 59.5% D. 99.5%

61. The exciting line in an experiment is 5460 Å and the stokes line is at 5520 Å. Find the wavelength of the anti-stokes line.

A. 5401 Å B. 3202 Å
C. 1105 Å D. 7805 Å

62. An α-particle of energy 2 × 10^{-13} J is scattered of an aluminium atom through an angle of 90°. Calculate the distance of closest approach.

Atomic number of Al is 13,

$$e = 1.6 \times 10^{-19}\ C$$

and $4\pi\epsilon_0 = 1 \times 10^{-10}$

A. 4.169 × 10^{-14} m
B. 1.169 × 10^{-14} m
C. 2.014 × 10^{-14} m
D. 0.169 × 10^{-14} m

63. Consider a monovalent metal of density 6.0 × 10^{22} electrons per cm^3. Assuming that θ_D = 300 K and T_C = 0.3 K, determine N(0)*g*.

A. 0.10 B. 0.14
C. 0.23 D. 0.34

64. Find the energy release, if two $_1H^2$ nuclei can fuse together to form $_2He^4$ nucleus. The binding energy per nucleon of H^2 and He^4 is 1.1 MeV and 7.0 MeV respectively.

A. 21.5 MeV B. 23.6 MeV
C. 31.5 MeV D. 11.5 MeV

65. What value of series resistance is required when three 10-watt, 10-volt, 1000 mA zener diodes are connected in series to obtain a 30-volt regulated output from a 45 volt d.c. power source?

A. 20Ω B. 15Ω

C. 25Ω D. 30Ω

66. The emitted radiant energy from a piece of metal is measured and the temperature is found to be 1065°C assuming a surface emissivity of 0.82. It was later found out that the true emissivity is 0.75. The error in temperature measurement.

A. –30°C B. –45°C

C. 30°C D. –60°C

67. If the electrostatic potential at a point (x, y) is given by $V = (2x + 4y)$ volts, the electrostatic energy density at that point (in J/m^3) is

A. $5\varepsilon_0$ B. $10\varepsilon_0$

C. $20\varepsilon_0$ D. $\frac{1}{2}\varepsilon_0(2x+4y)^2$

68. Find the magnetic moment, in Bohr magnetons, of an atom in the state $^3P_2$. In how many sub-states will the state split, if the atom is put in a weak magnetic field?

A. 12 B. 7

C. 9 D. 5

69. The matrix $A = \begin{bmatrix} a & h \\ h & b \end{bmatrix}$ is transformed to the diagonal form $D = T^{-1} AT$, where $T = \begin{bmatrix} \cos\theta & \sin\theta \\ -\sin\theta & \cos\theta \end{bmatrix}$. Find the value of θ which gives this diagonal transformation.

A. $\frac{1}{2}\tan^{-1}\frac{2h}{b-a}$ B. $\frac{1}{3}\tan^{-1}\frac{2h}{a-b}$

C. $\frac{1}{5}\tan^{-1}\frac{h}{a-b}$ D. $\frac{1}{4}\tan^{-1}\frac{3h}{b-a}$

70. A memory system of size 16K bytes is required to be designed using memory chips which have 121 address lines and 4 data lines each. Then number of such chips required to design the memory system is

A. 2 B. 4

C. 8 D. 16

71. Consider a radiation cavity of volume v at temperature T. The density of states at enrgy E of the quantized radiation (photons) is:

A. $\frac{8\pi v}{h^3c^3}E^2$ B. $\frac{8\pi v}{h^3c^3}E^{3/2}$

C. $\frac{8\pi v}{h^3c^2}E$ D. $\frac{8\pi v}{h^3c^2}E^{1/2}$

72. For the dominant modes in a rectangular waveguide with breadth 10 cm, the guide wavelength for a signal of 2.5 GHz will be

A. 12 cm B. 15 cm

C. 18 cm D. 20 cm

73. If the escape velocity from the surface of a spherical planet of mass M is given by $\sqrt{\frac{GM}{2R}}$, the radius of the planet is

A. $\frac{R}{2}$ B. R

C. 2R D. 4R

74. The phase velocity of ocean wave is $\sqrt{\frac{g\lambda}{2\pi}}$, where g is the acceleration due to gravity, then group velocity of ocean wave is

A. $\frac{v_p}{2}$ B. v_p

C. 0 D. $\frac{v_p}{4}$

75. The wave function in the ground state of hydrogen atom is given as

$$\psi = Ae^{-r/a}$$

where r measures distance from nucleus and a is constant. The value of A is:

A. $\frac{1}{\sqrt{\pi a}}$ B. $\frac{1}{\sqrt{\pi a^3}}$

C. $\sqrt{\pi a}$ D. $\frac{1}{\sqrt{\pi a^5}}$

ANSWERS

1	2	3	4	5	6	7	8	9	10
A	D	C	D	A	C	B	A	A	A
11	**12**	**13**	**14**	**15**	**16**	**17**	**18**	**19**	**20**
A	C	A	B	B	A	D	C	C	B
21	**22**	**23**	**24**	**25**	**26**	**27**	**28**	**29**	**30**
C	B	B	A	B	C	C	C	C	D
31	**32**	**33**	**34**	**35**	**36**	**37**	**38**	**39**	**40**
A	B	B	C	A	A	C	A	A	B
41	**42**	**43**	**44**	**45**	**46**	**47**	**48**	**49**	**50**
B	C	A	A	B	B	C	A	A	C
51	**52**	**53**	**54**	**55**	**56**	**57**	**58**	**59**	**60**
B	A	A	D	A	A	A	C	B	C
61	**62**	**63**	**64**	**65**	**66**	**67**	**68**	**69**	**70**
A	A	B	B	B	A	B	D	A	C
71	**72**	**73**	**74**	**75**					
A	B	D	A	B					

EXPLANATORY ANSWERS

1. The seating arrangement is shown in the fig. Hence, Q is just left of R.

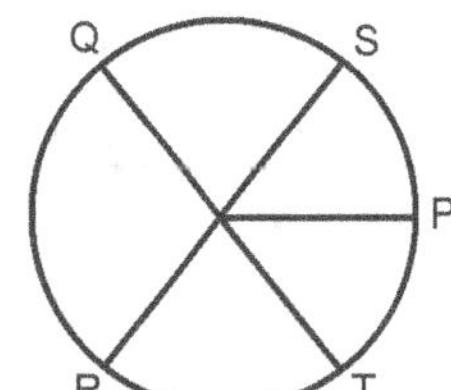

2. A. $L \xrightarrow{+2} N \xrightarrow{+2} P$

B. $V \xrightarrow{+2} X \xrightarrow{+2} Z$

C. $S \xrightarrow{+2} U \xrightarrow{+2} W$

D. $B \xrightarrow{+2} D \xrightarrow{+3} G$

From the above operation, it is clear that the alternative (D) is different from the rest four groups.

3. Total numbers of members = 108

No of men = $108 \times \frac{2}{3} = 36 \times 2 = 72$

$\therefore$ No. of women = 108 – 72 = 36

No. of unmarried women = 9

$\therefore$ No. of married women = 36 – 9 = 27

4. Dots are placed in a symmetrical order to start with, when dot 1 is connected to 9 with straight line, the line is bound to pass through dot 6. Similarly, when 9 is joined to 5, the line joined with 8 also and so on.

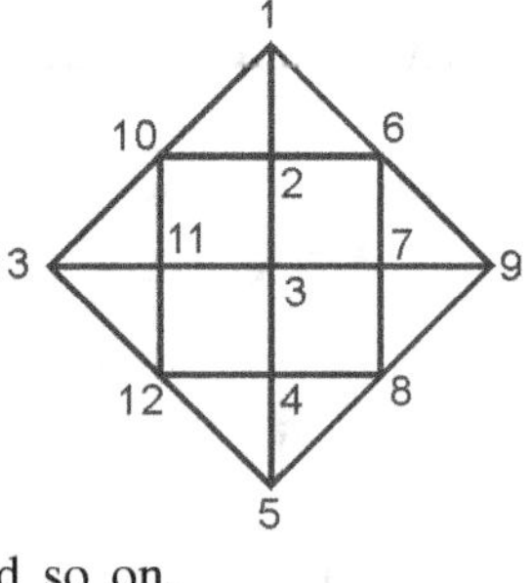

After, all the needed lines have been drawn, the resulting figure was above with 20 triangles.

5. Hypotenuse

$AB = \sqrt{3^2 + 4^2} = 5$

Perpendicular,

$CD = \frac{4 \times 3}{5} = \frac{12}{5} = DC'$

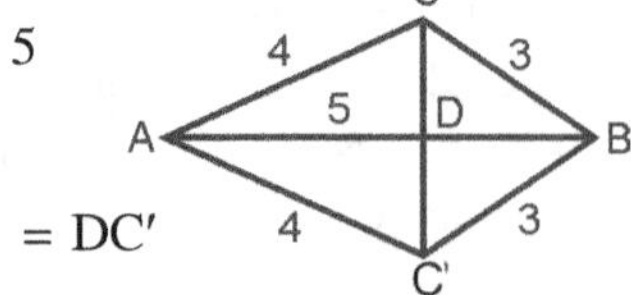

Turning ABC′ through 90° make the planes ABC and ABC′ perpendicular to one another, then CD is perpendicular to C′D in the same plane. So, CDC′ is right angles tringle with CC′ as hypotenuse, $(CC')^2 = CD^2 + C'D^2$

$$= \left(\frac{12}{5}\right)^2 + \left(\frac{12}{5}\right)^2$$

$$\therefore \quad CC' = \frac{12\sqrt{2}}{5}.$$

6.

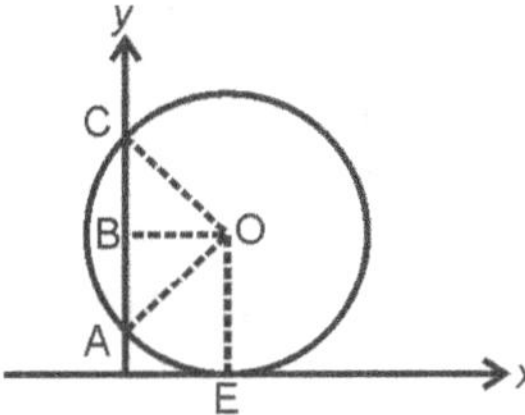

Let centre of the circle is O = (α, 5)

Given, AC = 6 units

Let BO is ⊥ar drawn on chord AC.

$$AB = BC = 3 \text{ units}$$

From single-angled triangle ΔABO,

$$(BO)^2 + (AB)^2 = (AO)^2$$

$$(\alpha)^2 + (3)^2 = (5)^2$$

$$\alpha^2 = 5^2 - 3^2 = 16$$

$$\alpha = \sqrt{16} = 4$$

∴ Centre of circle = (4, 5).

7. Time of information

= 1:40 pm = 13:40

According to question,

= (13:40 – 3:30) + 1:20

= 10:10 + 1:20 = 11:30.

8. Second figure in each row consists of first arrow of the first fig. as such as the second one in an inverted position.

The third figure, consists of the first arrow of first figure in an inverted position and the second arrow as such.

9.
$$A = 3B \qquad ...(i)$$

Four years ago their ages,

$$C - 4 = 2(A - 4) \qquad ...(ii)$$

and
$$A + 4 = 31 \qquad (iii)$$

$$\therefore \quad A = 31 - 4 = 27 \text{ years}$$

From equation (*i*), we get

$$3B = 27$$

$$\Rightarrow \quad B = 9 \text{ years}$$

From equation (*ii*), we get

$$C - 4 = 2(27 - 4)$$

$$= 2 \times 23$$

$$\Rightarrow \quad C = 46 + 4 = 50 \text{ years.}$$

10. Suppose the centre of sphere is A and radius *r*, AC is ⊥ar draw from A to side OD.

$$AC = r \text{ cm}$$

From rt. ΔOAC,

$$\sin 30° = \frac{AC}{OA} = \frac{r}{OA}$$

$$\Rightarrow \quad OA = r \text{ cosec } (30°)$$

$$= 2r$$

Now, height of conical vessel

$$OB = 10.5$$

Height, $OB = OA + AB = 2r + r$

$$\Rightarrow \quad 10.5 = 3r$$

$$\Rightarrow \quad r = 3.5 \text{ cm.}$$

11. Distance covered by *x* in 50 chances

= 49(5 – 1) + 5

= 49 × 4 + 5 = 201 cm

Distance covered by *y* in 50 chances

= 49(6 – 3) + 6 = 49 × 3 + 6

= 153 cm

Distance covered by *z* in 50 chances

= 49(7 – 2) + 7

= 49 × 5 + 7 = 252 cm

Hence, height of the shortest pillar is 153 cm.

12. If *a* cm is the length of one side of the smallest triangle, then

$$\frac{\sqrt{3}}{4}a^2 = 100$$

$$\therefore \quad a^2 = \frac{100 \times 4}{\sqrt{3}} = \frac{400}{\sqrt{3}}$$

But the side of the largest Δ will be 8*a* cm.

∴ Area of the largest Δ

$$= \frac{\sqrt{3}}{4}(8a)^2$$

$$= \frac{\sqrt{3}}{4} \cdot 64a^2$$

$$= \frac{\sqrt{3}}{4} \times 64 \times \frac{400}{\sqrt{3}}$$

$$= 6400 \text{ cm}^2 = 0.64 \text{ m}^2.$$

13. $\xrightarrow[\text{Savita}]{10^{th}} \xleftarrow[\text{Lazy}]{20^{th}} \xleftarrow[\text{Lazy}]{25^{th}}$

Difference of two positions of Lazy from the right = 25 – 20 = 5.

Hence, initially there are 5 ladies between Savita and Lazy. Therefore, an interchanging the positions Savita's position from the left

$= 10 + 5 = 15^{th}$

∴ Total number of ladies

= (Initial position of Lazy from right + final position of Savita from left) – 1

= (20 + 15) – 1 = 34.

14. According to Aman, date of birth of his elder brother = April (14 and 15) and according to his mother the date of birth of her son

= April (15 and 16)

Therefore, the date of birth of Aman's elder brother is 15th April.

15.
$$\iint_S \vec{F} \cdot \hat{n}\, ds = \iiint \text{div } F\, dV$$

$$= \iiint \left(\hat{i}\frac{\partial}{\partial x} + \hat{j}\frac{\partial}{\partial y} + \hat{k}\frac{\partial}{\partial z} \right) \left(x\hat{i} + y\hat{j} + z\hat{k} \right) dV$$

$$= \iiint 3\, dV$$

Putting the value $x = r \sin\theta \cos\phi$

$y = r \sin\theta \sin\phi$

$z = r \cos\theta$, we get

$$= 3\iiint \left(r^2 \sin\theta\, dr\, d\theta\, d\phi\right)$$

$$= 3\int_0^{\pi} d\phi \int_0^{\pi/2} \sin\theta\, d\theta \int_0^2 r^2 dV$$

$$= 3 \times \pi \times (-\cos\theta)_0^{\pi/2} \cdot \left(\frac{r^3}{3}\right)_0^2$$

$$= 3\pi \times (0+1)\left(\frac{2^3}{3}\right)$$

$$= \pi \times 8 = 8\pi.$$

16. The man starts walking from starting point O, 200 m to A towards north. From A, he turns right to go east. Distance from A to B is 800 m. At B, he again turns right to walk south. Distance from B to D is 800 m.

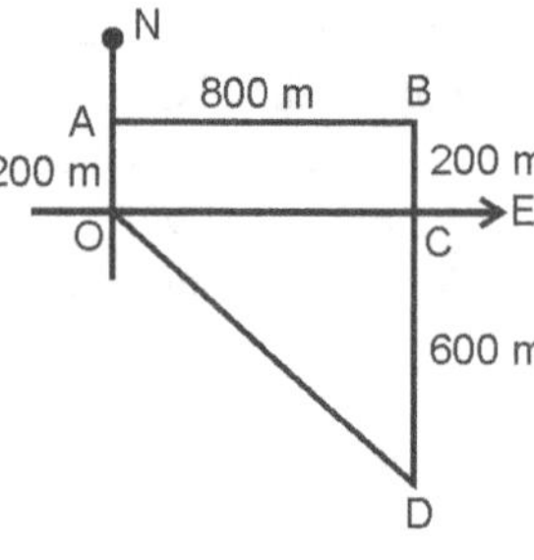

In rt. angled triangle OCD,

OC = 800 m

CD = BD – BC

= 800 – 200 = 600 m

In Δ OCD,

$OD^2 = OC^2 + CD^2$

$= (800)^2 + (600)^2$

= 10,00,000

∴ OD = 1000 m

17. We have,

$4^2 + 2^2 + 1^2 = 16 + 4 + 1 = 21$

$5^2 + 3^2 + 8^2 = 25 + 9 + 64 = 98$

$6^2 + 7^2 + 3^2 = 36 + 49 + 9$

$= 94$

Hence, the number is 94.

18. Probability for light to be green $= \frac{25}{60} = \frac{5}{12}$

Probability for light not to be green

$$= 1 - \frac{5}{12} = \frac{7}{12}.$$

19. $a^2 = 2r^2$

Area of the shaded portion of the circle

$$= 4 \times \frac{4}{7}$$

$\pi r^2 - a^2 = \pi r^2 - 2r^2$

$= r^2(\pi - 2)$

$$= 4 \times \frac{4}{7}$$

The diagonal of a square bisect each other at 90°.

So, $r^2(\pi - 2) = \dfrac{4 \times 4}{7}$

$$r^2 \times \left(\frac{22}{7} - 2\right) = \frac{4 \times 4}{7}$$

$$r^2 \times \left(\frac{22-14}{7}\right) = \frac{4 \times 4}{7}$$

$$\Rightarrow \quad r^2 = \frac{4 \times 4}{8} \Rightarrow r^2 = 2$$

or $\quad r = \sqrt{2}$

20. The co-ordinates of Q and R being the same QR is parallel to x-axis.

So, PT, being the x-axis.

Now, QR = 2 units

PT = 4 units

QR ∥ PT

So, PQRT is a trapezium.

Area of quadrilateral PQRS

= Area of PQRT – Area of PST

$$= \left(\frac{2+4}{2}\right) \times 4 - 4 \times \frac{1}{2}$$

= 10.

21.
$$\vec{E} = \frac{Q\hat{r}}{4\pi \epsilon_0 r^2}$$

$$\vec{\nabla} \cdot \vec{E} = \vec{\nabla} \cdot \frac{Q\hat{r}}{4\pi \epsilon_0 r^2}$$

$$= \frac{Q}{4\pi \epsilon_0} \vec{\nabla} \frac{\hat{r}}{r^2}$$

$$= \frac{Q}{4\pi \epsilon_0} \cdot \vec{\nabla} \cdot \frac{\vec{r}}{r^3}$$

But $\quad \vec{\nabla} \cdot \frac{\vec{r}}{r^3} = 0$

$\therefore \quad \vec{\nabla} \cdot \vec{E} = 0$

22. If orbit is circular, then

Attractive force = Centripetal force

$$\Rightarrow \quad \frac{GMm}{(R+H)^2} = \frac{8 R^2 m}{(R+H)^2} = \frac{mv_0^2}{R+H}$$

v_o = Orbital velocity

R = Radius of earth

$$\Rightarrow \quad v_0 = \frac{R}{R+H} \sqrt{[(R+H)g]} \qquad \text{...(1)}$$

If H << R

$\therefore \quad v_0 = \sqrt{Rg}$

Also orbital speed, $v_0 = \dfrac{2\pi(R+H)}{\pi}$

or $\quad T = \dfrac{2\pi(R+H)}{v_0}$

From equation (1), we get

$$T = 2\pi \frac{(R+H)}{R} \sqrt{\frac{R+H}{g}}$$

if H << R, then $\sqrt{\dfrac{R}{g}}$

or $\quad T = \dfrac{2\pi(R+H)}{v_0}$

$$T = 2\pi \sqrt{\frac{R}{g}}.$$

23. Magnetic field due to a long straight current carrying conductor

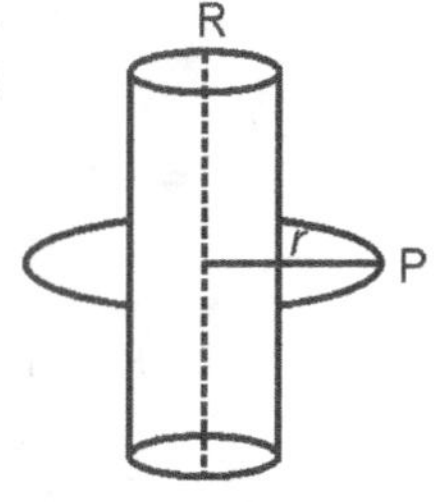

$$\oint \vec{B} \cdot \vec{dl} = \mu_0 \int \vec{j} \cdot \vec{ds}$$

$B.2\pi r = \mu_0$

[current crossing the bounded surface]

when $r > R$, current crossing bounded surface is I.

$$B.2\pi r = \mu_0 I$$

$$B = \frac{\mu_0}{4\pi} \cdot \frac{2I}{r}$$

$$B \propto \frac{1}{r}.$$

24. At absolute zero of temperature, all molecular motion ceases.

$\therefore$ From 2nd law of thermodynamics

$$dS = \frac{dQ}{T}$$

$$S = \frac{dQ}{T} = 0$$

25. We have, $V_2 = nV_1$, $V_4 = nV_3$

$$Q_1 = \text{Heat taken at upper term}$$
$$= RT_1 \ln n + RT_2 \ln n$$
$$= R(T_1 + T_2) \ln n$$

Now, $T_1V_2^{r-1} = T_2V_3^{r-1}$

$$\Rightarrow \quad V_3 = \left(\frac{T_1}{T_2}\right)^{1/(r-1)}$$

Similarly, $V_5 = \left(\frac{T_1}{T_2}\right)^{1/(r-1)} V_4$

$$V_6 = \left(\frac{T_1}{T_2}\right)^{1/(r-1)} V_1$$

Now, $Q_2 \to$ heat released at large temperature

$$= -RT_3 \ln\frac{V_6}{V_5}$$
$$= -RT_3 \ln\left(\frac{T_1}{T_2}\right)^{1/(r-1)} \times \frac{V_1}{V_4}$$
$$= +RT_3 \ln\left(\frac{T_1}{T_2}\right)^{1/(r-1)} \times \frac{V_2}{n^2V_3}$$
$$= RT_3 \ln\left(\frac{T_1}{T_2}\right)^{1/(r-1)} \cdot \frac{1}{n^2}\left(\frac{T_1}{T_2}\right)^{1/(r-1)}$$
$$= RT_3 \ln n$$
$$\Rightarrow \quad n = 1 - \frac{2T_3}{T_1 + T_2}$$

26. We have, $I = I_0 e^{ev/kT}$

$\therefore$ $I_1 = I_0 e^{ev_1/kT}$

and $I_2 = I_0 e^{ev_2/kT}$

Since $V_1 = 2V_2$

$$I_1 = I_0 e^{2ev_2/kT_1}$$

or $\frac{I_1}{I_2} = \frac{e^{2ev_2/kT}}{e^{ev_2/kT}} = e^{ev_2/kT}$

or $\frac{I_1}{I_2} = \frac{I_2}{I_0}$ [Since $I_2 = I_0 e^{ev_2/kT}$]

or $I_0 = \frac{I_2^2}{I_1}$.

27. We have, 0 – 10 A ammeter has accuracy of

$1\% = \frac{10}{100} = 0.1$

$\therefore$ Limiting error in reading 2.5 A is

$$= \frac{\text{Difference}}{\text{Actual reading}} \times 100$$
$$= \frac{0.1}{2.5} \times 100$$
$$= 4\%.$$

28. To go through the ionosphere, the angular frequency ω of a wave should be greater than the plasma frequency, $\omega_p = \sqrt{\frac{Ne^2}{\varepsilon_0 m}}$

The maximum electron density of a typical layer is $N \sim 10^{13}\ m^{-3}$

For an electron, $\frac{e^2}{\epsilon_0 m} = 3 \times 10^3\ m^3s^{-2}$

Hence, $\omega_p = \sqrt{3 \times 10^{16}} = 1.732 \times 10^8$

$$= 10^8$$

Hence, best rms is $10^8\ H_z$.

29. We have, $A = \begin{bmatrix} 1 & 0 \\ 2 & 4 \end{bmatrix}$

$$\lambda_1 = 1, 4$$

Eigen value of $A^{-1} = 1, \frac{1}{4}$

Eigen value of $A = 1, 4$

Eigen value of $I = 1, 1$

$\therefore$ Eigen values of $4A^{-1} + 3A + 2I$ are

$4(1) + 3(1) + 2(I) = 4 + 3 + 2 = 9$

or $4\left(\frac{1}{4}\right) + 3(4) + 2(1)$

$$= 1 + 12 + 2 = 15.$$

30. $\begin{bmatrix} a(a-2) & ab \\ b(a-2) & b^2 \end{bmatrix} = P$

$$P' = \begin{bmatrix} a(a-2) & b(a-2) \\ ab & b^2 \end{bmatrix}$$

$$= \frac{1}{2}(P + P')$$

$$= \frac{1}{2}\left\{\begin{bmatrix} 2a(a-2) & ab + ab - 2b \\ ab - 2b + ab & b^2 + b^2 \end{bmatrix}\right\}$$

$$= \begin{bmatrix} a(a-2) & b(a-1) \\ b(a-1) & b^2 \end{bmatrix}$$

31. We know that,

$$E^2 = p^2c^2 + m^2c^4 \quad [\because E = mc^2]$$

$$(2\,mc^2)^2 = p^2c^2 + m^2c^4$$

$$4m^2c^4 = p^2c^2 + m^2c^4$$

$$\Rightarrow \quad p^2c^2 = 4m^2c^4 - m^2c^4$$

$$\Rightarrow \quad p^2c^2 = 3m^2c^4$$

$$\Rightarrow \quad p^2 = 3m^2c^2$$

$$\therefore \quad p = \sqrt{3}\,mc$$

32. We know that,

$$\vec{H} = \frac{1}{\mu_0 c}\vec{E}$$

$$\Rightarrow \quad \left|\frac{E}{H}\right| = \left|\frac{E_0}{H_0}\right| = \mu_0 C$$

$$\therefore \quad E = \text{volt/m}$$

$$H = \text{amp} - \text{turn/m}$$

Hance, ratio,

$$Z_0 = \frac{\text{volt/m}}{\text{amp} - \text{turn/m}}$$

$$= \frac{\text{volt}}{\text{amp}} = \text{ohm}$$

which is the unit of the resistance.

33. Suppose the process is carried out reversibly by heating the water through the baths of steadily increasing temperature. Then, change in entropy is given by

$$dS = mc\int_{T_1}^{T_2}\frac{dT}{T} = mc\left(\log_e \frac{T_2}{T_1}\right)$$

$$= 2.3026\ mc\ \log_{10}\frac{T_2}{T_1}$$

$$= 2.3026 \times 1000 \times 4.2\ \log_{10}\frac{353}{293}$$

$$= 782\ \text{Jk}^{-1}$$

Hence, option (B) is correct.

34. Change in base-emitter voltage,

$$\Delta V_{BE} = 200\ \text{mV}$$

Change in base current,

$$\Delta I_g = 100\ \mu\text{A}$$

$\therefore$ Input resistance,

$$R_i = \frac{\Delta V_{BE}}{\Delta I_B} = \frac{200\,\text{mV}}{100\,\mu\text{A}}$$

$$= 2\ \text{k}\Omega.$$

35. As the individual components are pure sinusoidal their rms values are given by

$$HD = \frac{\sqrt{V_2^2 + V_3^2 + V_4^2 + \ldots}}{V_1}$$

$$V_{rms} = \frac{V_{peak}}{\sqrt{2}}$$

Hence, $$H.D. = \frac{\dfrac{\sqrt{(5)^2 + (7)^2 + (2)^2 + (3)^2}}{\sqrt{2}}}{\dfrac{10}{\sqrt{2}}}$$

$$= \frac{\sqrt{(5)^2 + (7)^2 + (2)^2 + (3)^2}}{10}$$

$$= 0.9327 = 93.27\%.$$

36. From Larmor's theorem,

$$W_i = g_i\frac{e}{2m}\cdot B$$

For orbital motion of an electron $g_i = 1$

$$W_i = \frac{e\hbar}{2m\hbar}\cdot B$$

$$= \frac{0.927 \times 10^{-23}\,\text{J/Wb/m}^2 \times 1\,\text{Wb/m}^2}{6.6 \times 10^{-34}}$$

$$= 8.8 \times 10^{10}\ \text{rev/sec}$$

37. We have for Bragg reflection

$$2d\sin\theta = n\lambda$$

For $n = 1, 2d \sin\theta = \lambda$

Here $d = 2.820$

$\theta = 8°35'$

$\therefore$ $\lambda = 2 \times 2.820 \times \sin 8°35'$

$= 2 \times 0.820 \times 0.1491 = 0.842$ Å.

38. Since number of nucleons is $_2He^4$ nucleus is 4, hence B.E. for $_2He^4$ = 28.0 MeV, similarly B.E. for H^2 nucleus (combination of one proton and one neutron) = 2.2 MeV.

Mass of $_2He^4$ nucleus = 2[Mass of proton] + 2 [Mass of neutron] – 28.0 MeV

Mass of $_1H^2$ nucleus = [Mass of proton] + [Mass of neutron] – 2.2 MeV

In fusion reaction energy released

$$\Delta E = 2[\text{Mass of } {}_1H^2] - [\text{Mass of } {}_2He^4]$$
$$= 2[M_p + M_n - 2.2] - [2M_p + 2M_n - 28.0]$$
$$= 23.6 \text{ MeV}.$$

39. Span of thermometer = 200°C – 150°C = 50°C

$$\therefore \text{ Maximum static error } = \frac{\pm 0.25 \times 50}{100} = \pm 0.125°C$$

40. dB voltage gain = $20 \log_{10} V_2/V_1$

or $15 = 20 \log_{10} V_2/V_1$

or $15/20 = \log_{10} V_2/V_1$

or $0.75 = \log_{10} V_2/0.8$

Taking antilogs, we get

Antilog $0.75 = \text{Antilog} (\log_{10} V_2/0.8)$

or $10^{0.75} = V_2/0.8$

$\therefore$ $V_2 = 10^{0.75} \times 0.8 = 4.5$ V

41. Output d.c. voltage $V_{dc} = 50$ V

diode resistance, $r_f = 25\ \Omega$

load resistance, $R_L = 800\ \Omega$

Let V_m be the maximum value of a.c. voltage required.

$$\therefore \quad V_{dc} = I_{dc} \times R_L = \frac{I_m}{\pi} \times R_L$$
$$= \frac{V_m}{\pi(r_f + R_L)} \times R_L \quad [\because I_m = \frac{V_m}{r_f + R_L}]$$

or
$$50 = \frac{V_m}{\pi(25 + 800)} \times 800$$

$$\therefore \quad V_m = \frac{\pi \times 825 \times 50}{800} = 162 \text{ V}$$

Hence, a.c. voltage of maximum value 162 V is required.

42. When the system has two energy states ε_1 and ε_2, we have

$$\omega_1 = Ce^{-\beta\varepsilon_1} \text{ and } \omega_2 = Ce^{-\beta\varepsilon_2}$$

$$\therefore \quad \frac{\omega_1}{\omega_2} = \frac{e^{-\beta\varepsilon_1}}{e^{-\beta\varepsilon_2}} = \exp.\left[(\varepsilon_2 - \varepsilon_1)/kT\right]$$

or
$$\log_e\left(\frac{\omega_1}{\omega_2}\right) = (\varepsilon_2 - \varepsilon_1)/kT$$

$$\therefore \quad T = \frac{\varepsilon_2 - \varepsilon_1}{k \log_e(\omega_1/\omega_2)}$$
$$= \frac{4.83 \times 10^{-21}}{(1.38 \times 10^{-23}) \log_e(e^2)}$$
$$= \frac{4.83 \times 10^{-21}}{1.38 \times 10^{-23} \times 2} = 175 \text{K}.$$

43. If the orbit is circular, then

Attractive force = centrifugal force

$$\Rightarrow \quad f = \left(\frac{dV}{dr}\right) = \frac{mv^2}{r} [V = kmr^3]$$
$$\Rightarrow \quad \frac{d}{dr}(kmr^2) = \frac{mv^2}{r}$$
$$\Rightarrow \quad 3\ kr^2 = \frac{v^2}{r}$$
$$\Rightarrow \quad v = r\sqrt{3kr}$$
$$\Rightarrow \quad r = a$$
$$\frac{v}{r} = a = a\sqrt{3ka}$$
$$\text{KE} = \frac{1}{2}mv^2$$
$$\Rightarrow \quad E = \frac{1}{2}\ m.a^2.3ka$$
$$E = \frac{3}{2}mka^3$$

44. The electromagnetic energy emitted by the

antenna in one second is E = 45000 J. Thus, the number of photons emitted in one second is

$$n = \frac{E}{h\nu}$$

$$= \frac{45000\text{ J}}{6.63\times10^{-34}\text{ Js}\times 4\times 10^{6}\text{Hz}}$$

$$= 1.7 \times 10^{31}.$$

45. The translational kinetic energy of the particle is $\frac{3}{2}$kT. Thus

$$\frac{1}{2}m\,(C_{rms})^2 = \frac{3}{2}\text{kT}$$

$$\therefore \quad m = \frac{3\text{kT}}{(C_{rms})^2}$$

Here T = 27°C = 300 K,

and C_{rms} = 1 m/sec.

$$\therefore \quad m = \frac{3\times(1.38\times10^{-23})\times300}{(1)^2}$$

$$= 1.24 \times 10^{-20}\text{ kg.}$$

46. λ = 2537 Å = 2537 × 10^{-10} m

Let excitation potential be V

$$\therefore \quad eV = h\nu = \frac{hc}{\lambda} \quad \text{or} \quad V = \frac{hc}{e\lambda}$$

$$V = \frac{6.6\times10^{-34}\times3\times10^{8}}{1.6\times10^{-19}\times2537\times10^{-10}}$$

$$= 4.9\text{ volts.}$$

47. The diamond structure consists of two inter-penetrating fcc lattices displaced along the body diagonal of the cubic cell by $\frac{1}{4}$th the length of that diagonal. The nearest neighbour distance (d) is, therefore, given by

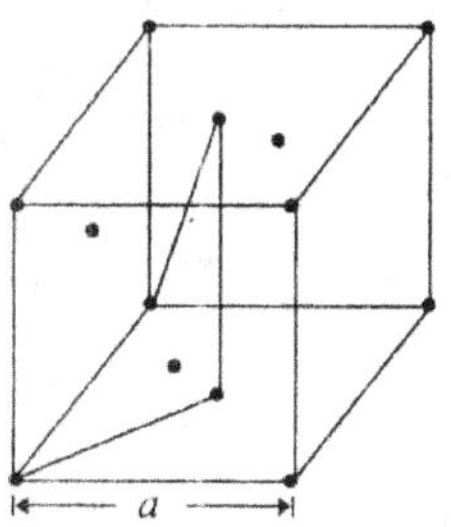

$$d = \frac{1}{4}\times \text{ length of the body diagonal}$$

If a is the edge length of the cubic cell, the length of the body diagonal is

$$\sqrt{3}a = 1.732\times3.56\text{ Å}$$

or $$d = \frac{1}{4}\times1.73\times3.56\text{ Å} = 1.54\text{ Å}.$$

48. Here $N_d = 10^{15}$/cc, $m_n^* = m$; $E_c - E_d = 0.05$ eV

The electron density in donor state is,

$$n_d = \frac{N_d}{1+\exp\left(\frac{E_d - E_F}{kT}\right)} = \frac{1}{2}N_d$$

(with half the donor states ionised)

or $$1+\exp\left(\frac{E_d - E_F}{kT}\right) = 2$$

or $$\exp\left(\frac{E_d - E_F}{kT}\right) = 1 = \exp(0)$$

$$\therefore \quad E_d = E_F$$

But electron density in conduction band is given by

$$n = N_C \exp\left(-\frac{E_C - E_F}{kT}\right)$$

or $$\frac{1}{2}N_d = N_C \exp\left(-\frac{E_C - E_F}{kT}\right)$$

$$= N_C \exp\left(-\frac{0.05}{kT}\right)$$

where $$N_C = \left(\frac{2\pi mkT}{h^2}\right)^{3/2}$$

$$\simeq 2.25\times10^{19}\text{ /cc (for T = 300 K)}$$

Thus $$\frac{1}{2}N_d = 2.25\times10^{19}\exp\left(-\frac{0.05}{kT}\right)$$

or $$\frac{1}{2}\times10^{15} = 2.25\times10^{19}\exp\left(-\frac{0.05}{kT}\right)$$

or $$\exp\left(-\frac{0.05}{kT}\right) = \frac{10^{15}}{2\times2.25\times10^{19}}$$

or $$\exp\left(\frac{0.05}{kT}\right) = \frac{4.5\times10^{19}}{10^{15}} = 4.5\times10^{4}$$

$$\frac{0.05}{kT} = \ln\,[4.5\times10^{4}] = 10.77$$

or $$T = \frac{4.668 \times 10^{-3}}{26 \times 10^{-3}} \times 300 = 53.8 \text{ K}$$

or $$kT = \frac{0.05}{10.77} = 4.668 \times 10^{-3} \text{ J}$$

Again we know that,

$$k \times 300 = 26\, m_e V$$

$$\therefore \quad \frac{kT}{k + 300} = \frac{4.668 + 10}{26 \times 10^{-3}}$$

or $$T = \frac{4.668 \times 10^{-3}}{26 \times 10^{-3}} \times 300$$
$$= 53.8 \text{ K}.$$

49. If A_1 and A_2 are the mass numbers of the new nuclei, then $A_1 = \frac{1}{3} \times 235$ and $A_2 = \frac{2}{3} \times 235$.

Therefore, the radii of the new numbers are

$$R_1 = R_0 A_1^{1/3} = 1.4 \times \left(\frac{235}{3}\right)^{1/3} = 5.99 \text{ fm}$$

$$R_2 = R_0 A_2^{1/3} = 1.5 \times \left(235 \times \frac{2}{3}\right)^{1/3} = 7.55 \text{ fm}.$$

50. The total number of ways W of distributing of identical particles (1) and (2) is

$$W = \prod_{i=1}^{n} \frac{(N_i + g_i - 1)!}{N_i!(g_i - 1)!}$$

$$W = \frac{(2+3-1)!}{2!(3-1)!} = \frac{4!}{2!2!}$$

$$= \frac{4 \times 3 \times 2 \times 1}{2 \times 2} = 6.$$

51. Power density spectrum

$$S_n = kT = 7 \times 10^{-21}$$

Input resistance, $R = 50 \times 10^3\ \Omega$

Bandwidth $= 100 \times 10^3$ Hz

Noise voltage $E_n = 2\sqrt{k'TR\Delta f}$

$$= 2 \times \sqrt{7 \times 10^{-21} \times 50 \times 10^3 \times 100 \times 10^3}$$
$$= 11.83 \text{ mV}$$

52. First Lyman series,

$$\nu_1 = \frac{1}{\lambda_1} = R_H\left[1 - \frac{1}{4}\right]$$

$$= \frac{3}{4} R_H$$

Frequency for the first Balmer series

$$\nu = R_H\left[\frac{1}{2^2} - \frac{1}{n_2^2}\right]$$

$$n_2 = 3, 4, 5,$$

$$= R_H\left[\frac{1}{4} - \frac{1}{9}\right] = \frac{5}{36} R_H$$

$\therefore$ Their ratio

$$= \frac{\frac{3}{4} R_H}{\frac{5}{36} R_H} = \frac{3}{4} \times \frac{36}{5} = \frac{27}{5}.$$

53. We know that,

$$\nu = \nu_0 \pm \nu_m$$

$$\therefore \quad \nu_1 = \nu_0 + \nu_m$$

and $$\nu_2 = \nu_0 - \nu_m$$

$$\therefore \quad \nu_1 - \nu_2 = 2\nu_m$$

$$\frac{c}{\lambda_1} - \frac{c}{\lambda_2} = \frac{2c}{\lambda_m}$$

or $$\lambda_m = \left[\frac{2\lambda_1\lambda_2}{\lambda_1 - \lambda_2}\right]$$

$\Rightarrow$ $\lambda_2 = 4554$ Å and $\lambda_1 = 4178$ Å

$$\therefore \quad \lambda_m = \frac{2 \times 4554 \times 4178}{4554 - 4178}$$
$$= 1.012 \times 10^5 \text{ Å}.$$

54. Modulation index,

$$m = \frac{V_{max} - V_{min}}{V_{max} + V_{min}}$$

Here, $V_{max} = 10$ V

$V_{min} = 5$ V

$$\therefore \quad m = \frac{10 - 5}{10 + 5} = \frac{1}{3} = 0.33.$$

55. $$\Delta T \propto z^4$$

For Li^{++} and H, $z = 3$ and I respectively,

$$\therefore \quad \frac{\Delta T_{Li^{++}}}{\Delta T_H} = \frac{(3)^4}{(1)^4} = 81$$

or $\Delta T_{Li^{++}} = 81\, (\Delta T_H)$.

$= 81 \times (0.365\ \text{cm}^{-1})$
$= 29.6\ \text{cm}^{-1}$.

56. As maximum radiant intensity is provided by

$$\lambda_m T = b \quad \text{(wein laws)}$$

or, $$\lambda_m = \frac{b}{T} \quad ...(1)$$

Also from stefan Boltzmann law

$$E \propto T^4$$

$$\Rightarrow \frac{E_{01}}{E_{02}} = \left(\frac{T_1}{T_2}\right)^4 = \left(\frac{\lambda_{m_2}}{\lambda_{m_1}}\right)^4 \quad \text{[using 1]}$$

$$\frac{E_{01}}{E_{02}} = \left(\frac{600}{200}\right)^4$$

$$\therefore E_{01} : E_{02} = 81$$

57. Conductivity of metal in terms of relaxation time is given by the relation

$$\sigma = \frac{Ne^2\tau}{m}$$

where N is the number of charge carriers and τ is the relaxation time.

$\sigma = 4 \times 10^7$ mho/m;
$N = 2 \times 10^{28}/\text{m}^3$; $\tau = ?$
$e = 1.6 \times 10^{-19}$ coulomb;
$m = 9.1 \times 10^{-31}$ kg

$$\tau = \frac{\sigma.m}{Ne^2} = \frac{4 \times 10^7 \times 9.1 \times 10^{-31}}{2 \times 10^{28} \times (1.6 \times 10^{-19})^2}$$

or, $$\tau = 7.1 \times 10^{-14}\ \text{sec.}$$

58. The decay scheme is

$${}_{17}C^{33} \rightarrow {}_{16}S^{33} + {}_{1}e^0 + \nu + E_\beta$$

When this proton emits with a maximum energy, the neutrino energy will be zero and the daughter nucleus S^{33} will be formed in the ground state

$$\therefore \quad E_\beta = \frac{3}{5}\frac{e^2A^{2/3}}{4\pi \epsilon_0 R_0} - 1.80\ \text{MeV}$$

or $$\frac{3}{5}\frac{e^2A^{2/3}}{4\pi \epsilon_0 R_0} = 6.1 \times 1.6 \times 10^{-13}\ \text{joule}$$

or $$R_0 = \frac{3}{5}\frac{e^2A^{2/3}}{4\pi \epsilon_0 \times 6.1 \times 1.6 \times 10^{-13}}$$

$$= \frac{3}{5}\frac{(1.6 \times 10^{-19})^2 (33)^{2/3} \times 9 \times 10^9}{6.1 \times 1.6 \times 10^{-13}}$$

$$= 1.41 \times 10^{-15}$$

$$\therefore \quad R = R_0\ A^{1/3}$$

$$= 1.41 \times 10^{-15} \times (33)^{1/3}$$

$$= 4.54 \times 10^{-15}\ \text{m.}$$

59. The given region is as shown below

$$f = 30\ \text{GHz}$$

$$\text{VSWR} = \frac{1+|\rho|}{1-|\rho|}$$

We find

$$\rho = \frac{\eta_2 - \eta_1}{\eta_2 + \eta_1} = \frac{\sqrt{\frac{\mu_2}{\epsilon_2}} - \sqrt{\frac{\mu_1}{\epsilon_1}}}{\sqrt{\frac{\mu_2}{\epsilon_2}} + \sqrt{\frac{\mu_1}{\epsilon_1}}}$$

$$= \frac{\frac{1}{2} - 1}{\frac{1}{2} + 1} = \frac{-1}{3}$$

VSWR at the interface

$$= \frac{1 + \frac{1}{3}}{1 - \frac{1}{3}} = 2$$

60. $$f_r = \frac{1.44}{(R_1 + 2R_2)C_{ext}}$$

$$= \frac{1.44}{(2.2\ \text{k}\Omega + 9.4\ \text{k}\Omega)\ 0.022\mu\text{F}}$$

$$= 5.64\ \text{kHz}$$

$$\text{Duty cycle} = \left(\frac{R_1 + R_2}{R_1 + 2R_2}\right) \times 100\%$$

$$= \left(\frac{2.2\ \text{k}\Omega + 4.7\ \text{k}\Omega}{2.2\ \text{k}\Omega + 9.4\ \text{k}\Omega}\right) 100\%$$

$$= 59.5\%$$

61. The stokes and anti-stokes lines have the same wave number displacement with respect to the exciting line. The wave number of the exciting line is

$$\nu = \frac{1}{5460 \times 10^{-8}\ \text{cm}} = 18315\ \text{cm}^{-1}$$

and that of the stokes line is

$$\frac{1}{5520 \times 10^{-8}\,\text{cm}} = 18116 \text{ cm}^{-1}$$

Thus, the wave number displacement is

$$\Delta\nu = 18315 - 18116 = 199 \text{ cm}^{-1}$$

$\therefore$ The wave number corresponding to the anti-stokes line would be given by

$$\nu + \Delta\nu = 18315 + 199 = 18514 \text{ cm}^{-1}$$

The corresponding wavelength is

$$\frac{1}{18514 \text{ cm}^{-1}} = 5.401 \times 10^{-5} \text{ cm} = 5401 \text{ Å}.$$

62. $$d = \left(\frac{2Ze^2}{4\pi \in_0 mv^2}\right)\left(1 + \text{cosec}\frac{\theta}{2}\right)$$

Here, $Z = 13$

$e = 1.6 \times 10^{-19}$ C

$\frac{1}{2}mv^2 = 2 \times 10^{-13}$ J

$mv^2 = 4 \times 10^{-13}$ J

$\theta = 90°$

$\text{cosec}\frac{90}{2} = J_2 = 1.414$

$4\pi\in_0 = 1 \times 10^{-10}$ (given)

$$d = \left[\frac{2 \times 13 \times (1.6 \times 10^{-19})^2}{10^{-10} \times 4 \times 10^{-13}}\right] (1 + 1.414)$$

$d = 4.169 \times 10^{-14}$ m.

63. We know that the Fermi energy of the standard metal is $E_F = 5.57$ eV, the Fermi wave number $k_F = 1.21 \times 10^8$ per cm and Fermi velocity is $v_F = 1.4 \times 10^8$ cm/sec.

$$T_C \cong \theta_D \exp\left[-\frac{1}{gN(0)}\right]$$

$$\therefore \quad gN(0) = -\frac{1}{\log\left(\frac{T_C}{\theta_D}\right)} = -\frac{1}{\log\left(\frac{0.3}{300}\right)}$$

$= 0.14.$

64. Since number of nucleons is $_2He^4$ nucleus is 4, hence B.E. for $_2He^4$ = 28.0 MeV, similarly B.E. for H^2 nucleus (combination of one proton and one neutron) = 2.2 MeV.

Mass of $_2He^4$ nucleus = 2[Mass of proton] + 2 [Mass of neutron] – 28.0 MeV

Mass of $_1H^2$ nucleus = [Mass of proton] + [Mass of neutron] – 2.2 MeV

In fusion reaction energy released

ΔE = 2 [Mass of $_1H^2$] – [Mass of $_2He^4$]

$= 2[M_p + M_n - 2.2] - [2M_p + 2M_n - 28.0]$

$= 23.6$ MeV

65. Figure shows the desired circuit. The worst case is at no load because then zeners carry the maximum current.

Voltage rating of each zener, V_Z = 10 V

Current rating of each zener, I_Z = 1000 mA

Input unregulated voltage, E_i = 45 V

Regulated output voltage,

E_o = 10 + 10 + 10 = 30 V

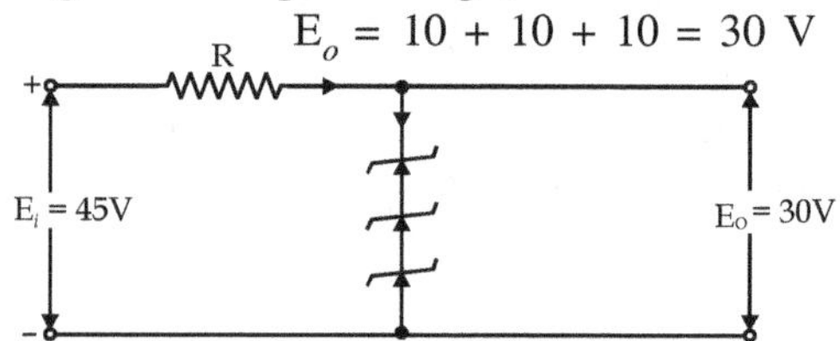

Let R ohms be the required series resistance.

Voltage across R = $E_i - E_o$ = 45 – 30 = 15 V

$$R = \frac{E_i - E_o}{I_Z}$$

$$= \frac{15\,\text{V}}{1000\,\text{mA}} = 15\Omega$$

66. Absolute temperature with emissivity of 0.82 is

= 1065 + 273 = 1338 K

$\therefore$ Apparent absolute temperature is

$T_a = (0.82)^{-1/4}$ (1338) = 1273 K

Actual absolute temperature when the emissivity is 0.75

$= (0.75)^{-1/4}$ (1273) = 1368 K

Actual temperature = 1368 – 273 = 1095°C

Hence, error in temperature measure

= 1065 – 1095 = – 30°C

67. Given

$V = (2x + 4y)$ volts.

$$E_x = -\frac{\partial V}{\partial x} = -2$$

$$E_y = -\frac{\partial V}{\partial y} = -4$$

$$\overline{E} = -2\hat{i} - 4\hat{j}$$

$$|\overline{E}| = \sqrt{(2)^2 + (4)^2} = \sqrt{20}$$

The expression for energy density is given by

$$U_E = \frac{1}{2} \epsilon_0 E^2$$

$$= \frac{1}{2} \epsilon_0 \times 20$$

$$= 10 \epsilon_0$$

68. The magnetic moment of an atom in which LS coupling holds has the magnitude

$$|\vec{\mu}_J| = g\frac{e}{2mc}|\vec{J}| = g.\frac{e}{2mc}\sqrt{\vec{J}(\vec{J}+1)}\frac{h}{2\pi}$$

$$= g.\sqrt{J(J+1)}\,\mu_B$$

where, $\mu_B = \dfrac{eh}{4\pi mc}$ is the Bohr magneton and g is Lande's g-factor given by

$$g = 1 + \frac{J(J+1) - L(L+1) + S(S+1)}{2J(J+1)}$$

For the given state $^3P_2$, we have
L = 1, S = 1, and J = 2 so that

$$g = 1 + \frac{2(2+1) - 1(1+1) + 1(1+1)}{2 \times 2(2+1)}$$

$$= 1 + \frac{6-1+2}{4\times 3} = 1 + \frac{1}{2} = \frac{3}{2}$$

$$\therefore \quad |\vec{\mu_J}| = \frac{3}{2}\sqrt{2(2+1)}\,\mu_B = \frac{3}{2}\sqrt{6}\,\mu_B$$

The number of weak-field substances is

$$(2J + 1) = (2 \times 2 + 1) = 5$$

69. $T = \begin{bmatrix} \cos\theta & \sin\theta \\ -\sin\theta & \cos\theta \end{bmatrix} \therefore T^{-1} = \begin{bmatrix} \cos\theta & -\sin\theta \\ \sin\theta & \cos\theta \end{bmatrix}$

Now T^{-1} AT

$$= \begin{bmatrix} \cos\theta & -\sin\theta \\ \sin\theta & \cos\theta \end{bmatrix} \begin{bmatrix} a & h \\ h & b \end{bmatrix} \begin{bmatrix} \cos\theta & \sin\theta \\ -\sin\theta & \cos\theta \end{bmatrix}$$

$$= \begin{bmatrix} a\cos\theta - h\sin\theta & h\cos\theta - b\sin\theta \\ a\sin\theta + h\cos\theta & h\sin\theta + b\cos\theta \end{bmatrix} \begin{bmatrix} \cos\theta & \sin\theta \\ -\sin\theta & \cos\theta \end{bmatrix}$$

$$= \begin{bmatrix} a\cos^2\theta - 2h\sin\theta\cos\theta + b\sin^2\theta & (a-b)\sin\theta\cos\theta - h\sin^2\theta + h\cos^2\theta \\ (a-b)\sin\theta\cos\theta + h\cos^2\theta - h\sin^2\theta & a\sin^2\theta + 2h\sin\theta\cos\theta + b\cos^2\theta \end{bmatrix}$$

$$= \begin{bmatrix} a\cos^2\theta - h\sin 2\theta + b\sin^2\theta & (a-b)\sin\theta\cos\theta + h\cos 2\theta \\ (a-b)\sin\theta\cos\theta + h\cos 2\theta & a\sin^2\theta + h\sin 2\theta + b\cos^2\theta \end{bmatrix}$$

$$= \begin{bmatrix} d_1 & 0 \\ 0 & d_2 \end{bmatrix} \quad \text{Being diagonal matrix}$$

$\therefore$ $(a - b) \sin\theta \cos\theta + h \cos 2\theta = 0$

or $\quad \tan 2\theta = \dfrac{2h}{b-a}$

or $\quad \theta = \dfrac{1}{2}\tan^{-1}\dfrac{2h}{b-a}$

70. 12 adder + 4 data lines

bit chip $= 2^{12} \times 4 = 16$ K bits/chip

Memo = 16 K bytes = 16 K × 8 bits

Number of chips

$$= \frac{16\,K \times 8}{16\,K} = 8.$$

71. For photon, BE statistics is applicable.

For photons, $\quad p = \dfrac{h}{\lambda} = \dfrac{h\nu}{c}$

$$dp = \frac{h\,d\nu}{c}$$

The density of states for photons between p and $p + dp$ is

$$g(p)\,dp = \frac{4\pi p^2 dp}{h^3/V}$$

$$g(\nu)\,d\nu = 4\pi V \cdot \frac{\nu^2}{c^3} \cdot d\nu$$

Since, two independent direction of polarisation

$$g(\nu)\,d\nu = \frac{8\pi V}{c^3} \cdot \nu^2 d\nu$$

Since, $\quad h\nu = E$

$$hd\nu = dE$$

$$\therefore \quad g(E)dE = \frac{8\pi VE^2}{h^2c^3}\cdot\frac{dE}{h}$$

$$= \frac{8\pi V}{h^2c^3}\cdot E^2 dE.$$

72. Dominant mode is TE_{10} mode, and f_c

$$= \frac{c}{2}\sqrt{\frac{m^2}{a^2}+\frac{n^2}{b^2}}$$

For TE_{10} mode,

$$f_c = \frac{c}{2a} = \frac{3\times10^8}{2\times10\times10^{-2}}$$

$$= 0.15 \times 10^{10} \text{ Hz}$$

The guide wavelength,

$$\lambda_g = \frac{\lambda_0}{\sqrt{1-\left(\frac{f_c}{f}\right)^2}} = \frac{3\times10^8/2.5\times10^9}{\sqrt{1-\left(\frac{1.5}{2.5}\right)^2}}$$

$$= 15 \text{ cm}.$$

73. Escape velocity $= \sqrt{\frac{2GM}{r}}$

Given escape velocity for spherical planet of mass M $= \sqrt{\frac{GM}{2R}}$

Compare these two,

$$\sqrt{\frac{2GM}{r}} = \sqrt{\frac{GM}{2R}}$$

or $$\frac{2}{r} = \frac{1}{2R}$$

or $$r = 4R$$

74. As, $$v_p = \sqrt{\frac{g\lambda}{2\pi}} \quad ...(1)$$

Group velocity of ocean,

$$v_g = v_p - \lambda\frac{dv_p}{d\lambda}$$

From equation (1), we get

$$\frac{dv_p}{d\lambda} = \frac{1}{2}\lambda^{-\frac{1}{2}}\sqrt{\frac{g}{2\pi}}$$

$$\therefore \quad v_g = \sqrt{\frac{g\lambda}{2\pi}} - \frac{1}{2}\sqrt{\frac{g\lambda}{2\pi}} = \frac{1}{2}\sqrt{\frac{g\lambda}{2\pi}}$$

$$\therefore \quad v_g = \frac{v_p}{2}$$

75. $\int\psi^*\psi\, d\tau = 1$

$$\Rightarrow \int A\cdot e^{-r/a}A\cdot e^{-r/a}d\tau$$

$$\Rightarrow \quad A^2\int_0^\infty\int_0^\pi\int_0^{2\pi} e^{-2r/a}r^2dr\sin\theta\, d\theta\, d\phi = 1$$

We know that $d\tau = r^2dr\cdot\sin\theta\cdot d\theta\cdot d\phi$

$$\Rightarrow \quad A^2 - 4\pi\int_0^\infty e^{-2r/a}r^2dr = 1$$

$$\Rightarrow \quad A^2\cdot 4\pi\times\frac{\sqrt{3}}{\left(\frac{2}{a}\right)^3} = 1$$

$$\left[\text{using } \int_0^\infty e^{-ax}x^{m-1}dx = \frac{\sqrt{m}}{a^m}\right]$$

$$\therefore\ A^2\ .\ 4\pi \times \frac{2\times1}{2^3}a^3 = 1 \qquad [\text{As } m = 3]$$

or $$A = \frac{1}{\sqrt{\pi a^3}}$$

SET–3
CSIR–UGC (NET) PHYSICAL SCIENCES

PART-A

1. A person chewing a bubble gum did not experience ear pain in a jet plane while landing whereas another person not chewing a gum had ear pain. The reason could be
   A. Chewing gum is a pain killer
   B. Chewing equilibrates pressure on both sides of the ear drum
   C. Chewing gum closes the ear drum
   D. Chewing distracts the person

2. In a joint family, there are father, mother, 3 married sons and one unmarried daughter of the 2 sons have 2 daughters each and one has a son. How many female members are there in the family?
   A. 9 B. 3
   C. 2 D. 6

3. Vinod, Virendra, Savita and Sadhana are sitting around the table. Vinod is sitting on the right side of Virendra. Savita is in left of Sadhana. From the given responses indicate which pair is sitting infront of each other?
   A. Virendra – Sadhana
   B. Vinod – Sadhana
   C. Vinod – Virendra
   D. Savita – Vinod

4. A box of sticks of equal lengths is provided. The minimum number of sticks needed to build a frame to enclose a 3-dimensional volume is
   A. 6 B. 12
   C. 3 D. 8

5. If EARTHQUAKE is coded as MOGPENJOSM, the EQUATE will be coded as
   A. MENOPM B. MENOMP
   C. MJOGPM D. MNJOPM

6. The following table shows the percentage change in the consumption of electricity by five towns A, B, C, D and E from 2012 to 2014.

Town	*Percentage*	
	2012 to 2013	*2013 to 2014*
A	+8	−18
B	−15	+11
C	+6	+9
D	−7	−5
E	+13	−6

   If town E consumed, 5,00,000 units in 2012, how much did it consume in 2014?
   A. 3,71,000 units B. 5,31,100 units
   C. 5,51,000 units D. 5,71,000 units

7. For the equipments using integrated Circuit Board : 400, Capacitors 240 and Printed Circuit Boards : 120 to run with minimum down time, how many spares should be kept in the store respectively?
   A. 12, 4, 3 B. 12, 5, 4
   C. 5, 12, 4 D. 12, 4, 4

8. The drawing shows a cross-section where the land meets the sea. The section covered is 5 kms. On a hot day, in which direction, indicated by four arrows, is the wind most likely to blow?

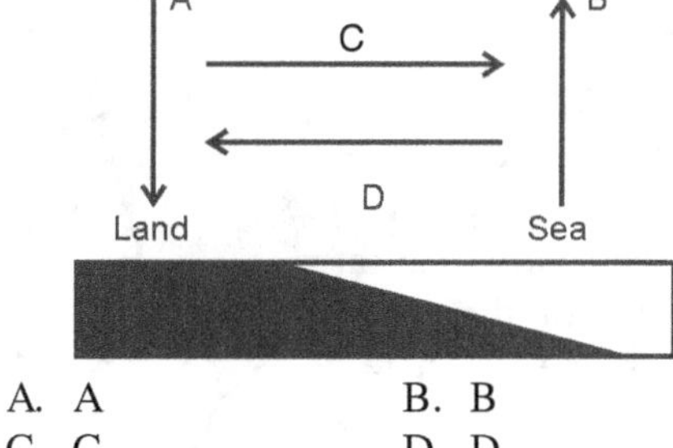

   A. A B. B
   C. C D. D

9. Three partners invested capital in the ratio 2 : 7 : 9. The time period for which each of them inverted was in the ratio of the reciprocals

of the amount invested. Find the share of the partners who brought in the highest capital, if the profit is ₹ 1080.

A. ₹ 120 B. ₹ 360
C. ₹ 540 D. ₹ 420

10. In a group of 36 persons, a total of 16 take tea while 9 take tea but hot coffee. How many persons in this group take coffee but not tea?

A. 20 B. 15
C. 10 D. 30

11. In the following series, find the term in place of question mark (?)

3, 8, 27, 112, 565, ?

A. 3400 B. 3396
C. 1596 D. 2266

12. In the figure section of a sphere of radius r_1 and centre O is shown. The right angle AOC is rotated about its vertical axis OC through 360°C, then generating a conical figure inside the hemisphere. Find the volume of the annual space between the canonical figure and the hemisphere.

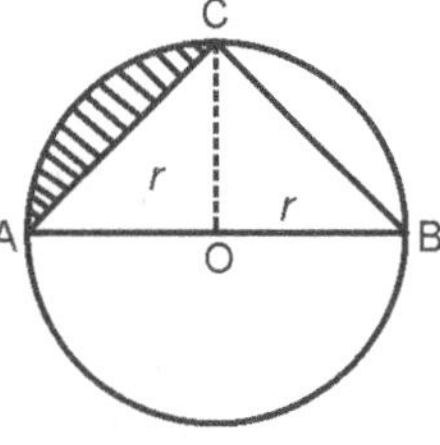

A. $\frac{\pi r^3}{3}$ B. $\frac{\pi r^3}{6}$

C. $\frac{\pi r^3}{4}$ D. $\frac{\pi r^2}{2}$

13. A point is chosen at random from a circular disc shown below. What is the probability that the point lies in the sector OAB? (where $\angle AOB = x$ radians)

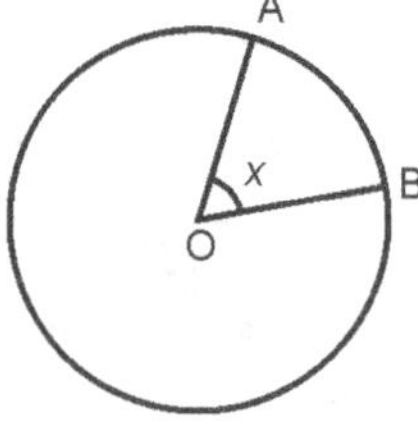

A. $\frac{2x}{\pi}$ B. $\frac{x}{\pi}$

C. $\frac{x}{2\pi}$ D. $\frac{x}{4\pi}$

14. How many squares are there in this figure?

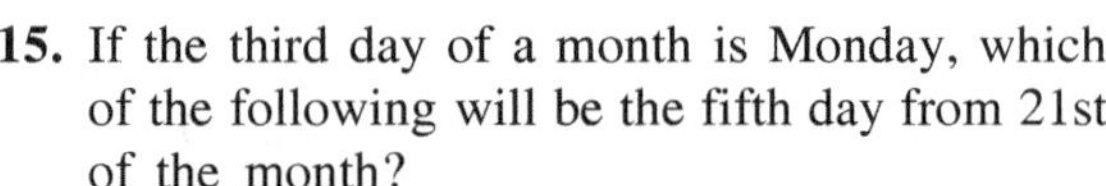

A. 9
B. 14
C. 15
D. 17

15. If the third day of a month is Monday, which of the following will be the fifth day from 21st of the month?

A. Tuesday B. Monday
C. Wednesday D. Thursday

16. A bus starts from the town P, in which the number of men is 2 times the number of women. In the town Q, 10 men gets down but 5 women enters in the bus. Now, the number of both becomes equal. How many passengers were initially in the bus?

A. 35 B. 40
C. 30 D. 45

17. FET tuned amplifier with $g_m = \frac{5mA}{V}$, r_d = 20 K has a resonant impedance of 20 kΩ. The gain resonance is given by

A. 200 B. 100
C. 50 D. 25

18. The position of A in a class is 5th from the top and the position of A is 7th from the bottom If C is the 6th place after A and C is between A and B. How many students are there in the class?

A. 25 B. 24
C. 21 D. 28

19. Vinod goes 25 km towards South from his fixed place. Then, after turning to his right he goes 30 km and then again turning to his, he goes 10 km. In the end, after turning to his left, he goes 10 km. In the end after turning to his left he goes 30 km. How far is the from his starting point?

A. 30 km B. 40 km
C. 35 km D. 45 km

20. A circular plot of lawn of diameter $2x$ metres surrounded by a pathway of width 2m. What is the total area of the pathway?

A. $4\pi (x + 1)$ sq.m B. $\pi(x + 2)$ sq.m
C. $\pi (x + 2)^2$ sq.m D. $2\pi (x + 3)$ sq.m

PART-B

21. For the function $\phi(x, y) = \frac{x}{x^2 + y^2}$, find the magnitude of the directional derivative along a line making an angle 30° with the positive x-axis at (0, 2).

A. $\frac{\sqrt{2}}{5}$ B. $\frac{\sqrt{3}}{8}$

C. $\frac{1}{\sqrt{2}}$ D. $\frac{\sqrt{3}}{5}$

22. To find the Lagrange's equations of motion for an electrical circuit comprising an inductance L and capacitance C. The condenser is charged to q coulombs and the current flowing in the circuit is i amperes.

A. $\frac{L}{C} + \dot{q} = 0$ B. $L^2\ddot{q} + \frac{q}{C} = 0$

C. $L\dot{q} + \frac{q}{C} = 0$ D. $L\ddot{q} + \frac{q}{C} = 0$

23. In a scattering of 2 eV protons from a crystal, the fifth maximum of the intensity is observed at an angle of 30°. Estimate the crystal's planar separation.

A. 0.100 nm B. 0.110 nm

C. 0.101 nm D. 0.201 nm

24. For a gas the critical pressure is 12.8 atm and the critical volume for a mole 70×10^{-6} m^3. Calculate the Van der Waals' constants of the gas and its critical temperature. 1 atm = 10^5 Nm^{-2}.

A. 18.2 K B. 20.5 K

C. 38.8 K D. 28.8 K

25. Let C be a circle $|z - 1| = 3$ in the complex plane, then $\int_c \frac{\cos z}{z - \pi} dz$, C being transversed clockwise, equals

A. $+\pi$ B. $-\pi$

C. -2π D. 2π

26. A cube has side l_0 when at rest. If the cube moves with velocity v parallel to its one edge, then its volume becomes

A. l_0^3 B. $l_0^3\left(1-\frac{v^2}{c^2}\right)^{-\frac{1}{2}}$

C. $l_0^3\left(1-\frac{v^2}{c^2}\right)$ D. $l_0^3\left(1-\frac{v^2}{c^2}\right)^{1/2}$

27. The projection of vector $\vec{a} = 2\hat{i} - 3\hat{j} + 6\hat{k}$ on vector $\vec{b} = \hat{i} + 2\hat{j} + 2\hat{k}$

A. $\frac{5}{3}$ B. $\frac{8}{3}$

C. $\frac{4}{3}$ D. $\frac{11}{3}$

28. The mean and standard deviation of a binomial distribution are 10 and 2 respectively. The value of P is

A. 1.0 B. 0.8

C. 0.6 D. 0.4

29. The Poisson's equation in CGS Gaussian system is:

A. $\nabla^2 V = -4\pi\rho$ B. $\nabla^2 V = 0$

C. $\nabla^2 V = -\frac{\rho}{\epsilon_0}$ D. $\nabla^2 V = -4\pi\sigma$

30. Neglecting variation of mass with velocity, the wavelength associated with electron having a kinetic energy, E is proportional to:

A. E^{-2} B. $E^{1/2}$

C. E D. $E^{-1/2}$

31. The combined form of first and second law of thermodynamics is given by

(P = Pressure, V = Volume, T = Temperature, U = Internal energy, S = Entropy, Q = Quantity of heat)

A. $TdS = dU - PdV$ B. $TdS = dU + PdV$

C. $dQ = TdS + PdV$ D. $dU = TdS + dQ$

32. The maximum current which can flow through a 20 k ohms resistor, rated 2W is

A. 40 mA B. 10 mA

C. 100 mA D. 1 mA

33. The circuit shown in Figure is functionally equivalent to

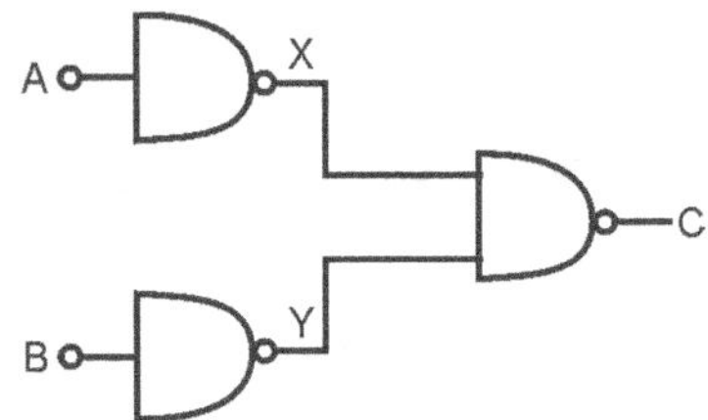

A. OR gate
B. AND gate
C. EX-OR gate
D. NOR gate

34. Given a parallel resonance circuit with Q = 40, f_0 = 440 Hz, and an admittance of 500 μ mho at resonance the resistance of the circuit is

A. 100 Ω
B. 4 MΩ
C. 300 kΩ
D. 2 kΩ

35. For an atom in the state of $^2D_{5/2}$ the Lande-*g* factor should be

A. 1.75
B. 1.33
C. 2
D. 1.20

36. NaCl has fcc lattice with a = 5.63Å, the spacing of {100} planes is

A. 2.82 Å
B. 5.64 Å
C. 1.41 Å
D. 4.23 Å

37. Given that $_3Li^7$ = 7.01816 amu, $_3Li^6$ = 6.01692 amu, $_0n^1$ = 1.00893 amu. The binding energy of a neutron in a $_3Li^7$ nucleus is

A. 7.17 MeV
B. 0.51 MeV
C. 1.04 MeV
D. 2.08 MeV

38. The final value of $L^{-1}\dfrac{2s+1}{s^4+8s^3+16s^2+s}$ is

A. 0
B. Infinity
C. 2
D. 1

39. $\begin{vmatrix} -2 & -9 & 5 \\ -5 & -10 & 7 \\ -9 & -21 & 14 \end{vmatrix}$, then $\lambda_1 + \lambda_2 + \lambda_3$ is equal to

A. –16
B. 2
C. –6
D. –14

40. The generalised co-ordinate θ for the motion of a simple pendulum oscillating in a vertical plane is

A. $\cos^{-1}\dfrac{x}{l}$

B. $\sin^{-1}\dfrac{y}{l}$

C. (A) and (B) both

D. None of these

41. If element with principal quantum number $n > 4$ were not allowed in nature, the number of possible element would be

A. 60
B. 32
C. 4
D. 64

42. Fermi function

$$f(\in) = \frac{1}{e^{(\in-\in_f)/kT}+1}$$

gives the probability of occupation of electrons per energy state. Then, the probability of number of electrons of absolute temperature (T = 0K), when $\in = \in_f$ is

A. 1
B. 0
C. ∞
D. $\dfrac{1}{2}$

43. A certain D-MOSFET is biased at V_{GS} = 0 V. Its data sheet specifies I_{DSS} = 20 mA and $V_{GS(off)}$ = –5 V. The value of the drain current

A. Is 0A
B. Cannot be determined
C. Is 20 mA
D. None of these

44. To measure the temperature of wide range from –200°C to 2200°C with greatest economy, we use

A. Thermocouple
B. Platinum
C. Thermistor
D. Semiconductor sensors

45. If the band gap of an alloy semiconductor is 1.98 eV, then calculate the wavelength of radiation that is emitted when electrons and holes in the material recombine directly

A. 6250 Å
B. 7250 Å
C. 5520 Å
D. 8125 Å

PART-C

46. Find the constant 'a' for which the vector $\vec{A} = (x+3y)\hat{i} + (y-2z)\hat{j} + (x+az)\hat{k}$ is solenoidal.
A. –4 B. –3
C. –1 D. –2

47. Water at temperature 100ºC cools in 10 minutes to 88ºC in a room of temperature 25ºC. The temperature of water after 20 minutes is
A. 50.9°C B. 70.5°C
C. 77.9°C D. 89.6°C

48. Consider a photon that scatters from an electron at rest. If the Compton's wavelength shift is observed to be triple the wavelength of the incident photon and if the photon scatters at 60º, the wavelength of the incident photon is
A. 2.03×10^{-13} m
B. 4.04×10^{-13} m
C. 6.09×10^{-12} m
D. 3.45×10^{-13} m

49. A plane electromagnetic wave travelling in +ve z-direction in an unbounded lossless dielectric medium with relative permeability $\mu_r = 1$ and relative permittivity $\epsilon_r = 3$ has a peak electric field intensity $E_0 = 6$ V/m. Find the speed of the wave.
A. 5.3×10^7 m/s
B. 7.3×10^7 m/s
C. 2.3×10^7 m/s
D. 4.3×10^7 m/s

50. A quantity of heat ΔH is transferred from a large heat reservoir at temp T_1 to another large heat reservoir at temp T_2, with $T_1 > T_2$ required for spontaneous transfer. The heat reservoir have such large capacities that there is no observable change in their temp. The entropy of the entire system has
A. Zero
B. Remains unchanged
C. Decrease
D. Increase

51. The circuit using BJT with β = 50 and V_{BE} = 0.7 V is shown in fig. The base current I_B and collector voltage V_C are respectively

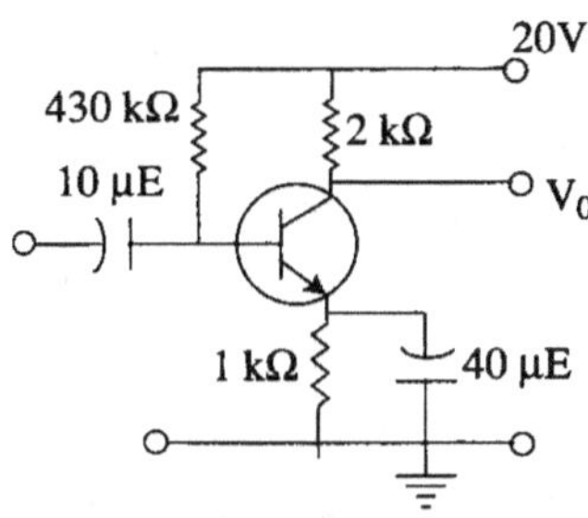

A. 50 μA and 10 Volts
B. 43 μA and 11.4 Volts
C. 40 μA and 16 Volts
D. 45 μA and 11 Volts

52. A low pass filter has an input $\frac{S}{N}$ of 20. The input voltage is 3 mV. The noise voltage is:
A. 1.67 mV B. 0.67 mV
C. 1.1 mV D. 0.3 mV

53. If 'R' is the distance between two hydrogen atoms, the Van der Waals interaction energy between them is proportional to
A. $\frac{1}{R^4}$ B. $\frac{1}{R}$
C. $\frac{1}{R^6}$ D. $\frac{1}{R^2}$

54. The total energy of an ionic solid is given by

$$U = -\frac{\alpha e^2}{4\pi \epsilon_0 r} + \frac{\beta}{r^9}$$

where α is Madelung constant r is the distance between the nearest neighbour in the crystal. If r_0 is the equilibrium separation then the constant β is given by
A. $\frac{\alpha e^2 r_0^8}{36\pi \epsilon_0}$ B. $\frac{2\alpha e^2 r_0^8}{9\pi \epsilon_0}$
C. $\frac{\alpha e^2 r_0^{10}}{36\pi \epsilon_0}$ D. $\frac{-\alpha e^2 r_0^{10}}{36\pi \epsilon_0}$

55. Mass m_p are accelerated through the same potential difference, the ratio of the wavelengths associated with an electron to that associated with proton is

A. $\frac{m_p}{m_e}$ B. $\sqrt{m_p / m_e}$

C. $\frac{m_e}{m_p}$ D. None of these

56. For cubic polynomial which takes the following values

$y(0) = 1$, $y(1) = 0$, $y(2) = 1$ and $y(3) = 10$, $y(4) = ...$

A. 42 B. 36

C. 24 D. 33

57. The J = 1 ← 0 transition in HCl occurs at 20.68 cm^{-1}. Regarding the molecule to be a rigid rotator, the wavelength of the transition J = 15 ← 14 is

A. 42μm B. 32μm

C. 22μm D. 52μm

58. The amount of energy released when all the nuclei in 1 kg of deuterium fuse by the following reaction

$6({}_1H^2) \rightarrow 2({}_2He^4) + 2p + 2n + 43$ MeV is:

A. 3.453×10^{10} J B. 3.453×10^{16} J

C. 3.453×10^{14} J D. 3.453×10^{12} J

59. To penetrate the coulomb barrier of a light nucleus, a proton must have a minimum energy of the order of

A. 1 MeV B. 1 eV

C. 1 GeV D. 1 keV

60. The maximum change in energy of a *p*-electron due to the precessional motion of its orbit in a magnetic field of 3×10^4 gauss is of the order of

A. 2.8×10^{-12} ergs B. 2.8×10^{-10} ergs

C. 2.8×10^{-8} ergs D. 2.8×10^{-16} ergs

61. If the radiated power of AM transmitter is 10 KW, the power in the carrier for modulation index of 0.6 is nearly

A. 8.47 KW B. 3.47 KW

C. 5.35 KW D. 6.37 KW

62. If the negative logic is used, the diode gate is shown in the given fig. will represent

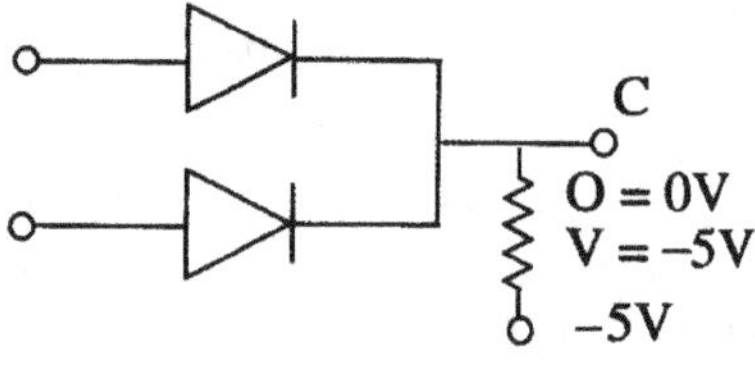

A. NAND gate B. NOR gate

C. AND gate D. OR gate

63. C^{14} disintegrates by β emission with an end point energy of 0.155 MeV. A β-particle with an energy of 0.025 MeV is emitted in a direction at 135 degrees to the direction of motion of the recoil nucleus. The momenta of the three particles involved in this disintegration is:

A. 0.269 MeV/C B. 0.179 MeV/C

C. 0.079 MeV/C D. 1.023 MeV/C

64. The saturation magnetisation of iron is 1.75×10^6 amp/metre. Assuming that the iron has a body Centred cubic structure with an edge length of 2.87 Å, find the average number of Bohr magnetons contributing to the saturation magnetisation per atom.

A. 1.23 Bohr magneton

B. 3.23 Bohr magneton

C. 0.23 Bohr magneton

D. 2.23 Bohr magneton

65. Calculate the mean free path of the molecules of a gas in a chamber of 10^{-6} mm of mercury pressure, assuming the molecular diameter to be 2Å. Take the temperature of the chamber to be 273 K and Boltzmann constant $k = 1.38 \times 10^{-23}$ J/K.

A. 162.9 m B. 262.9 m

C. 62.9 m D. 362.9 m

66. A uniform current I is flowing along the surface of a hollow conducting cylinder of radius a parallel to its axis. The magnetic induction inside the cylinder is

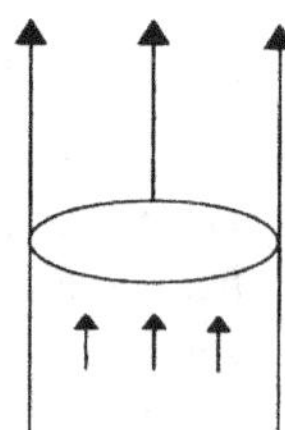

A. $\frac{I}{a}$ B. $\frac{I}{\pi a^2}$

C. $\frac{\mu_0 I}{2\pi a}$ D. 0

67. The Lagrangian of a particle of mass *m* moving in a plane is given by $L = \frac{1}{2}m(v_x^2 + v_y^2) + a(xv_y - yv_x)$ where v_x and v_y are velocity components and *a* is a constant. The canonical momenta of the particle are given by:

A. $p_x = mv_x - ay$ and $p_y = mv_y - ax$
B. $p_x = mv_x - ay$ and $p_y = mv_y + ax$
C. $p_x = mv_x + ay$ and $p_y = mv_y + ax$
D. $p_x = mv_x$ and $p_y = mv_y$

68. A plane electromagnetic wave travelling in vacuum is incident normally on a non-magnetic, non-absorbing medium of refractive index n. The incident (E_i), reflected (E_r) and transmitted (E_t) electric fields are given as

$E_i = E_{0i} \exp[i\,(k_i z - \omega t)]$,
$E_r = E_{0r} \exp[i\,(k_r z - \omega t)]$;
$E_t = E_{0t} \exp[i\,(k_t z - \omega t)]$

If $E_{0i} = 2$ V/m and $n = 1.5$, then the application of appropriate boundary conditions leads to:

A. $E_{0r} = \frac{4}{5}$ V/m, $E_{0t} = \frac{6}{5}$ V/m

B. $E_{0r} = -\frac{3}{5}$ V/m, $E_{0t} = \frac{7}{5}$ V/m

C. $E_{0r} = -\frac{2}{5}$ V/m, $E_{0t} = \frac{8}{5}$ V/m

D. $E_{0r} = -\frac{1}{5}$ V/m, $E_{0t} = \frac{9}{5}$ V/m

69. Which of the wave functions in the following figures have physical significance in the interval shown?

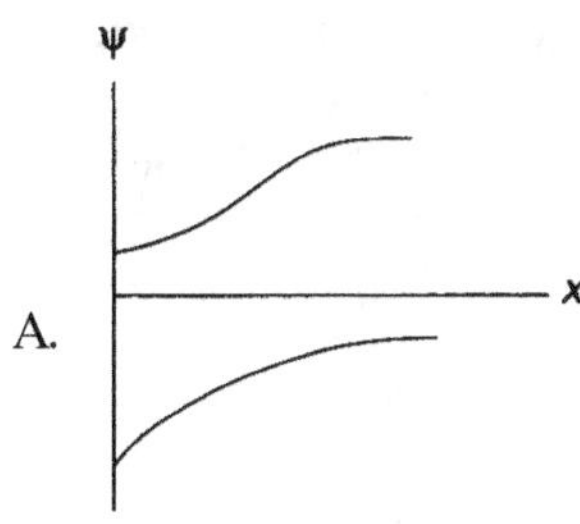

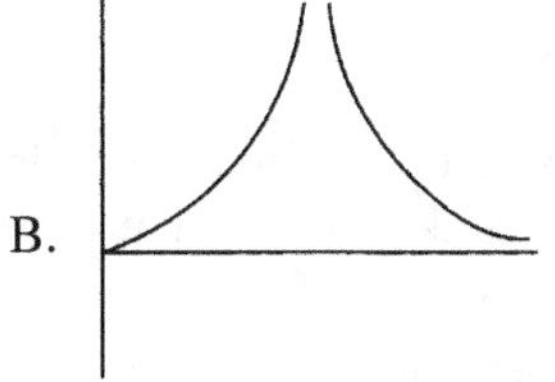

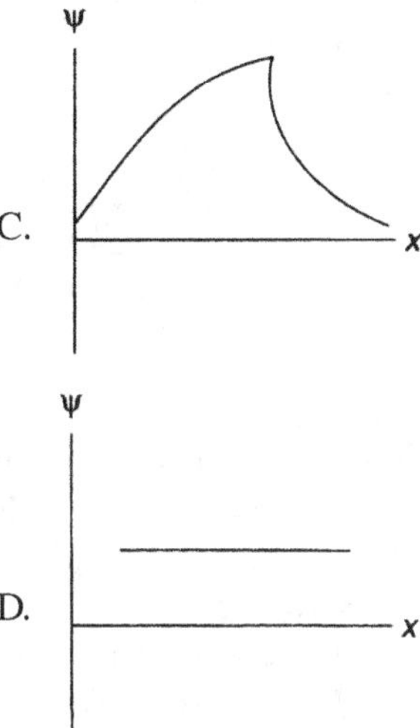

70. If the two sub-system 1 and 2 are in thermal equilibrium and the entropy σ of the total system must have maximum value with respect to small transfer of energy from one subsystem to the other, then the statistical temperature τ is defined as

A. $\frac{1}{\tau} = -\left(\frac{\partial \sigma}{\partial U}\right)$ B. $\frac{1}{\tau} = \left(\frac{\partial \sigma}{\partial U}\right)$

C. $\tau = -\left(\frac{\partial \sigma}{\partial U}\right)$ D. $\tau = \left(\frac{\partial \sigma}{\partial U}\right)$

71. A plane em wave of frequency 30 MHz travels in free space along the x-direction. The electric field component of the wave at a particular point of space and time is E = 6 Vm^{-1} along y-direction. Its magnetic field component B at this point would be

A. 2×10^{-8} T along z-direction
B. 6×10^{-8} T along x-direction
C. 2×10^{-8} T along y-direction
D. 6×10^{-8} T along z-direction

72. A simple pendulum has a length l and the mass is m. The bob is given a charge of q coulomb. The pendulum is suspended between the vertical plates of a charged parallel plate capacitor. If E is the electric field strength between the plates, the time period of the pendulum is given by

A. $2\pi\sqrt{\frac{l}{g}}$ B. $2\pi\sqrt{\frac{l}{\sqrt{g+\frac{qE}{m}}}}$

C. $2\pi\sqrt{\frac{l}{\sqrt{g-\frac{qE}{m}}}}$ D. $2\pi\sqrt{\frac{l}{\sqrt{g^2+\left(\frac{qE}{m}\right)^2}}}$

73. LASER are light source which give almost perfectly parallel beam of high intensity. If a 2K watt laser beam is concentrated by a lens into cross-sectional area about 10^{-6} cm^2, then the value of Poynting vector:

A. 2×10^{12} W/m^2 B. 2×10^{14} W/m^2
C. 2×10^{11} W/m^2 D. 2×10^{13} W/m^2

74. Boltzmann distribution of particles between different states under equilibrium at temperature T is given by

$$N_2 = N_1 \exp\left(\frac{-E_{12}}{kT}\right)$$

Vibrational states have equal spacings $h\upsilon$ as a first approximation. For a particular case exp $\left(\frac{-h\upsilon}{kT}\right)$ = 0.4. Out of N molecules, a number N_0 is in the ground state. Then N_0/N is nearest to:

A. 1/1.92 B. 1/1.68
C. 1/1.4 D. 0.6

75. The half lives of two radioactive substances A and B are respectively 1 hour and 2 hour. If initially the number of nuclei of both substances are the same, the ratio of their rate of disintegration after 2 hour is

A. 1 : 2 B. 2 : 3
C. 1 : 1 D. 1 : 3

ANSWERS

1	2	3	4	5	6	7	8	9	10
B	A	B	C	D	B	B	D	B	A
11	**12**	**13**	**14**	**15**	**16**	**17**	**18**	**19**	**20**
B	A	C	C	C	D	C	B	C	A
21	**22**	**23**	**24**	**25**	**26**	**27**	**28**	**29**	**30**
B	D	C	D	C	D	B	C	A	D
31	**32**	**33**	**34**	**35**	**36**	**37**	**38**	**39**	**40**
B	B	A	D	D	A	C	D	B	C
41	**42**	**43**	**44**	**45**	**46**	**47**	**48**	**49**	**50**
A	D	C	A	A	D	C	B	B	D
51	**52**	**53**	**54**	**55**	**56**	**57**	**58**	**59**	**60**
C	B	C	A	B	D	B	C	A	D
61	**62**	**63**	**64**	**65**	**66**	**67**	**68**	**69**	**70**
A	C	B	D	A	D	B	C	D	B
71	**72**	**73**	**74**	**75**					
A	D	D	B	C					

EXPLANATORY ANSWERS

1. Chewing gum stretches muscles in the jaw and throat that can cause the Eustachain tube to open. This allows air into the middle ear and equalizes the pressure.

2. Female members: Mother, 3 daughters-in-law, one daughter and 4 granddaughters. Thus, there are 9 female members in the family.

3. Their seating arrangement is shown below

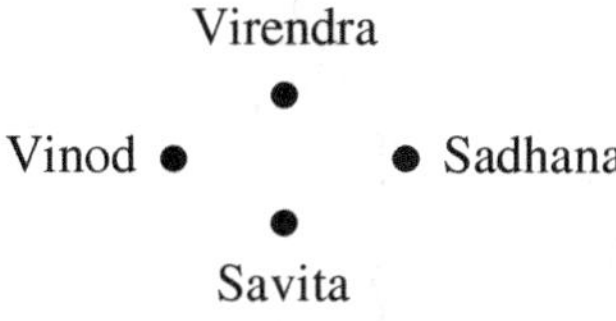

The required answer is B.

4. Consider a corner of a 3-dimensional room. Minimum sticks required to enclosed a 3-dimensional volume.

= AB.BC and BD

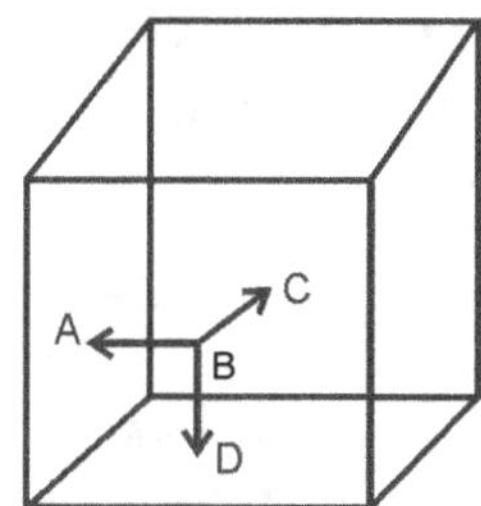

Hence, the number of minimum sticks = 3.

5. The alphabet in word EQUATE are taken from the given word EARTHQUAKE. Tally the letters from the coded word to get the answer code.

EARTHQUAKE → letters
MOGPENJOSM → codes
∴ EQUATE → letters to be coded
MNJOPM → Answer codes.

6. Unit consumes in 2012 = 5,00,000 units
13% of 5,00,000 = 65,000
∴ Consumption in 2013 = 565,000 unit
Required consumption
= 5,65,000 – 6% of 5,65,000
= 56,500 – 33,900
= 5,31,100 units.

7. Expected number of Component failures in Integrated Circuit Boards

$$= 400 \times \frac{3}{100} = 12$$

In Capacitors = $240 \times \frac{2}{100} = 4.8$

In Printed Circuit Boards

$$= 120 \times \frac{3.3}{100} = 3.96$$

∴ 12, 5 and 4 respectively of spares of IC Boards.
Capacitors and Printed Circuit Boards must be kept in store.

8. On a hot day, the heat from the land goes up and there will be vacuum space formed on the earths atmosphere. Hence, the wind from the sea blows from sea towards land, i.e., D.

9. Ratio of capital = 2 : 7 : 9

Ratio of time = $\frac{1}{2}:\frac{1}{7}:\frac{1}{9}$

∴ Ratio of investment

$$= 2\times\frac{1}{2}:7\times\frac{1}{7}:9\times\frac{1}{9}$$
$$= 1 : 1 : 1$$

∴ Required ratio = $\frac{1}{3}\times 1080$ = ₹ 360.

10.

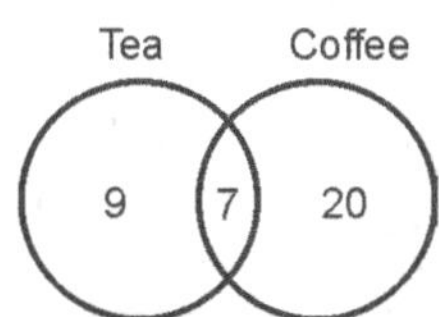

By the Venn diagram 16 persons take tea, while 9 persons take only tea.
Persons who take both tea and coffee
= 16 – 9 = 7
No. of persons who take coffee only
= 36 – (9 + 7) = 20.

11. We have,

$$2 \times 1 + 1 = 3$$
$$3 \times 2 + 2 = 8$$
$$8 \times 3 + 3 = 27$$
$$27 \times 4 + 4 = 112$$
$$112 \times 5 + 5 = 565$$
$$565 \times 6 + 6 = 3396$$

Hence, B is correct option.

12. Volume = $\frac{1}{3}\pi r^2 \times r = \frac{1}{3}\pi r^3$

[As figure generated by revolving the triangle AOC about the vertical axis OC will be a right circular cone of basic radius r and height r]
Volume of hemisphere AOB

$$= \frac{2}{3}\pi r^3$$

Hence, volume of annular shaded portion between cone and hemisphere is volume of hemisphere – volume of cone

$$= \frac{2}{3}\pi r^3 - \frac{1}{3}\pi r^3 = \frac{\pi r^3}{3}.$$

13. Area of whole circular disc = $\pi(OA)^2$

Area of sector OAB = $\frac{x}{360} \times \pi(OA)^2$

$\therefore$ Required probability = $\dfrac{\frac{x}{360} \times \pi \times (OA)^2}{\pi \times (OA)^2}$

$$= \frac{x}{360} = \frac{x}{2\pi}.$$

14. No. of squares = 9

No. of squares with sides twice that of small squares = 5

No. of squares with sides 3 times that of small squares = 1

Therefore, total number of squares

$= 9 + 5 + 1 = 15.$

15. 3rd day of month is Monday
5th day from 21st is 26th
$26 - 3 = 23$ days
23 days later, 23/7 leaves 2 days. Therefore, two days ahead of Monday will be Wednesday.

16. Let the initial no. of women be x.

$\therefore$ Initial no of men = $2x$

$\Rightarrow \quad 2x - 10 = x + 5$

$\Rightarrow \quad 2x - x = 5 + 10$

$\therefore \quad x = 15$

$\therefore$ Total number of the passengers initially

$= 15 \times 3 = 45.$

17. As, $A_V = g_m R$

$$R = r_d \parallel R_{max} = \frac{20 \times 20}{20 + 20}$$

$= 10\ k\Omega$

$\therefore \quad A_V = 5 \times 10^{-3} \times 10k$

$= 50.$

18. 5th, 11th
←5→A←6→C←5→B←8→

$\therefore$ Total number of students in the class

$= 5 + 6 + 5 + 8 = 24$

19.

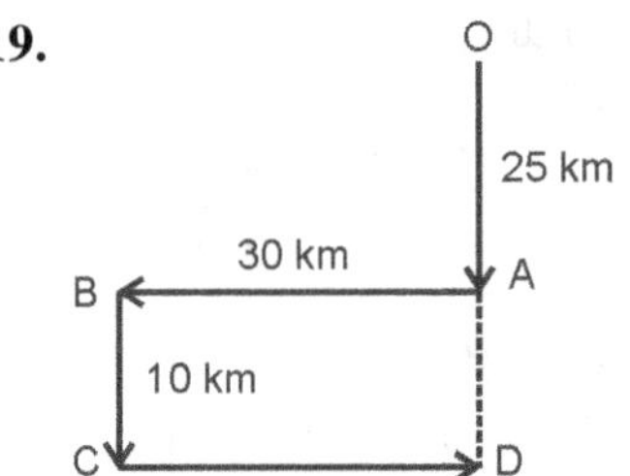

Total distance = OA + AD

AD = BC = 10 km

$\therefore$ Total distance = 25 + 10 = 35 km

20. Area of plot of lawn = πx^2 ...(*i*)
Area of circular plot including
Circular path way = $\pi(x + 2)^2$ ...(*ii*)
Now, area of pathway only

$= \pi(x + 2)^2 - \pi x^2$

$= \pi(x^2 + 4 + 2x - \pi x^2)$

$= \pi x^2 + 4\pi + 4\pi x - \pi x^2$

$= \pi(4 + 4x)$

$= 4\pi(x + 1)$ sq.m.

21. Directional derivative = $\vec{\nabla}\phi$

$$= \left(i\frac{\partial}{\partial x} + j\frac{\partial}{\partial y} + k\frac{\partial}{\partial z}\right)\frac{x}{x^2 + y^2}$$

$$= i\left(\frac{1}{x^2 + y^2} - \frac{x(2x)}{(x^2 + y^2)^2}\right) - j\frac{x(2y)}{(x^2 + y^2)^2}$$

$$- i\frac{y^2 - x^2}{(x^2 + y^2)^2} - j\frac{2xy}{(x^2 + y^2)^2}$$

Directional derivative at the point (0, 2)

$$= i\frac{4 - 0}{(0 + 4)^2} - j\frac{2(0)(2)}{(0 + 4)^2} = \frac{i}{4}$$

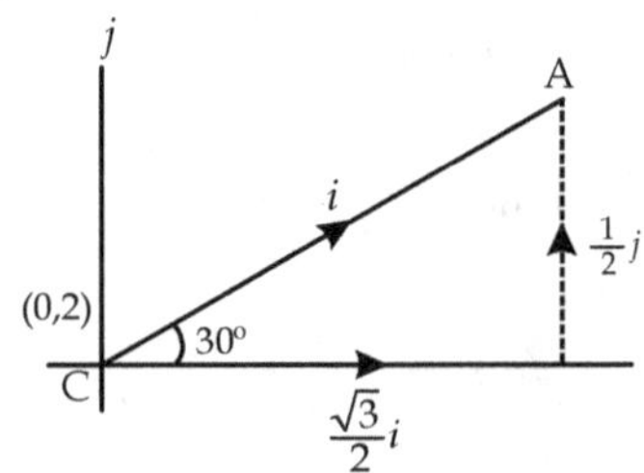

Directional derivative at the point (0, 2) in the direction $\vec{CA}$, *i.e.*, $\left(\frac{\sqrt{3}}{2}i + \frac{1}{2}j\right)$

$$= \frac{i}{4} \cdot \left(\frac{\sqrt{3}}{2} i + \frac{1}{2} j\right) \quad \left(\begin{array}{l} \vec{CA} = \vec{OB} + \vec{BA} \\ \quad = i\cos 30° + j\sin 30° \\ \quad = \cdot\left(\frac{\sqrt{3}}{2} i + \frac{1}{2} j\right) \end{array}\right)$$

$$= \frac{\sqrt{3}}{8}$$

22. For such a circuit the magnetic energy will be

$T_M = \frac{1}{2} Li^2 = \frac{1}{2} L\dot{q}^2$ and electrical energy

$V_E = \frac{1}{2} \frac{q^2}{C}$.

Therefore, Lagrangian can be represented as

$$L_E = \frac{1}{2} L\dot{q}^2 - \frac{q^2}{C}. \qquad ...(1)$$

Choosing q as the generalised co-ordinate, the equation of motion will be

$$\frac{d}{dt}\left(\frac{\partial L_E}{\partial \dot{q}}\right) - \frac{\partial L_E}{\partial q} = 0 \qquad ...(2)$$

But from eq. (1)

$$\frac{\partial L_E}{\partial \dot{q}} = L\dot{q} \quad \text{and} \quad \frac{\partial L_E}{\partial q} = -\frac{q}{C}.$$

So the eq. takes the form

$$L\ddot{q} + \frac{q}{C} = 0$$

23. Using Bragg's relation, $\lambda = (2d/n) \sin \phi$, where d is the crystal's plannar separation, we can infer the proton's kinetic energy:

$$E = \frac{v^2}{2m_p} = \frac{2\pi^2 h^2}{m_p \lambda^2} = \frac{n^2 \pi^2 h^2}{2m_p d^2 \sin^2 \phi},$$

which leads to

$$d = \frac{n\pi h}{\sin \phi \sqrt{2m_p E}}$$

$$= \frac{n\pi hc}{\sin \phi \sqrt{2m_p c^2 E}}.$$

Since $n = 5$ (the fifth maximum), $\phi = 30°$, $E = 2$ eV and $mpc^2 = 938.27$ MeV, we have

$$d = \frac{5\pi \times 197.33 \times 10^{-15} \text{MeVm}}{\sin 30 \sqrt{2 \times 938.27 \text{MeV} \times 2 \times 10^{-6} \text{MeV}}}$$

$= 0.101$ nm.

24. Since $\quad V_c = 3b$,

$$\therefore \quad b = \frac{V_c}{3} = \frac{70 \times 10^{-6}}{3}$$

$$= 23.3 \times 10^{-6} \text{ m}^3.$$

We have $\quad P_c = \frac{a}{27b^2}$

or $\quad a = 27b^2 P_c$

$$= 27 \times (23.3 \times 10^{-6})^2 \times (12.8 \times 10^5)$$

$$= 0.0188 \text{ Nm}^4.$$

$$T_c = \frac{8a}{27Rb}$$

$$= \frac{8 \times .0188}{27 \times 8.3 \times 23.3 \times 10^{-6}}$$

$$= 28.8 \text{ K}.$$

25. Pole: $z - \pi = 0$

$\Rightarrow \quad z = \pi \quad$ or $\quad z = 3.14$

Circle: $|z - 1| = 3$ is a circle with centre at $z = 1$ and radius 3 as shown in fig.

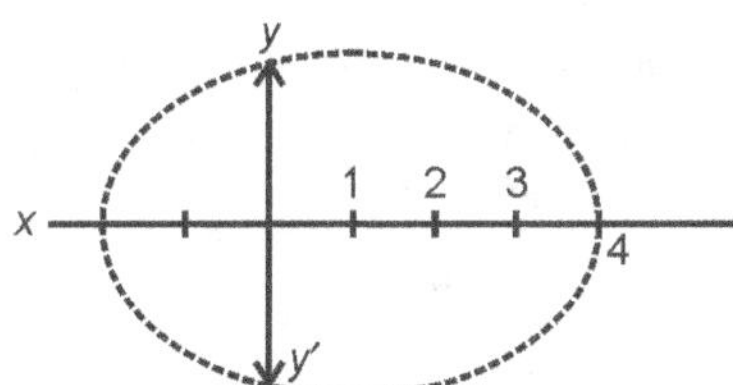

The integrand has simple pole at $z = \pi$

$\therefore$ Residue at $z = \pi$

$$\Rightarrow \lim_{z \to \pi} (z - \pi) \frac{\cos z}{(z - \pi)} = \cos \pi = -1$$

Hence, integral $= -1 \times 2\pi°$

$= -2\pi°$.

26. Let two system s and s' moving with velocity v relative to s along +ve direction of x-axis.

Volume of the cube in system

$$s = l_0^3$$

One edge of the cube = l_0
Along x-axis as observed by the observer on s',

$$l_x = l_0\sqrt{1-\frac{v^2}{c^2}}$$

∴ Volume of cube as observed from s'

$$l_x\, l_y\, l_z = l_0\sqrt{\left(1-\frac{v^2}{c^2}\right)} \times (l_0)\times(l_0)$$

$$= l_0^3\sqrt{1-\frac{v^2}{c^2}}$$

∴ $$v = l_0^3\left(1-\frac{v^2}{c^2}\right)^{1/2}.$$

27. Let θ → angle between the vectors $\vec{a}$ and $\vec{b}$.
Projection of $\vec{a}$ on $\vec{b}$ = a cos θ.
Also $\vec{a}\cdot\vec{b} = ab\cos\theta$

$$a\cos\theta = \frac{\vec{a}\cdot\vec{b}}{B}$$

$$= \frac{(2\hat{i}-3\hat{j}+6\hat{k})\cdot(\hat{i}+2\hat{j}+2\hat{k})}{\sqrt{(1)^2+(2)^2+(2)^2}}$$

$$= \frac{2-6+12}{\sqrt{9}} = \frac{8}{3}$$

∴ Projection of $\vec{a}$ on $\vec{b}$

$$= \frac{8}{3}.$$

28. Given $np = 10$, $npq = 2^2 = 4$

⇒ $$q = \frac{4}{10} = \frac{2}{5}$$

Now, $p = (1 - q)$

$$= \frac{2}{5} = 0.6.$$

29. In the region where there exists a distribution of charge of volume charge density (*i.e.*, charge per unit volume) ρ, the differential form of Gauss's law is

$$\text{div } \bar{E} = 4\pi\rho$$

[in CGS Gaussian system]

We have $E = -\text{grad } V$

∴ $\text{div }(-\text{ grad } V) = 4\pi\rho$

$$-\bar{\nabla}\cdot\nabla V = 4\pi\rho$$

or $$\nabla^2 V = -4\pi\rho$$

30. We know

$$\lambda = \frac{h}{mv}$$

and $$E = \frac{1}{2}mv^2$$

or $$mv = \sqrt{2mE}$$

∴ $$\lambda = \frac{h}{\sqrt{2mE}}$$

If h and m are constant

$$\lambda \propto \frac{1}{\sqrt{E}} \text{ or } \lambda \propto E^{-1/2}.$$

31. According to first law of thermodynamics

$$dQ = dU + PdV \quad ...(1)$$

According to second law of thermodynamics

$$dS = \frac{dQ}{T} \quad ...(2)$$

combined form of equation (1) and (2), we get

$$TdS = dU + PdV.$$

32. $$P = I^2R$$

$$2W = I^2(20\text{ K})$$

or $$I^2 = \frac{2}{20\times10^3} = 1\times10^{-4}\text{A}$$

$$I = 10^{-2}\text{ A}$$

$$I = 10\text{ mA}$$

33. Circuit

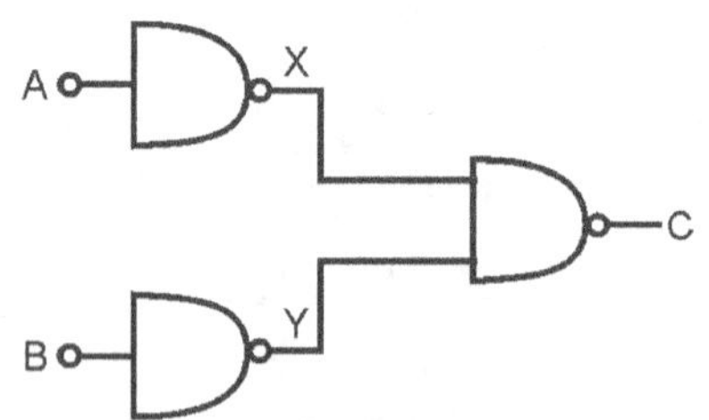

Truth Table for this circuit is

A	B	X	Y	C
0	0	1	1	0
0	1	1	0	1
1	0	0	1	1
1	1	0	0	1

which is truth table for OR gate.

34. For parallel resonance circuit

$$Q = \frac{1}{\omega CR}$$

$$\Rightarrow \qquad Q = \frac{\omega L}{R}$$

Using this relation we get 2 kΩ

35. The lande g-factor is

$$g = 1 + \frac{J(J+1)+S(S+1)-L(L+1)}{2J(J+1)}$$

For term $^2D_{5/2}$

$$L = 2,\ S = \frac{1}{2},\ J = \frac{5}{2}$$

$$g = 1 + \frac{\frac{5}{2}\left(\frac{5}{2}+1\right)+\frac{1}{2}\left(\frac{1}{2}+1\right)-2(2+1)}{2\frac{5}{2}\left(\frac{5}{2}+1\right)}$$

$$= 1.20.$$

36. Interplaner spacing of lattice planes for fcc lattice for {100} plane is $\frac{a}{2}$

Here $\quad a = 5.63$ Å

So $\quad d_{100} = \frac{5.63}{2}$ Å

$= 2.8155$ or 2.82 Å

37. Mass of $_3Li^6$ and $_0n^1$ is

$= 6.01692 + 1.00893$

$= 7.02585$ amu

Mass of $\quad _3Li^7 = 7.01816$ amu

Mass defect Δm $= 7.02585 - 7.01816$

$= 0.00769$ amu

The binding energy $= 0.00769 \times 931.4812$

$= 7.17$ MeV

Binding energy per nucleon

$$= \frac{7.17}{7} \text{ MeV}$$

$$= 1.04 \text{ MeV.}$$

38. $\lim_{t\to\infty} f(t) = \lim_{s\to 0} SF(s)$

$$\lim_{s\to 0} \frac{s(2s+1)}{s^4+8s^3+16s^2+s}$$

$$\lim_{s\to 0} \frac{2s+1}{s^3+8s^2+16s+1}$$

$$= 1.$$

39. The sum of the eigen values of matrix is equal to the trace of the matrix. Trace of the matrix is the sum of the elements on the principal diagonal of matrix.

$\therefore \quad \lambda_1 + \lambda_2 + \lambda_3 = -2 - 10 + 14$

$= 2.$

40. For the motion of a simple pendulum oscillating in a vertical plane, we have

$$x = l \sin\theta$$

$$\Rightarrow \qquad \theta = \sin^{-1}\frac{x}{l}$$

$$y = l \cos\theta$$

$$\Rightarrow \qquad \theta = \cos^{-1}\frac{y}{l}.$$

41. Total possible states are

$= \Sigma 2n^2 = 2[1 + 4 + 9 + 16]$

$= 2[30] = 60.$

42. As, $\qquad f(\in) = \dfrac{1}{e^{(\in-\in_f)/kT}+1}$

at $\qquad T = 0K$

and $\qquad \in = \in_f$

$$e^{(\in-\in/kT)} = e^0 = 1$$

$$\text{Probability} = \frac{1}{1+1} = \frac{1}{2}.$$

43. Since $\qquad V_{GS} = 0$ V,

$I_D = I_{DSS}$

as $\qquad I_{DSS} = 20$ mA

$I_D = 20$ mA.

44. Thermocouple : –200°C to 2200°C
Platinum : –100°C to 850°C
Thermistors : –100°C to 300°C.

45. As, $E_g = h\nu = \dfrac{hc}{\lambda}$

or
$$\lambda = \frac{hc}{E_g}$$
$$= \frac{6.6\times10^{-34}\times3\times10^{8}}{1.98\times1.6\times10^{-19}}$$
$$= \frac{6.6\times3\times10^{-7}}{1.98\times1.6} = 6250 \text{ Å}$$

46. Vector $\vec{A}$ is said to be solenoidal if its divergence is zero, *i.e.*,
$$\text{div}\,\vec{A} = 0$$
$$\text{div}\,\vec{A} = \vec{\nabla}\cdot\vec{A}$$
$$= \left(\hat{i}\frac{\partial}{\partial x}+\hat{j}\frac{\partial}{\partial y}+\hat{k}\frac{\partial}{\partial z}\right)\cdot\left[(x+3y)\hat{i}+(y-2z)\hat{j}+(x+az)\hat{k}\right]$$
$$\text{div}\,\vec{A} = \frac{\partial}{\partial x}(x+3y)+\frac{\partial}{\partial y}(y-2z)+\frac{\partial}{\partial z}(x+az)$$
$$= 1 + 1 + a = 2 + a$$

For solenoidal vector $\text{div}\,\vec{A} = 0$
$$\Rightarrow \quad 2 + a = 0$$
$$a = -2.$$

47. Here we apply "Newton's law of cooling" which states that the rate of decrease of the temperature of a body is proportional to the difference between the temperature of the body and that of the medium;

i.e., $$\frac{dT}{dt} = -k(T - T_0)$$

Where T is the temperature of the body at time t and T_0 the constant temperature of the medium.

Thus, $$\frac{dT}{dt} = -k(T-25)$$

or $$\frac{dT}{T-25} = -k\,dt$$

On integrating, $\log (T - 25) = -kt + c_1$ ...(*i*)

Now $T = 100,\ t = 0 \quad \therefore \log 75 = c_1$

Substituting in (*i*), we get
$$\log (T - 25) = -kt + \log 75$$
$$\Rightarrow \log \frac{T-25}{75} = -kt \qquad ...(ii)$$

Also T = 88 when t = 10 minutes,
$$\therefore \log \frac{88-25}{75} = -10k, \text{ giving}$$
$$k = \frac{1}{10}\log\frac{75}{63} = \frac{1}{10}\log\frac{25}{21}$$

Substituting in (*ii*), we have
$$\log\frac{T-25}{75} = \left(-\frac{1}{10}\log\frac{25}{21}\right)t \qquad ...(iii)$$

Putting t = 20 in (*iii*), we have
$$\log\frac{T-25}{75} = -2\log\frac{25}{21}$$
$$\therefore \quad \frac{T-25}{75} = \left(\frac{25}{21}\right)^{-2}$$
$$\Rightarrow \quad T = 25 + 75\left(\frac{21}{25}\right)^2 = 77.9°\text{C}.$$

48. In the case where the photons scatter at $\theta = 60°$ and since $\Delta\lambda = 3\lambda$, the wave shift relation yields
$$3\lambda = \frac{h}{m_e c}(1-\cos 60).$$
which in turn leads to
$$\lambda = \frac{h}{6m_e c} = \frac{\pi hc}{3m_e c^2}$$
$$= \frac{3.14\times197.33\times10^{-15}\,\text{MeV m}}{3\times0.511\,\text{MeV}}$$
$$= 4.04 \times 10^{-13}\text{ m}.$$

49. $$E_0 = \sqrt{E_{0x}^2 + E_{0y}^2} = 6 \text{ V/m},$$
$$\epsilon_r = 3,\ \mu_r = 1$$

Speed of electromagnetic wave

$$v = \frac{1}{\sqrt{\mu \in}} = \frac{1}{\sqrt{\mu_r \mu_0 \in_r \in_0}}$$

$$= \frac{c}{\sqrt{\mu_r \in_r}} = \frac{3 \times 10^8}{\sqrt{1 \times 3}}$$

$$= 0.73 \times 10^8 \text{ m/s} = 7.3 \times 10^7 \text{ m/s}.$$

50. $$\Delta S_1 = \frac{\Delta H_1}{T_1} = -\frac{\Delta H}{T_1}$$

$$\Delta S_2 = \frac{\Delta H_2}{T_2} = \frac{\Delta H}{T_2}$$

$$\Delta S = -\frac{\Delta H_1}{T_1} + \frac{\Delta H}{T_2}$$

$$= \Delta H \frac{(T_1 - T_2)}{T_1 T_2}$$

Since $T_1 > T_2$

Therefore ΔS increases.

51. $$I_C \simeq \beta I_B \simeq I_E$$

Also $I_E = I_C + I_B = (\beta + 1) I_B$

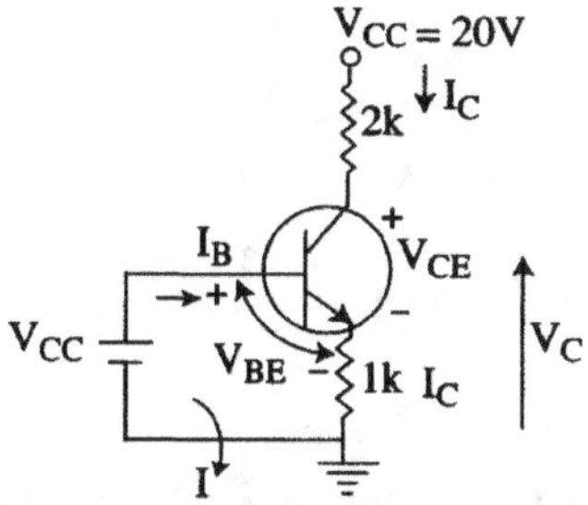

$V_{CC} = 20V$, 2k, I_C, I_B, V_{CE}, V_{CC}, V_{BE}, 1k, I_C, V_C, I

In loop 1, $20 = -0.7 + I_E \times 1\ k\Omega$

$$I_E = 20.7 \text{ mA}$$

$$\therefore \quad I_B = \frac{I_E}{\beta+1} = \frac{20.7}{51} = 40\ \mu A$$

$$V_C = V_{CC} - I_C \times 2k - I_E \times 2k - V_{CE}$$

$$= 20 - 3 \times 20 \text{ mA} \times 10^3 - 0.7$$

$$\simeq 16 \text{ V}.$$

52. Signal to noise ratio is

$$\frac{S}{N} = \frac{V_s^2}{V_n^2}$$

$$\therefore \text{ Noise voltage } V_n = \frac{V_s}{\sqrt{S/N}} = \frac{3}{\sqrt{20}}$$

$$= 0.67 \text{ mV}.$$

53. The Van der Waals interaction is weak but present everywhere. This interaction energy is given by

$$= -\frac{\alpha}{(4\pi\varepsilon_0)^2}(1 + 3\cos^2\theta)\frac{p^2}{R^6}$$

or $$\propto \frac{1}{R^6}.$$

54. The total energy

$$U = -\frac{\alpha e^2}{4\pi \in_0 r} + \frac{\beta}{r^9}$$

For equilibrium separation r_0, minimum energy

$$\left.\frac{dU}{dr}\right|_{r=r_0} = 0$$

$$= -\left[-\frac{\alpha e^2}{4\pi \in_0 r_0^2}\right] + \left[-\frac{9\beta}{r_0^{10}}\right] = 0$$

$$\Rightarrow \quad \frac{9\beta}{r_0^{10}} = \frac{\alpha e^2}{4\pi \in_0 r_0^2}$$

$$\beta = \frac{\alpha e^2}{36\pi \in_0} r_0^8.$$

55. Wavelength associated with an electron

$$\lambda_e = \frac{h}{\sqrt{2m_e E}}$$

and $$\lambda_p = \frac{h}{\sqrt{2m_p E}}$$

$$E \to eV$$

or $$\lambda_e = \frac{h}{\sqrt{2m_e eV}}$$

and $$\lambda_p = \frac{h}{\sqrt{2m_p eV}}$$

$$\therefore \quad \frac{\lambda_e}{\lambda_p} = \sqrt{\frac{m_p}{m_e}}$$

56.

x	x	Δ	Δ^2	Δ^3
0	0			
		0		
1	0			
		–1	2	
2	1			6
		1	8	
3	10			
		9		

Here $h = 1$

Hence using formula

$$x = x_0 + ph$$

and taking $x = 0$,

we get $p = x$

$$y(x) = 1 + x(-1) + \frac{x.(x-1)}{2}\cdot 2 + \frac{x.(x-1)(x-2)}{6}(6)$$

$$= x^3 - 2x^2 + 1 \rightarrow p$$

This is the polynomial for above tabulate

For $x = 4$, $y(4) = 1 + 4(-1) + 12 + 24$

$= 33.$

57. The wave number of the radiation absorbed in a rotational transition from J to J + 1 is given by

$$\nu = 2B\ (J + 1)$$

For a transition from J = 0 to J = 1, we have

$$\nu = 2B$$

But $\nu = 20.68\ cm^{-1}$ (given)

$\therefore$ $2B = 20.68$

$B = 10.34\ cm^{-1}$

Again, the wave number of the radiation absorbed in J = 15 ← 14 is given by

$$\nu = 2B\ (J + 1),$$

where J refers to lower state

$= 2B(14 + 1) = 30 \times 10.34$

$= 310.2\ cm^{-1}$

The corresponding wavelength is

$$\lambda = \frac{1}{\nu} = \frac{1}{310.2}\ cm = 32 \times 10^{-4}\ cm$$

$= 32\mu m.$

58. 2 kg of deuterium contains 6.023×10^{26} atoms.

1 kg of deuterium contains $\left[\frac{6.023\times 10^{26}}{2}\right]$ atoms.

Therefore, energy released due to 1 kg of deuterium by fusion is given by

$$U = \left(\frac{43}{6}\right)\left(\frac{6.023\times 10^{26}}{2}\right)\ MeV$$

$= 2.158 \times 10^{27}$ MeV

$= 2.158 \times 10^{27} \times 10^{6} \times 1.6 \times 10^{-19}$ J

$U = 3.453 \times 10^{14}$ J.

59. The coulomb barrier of a light nucleus is

$$V = \frac{Q_1Q_2}{A}.$$

Let $Q_1 \approx Q_2 \approx e, \simeq r \approx 1$ fm

So, $$V = \frac{e^2}{r}$$

$$= \frac{\hbar C}{r}\left(\frac{e^2}{\hbar C}\right)$$

$$= \frac{197}{1}\cdot\frac{1}{137} = 1.44\ MeV.$$

60. The max. energy change

$$\Delta E = \frac{e\hbar}{2m_0c}B_z(\Delta M_L)$$

$$= \frac{1.6\times 10^{-19}\times 6.6\times 10^{-27}}{2\times 9.1\times 10^{-31}\times 2 \times 3.14\times 3\times 10^{10}}\times 3\times 10^{4}$$

$= 2.8 \times 10^{-16}$ ergs.

61. As $$P_t = P_c\left(1+\frac{m^2}{2}\right)$$

$\Rightarrow$ $$10 = P_c\left(1+\frac{0.6^2}{2}\right)$$

$\Rightarrow$ $P_c = 8.47$ KW

62. It is seen that when either A or B both are at zero potential, current flow through R, thereby bringing the potential of C to zero level, thus logic output is zero. When both of them are at 5 V no current can flow and the voltage of C stays at –5 V, *i.e.,* the logic output of 1.

63.

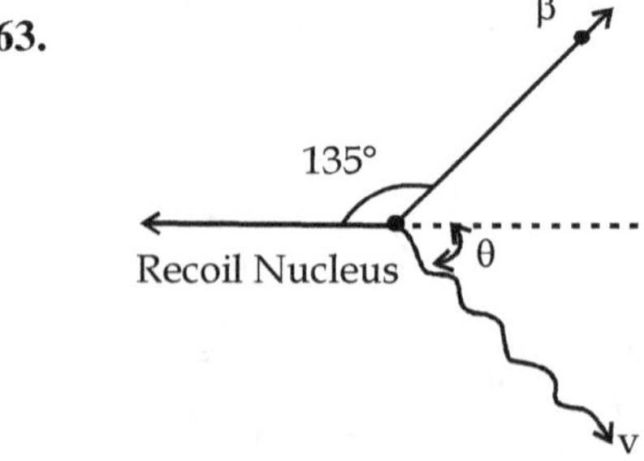

We know that the end point energy

$$E_0 = E_\nu + E_\beta$$

$$\therefore \quad E_\nu = E_0 - E_\beta$$

$$= 0.155 - 0.025 = 0.130 \text{ MeV}$$

Hence, the momentum of the neutrino

$$p_\nu = \frac{E_\nu}{c} = 0.13 \text{ MeV/C}$$

Momentum of a β-particle can be obtained from the relation

$$p_\beta = \sqrt{2ME_\beta}$$

$$= \sqrt{(2 \times 9.1091 \times 10^{-31} \times 0.025 \times 1.6 \times 10^{-12})}$$

$$= 0.158 \text{ MeV/C}$$

Using conservation of momentum of the system, we have

$$p_\beta \sin 45° = p_\nu \sin\theta$$

or, $$\sin\theta = \left(\frac{p_\beta}{p_\nu}\right)\sin 45° = 0.859$$

and $$p_R = p_\beta \cos 45° + p_\nu \cos\theta$$

$$= 0.158\left(\frac{1}{\sqrt{2}}\right) + 0.13\sqrt{[1-(0.859)^2]}$$

$$= 0.179 \text{ MeV/C}$$

64. We have for saturation magnetisation

$$M_S = n\mu$$

where n is the total number of atoms per unit volume and μ is the dipole moment of each atom. Now, the volume of each cubic cell is $(2.87 \times 10^{-10})^3$ m^3. For the body centred cubic cell, there are two atoms per cubic cell. Therefore,

$$n = \frac{2}{\left(2.87 \times 10^{-10}\right)^3}$$

$$= \frac{2 \times 10^{30}}{(2.87)^3}\text{m}^{-3}$$

Hence $$\mu = \frac{M_S}{n} = \frac{1.75 \times 10^6 \times (2.87)^3}{2 \times 10^{30} \times 9.27 \times 10^{-24}}$$ Bohr magnetons

Since 1 Bohr magneton = 9.27×10^{-24} A.m^2

or $\mu = 2.23$ Bohr magneton.

65. We know that

$$\lambda = \frac{1}{(\sqrt{2}).\pi d^2 n} = \frac{kT}{(\sqrt{2}).\pi d^2 P}$$

(when $n = P/kT$)

Given $k = 1.38 \times 10^{-23}$ J/K,

$T = 273$ K

$P = 10^{-6}$ mm of mercury

$= 10^{-9}$ m of mercury

$= 10^{-9} \times (13.6 \times 9.8 \times 10^{-3})$ N/m^2

$d = 2\text{Å} = 2 \times 10^{-10}$ m

$$\therefore \lambda = \frac{(1.38 \times 10^{-23})(273)}{(\sqrt{2}).3.14 \times (2 \times 10^{-10})^2 \times (13.6 \times 10^{-3} \times 9.8)10^{-9}}$$

$$= 162.9 \text{ metre.}$$

66. Outside the cylinder

$$\oint B.dl = \mu_0 I$$

$$B.2\pi r = \mu_0 I$$

$$B = \frac{\mu_0 I}{2\pi r}$$

Inside the cylinder

$$\oint \overline{B}.\overline{dl} = 0$$

which gives us

$$\overline{B} = 0$$

67. $$L = \frac{1}{2}m(v_x^2 + v_y^2) + a(xv_y - yv_x)$$

So, $$p_x = \frac{\partial L}{\partial \dot{x}} = \frac{\partial L}{\partial v_x} = mv_x - ay$$

$$p_y = \frac{\partial L}{\partial \dot{y}} = \frac{\partial L}{\partial v_y} = mv_y + ax$$

68. We know

$$\frac{E_{0r}}{E_{0i}} = \frac{n_1 - n_2}{n_2 + n_1}$$

$$\frac{E_{0t}}{E_{0i}} = \frac{2n_1}{n_2 + n_1}$$

$$\Rightarrow \quad E_{0r} = E_{0i}\left[\frac{1-\frac{n_2}{n_1}}{\frac{n_2}{n_1}+1}\right]$$

$$= 2\times\frac{1-1.5}{1.5+1} = -2\times\frac{0.5}{2.5}$$

$$= -\frac{2}{5}\text{ V/m}$$

and for $E_{0t} = E_{0i}\times\dfrac{2}{1+\frac{n_2}{n_1}}$

$$= 2\times 2\times\frac{1}{5}\times 2$$

$$E_{0t} = \frac{8}{5}\text{ V/m.}$$

69. Wave function (A) is physically admissible wave function as it satisfy the conditions of finiteness, uniqueness and continuity. However, others are not as (D) is double valued, (C) is goes to infinity and (B) has a discontinuous derivative.

70. If σ_1 and σ_2 → entropies of the subsystems 1 and 2, then additive property of entropy

$$\sigma = \sigma_1 + \sigma_2 \quad ...(1)$$

Also, $\sigma = \sigma(U_1, U_2)$ ...(2)

and $U = U_1 + U_2$ ...(3)

Then $\delta\sigma = \delta\sigma_1 + \delta\sigma_2$

$$= \left(\frac{\partial\sigma_1}{\partial U_1}\right)\delta U_1 + \left(\frac{\partial\sigma_2}{\partial U_2}\right)\delta U_2 \quad ...(4)$$

and $\delta U = \delta U_1 + \delta U_2$ ...(5)

For thermal equilibrium, we have

$$\delta U = \delta U_1 + \delta U_2 = 0$$

or $\delta U_2 = -\delta U_1$ ...(6)

and $$\delta\sigma = \left(\frac{\partial\sigma_1}{\partial U_1}\right)\delta U_1 + \left(\frac{\partial\sigma_2}{\partial U_2}\right)\delta U_2 = 0 \quad ...(7)$$

From equations (6) and (7)

$$\delta\sigma = \left[\frac{\partial\sigma_1}{\partial U_1} - \frac{\partial\sigma_2}{\partial U_2}\right]\delta U_1 = 0$$

δU_1 is arbitrary variation, hence, $\delta U_1 \neq 0$

$$\therefore \quad \frac{\partial\sigma_1}{\partial U_1} = \frac{\partial\sigma_2}{\partial U_2}$$

or we can define quantity τ by

$$\frac{1}{\tau} = \left(\frac{\partial\sigma}{\partial U}\right).$$

71. As, $B = \dfrac{E}{C} = \dfrac{6}{3\times10^8} = 2\times10^{-8}$ T

along z-direction.

The direction of travel of em wave is in the direction vector $\vec{E}\times\vec{B}$.

72. Acceleration produced due to electric field.

$$a = \frac{qE}{m}, \text{ along horizontally.}$$

Acceleration due to gravity = g, acting vertically downwards

Net acceleration, $g' = \sqrt{g^2 + a^2}$

$$= \sqrt{g^2 + \left(\frac{qE}{m}\right)^2}$$

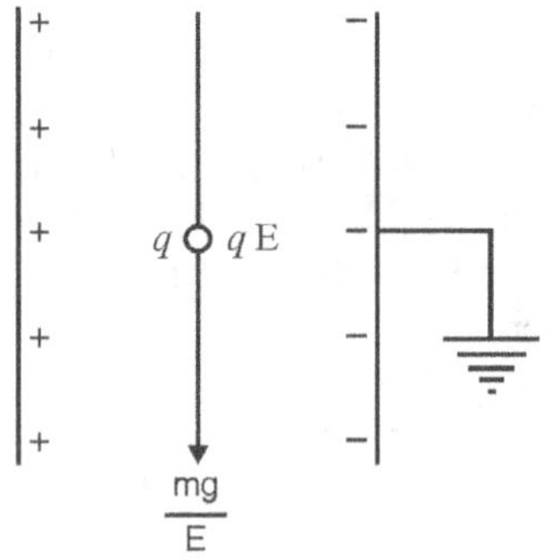

$$\therefore \quad T_2 = 2\pi\sqrt{\frac{l}{g'}}$$

$$= 2\pi\sqrt{\frac{l}{\sqrt{g^2 + \left(\frac{qE}{m}\right)^2}}}.$$

73. Power = 2K watt = 2×10^3 W

Cross-sectional area = 10^{-6} cm^2

$$\text{Poynting vector } S = \frac{P}{A}$$

$$= \frac{2 \times 10^3 \text{ W}}{10^{-6}(10^{-2}\text{ m})^2}$$

$$= 2 \times 10^{3+10} \text{ W/m}^2$$

$$S = 2 \times 10^{13} \text{ W/m}^2.$$

74. $$N = N_0 \exp\left(\frac{-h\upsilon}{kT}\right)$$

$$= N_0 [1 + (0.4) + (0.4)^2 + (0.4)^3 + ...]$$

As $\exp.\left(\frac{-h\upsilon}{kT}\right) = 0.4$ (given)

$$= N_0 (1.68) \text{ nearly.}$$

75. Given $T_A = 1$ hr

$T_B = 2$ hr

and $t = 2$ hr

According to decay law, the rate of disintegration at any instant is

$$\frac{dN}{dt} = -N\lambda$$

∴ After 2 hour, the ratio of rate of disintegrations of A and B is

$$\frac{\left(\frac{dN}{dt}\right)_A}{\left(\frac{dN}{dt}\right)_B} = \frac{N_A\lambda_A}{N_B\lambda_B} = \frac{N_A(0.693/T_A)}{N_B(0.693/T_B)}$$

$$= \frac{N_A T_B}{N_B T_A}$$

But from $N = N_0\left(\frac{1}{2}\right)^{t/T}$,

$$N_A = N_0\left(\frac{1}{2}\right)^{2/1}$$

and $$N_B = N_0\left(\frac{1}{2}\right)^{2/2}$$

or $$\frac{\left(\frac{dN}{dt}\right)_A}{\left(\frac{dN}{dt}\right)_B} = \frac{N_0\left(\frac{1}{2}\right)^{2/1} \times 2}{N_0\left(\frac{1}{2}\right)^{2/2} \times 1} = 1.$$

SET–4
CSIR–UGC (NET) PHYSICAL SCIENCES

PART-A

1. Inner planets of the solar system are rocky, whereas outer planets are gaseous. One of the reasons for this is that

A. solar heat drove away the gases to the outer region of the solar system
B. gravitational pull of the sun pulled all rocky material to the inner solar system
C. outer planet are larger than the inner plants
D. comets delivered the gases materials to the outer planets

2. Two boys A and B are at two diametrically opposite points on a circle. At one instant the two start running on the circle; A anticlockwise with constant speed v and B clockwise with constant speed $2v$. In 2 minutes, they pass each other for the first time. How much later will they pass each other for the second time?

A. 1 minute B. 2 minutes
C. 3 minutes D. 4 minutes

3. A man can row three quarters of a kilometer against the stream in 11¼ minutes and return in 7½ minutes. Find the speed of the man in still water.

A. 3 km/hr B. 4 km/hr
C. 5 km/hr D. 6 km/hr

4. Find the number of different permutations of the letters of the word BANANA.

A. 60 B. 70
C. 40 D. 50

5. Living beings get energy from food through the process of aerobic respiration. One of the reactants is

A. carbon dioxide B. water vapour
C. oxygen D. phosphorus

6. Six sides of the block are coloured Green, Blue, Red, Yellow, Orange, White in the following manner :

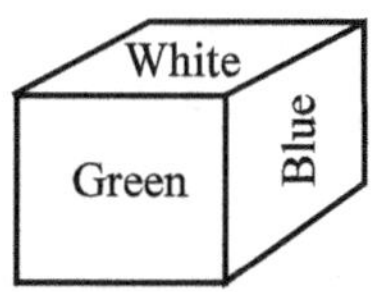

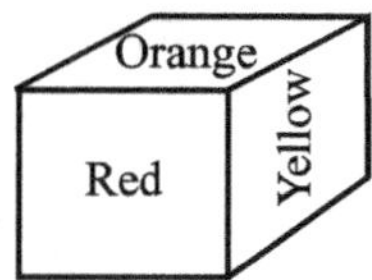

When Blue is on top, which colour will be at the bottom?

A. Orange B. Red
C. White D. Yellow

7. In the fig. EF is parallel to BC, FG is parallel to AB, AE is equal to FG = 4, EF = 3, what is BC?

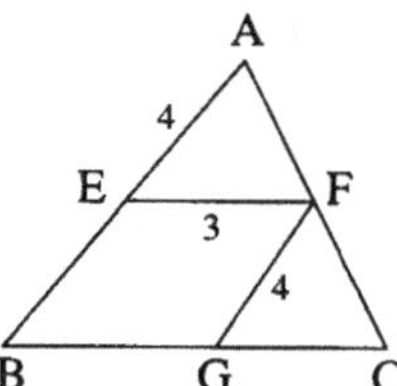

A. 6 B. 7
C. 9 D. 8

8. If → stands for subtract, ← stands for add, ↑↑ stands for multiply, ↓↓ stands for divide, ↔ for greater than, ⟷ stands for equal to, then which of the following alternatives is true?

A. 4 ← 6 ↑↑ 2 ⟷ 3 → 12 ← 12
B. 10 ↓↓ 5 ↑↑ 5 ⟷ 9 → 3 ← 4
C. 15 ↑↑ 2 → 5 ⟷ 12 ↓↓ 4 ← 3
D. 13 ↓↓ 13 ← 1 ↔ 20 → 5 ↑↑ 2

9. A farmer took a loan at 12% per annum at SI. After 4 years, he settled the loan by paying ₹ 2442, what was the principal amount?

A. ₹ 1650 B. ₹ 1825
C. ₹ 1320 D. ₹ 2140

10. How many circles are there in the figure given below?

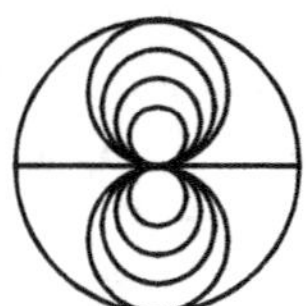

A. 5 B. 6
C. 8 D. 9

11. A peacock perched on the top of a 12 m high tree spots a snake moving towards its hole at the base of the tree from a distance equal to thrice the height of the tree. The peacock flies towards the snake in a straight line and they both move at the same speed. At what distance from the base of the tree will the peacock catch the snake?

A. 16 m B. 18 m
C. 14 m D. 12 m

12. Which one number can be placed at the sign of interrogation?

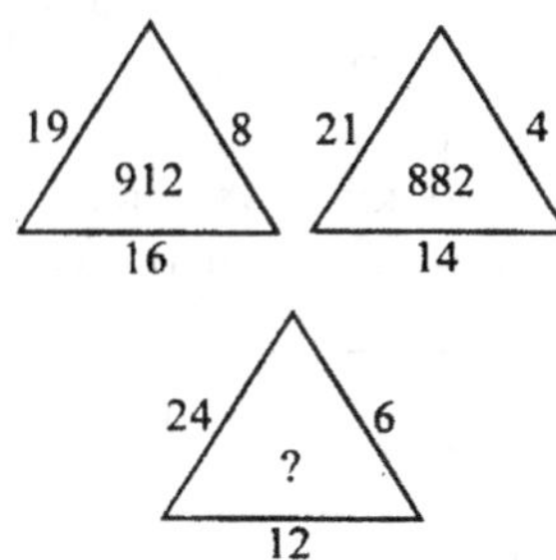

A. 1356 B. 862
C. 1234 D. 864

13. Which of the following pairs of numbers of the dice given below does not correctly give the numbers on the opposite side?

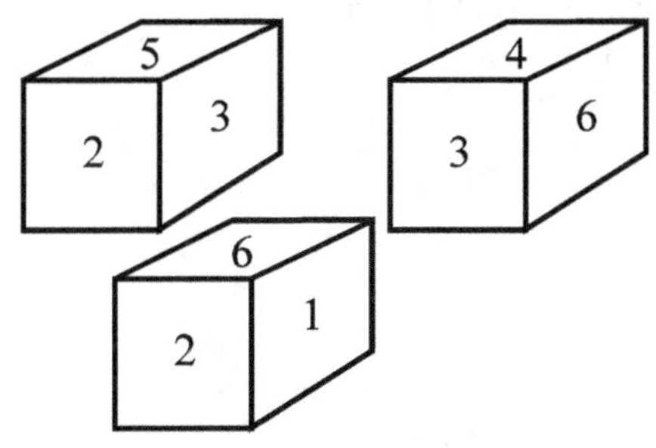

A. 2 – 4 B. 4 – 1
C. 3 – 1 D. 6 – 5

14. Consider the diagram given below:

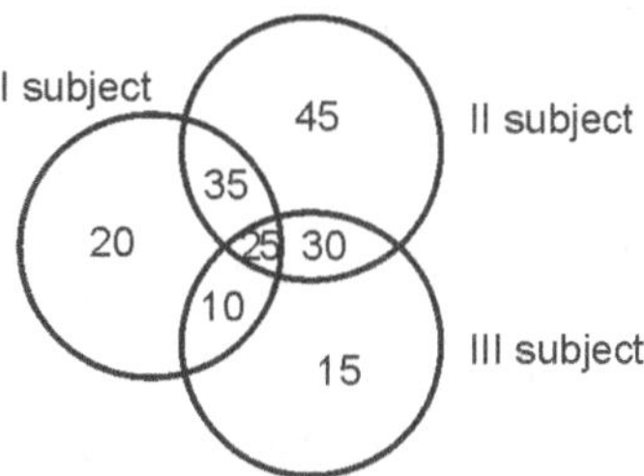

If 500 students appeared in an examination. How many students appeared at least in two subjects?

A. 200 B. 100
C. 150 D. 50

15. There are eight bags of rice looking alike, seven of which have equal weight and one is slightly heavier. The weighing balance is of unlimited capacity. Using this balance, the minimum number of weighing required to identify the heavier bag is

A. 8 B. 3
C. 2 D. 4

16. In a coding system, VINOD is written as TGLMB, then VIRENDRA will be coded as

A. TGPCLBPY
B. TGQRBPYL
C. TGPCRBPZ
D. TGBQRLYR

17. If the base of a triangle is made double and its height is half, what will be the ratio of the area of the original triangle to that of the new triangle?

A. 1 : 1 B. 1 : 2
C. 2 : 3 D. 2 : 1

18. Two missiles speed directly towards each other, one at 12000 miles per hour and the other at 18,000 miles per hour. Initially they are at a distance of 1115 miles from each other. How far apart they would be exactly 30 second before they collide?

A. 50 miles B. 11.15 miles
C. 100 miles D. 250 miles

19. The question fig. is folded to form a box, choose, the box similar to box formed.

Question Figure:

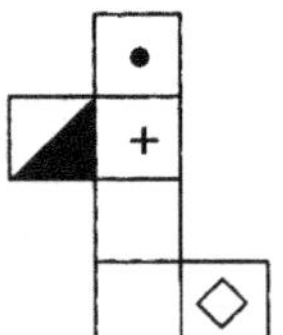

Answer Figures:

 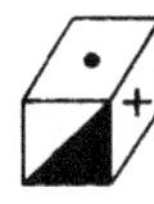 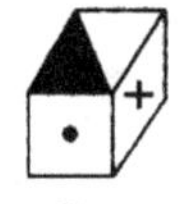 

A B C D

20. In the given figure of a triangle PQR, if the points S, T, U, V are joined together to form a quadrilateral STUV, then how many triangles will have in the resultant figure

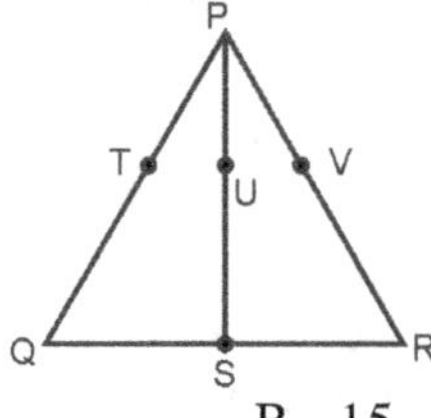

A. 11 B. 15
C. 13 D. 17

PART-B

21. The volume (V) versus temperature (T) graphs for a certain amount of a perfect gas at two pressures P_1 and P_2 are shown in fig. It follows from the graphs that

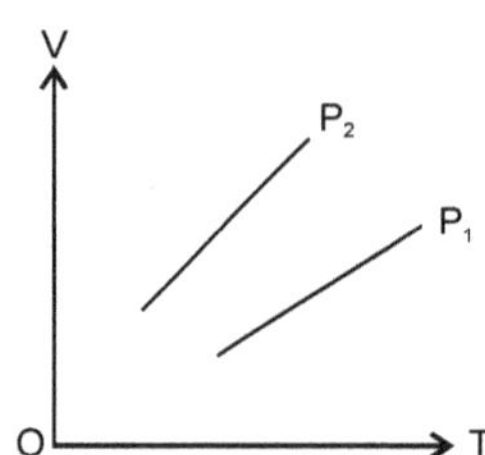

A. $P_1 < P_2$ B. $P_1 > P_2$
C. $P_1 = P_2$ D. None of these

22. The binding energy per nucleon for the parent nucleus is E_1 and that for the daughter nuclei is E_2, then

A. $E_1 > E_2$ B. $E_2 > E_1$
C. $E_1 = E_2$ D. $E_1 = 2E_2$

23. A box contain 5 black and 5 red balls. Two balls are randomly picked one after another from the box, without replacement. The probability to both balls being red is

A. $\frac{2}{9}$ B. $\frac{1}{9}$

C. $\frac{3}{20}$ D. $\frac{19}{90}$

24. A γ-ray of energy 2.2 MeV produces an electron-positron pair. Then, the energy imparted to each of the charge particles is nearly

A. 1.59 MeV B. 0.59 MeV
C. 2.59 MeV D. 1.01 MeV

25. Two point charges Q and –Q are located on two opposite corners of a square as shown in fig. If the potential at the corner A is taken as 1 V, then the potential at B, the centre of the square will be

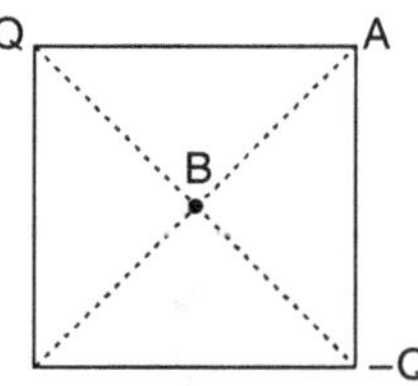

A. 0 V B. 1 V
C. 2 V D. 1.5 V

26. If pressure is increased on piece of wax, the melting point of wax

A. increases
B. decreases
C. remains constant
D. decreases at first, then increases

27. For a transistor circuit

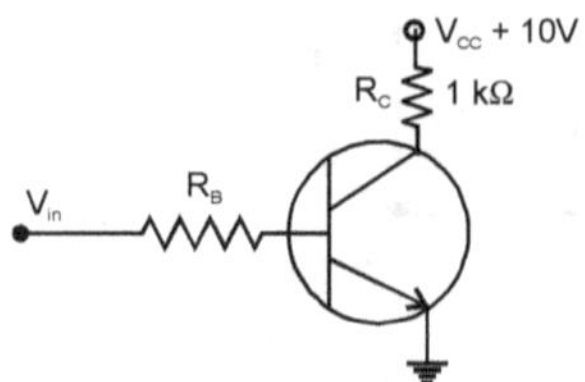

V_{CE}, when $V_{IN} = 0$ V

A. 5 V B. 10 V
C. 15 V D. 12 V

28. The numerical value of the radius of the first orbit of hydrogen as

A. 0.0529 nm B. 0.0295 nm
C. 0.1123 nm D. 0.1789 nm

29. An ideal gas heat engine is operating between 227°C and 127°C. It absorbs 10^4 J of heat at the higher temperature. The amount of heat converted into work is

A. 3000 J B. 2000 J
C. 4000 J D. 1000 J

30. The equation $4\,{}_1^1H^+ \rightarrow {}_2^4He^{2+} + 2\,{}_0e^{-1} + 26\,\text{MeV}$ represents:

A. fusion B. fission
C. β-decay D. γ-decay

31. The duration of randar pulse is 10^{-6} s. The uncertainty in its energy would be

A. 1.05×10^{-28} J B. 1.05×10^{-21} J
C. 1.05×10^{-25} J D. 0

32. A RF signal is amplitude modulated to a depth of 100% by a sinusoidal signal. The ratio of modulated signal power to unmodulated carrier power is

A. $\frac{3}{2}$ B. $\frac{1}{2}$
C. $\frac{1}{3}$ D. $\frac{1}{4}$

33. If n_ϕ and n for an electron in an elliptical orbit are 1 and 2 respectively, then the ratio of semi-major axis and semi-minor axis is

A. 0.5 B. 2
C. 0.25 D. 1

34. E_F and E_f are the Fermi levels of sodium at 0 K and 10000 K, E_F for sodium is 3 eV, then $\frac{E_f}{E_F}$ is

A. 21 B. 0.02
C. 1.93 D. 0.93

35. Two events, separated by a special distance 9×10^9 m are simultaneous in one inertial frame. The time interval between these two events in a frame moving with a constant speed $0.8c$ (where the speed of light $c = 3 \times 10^8$ m/s) is

A. 20 s B. 40 s
C. 60 s D. 30 s

36. The period of oscillation for compound pendulum is

A. $2\pi\sqrt{\frac{(k^2+l^2)}{gl}}$ B. $2\pi\sqrt{\frac{gl}{k^2+l^2}}$
C. $2\pi\sqrt{\frac{(k^2+l^2)}{mgl}}$ D. $2\pi\sqrt{\frac{mgl}{(k^2+l^2)}}$

37. In Fig. XY is an infinite line charge distribution. P and Q are points as shown. The ratio of electric field at P and Q is

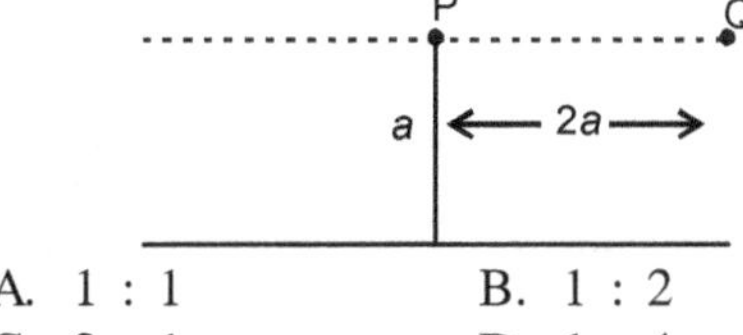

A. 1 : 1 B. 1 : 2
C. 2 : 1 D. 1 : 4

38. Isothermal compressibility K_F of a substance is defined as $K_T = -\frac{1}{V}\left(\frac{\partial V}{\partial P}\right)_T$. Its value for n moles of an ideal gas will be

A. $\frac{1}{P}$ B. $\frac{n}{P}$
C. $-\frac{1}{P}$ D. $-\frac{n}{P}$

39. A condenser of 250 μF is connected in parallel to a coil of inductance 0.16 mH and effective resistance 20 Ω. The resonant frequency will be

A. 8×10^5 Hz B. 8.5×10^6 Hz
C. 7.5×10^4 Hz D. 6×10^5 Hz

40. The duration of radar pulse is 10^{-6} s. The uncertainty in its energy would be

A. 1.05×10^{-35} J B. 1.05×10^{-28} J
C. 0 D. 1.05×10^{-21} J

41. Consider the physical system whose Hamiltonian H and initial state $|\psi_0>$ are given by

$$H = \in\begin{pmatrix} 0 & i & 0 \\ -i & 0 & 0 \\ 0 & 0 & -1 \end{pmatrix}, |\psi_0> = \frac{1}{\sqrt{5}}\begin{pmatrix} 1-i \\ 1-i \\ 1 \end{pmatrix}, \in \text{has}$$

dimension of energy. The prob of measuring $E_1 = \in$

A. $\frac{4}{5}$ B. $\frac{1}{5}$

C. $\frac{2}{5}$ D. $\frac{3}{5}$

42. One kilogram of ice melts at 0°C into water at the same temperature. The change in entropy is (in cal/K)

A. 293 B. 0.293

C. ∞ D. 0

43. A silicon diode is in series with a 1.0 kΩ resistor and a 5 V battery. If the anode is connected to the positive battery terminal, the cathode voltage with respect to the negative battery terminal is

A. 5.7 V B. 4.3 V

C. 0.3 V D. 0.7 V

44. A 10 MHz clock frequency is applied to a cascaded counter consisting of a modulus-5 counter, a modulus-8 counter, and two modulus-10 counters. The lowest output frequency possible is

A. 5 kHz B. 25 kHz

C. 2.5 kHz D. 10 kHz

45. A Rf carrier of 12 kV at 1 MHz is amplitude modulated by a 1 kHz signal of 6 kV peak. The modulation pattern is observed on a CRO caliborated suitably. The voltage indicated will be

A. 36 kV B. 22 kV

C. 14 kV D. 28 kV

PART-C

46. What are the eigen values of the given matrix

$$A = \begin{bmatrix} 7 & 0 & 0 \\ 0 & 1 & -i \\ 0 & i & -1 \end{bmatrix}$$

A. $7, \sqrt{2}, -\sqrt{2}$ B. $-7, -\sqrt{2}, -\sqrt{2}$

C. $7, \sqrt{3}, -\sqrt{3}$ D. $7, \sqrt{2}, \sqrt{2}$

47. The correct curve between intensity of magnetisation (I) and magnetic field (H) for a ferromagnetic substance is given by

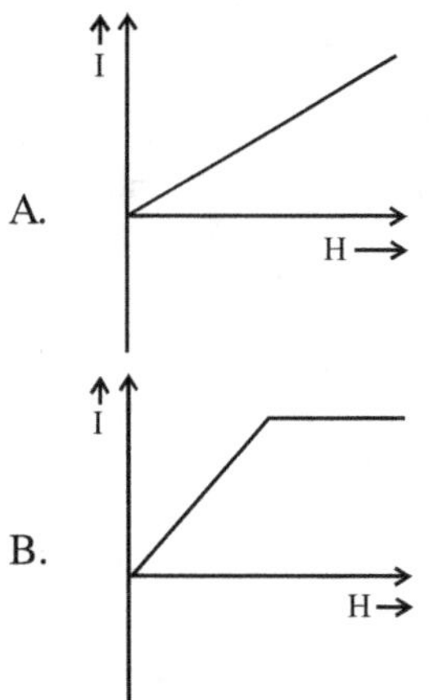

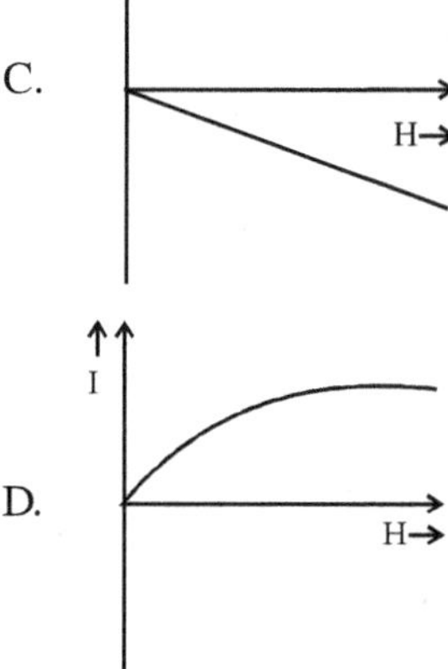

48. The independent solution of the equation $\frac{d^3y}{dx^3} + \frac{6d^2y}{dx^2} + \frac{11dy}{dx} + 6y = 0$ are

A. e^x, e^{2x} and e^{3x}

B. e^{-x}, e^{-2x} and e^{-3x}

C. $\frac{1}{x}$, x^2 and x^3

D. $\sin x$, $\cos 2x$ $\cos 3x$

49. In a simple cubic lattice $d_{100} : d_{110} : d_{111}$ is :

A. 6 : 3 : 2 B. $6 : 3 : \sqrt{2}$

C. $\sqrt{6} : \sqrt{3} : \sqrt{2}$ D. $\sqrt{6} : \sqrt{3} : \sqrt{4}$

50. If A and B are two elements such that P(A) = $\frac{2}{3}$, $P(B) = \frac{3}{4}$, $P(A \cap B) = \frac{1}{2}$, then $P(A \cup B)$ =

A. $\frac{11}{12}$ B. $\frac{16}{19}$

C. $\frac{21}{23}$ D. $\frac{7}{12}$

51. The earth revolves round the sun in elliptical orbit with sun at centre of the foci in figure. The orbital speed of the earth is maximum near the point

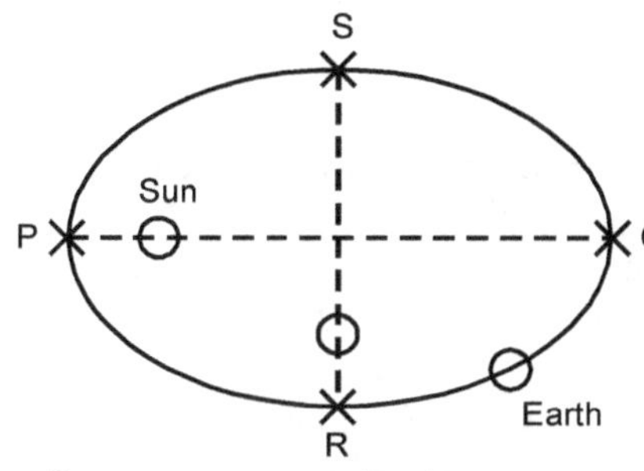

A. Q B. R
C. S D. P

52. The electric flux passing through a hemispherical surface of radius R placed in an electric field $\vec{E}$ with the axis parallel to the field is

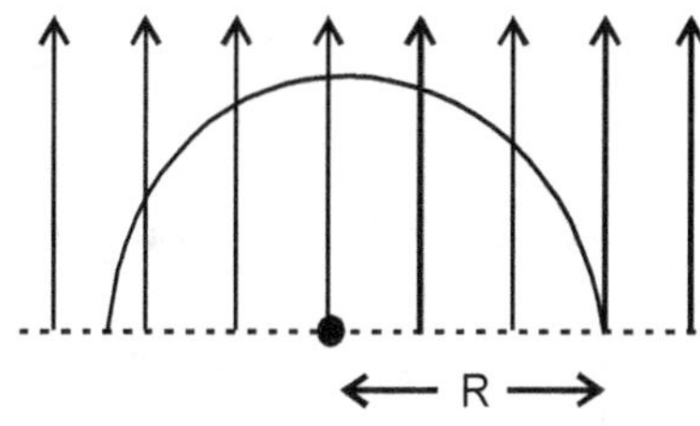

A. $2\pi RE$ B. πR^2E
C. $2\pi R^3E$ D. $2\pi R^2E$

53. The bob of a simple pendulum moves in a horizontal circle as, shown in figure. Find the angular frequency of the circular motion in terms of angle θ and the length, *l*, of the rod (conical pendulum).

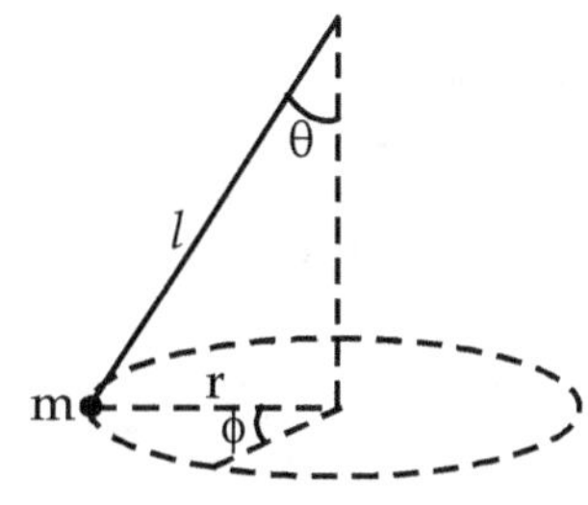

A. $\sqrt{\frac{g}{l\cos\theta}}$ B. $\sqrt{\frac{l}{g\cos\theta}}$

C. $\sqrt{\frac{g}{l\sin\theta}}$ D. $\sqrt{gl\cos\theta}$

54. According to Maxwell's law of distribution of velocities of molecules, the most probable velocity is

A. Greater than the mean velocity
B. Equal to the mean velocity
C. Equal to root mean square velocity
D. Less than root mean square velocity

55. An AM modulater has output $\pi(t)$ = A cos 400 πt + B cos 380π*t* + B cos 220πt
The carrier power is 100 W and the efficiency is 40%. The value of A and B are

A. 22.36, 13.46 B. 14.14, 8.16
C. 30, 20 D. 50, 10

56. The potential energy between a pair of atoms is given as $U = -\frac{\alpha}{r^6} + \frac{\beta}{r^{12}}$. The equilibrium-interatomic separation will be

A. $\left(\frac{\alpha}{2\beta}\right)^{1/6}$ B. $\left(\frac{2\beta}{\alpha}\right)^{1/6}$

C. $\frac{2\beta}{\alpha}$ D. $\frac{\beta}{\alpha}$

57. Two spherical nuclei have mass numbers 216 and 64 with their radii R_1 and R_2 respectively. The ratio $\frac{R_1}{R_2}$ is

A. 1.0 B. 1.5
C. 2.0 D. 2.5

58. The logic expression for the output Y of the following circuit is

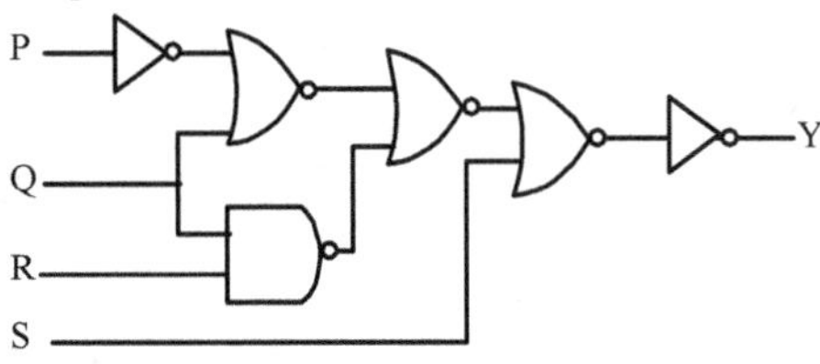

A. $\overline{\overline{\overline{P}+Q}+\overline{QR}}+S$ B. $\overline{\overline{\overline{P}+Q}+\overline{QR}+S}$

C. $\overline{\overline{P}+Q+\overline{\overline{QR}}}+S$ D. $\overline{\overline{\overline{P}+Q}+\overline{QR}}+\overline{S}$

59. For the circuit shown below, calculate the output voltage V_0. What would V_0 be if the polarity of 2 V battery is reversed at terminal B? (Assume the operational amplifier to be ideal).

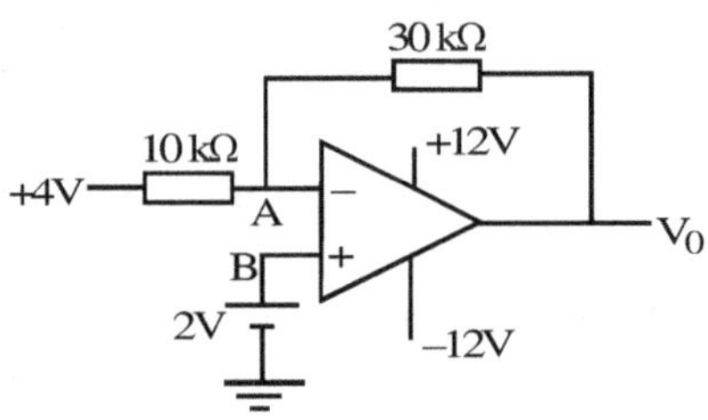

A. 12 V B. 14 V
C. 16 V D. 18 V

60. A neutron of mass $m_n = 10^{-27}$ kg is moving inside a nucleus. Assume the nucleus to be a cubical box of size 10^{-14} m with impenetrable walls. Take $\hbar \simeq 10^{-34}$ Js and 1 MeV $\simeq 10^{-13}$ J. An estimate of the energy in MeV of the neutron is

A. 80 MeV B. $\frac{1}{8}$ MeV

C. 8 MeV D. $\frac{1}{80}$ MeV

61. The correct plot for the equivalent one dimensional potential for an attractive inverse fourth law of force :

A.

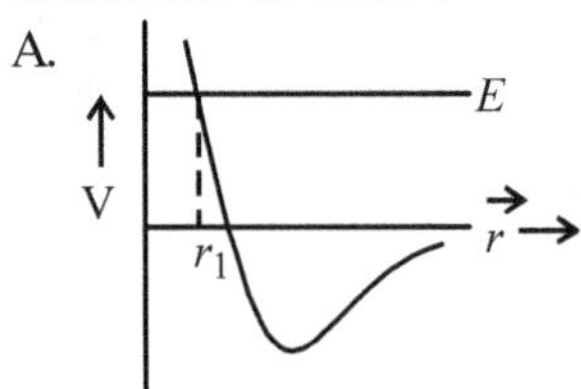

B.

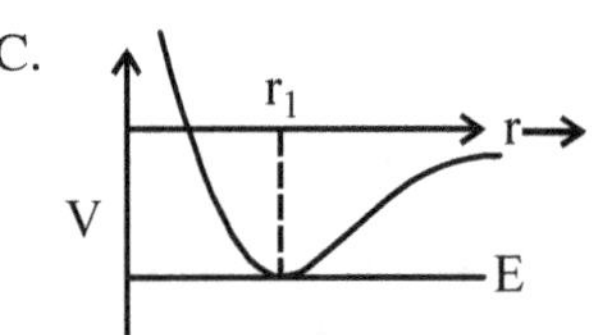

C.

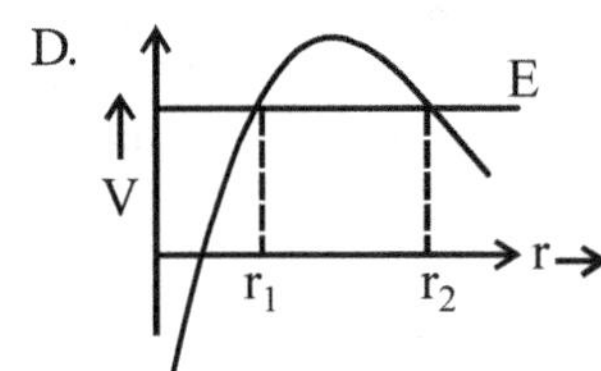

D. (graph of V against r with E, r_1, r_2)

62. The separation of the lines in the far Infrared spectrum of HBr is 16.90×10^{-10} cm, its moment of inertia should be around

A. 6.66×10^{-40} gm cm^2
B. 3.30×10^{-38} gm cm^2
C. 3.30×10^{-38} gm cm^2
D. 3.30×10^{-40} gm cm^2

63. When two ultraviolet beams of wavelengths λ_1 = 280 nm and λ_2 = 490 nm fall on a lead surface, they produce photoelectrons with maximum energies 8.57 eV and 6.67 eV, respectively. Estimate the numerical value of the Planck constant

A. 6.62×10^{-34} Js
B. 6.12×10^{-34} Js
C. 5.67×10^{-34} Js
D. 4.32×10^{-34} Js

64. What is the entropy change of water when 1000 gm of water are heated from 20°C to 80°C. Given that specific heat of water has a constant value 4.2 J/gm-°C.

A. 582 J/K B. 475 J/K
C. 782 J/K D. 975 J/K

65. A 160 PF capacitor, an indicator of 160 ± 10% μH and a resistor of 1200 ± 10 Ω are connected in series. If all the three components are ± 0% and resonant frequency is $f_r = \frac{1}{2\pi}\sqrt{\frac{1}{LC}}$, the resonant frequency of the combination is

A. 5 MHz B. 1 MHz
C. 2 MHz D. 3 MHz

66. In DAC circuit shown in the figure below, V_R = 10 V and R = 10 kΩ

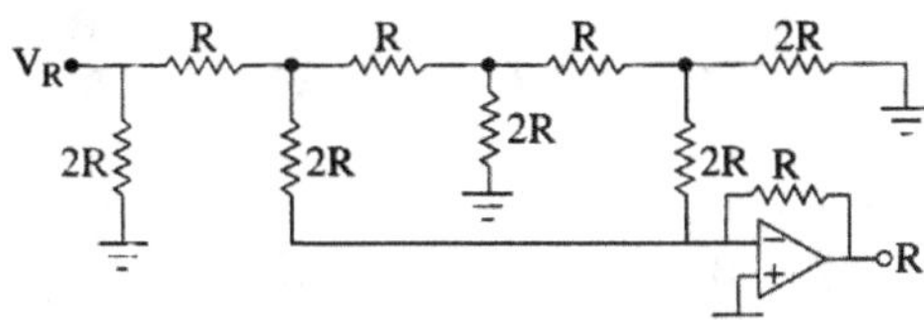

the current i is
A. 250 μA B. 125 μA
C. 62.5 μA D. 31.25 μA

67. In a crystalline solid, the energy band structure (E-k relation for an electron of mass m is given by $E = \frac{\hbar^2 k(2k-3)}{2m}$. The effective mass of the electron in the crystal is

A. m B. $\frac{2}{3}m$
C. $\frac{m}{2}$ D. $2m$

68. In an experiment with benzene the wavelengths of a pair of stokes and antistokes lines were measured to be 4554 Å and 4178 Å respectively. Calculate the wavelength of the corresponding infra-red absorption line.
A. 1.012×10^5 Å B. 2.031×10^5 Å
C. 4.321×10^5 Å D. 0.012×10^5 Å

69. The Mesen theory of nuclear forces assumes the virtual exchange of pions. If a nucleon emits a virtual pions of rest mass 270 m_e, the range of nuclear force is
A. 1.23 fermi B. 1.43 fermi
C. 3.25 fermi D. 2.24 fermi

70. A CDS cell has a dark resistance of 100 kΩ and a resistance of 30 kΩ in a day light beam. Find the resistance of the cell after 10 ns of application of a beam. The time constant is 72 ns.

A. 42.3 kΩ B. 39.1 kΩ
C. 21.3 kΩ D. 22.9 kΩ

71. If the wavelength of the first line of the Lyman series of hydrogen is 1215 Å, the wavelength of the second line of the series is
A. 1825 Å B. 1225 Å
C. 1025 Å D. 1525 Å

72. In an amplitude modulated system, if the total power is 600 W and the power in carrier is 400 W, then the modulation index is
A. 1 B. 0.75
C. 0.5 D. 0.9

73. The 8 bit shift register and D flip-flop shown in fig. is synchronized with same clock. The D flip-flop is initially cleared

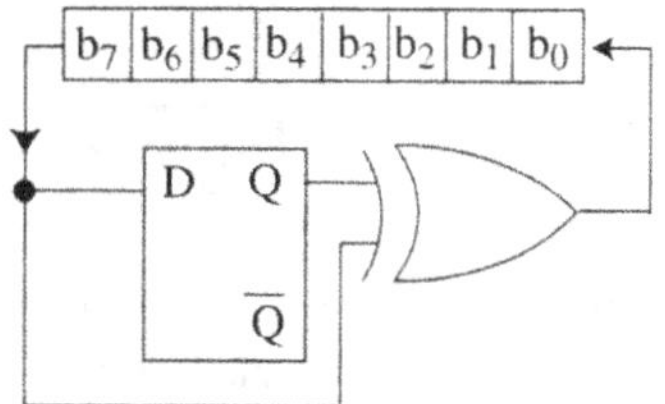

The circuit act as—
A. Binary to Excess-3 code convertor
B. Binary to 1's complement convertor
C. Binary to Gray code convertor
D. Binary to 2's complement convertor

74. If V_B is the built-in potential and $\pm V_a$ is the applied voltage (positive sign for reverse bias and negative sign for forward bias), then the junction capacitance of an abrupt p-n junction is proportional to
A. $(V_\beta \pm V_\alpha)$ B. $(V_\beta \pm V_\alpha)^{1/2}$
C. $(V_\beta \pm V_\alpha)^{-1/3}$ D. $(V_\beta \pm V_\alpha)^{-1/2}$

75. A solid cylindrical conductor of radius R has a uniform current density. The magnetic field H—inside the conductor at a distance r from the axis of the conductor is

A. $\frac{Ir}{4\pi R^2}$ B. $\frac{I}{2\pi r}$

C. $\frac{I}{4\pi r}$ D. $\frac{\overline{Ir}}{2\pi R^2}$

ANSWERS

1	2	3	4	5	6	7	8	9	10
A	D	C	A	C	D	A	B	A	D
11	**12**	**13**	**14**	**15**	**16**	**17**	**18**	**19**	**20**
A	D	B	B	C	A	A	D	B	A
21	**22**	**23**	**24**	**25**	**26**	**27**	**28**	**29**	**30**
A	B	A	B	B	A	B	A	B	A
31	**32**	**33**	**34**	**35**	**36**	**37**	**38**	**39**	**40**
A	A	A	D	B	A	A	A	A	B
41	**42**	**43**	**44**	**45**	**46**	**47**	**48**	**49**	**50**
C	A	B	C	A	A	B	B	B	A
51	**52**	**53**	**54**	**55**	**56**	**57**	**58**	**59**	**60**
D	B	A	D	B	B	B	B	C	B
61	**62**	**63**	**64**	**65**	**66**	**67**	**68**	**69**	**70**
D	D	A	C	B	C	C	A	B	B
71	**72**	**73**	**74**	**75**					
C	A	C	D	D					

EXPLANATORY ANSWERS

1. We know that the solar system contains eight planets—the four rocky inner planets are Mercury, Venus, Earth and Mars and then the four gas giants comprising Jupiter, Saturn, Uranus and Neptune.

The reason is that, when the solar system was born, most of the gases near the sun were soon either vapourised and blown away by the solar wind, hence only rock materials and heavy metal were left to form the inner planets.

2. Let A and B meet at point 'C' after running 2 minutes.

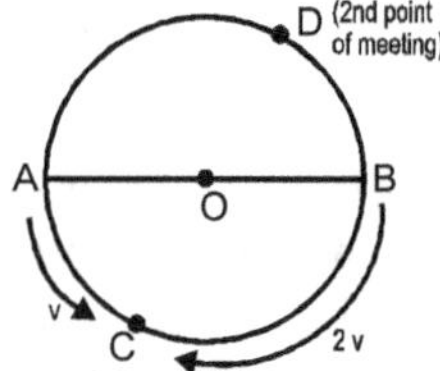

So, distance ACB $= \frac{1}{2} \times$ (Perimeter of circular path)

Distance travelled by 'A' in 2 minutes

$$AC = 2v$$

Distance travelled by 'B' in 2 minutes

$$BC = 2(2v) = 4v$$

$\frac{1}{2} \times$ (Perimeter of circle)

$= AC + BC = 2v + 4v = 6v$

Perimeter of circle $= 12v$

Now, from formula,

Perimeter of circle $= 2\pi r$ {where r = radius}

$$2\pi r = 12v$$

$$r = \frac{6v}{\pi} \quad ...(i)$$

Again, let they meet 2nd time at point D after time 't' minutes.

So, distance travelled by 'B' in t minutes

$$CAD = 2vt$$

Distance travelled by 'A' in t minutes

$$CBD = vt$$

From figure,

$$CAD + CBD = 2\pi.(r) \text{ \{Perimeter of circle\}}$$

$$2vt + vt = 2\pi.r$$

From equation (i),

$$r = \frac{6v}{\pi}$$

$$3vt = 2\pi \cdot \frac{6v}{\pi}$$

$$3vt = 12v$$

$$t = \frac{12v}{3v}$$
t = 4 minutes.

3. Upstream speed = $\dfrac{3/4}{\dfrac{45}{4 \times 60}}$ = 4 km/hr

Downstream speed = $\dfrac{3/4}{\dfrac{15}{2 \times 60}}$ = 6 km/hr

∴ Speed of the man in still water

$$= \frac{1}{2}(6 + 4) = 5 \text{ km/hr.}$$

4. BANANA
3A's, 2N's, B, *i.e.,* 6 letters, 3 alike of one type and 2 of another type. Number of words taken all at a time is $\dfrac{6!}{3!2!} = \dfrac{6 \times 5 \times 4}{2} = 60.$

5. Aerobic respiration uses oxygen to get the energy from food. Living things that use aerobic respiration are called aerobes. As a result of aerobic respiration ATP is released from food. The energy released is used by the cell to perform its functions. Enzymes are used in this process.

6. The coloured sides of the block which are clearly understood to be the opposites are: White – Orange, Blue – Yellow and Green – Red. So, when blue is on the top, yellow will be at the bottom.

7. Since, EF is parallel to BC and FG is parallel to AB. Hence, BEFG is a parallelogram.
So, FG = BE and FG = AE (given)
So, AE = BE and E = is mid-point of AB.
Since, EF is parallel to BC, F is the mid-point of AC.

So, $EF = \dfrac{1}{2}BC$

$BC = 2EF = 6$

8. A. $4 + 6 \times 2 = 3 - 12 + 12$
$16 = 3$
B. $10 \div 5 \times 5 = 9 - 3 + 4$
$10 = 10$
C. $15 \times 2 - 5 = 12 \div 4 + 3$
$25 = 6$
D. $13 \div 13 + 1 > 20 - 5 \times 2$
$2 > 10$

9. Let principal = ₹ x, then

$$x + \frac{x \times 12 \times 4}{100} = 2442$$

$$\Rightarrow \quad \frac{37x}{25} = 2442$$

$$\Rightarrow \quad x = \frac{2442 \times 25}{37} = ₹1650.$$

10.

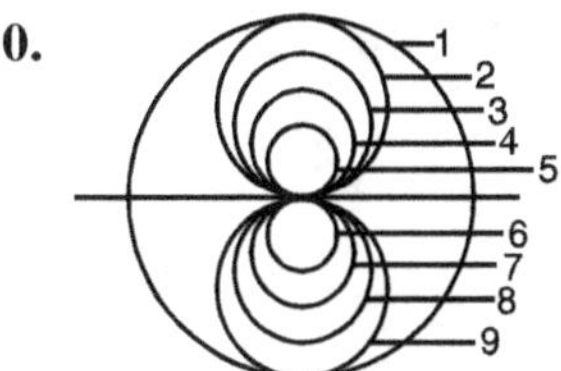

There is 1 main circle, 4 circles on the top of the horizontal lines and 4 circles below it.
So, the total number of circles is 1 + 4 + 4 = 9.

11. Height of tree AB = 12 m.
Distance of snake from its hole BC = 36 m.
Let the Snake and Peacock meets at point D such that BD = x m.

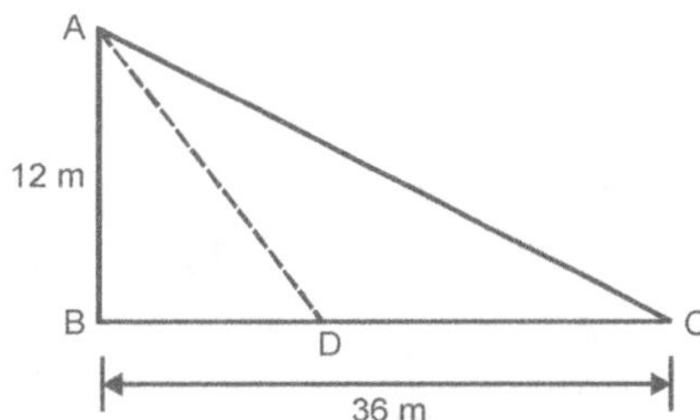

As speed of two are same, so in equal time, distance AD = CD = $(36 - x)$ m.
Again, from right ΔABD

$$AB = 12 \text{ m}$$
$$BD = x \text{ m}$$
$$AD = (36 - x)\text{m}$$
$$(AD)^2 = (AB)^2 + (BD)^2$$
$$(36 - x)^2 = (12)^2 + (x)^2$$
$$1296 + x^2 - 72x = 144 + x^2$$
$$72x = 1296 - 144$$
$$72x = 1152$$

$$x = \frac{1152}{72} = 16 \text{ m.}$$

12. $912 = 19 \times 2\ (16 + 8)$

$882 = 21 \times 2\ (7 + 14)$

and $? = 24 \times 2\ (6 + 12)$

$= 864.$

13. After observing the views of the same dice, the sides that can be clearly understood to be the opposites are : 2 – 4, 3 – 1 and 5 – 6.

14. No. of students who appeared in at least two subjects

$= 35 + 30 + 10 + 25$

$= 100.$

15. Let us consider category of bag

$A_1\ A_2\ A_3\ B_1\ B_2\ B_3\ C_1\ C_2$

Ist weight A *Vs* B.

Case I: $A_1\ A_2\ A_3 = B_1\ B_2\ B_3$

Case II: $A_1\ A_2\ A_3 \neq B_1\ B_2\ B_3$

Either C_1 or C_2 is heavier, either A or B would be heavier (say A > B)

2nd weight,

C_1 *Vs* C_2, if $C_1 > C_2$, then C_1

If $C_1 < C_2$, then C_2

If $A_1 < A_2$, then A_2

A_1 *Vs* A_2 if $A_1 = A_2$, then A_3

If $A_1 > A_2$, then A_1.

16. As

V I N O D
–2 –2 –2 –2 –2
T G L M B

Same as

V I R E N D R A
–2 –2 –2 –2 –2 –2 –2 –2
T G P C L B P Y

17. Let the base of the triangle = *a* and height = *b*

∴ Area of the original triangle

$$= \frac{1}{2} \times a \times b = \frac{ab}{2}$$

According to questions,

Base of the new triangle = $2a$ and height of the new triangle = $\frac{b}{2}$

∴ Area of the new triangle

$$= \frac{1}{2} \times 2a \times \frac{b}{2} = \frac{ab}{2}$$

Hence, ratio of their areas

$$= \frac{ab}{2} : \frac{ab}{2} = 1 : 1.$$

18. The two missiles approach one another at a speed of (12,000 + 18,000) miles per hour

= 30,000 miles per hour

= 500 miles per minute

Thus, 30 sec. before collision distance between them

$$= \frac{500}{2} = 250 \text{ miles}$$

19. Question figure is same as B when fold to form a cube, the half shaded face will lie opposite the face bearing the rhombus.

20.

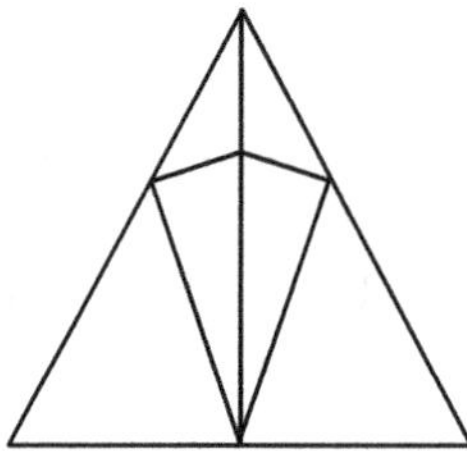

8 + 3 = 11

21. At a given temperature T_1

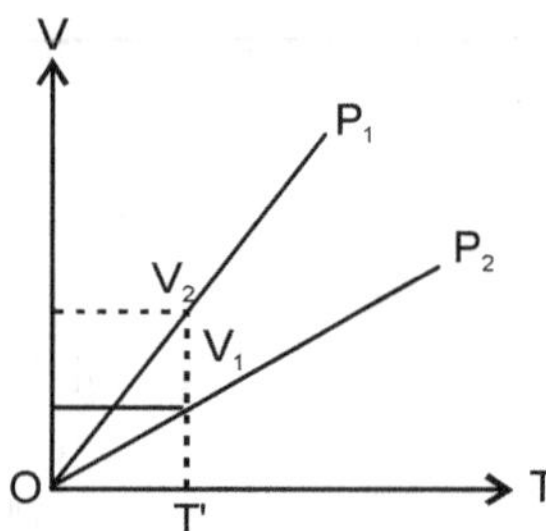

From the graph, we see that

$V_1 < V_2$

∴ $P_1 > P_2$

22. As energy is released, binding energy per nucleon of products is more than that of reactants.

Then, $E_2 > E_1$.

23. The probability of drawing a red ball = $\frac{5}{10}$.

If the ball is not replaced, the box will have a ball, so probability of drawing the red ball in next chance = $\frac{4}{9}$

Therefore, the probability of drawing 2 balls

$$= \frac{5}{10} \times \frac{4}{9} = \frac{2}{9}$$

24. 1.02 MeV is used in pair production. So, total energy imparted = 2.2 – 1.02

$$= \frac{1.18}{2} = 0.59 \text{ MeV}$$

25. Since diagonal of a square cut orthogonally, therefore, it becomes a equipotential surface. It will be contain the same potential.

26. Wax expand on melting, the quantity $(V_2 - V_1)$ is positive, and so $\frac{dp}{dT}$ is +ve, which means the melting point of wax type substance rises with increase in pressure.

27. When V_{in} = 0V, the transistor is in out off (acts like an open switch) and

$$V_{CE} = V_{CC} = 10 \text{ V}$$

28. r_n for hydrogen atom for Ist orbit

$$r_H = \frac{h^2 \epsilon_0}{\pi m e^2}$$

$$= \frac{6.6 \times 10^{-34} \times 8.85 \times 10^{-12}}{3.14 \times 9.1 \times 10^{-31} \times (1.6 \times 10^{-19})^2}$$

= 0.0529 nm

29. As, $\eta = 1 - \frac{T_2}{T_1}$

$$= 1 - \frac{273+127}{273+227} = 1 - \frac{400}{500} = \frac{1}{5}$$

$$W = \eta\, Q_1 = \frac{1}{5} \times 10^4 = 2000 \text{ J}$$

30. During nuclear fusion, two or more lighter nuclei combine to form a heavier nucleus.

31. As, $\Delta E\, \Delta t \geq \hbar$

or $\Delta E = \frac{\hbar}{\Delta t}$

$$= \frac{6.6 \times 10^{-34}}{2 \times \pi \times 10^{-6}}$$

$$= \frac{1.05 \times 10^{-34} \text{ Js}}{10^{-6} \text{ s}}$$

ΔE = 1.05 × 10^{-28} J

32. As, $P_t = P_c \left(1 + \frac{m^2}{2}\right)$

$$\frac{P_t}{P_c} = 1 + \frac{m^2}{2} = 1 + \frac{1}{2}$$

$$= \frac{3}{2}$$

33. For an ellipse $(1 - \epsilon^2) = \frac{b^2}{a^2}$, where a and b are the semi-major and semi-minor axes respectively.

Thus, $\frac{b^2}{a^2} = \frac{n_\phi^2}{n^2}$

or $\frac{b}{a} = \frac{n_\phi}{n}$

$n_\phi = 1;\; n = 2$

Ratio of semi-major axis a and semi-minor axis is

$$\frac{a}{b} = \frac{n}{n_\phi} = \frac{2}{1}$$

34. We have

$$E_f = E_F\left[1 - \left(\frac{\pi^2}{12}\right)\left(\frac{k_B T}{E_F}\right)^2\right]$$

$$= E_F\left[1 - \frac{\pi^2}{12} \times \frac{1.38 \times 10^{-23} \times 10000}{3 \times 1.6 \times 10^{-19}}\right]$$

or $\frac{E_f}{E_F} = \left[1 - \frac{(3\cdot14)^2}{12} \times \frac{1.38}{3 \times 1.6}\right]$

= 1 – 0.07 = 0.93

35. As, $t_2 - t_1 = \frac{\frac{v}{c^2}(x_2 - x_1)}{\sqrt{1 - \frac{v}{c^2}}}$

$$= \frac{0.8\frac{c}{c^2} \times 9 \times 10^9}{0.6} = 40 \text{ sec}$$

36. For compound pendulum

$$T = \frac{2\pi}{\omega} = 2\pi\sqrt{\frac{I}{mgl}}$$

where $\omega = \sqrt{\frac{mgl}{I}}$

If $k \to$ Radius of gyration, then
$I = mk^2 + ml^2$

$$\Rightarrow T = 2\pi\sqrt{\frac{mk^2 + ml^2}{mgl}} \Rightarrow T = 2\pi\sqrt{\frac{k^2 + l^2}{gl}}$$

37. The electric field due to an infinite line charge distribution at point P.

$$\vec{E_1} = \frac{1}{2\pi \epsilon_0}.\frac{\lambda}{a}$$

and that is due to an infinite line charge distribution at point Q.

$$\vec{E_2} = \frac{1}{2\pi \epsilon_0}.\frac{\lambda}{a}$$

Their ratio,

$$E_1 : E_2 = \frac{\frac{1}{2\pi \epsilon_0}.\frac{\alpha}{a}}{\frac{1}{2\pi \epsilon_0}.\frac{\alpha}{a}} = 1 : 1$$

38. Since, $PV = nRT$

or $V = \frac{nRJ}{P}$

Also, $K_T = -\frac{1}{V}\left(\frac{\partial V}{\partial P}\right)_T = -\frac{1}{V}.\frac{nRT}{\left(-P^2\right)}$

$$= \frac{PV}{P.PV} = \frac{1}{P}$$

39. As, $f_0 = \frac{1}{2\pi}\sqrt{\frac{1}{LC} - \frac{R^2}{L^2}}$

$$\Rightarrow f_0 = \frac{1}{2\pi}\sqrt{\frac{1}{LC} - \frac{R^2}{L^2}}$$

$$= \frac{1}{2\pi}\sqrt{\frac{1}{250 \times 10^{-6} \times 0.16 \times 10^{-3}} - \frac{20 \times 20}{\left(0.16 \times 10^{-3}\right)^2}}$$

$= 8 \times 10^5$ Hz

40. $\Delta E \, \Delta t \geq \hbar$

or $\Delta E = \frac{\hbar}{\Delta t} = \frac{6.6 \times 10^{-34}}{2 \times \pi \times 10^{-6}}$

$$= \frac{1.05 \times 10^{-34} \text{ J-s}}{10^{-6} \text{s}}$$

$$\Delta E = 1.05 \times 10^{-28} \text{ J}$$

41. $P_1(E_1) = | < \phi_1 | \psi_0 > |^2$

$$|\phi_1 > = \frac{1}{\sqrt{2}}\begin{pmatrix} 1 \\ -i \\ 0 \end{pmatrix}$$

$$P_1(E_1) = |\sqrt{\frac{2}{5}} < \phi_1 | \phi_2 >|^2 = \frac{2}{5}$$

42. Change in entropy

$$dS = \frac{dQ}{T} = \frac{1000 \times 80}{273} = 293 \text{ cal/K}$$

$dQ = m\,L$

L = Latent heat of vaporization

43. The cathode voltage with respect to the negative battery terminal is—

$$= V_{BIAS} - V_F$$

For Silicon $V_F = 0.7$ V

$V_{BIAS} = 5$V

$\therefore \quad V_R = (5 - 0.7)$ V

$V_R = 4.3$ V

44. The overall modulus configuration for cascaded counter (consisting one mod-5, a mod-8 and 2-mod-10 counter) is

$= 5 \times 8 \times 10 \times 10 = 4000$

$\therefore$ The lowest output frequency possible is

$$= \frac{10 \text{ MHz}}{4000} = \frac{10 \times 10^6}{4000} \text{Hz}$$

$= 2.5$ kHz

45. Voltage observed on CRO (peak-to-peak)

$= (12 + 6) \times 2$

$= 18 \times 2$

$= 36$ kV

46. $A = \begin{pmatrix} 7 & 0 & 0 \\ 0 & 1 & -i \\ 0 & i & -1 \end{pmatrix}$

$$|A - \lambda I|\ \Psi = 0$$

$$\therefore \quad |A - \lambda I| = 0$$

$$\begin{pmatrix} 7 & 0 & 0 \\ 0 & 1 & -i \\ 0 & i & -1 \end{pmatrix} - \lambda \begin{pmatrix} 1 & 0 & 0 \\ 0 & 1 & 0 \\ 0 & 0 & 1 \end{pmatrix} = 0$$

$$\begin{pmatrix} 7-\lambda & 0 & 0 \\ 0 & 1-\lambda & -i \\ 0 & i & -1-\lambda \end{pmatrix} = 0$$

$$(7-\lambda)\,[(1-\lambda)(-1-\lambda) + i^2] = 0$$

$$(7-\lambda)\,[-(1-\lambda^2) - 1] = 0$$

$$(7-\lambda)(\lambda^2 - 2) = 0$$

$$\therefore \lambda = 7, \sqrt{2}, -\sqrt{2}$$

47. The intensity of magnetisation increases for a ferromagnetic substance with the applied magnetic field and becomes constant, when the domains get perfectly aligned w.r.t. the external magnetic field.

48. $\dfrac{d^3y}{dx^3} + 6\dfrac{d^2y}{dx^2} + \dfrac{11dy}{dx} + 6y = 0$

Let, $D = \dfrac{d}{dx}$

$$D^3y + 6D^2y + 11Dy + 6y = 0$$

$$\left(D^3 + 6D^2 + 11D + 6\right)y = 0$$

$$\therefore \quad D^3 + 6D^2 + 11D + 6 = 0$$

$$(D+1)\left(D^2 + 5D + 6\right) = 0$$

$$(D+1)(D+2)(D+3) = 0$$

$$D = -1, -2, -3.$$

$$y = e^{-x}, e^{-2x}, e^{-3x} \quad ...(b)$$

49. $d_{hkl} = \dfrac{a}{\sqrt{h^2 + k^2 + l^2}}$

where a is the interatomic separation.

$$d_{100} = 1\frac{a}{\sqrt{1^2 + 0^2 + 0^2}} = a$$

$$d_{110} = \frac{a}{\sqrt{1^2 + 1^2 + 0^2}} = \frac{a}{\sqrt{2}}$$

$$d_{111} = \frac{a}{\sqrt{1^2 + 1^2 + 1^2}} = \frac{a}{\sqrt{3}}$$

$$= \sqrt{6} : \sqrt{3} : \sqrt{2} \quad ...(c)$$

50. P (A ∪ B) = P(A) + P(B) – P (A ∩ B)

$$= \frac{2}{3} + \frac{3}{4} - \frac{1}{2}$$

$$= \frac{8 + 9 - 6}{12}$$

$$= \frac{11}{12}$$

51. Gravitational force is a central force. Angular momentum is conserved.

$$m\vec{v} \times \vec{r} = \text{constant}$$

$$v \propto \frac{1}{r}$$

At, Q, R, S $\vec{v}$ and $\vec{r}$ are at 90°.

And it is maximum at P.

52. Electric flux,

$$\phi = \int \vec{E} \cdot \vec{ds}$$

$\int ds = \pi r^2 \rightarrow$ surface area of the hemispherical surface of radius r

$$\phi = E\pi R^2$$

$$\phi = \pi R^2 E$$

53. $T = \dfrac{1}{2}mr^2\dot{\phi}^2 = \dfrac{1}{2}ml^2 \sin^2\theta\dot{\phi}^2$

$$V = -mgl\cos\theta$$

$$L = \frac{1}{2}ml^2 \sin^2\theta\,\dot{\phi}^2 + mgl\cos\theta$$

For ϕ variable $\dfrac{\partial L}{\partial \phi} = ml^2 \sin^2\theta\,\dot{\phi}$

$$\frac{\partial L}{\partial \phi} = 0$$

so that Lagrange's equation is

$$ml^2 \sin^2\theta\, \ddot{\phi} = 0$$

or $\quad \ddot{\phi} = 0$ (as θ = const.)

or $\quad \dot{\phi}$ = const. = ω

Note : Lagrangian is a function of θ so we can write

$$\frac{d}{dt}\left(\frac{\partial L}{\partial \dot{\theta}}\right) - \frac{\partial L}{\partial \theta} = 0$$

and can put derivatives

$$\frac{\partial L}{\partial \dot{\theta}} = 0,\ \frac{\partial L}{\partial \theta} = ml^2 \sin\theta\cos\theta\dot{\phi}^2 - mgl\sin\theta$$

to get $\; ml^2\sin\theta\cos\theta\,\dot{\phi}^2 - mgl\sin\theta = 0$

or $\dot{\phi}^2 = \dfrac{g}{l\cos\theta}$ or $\omega = \dot{\phi} = \sqrt{\dfrac{g}{l\cos\theta}}$

54. Maxwell's distribution of velocities law yields.

Rms velocity, $V_{rms} = \sqrt{\dfrac{3kT}{m}}$

Mean velocity, $V_{mean} = \sqrt{\dfrac{6kT}{\pi m}}$

$\therefore$ Most probable velocity,

$$U_p\sqrt{\frac{2kT}{m}}$$

Clearly, $\quad U_p < U_{rms}$

55. Carrier power,

$$P_C = \frac{A^2}{2} = 100\,W$$

A = 14.14

$$E_{eff} = \frac{P_{sb}}{P_c + P_{sb}} = \frac{40}{100}$$

P_{sb} = 66.67 W

$$P_{sb} = \frac{1}{2}B^2 + \frac{1}{2}B^2 = 66.67$$

B = 8.161

56. The PE of the molecule is given by

$$U = -\frac{\alpha}{r^6} + \frac{b}{r^{12}}$$

At $r = r_0$ U = U_{min}

or $\left.\dfrac{dU}{dr}\right|_{r=r_0} = 0$

$$\Rightarrow \frac{d}{dr}(-\alpha r^{-6} + \beta r^{-12})_{r=r_0} = 0$$

$$\Rightarrow \left[+6\alpha r^{-7} - 12Br^{-13}\right]_{r=r_0} = 0$$

or $6\alpha = 12\beta\dfrac{r_0^{-13}}{r_0^{-7}}$

or $\dfrac{\alpha}{2\beta} = r_0^{-6} \qquad \Rightarrow r_0^6 = \dfrac{2\beta}{\alpha}$

$$\Rightarrow r_0 = \left(\frac{2\beta}{\alpha}\right)^{1/6}$$

57. Radius of nuclei of mass number A is determined as

$R = R_0A^{1/3}$ where $R_0 = 1.2 \times 10^{-15}$ fm.

for $\quad \dfrac{R_1}{R_2} = \left(\dfrac{A_1}{A_2}\right)^{\frac{1}{3}}$

$$\frac{R_1}{R_2} = \left(\frac{216}{64}\right)^{\frac{1}{3}} = \frac{6}{4}$$

$\therefore R_1 : R_2$ = 1.5

58.

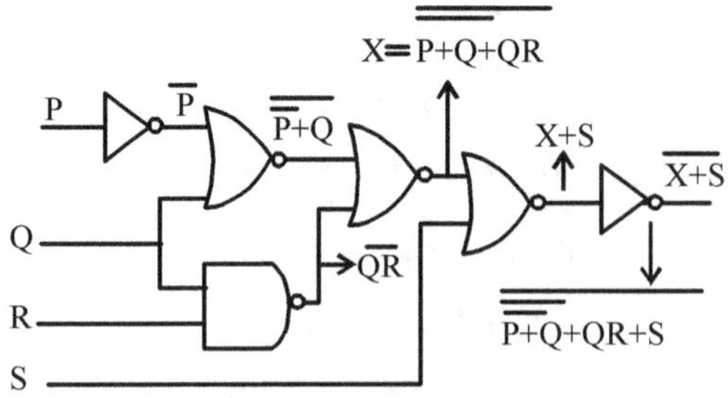

59. For an ideal amplifier.

At point A, voltage induced will be +2V.

Applying Kirchhoff's loop rule.

$$\frac{V_i - V_A}{R_A} = \frac{V_A - V_0}{R_B} \quad ...(1)$$

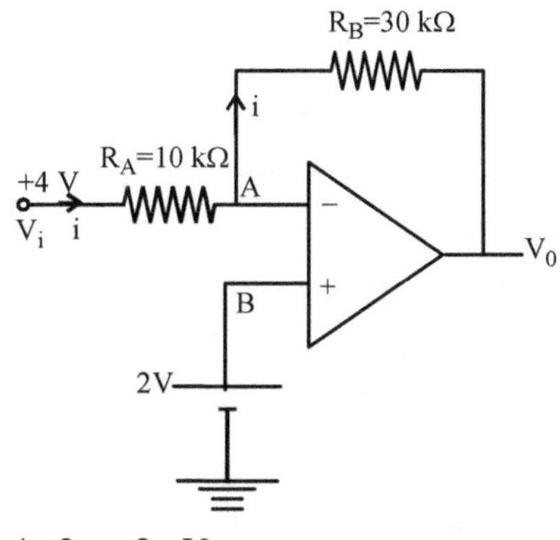

$$\frac{4-2}{10\,\text{k}\Omega} = \frac{2-V_0}{30\,\text{k}\Omega}$$

$6 = 2 - V_0$

$V_0 = 2 - 6 = -4$

When the polarity of the 2V battery is reversed. The voltage developed at point A will be –2V

From equation (1)

$$\frac{V_i - V_A}{R_A} = \frac{V_A - V_0}{R_B}$$

$$-\frac{4-(-2)}{10\,\text{k}\Omega} = \frac{-2-V_0}{30\,\text{k}\Omega}$$

$6 \times 3 = 2 + V_0$

$18 = -2 + V_0$

$V_0 = -2 + 18 = 16$ V.

60. $L = 10^{-14}$ m

$m_n = 10^{-27}$ kg

$\Delta x\, \Delta p \simeq \hbar$

$$\Delta p \sim p = \frac{\hbar}{\Delta x} = \frac{10^{-34}}{10^{-14}}$$

$p = 10^{-20}$

$$E = \frac{p^2}{2m}$$

$$= \frac{\left(10^{-20}\right)^2}{2\times 10^{-27}} = \frac{10^{-40}}{2\times 10^{-27}}$$

$$= \frac{1}{2}\times 10^{-13}$$

$$= \frac{1}{2}\times 1\,\text{MeV}$$

$= 0.5$ MeV

61. $E = V_{eff} + \frac{1}{2} m\dot{r}^2$

where $V_{eff} = V + \frac{l^2}{2mr^2}$

where l is the angular momentum.

According to the question,

$$F(r) = \frac{K}{r^4}$$

$$V(r) = -\int F(r)dr.$$

$$V(r) = \frac{k}{3r^3}$$

$$V_{eff} = \frac{k}{3r^3} + \frac{l^2}{2mr^2}.$$

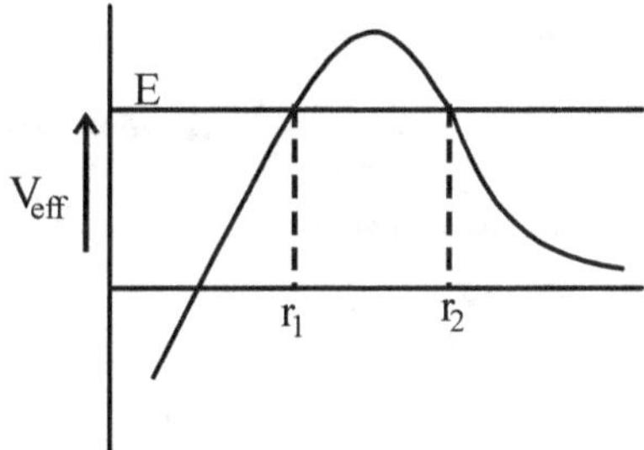

62. The separation

$2B = 16.90 \times 10^{-10}$ cm

$B = 8.45 \times 10^{-10}$ cm

Now, $I = \frac{h}{8\pi^2 BC}$

$= 3.30 \times 10^{-40}$ gm cm^2

Using $h = 6.6 \times 10^{-27}$ erg-sec

63. Kinetic energies of the emitted electrons as $K_1 = hc/\lambda_1 - W$ and $K_2 = hc/\lambda_2 - W$; the difference between the two expressions is given by $K_1 - K_2 = hc(\lambda_2 - \lambda_1)/(\lambda_1\lambda_2)$, hence

$$h = \frac{K_1 - K_2}{c} \frac{\lambda_1\lambda_2}{\lambda_2 - \lambda_1}$$

Since, 1 eV = 1.6×10^{-19} J, the numerical value of h follows at once:

$$h = \frac{(8.57 - 6.67) \times 1.6 \times 10^{-19}\,\text{J}}{3 \times 10^{8}\ \text{ms}^{-1}}$$

$$\times \frac{(280 \times 10^{-9}\,\text{m})(490 \times 10^{-9}\ \text{m})}{490 \times 10^{-9}\ \text{m} - 280 \times 10^{-9}\,\text{m}} \simeq 6.62 \times 10^{-34}\,\text{Js.}$$

64. Suppose the process is carried out reversibly by heating the water through the baths of steadily increasing temperature. Then change in entropy is given by

$$dS = mc \int_{T_1}^{T_2} \frac{dT}{T} = mc\left(\log \frac{T_2}{T_1}\right)$$

$$= 2.3026\, mc \log_{10} \frac{T_2}{T_1}$$

$$= 2.3026 \times 1000 \times 4.2 \times \log_{10} \frac{353}{293}$$

$$= 782\ \text{J/K.}$$

65. When all the components have zero error,

$L = 160\mu\text{H} = 160 \times 10^{-6}$ H

and $C = 160\text{pF} = 160 \times 10^{-12}$ F

∴ Resonant frequency,

$$f_r = \frac{1}{2\pi}\sqrt{\frac{1}{LC}}$$

$$= \frac{1}{2\pi}\sqrt{\frac{1}{160 \times 10^{-6} \times 160 \times 10^{-12}}}$$

$$= 1\ \text{MHz}$$

66. $V_+ = 0$

$R = 10\ \text{k}\Omega$

$V_+ = V_-$

$\Rightarrow \quad V_- = 0$

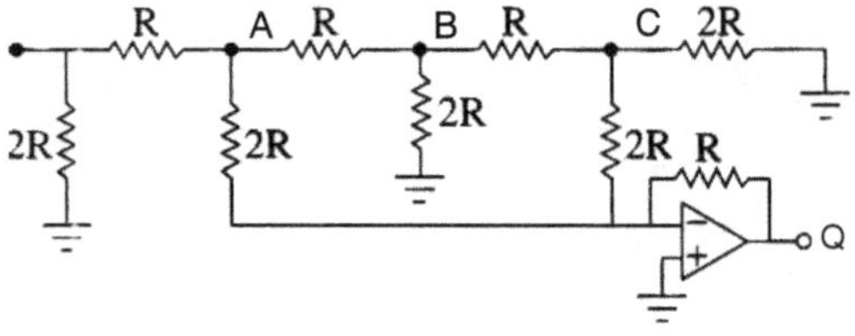

At node A

$$\frac{V_A - V_R}{R} + \frac{V_B - V_A}{R} + \frac{V_A - V_-}{2R} = 0$$

$$5V_A - 2V_B - 2V_R = 0$$

At node B

$$\frac{V_B - V_A}{R} + \frac{V_B - V_C}{R} + \frac{V_C}{2R} = 0$$

$$5V_B - 2V_A - 2V_C = 0$$

At node C

$$\frac{V_C - V_B}{R} + \frac{V_C - V_-}{2R} + \frac{V_C}{2R} = 0$$

$$4V_C - 2V_B = 0$$

Solve $\quad V_A = 5$ V, $V_B = 2.5$

And $\quad V_C = 1.25$

$$i = \frac{V_C}{2R}$$

$$= \frac{1.25}{2 \times 10 \times 10^{3}} = 62.5\ \mu\text{A}$$

67.

$$m = \frac{\hbar^2}{\dfrac{\partial^2 E}{\partial k^2}}$$

$$E = \frac{\hbar^2\left[2k^2 - 3k\right]}{3m}$$

$$E = \frac{2k^2\hbar^2}{2m} - \frac{\hbar^2 k}{m}$$

$$\frac{\partial E}{\partial k} = \frac{2\hbar^2}{2m}(2k)\frac{\hbar^2}{m}$$

$$\frac{\partial E}{\partial k} = \frac{4\hbar^2 k}{2m} - \frac{\hbar^2}{m}$$

$$\frac{\partial^2 E}{\partial k^2} = \frac{4\hbar^2}{2m}$$

$$m = \frac{\hbar^2}{2\hbar^2/m} = \frac{m}{2}$$

68. We know

$$v = v_0 \pm v_m$$

$$\therefore \quad v_1 = v_0 + v_m$$

and $v_2 = v_0 - v_m$

$\therefore \quad v_1 - v_2 = 2v_m$

$$\frac{c}{\lambda_1} - \frac{c}{\lambda_2} = \frac{2c}{\lambda_m}$$

$$\lambda_m = \left[\frac{2\lambda_1\lambda_2}{\lambda_1 - \lambda_2}\right]$$

$$\lambda_2 = 4554 \text{ Å}$$

$$\lambda_1 = 4178 \text{ Å}$$

$$\lambda_m = \frac{2 \times 4554 \times 4178}{4554 - 4178}$$

$$= 1.012 \times 10^5 \text{ Å}$$

69. From Einstein's mass energy relates

$$\Delta E = \Delta mc^2$$

Again from the uncertainty principle

$$\Delta E \,.\, \Delta t = \hbar$$

we get, $\Delta t = \dfrac{\hbar}{\Delta E} = \dfrac{\hbar}{\Delta mc^2}$

Assuming that the emitted travels at the speed of light, distance travelled by it during this time, is given by

$$r_0 = c.\Delta t$$

$$= c.\frac{\hbar}{\Delta\, mc^2} = \frac{\hbar}{\Delta mc}$$

$$\therefore \quad r_0 = \frac{\left[1.0545 \times 10^{-34} \text{ J-s}\right]}{270 \times \left(9.1 \times 10^{-31} \text{mg}\right) \times \left(3 \times 10^8 \text{ m/s}\right)}$$

$$= 1.43 \times 10^{-15} \text{ m}$$

$$= 1.43 \text{ fermi}$$

70. The resistance of cell

$$R_t = + (R_f - R_i)\left[1 - \exp\left(-\frac{t}{\tau}\right)\right]$$

$$= 30 + (100 - 30)\left[1 - \exp\left(-\frac{10}{72}\right)\right]$$

$$= 39.1 \text{ k}\Omega$$

71. The wavelengths of the Lyman series of H-atom are given by

$$\frac{1}{\lambda} = R_H\left(\frac{1}{1^2} - \frac{1}{n^2}\right) \quad n = 2, 3, 4$$

for the first line, $\lambda = 1215$ Å, $n = 2$

$$\therefore \quad \frac{1}{1215 \text{ Å}} = \frac{3}{4} R_H$$

or $R_H = \dfrac{4}{3 \times 1215} \text{Å}^{-1}$

For the second line, $(\lambda = 3\lambda, n = 3)$

$$\therefore \quad \frac{1}{\lambda} = \frac{4}{3 \times 1215}\left(\frac{1}{1^2} - \frac{1}{3^2}\right)$$

$$= \frac{4}{3 \times 1215} \times \frac{8}{9} \text{Å}^{-1}$$

$$\lambda = \frac{3 \times 1215 \times 9}{4 \times 8} = 1025 \text{ Å}$$

72. Total power

$$P_t = P_C + P_s$$

$$= \frac{A^2_C}{2} + \frac{A^2_C}{4}\mu^2$$

$$= \frac{A^2_C}{2}\left(1 + \frac{\mu^2}{2}\right) = 600 \text{ W}$$

$$P_C = \frac{A^2_C}{2} = 400 \text{ W}$$

$$\therefore \quad \frac{600}{400} = 1 + \frac{\mu^2}{C}$$

$$\Rightarrow \quad \frac{\mu^2}{2} = \frac{1}{2}$$

$\therefore$ Modulation index, $\mu = 1$

73. The output of XOR gate is

$$Z = b_{i+1} \oplus b_i$$

and this output shift the register to left

Initially $Z = 0$

After Ist clock $Z = b_7 \oplus 0 = b_7$

After 2nd clock $Z = b_7 \oplus b_6$

After 3rd clock $Z = b_6 \oplus b_5$

After 4th clock $Z = b_5 \oplus b_4$

Gray code converter.

74. Junction capacitance is defined as

$$C = \frac{\in A}{X}\text{farad} = \frac{\in}{X}\text{farad}/\text{m}^2$$

$\in$ is constant for given material

$$C \propto \frac{1}{X}$$

when X is total depletion width

$$X \approx 10^{-6}\,(V_\beta \pm V_\alpha)^{1/2}$$

$\therefore$ Capacitance $\propto \left(V_\beta \pm V_\alpha\right)^{-1/2}$

75. As, $B.dl = \mu_0 I$

For cylindrical conductor,

$$B.2\pi r = \frac{\mu_0 I r^2}{R^2}$$

$$\bar{B} = \frac{\mu_0 I \bar{r}}{2\pi R^2}$$

$$\bar{H} = \frac{\bar{B}}{\mu_0}$$

$$\bar{H} = \frac{\overline{Ir}}{2\pi R^2}$$

SET–5
CSIR–UGC (NET) PHYSICAL SCIENCES

PART-A

1. A sphere of radius 4 cm is curved from a homogeneous sphere of radius 8 cm and mass 160 g. The mass of the smaller sphere is

A. 20 g B. 50 g
C. 30 g D. 60 g

2. Two persons A and B travel a distance of 25 km from M and N with the speed of 2 kmh^{-1} and 3 kmh^{-1} respectively. After reaching M; B returns immediately and meets A at the point-O. The distance of O from M is

A. 25 km B. 20 km
C. 18 km D. 22 km

3. In an election, one of the two candidates gets 40% votes and loses by 100 votes. Then, the total number of votes is

A. 400 B. 500
C. 600 D. 700

4. Two trains are running at 40 km/hr and 20 km/hr respectively in the same direction. Fast train completely passes a man sitting in the slower train in 5 seconds. Find the length of the fast train.

A. $27\frac{7}{9}$ m B. 27 m

C. $23\frac{2}{9}$ m D. 23 m

Directions (Q. 5): *In the following question, which one number can be placed at the sign of interrogation?*

5.

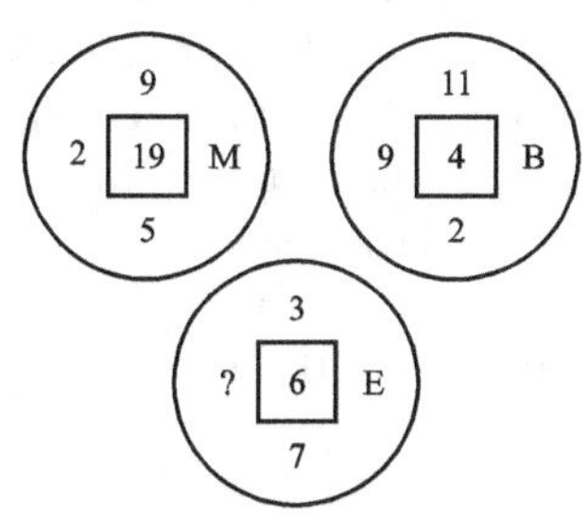

A. 1 B. 3
C. 9 D. 13

6. In a certain code language, HOTEL has been coded as 55. How will you code BORE in the same code language?

A. 56 B. 30
C. 36 D. 46

7. A student who secures 20% marks in an examination fails by 30 marks. Another student who secures 32% gets 42 marks more than those required to pass. The percentage of marks required to pass is

A. 20% B. 25%
C. 28% D. 30%

8. The number of squares in the figure below is:

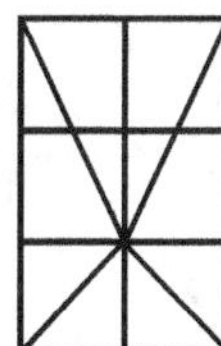

A. 6 B. 10
C. 8 D. 12

9. If perimeter of a right angled triangle is six times its smallest side, then the three sides of this triangle are in the ratio of:

A. 13 : 5 : 12 B. 13 : 12 : 5
C. 12 : 5 : 13 D. 13 : 5 : 10

10. A room 8 metres long, 6 metres broad and 3 metres high has two windows of size 1½ m × 1 m and a door 2 m × 1 ½ m.
Find the cost of papering the walls with paper 50 cm wide at 25 p. per metre.

A. ₹ 39 B. ₹ 30
C. ₹ 36 D. ₹ 42

Direction (Qs. No. 11): *In the following question, understand the arrangement pattern and then select the right answer from the given options.*

11. Mini is to the right of Rajni but to the left of Panas. Saya is to the right of Mini but to the left of Jaya. Who is on the extreme left if all the girls are facing North?

A. Jaya B. Mini

C. Rajni D. Saya

12. A shopkeeper has 50 kgs of rice. He sells a part of it at 20% profit and the rest at 40% profit. If he gains 25% on the whole, find the quantity of each part.

A. 12.5 kgs and 37.5 kgs

B. 37.5 kgs and 12.5 kgs

C. 23.5 kgs and 21.5 kgs

D. 21.5 kgs and 23.5 kgs

13. Which one number can be placed at sign of interrogation?

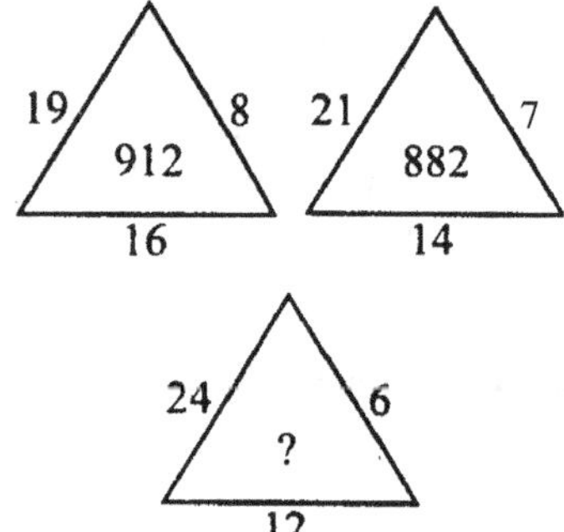

A. 1356 B. 862

C. 1234 D. 864

14. Two clocks begin to strike 12 together. One strikes its strokes in 33 seconds and the other in 22 seconds. What is the interval between the 6th stroke of the first and 8th stroke of the second?

A. 3 seconds

B. 1 second

C. 11 seconds

D. strikes at the same time

15. The number of rectangles in this figure are:

A. 21

B. 24

C. 23

D. 25

16. If the income tax is decreased by 26%, a man's net income increases by $\frac{2}{3}\%$. The rate of income tax is:

A. $3\frac{1}{2}\%$ B. $2\frac{1}{2}\%$

C. $1\frac{1}{2}\%$ D. 3%

17. The ratio of ages of Namrata and Divya is 4 : 3. The sum of their ages is 28 years. The ratio of their ages after 4 years will be:

A. 3 : 4 B. 5 : 4

C. 5 : 6 D. 6 : 5

18. The sum of digits of a three-digit number is 10 and the digit in the middle of this three digit number is equal to the sum of the remaining two digits. If the first and the third digits are interchanged, the value of this number increases by 99. Find the number.

A. 385 B. 253

C. 154 D. 374

19. There are 4 white and 4 black balls in a bag and 3 balls are drawn at random. If balls of same colour are identical, the probability that none of them is black, is :

A. 1/4

B. 1/14

C. 1/2

D. None of these

20. One-third of a certain journey was covered at the rate of 25 km per hour, one-fourth at the rate of 30 km per hour and the rest at 50 km per hour. What is the average speed per hour for the whole journey?

A. $33\frac{1}{3}$ kmph B. $44\frac{1}{4}$ kmph

C. $22\frac{1}{2}$ kmph D. 33 kmph

PART-B

21. The period of oscillation of a simple pendulum is $T = 2\pi\sqrt{\frac{L}{g}}$. Measured the value of L is 20 cm known to 1 mm accuracy and time for 100 oscillations of the pendulum is found to be 90s using a wristwatch of 1 s resolution. The accuracy in the determination of g is

A. 1% B. 2%
C. 3% D. 4%

22. In a refrigerator, heat from inside at 277 K is transferred to a room at 300 K. How many joules of heat shall be delivered to the room for each joule of electrical energy consumed ideally?

A. 12 J B. 10 J
C. 11 J D. 13 J

23. A cylinder is placed in a uniform electric field $\vec{E}$ with its axis parallel to the field. The total electric flux through the cylinder is

A. 0 B. ∞
C. 1 D. 100

24. A 10V zoner diode along with a series resistance is connected across a 40 V supply. The minimum value of the resistance required, if the maximum zener current is 50 mA is

A. 500 Ω B. 300 Ω
C. 400 Ω D. 600 Ω

25. The area of triangle whose base is given by $\vec{a} = 5\hat{i} - 3\hat{j} + 4\hat{k}$ and $\vec{b} = \hat{j} - \hat{k}$ is

A. $\frac{\sqrt{61}}{2}$ B. $\frac{\sqrt{51}}{2}$

C. $\frac{\sqrt{50}}{2}$ D. $\frac{\sqrt{14}}{2}$

26. An electromagnetic wave going through vacuum is described by $E = E_0 \sin(kx - \omega t)$ and $B = B_0 \sin(kx - \omega t)$ then—

A. $E_0B_0 = \omega k$ B. $E_0\omega = B_0k$
C. $E_0k = B_0\omega$ D. None of these

27. The phase velocity of ocean wave is $\sqrt{\frac{g\lambda}{2\pi}}$, where g is the acceleration of gravity, then group velocity of ocean wave is—

A. v_p B. $\frac{v_p}{2}$

C. $\frac{v_p}{4}$ D. 0

28. For a transistor circuit

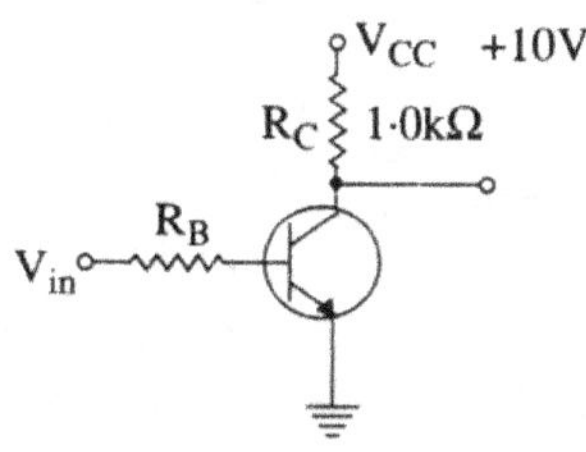

V_{CE} when $V_{IN} = 0$ V

A. 0 V B. 5 V
C. 2.5 V D. 10 V

29. A reversible engine cycle is shown in fig. following T-S diagram. The efficiency of engine is

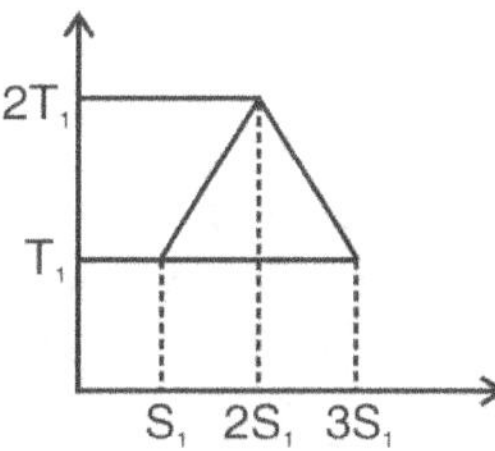

A. $\frac{1}{4}$ B. $\frac{1}{2}$

C. $\frac{1}{3}$ D. $\frac{1}{5}$

30. When an 8 bit serial in/serial out is used for a 24 μs time delay, the clock frequency must be

A. 333 kHz B. 111 kHz
C. 222 kHz D. 234 kHz

31. A 0-300 V voltmeter has an error of ± 2% of full scale deflection. What would be the range of readings if true voltage is 30 V?

A. 29.4 V —30.6 V
B. 20 V —40 V
C. 24 V — 36 V
D. None of these

32. The total number of Zeeman components observed in an electronic transition $^2D_{5/2} \rightarrow {}^2P_{3/2}$ of an atom in a weak field is

A. 6 B. 10
C. 4 D. 12

33. The lattice system in three dimensionals with least symmetry elements is

A. Triclinic B. Tetragonal
C. Cubic D. Orthorhombic

34. Which is wrong in the following?

A. Photoelectric cross-section increases with atomic number (Z) for a given energy
B. A free electron can not absorb photons
C. Pair production takes place at all photon energies
D. ^{208}Pb is a doubly magic nucleus

35. Knowing the decay constant λ of a nucleus, the probability of decay of the nucleus during the time from 0 to t is

A. $1 - e^{-\lambda t}$ B. $1 - e^{\lambda t}$
C. $e^{-\lambda t}$ D. $e^{\lambda t}$

36. The magnetic bending radius of a 400 GeV particle is 15 kg gauss is

A. 8.8 km B. 97 m
C. 880 m D. None of these

37. A sensitive way to measure the mass of the electron neutrino is to measure

A. The angular distribution in electron neutrino scattering
B. The electron energy spectrum in β-decay
C. The neutrino flux from the sun
D. None of these

38. When 1×10^{12} electrons are transferred from one conductor to another of a capacitor, a Potential difference of 10 V develops between the two conductors. The capacitance of the capacitor is

A. 1.2×10^{-5} F B. 1.6×10^{-7} F
C. 2.1×10^{-6} F D. 1.6×10^{-8} F

39. Forward biasing of p-n-junction offers

A. high resistance
B. zero resistance
C. low resistance
D. infinite resistance

40. In HCl molecule, the energy gap between the two vibrational levels is 0.36 eV. Its zero point energy will be

A. 0.12 eV B. 0.10 eV
C. 0.48 eV D. 0.18 eV

41. Let $M = \begin{bmatrix} 1 & 1 & 1 \\ -1 & 1 & 2 \\ 2 & 2 & 0 \\ -1 & 0 & 1 \end{bmatrix}$, then the rank of M is equal to

A. 3 B. 4
C. 2 D. 1

42. The electric potential due to a linear quadrupole varies inversely with

A. r B. r^2
C. r^3 D. r^4

43. The de-Broglie wavelength of material particles which are in thermal equilibrium at temperature T is

A. $\dfrac{h}{\sqrt{2mkT}}$ B. $\dfrac{h}{\sqrt{3mkT}}$

C. $\dfrac{h}{\sqrt{muT}}$ D. $\dfrac{h}{\sqrt{2kT}}$

44. In cyclic process

A. Work done is zero
B. Work done by the system is equal to the quantity of heat given to the system
C. Work done does not depend on the quantity of heat given to the system
D. The internal energy of the system increases

45. The numerical value of the radius of the first orbit of hydrogen as

A. 0.529 nm
B. 0.0529 Å
C. 5.29 Å
D. 0.0529 nm

PART-C

46. In an X-ray tube, X-rays are produced by electrons accelerated by V volt. The maximum frequency of the X-rays is

A. ehV B. $\frac{hV}{e}$

C. $\frac{eh}{V}$ D. $\frac{eV}{h}$

47. A box contain 5 black and 5 red balls. Two balls are randomly picked one after another from the box, without replacement. The probability for both balls being red is

A. $\frac{1}{90}$ B. $\frac{1}{5}$

C. $\frac{19}{90}$ D. $\frac{2}{9}$

48. In free space E $(z, t) = 50 \cos(\omega t - \beta z)\ \hat{a}_x$ (V/m). Find the average power crossing a circular area of radius 2.5 m in the plane z = constant.

A. 45.1 W B. 55.1 W

C. 65.1 W D. 75.1 W

49. A rectangular hollow metal waveguide is required to be so designed to propagate a 9375 MHz signal in its TE_{10} mode that the guide wavelength equals the cut-off wavelength. The value of 'a' is breadth or the wider dimension of the waveguide. [Take $b = \frac{a}{2}$].

A. 0.112 m B. 0.09 m

C. 0.05 m D. 0.016 m

50. A 4-bit D/A converter produces an output voltage of 4.5 V for an input code of 1001. The value of the output voltage for an input code of 0011 is

A. 1.5 V B. 3.5 V

C. 0.5 V D. 2.5 V

51. When light of a given wavelength is incident on a metallic surface, the stopping potential for the photoelectrons is 3.2 V. If a second light source whose wavelength is double that of the first is used, the stopping potential drops to 0.8 V. From this data, the wavelength of the first radiation is

A. 1.2×10^{-5} m B. 3.5×10^{-8} m

C. 2.6×10^{-7} m D. 2.6×10^{-6} m

52. A satellite of radius a revolves in the circular orbit about a planet of radius b with period P. If the shortest distance between their surfaces is c, then the mass of the planet is

A. $4\pi^2 (a - b - c)^3 / GP$

B. $4\pi^2 (a + b + c)^2 / G^2P$

C. $4\pi^2 (a + b + c)^3 / GP^2$

D. $4\pi^2 (a - b + c)^3 / GP^2$

53. The transistor gain of the circuit shown in the figure is given by

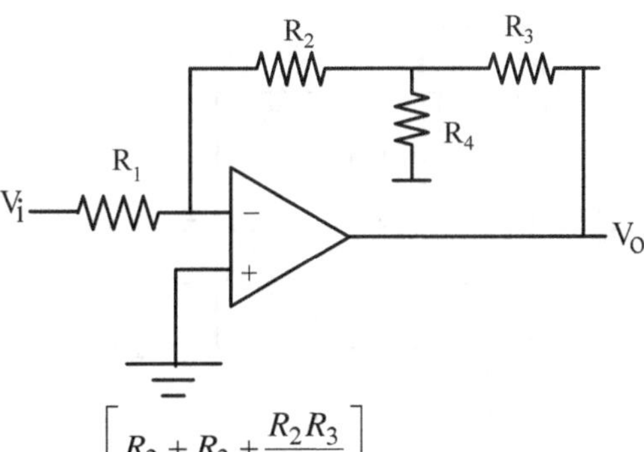

A. $-\left[\dfrac{R_2 + R_3 + \dfrac{R_2R_3}{R_4}}{R_1}\right]$

B. $-\left[\dfrac{\dfrac{R_3R_4}{R_3R_4} + R_2}{R_1}\right]$

C. $-\left[\dfrac{\dfrac{R_2R_4}{R_2R_4} + R_3}{R_1}\right]$

D. $-\left[\dfrac{R_2 + R_3}{R_1}\right]$

54. A carnot's engine whose low temperature reservoir is at 7°C has an efficiency 50%. It is desired to increase the efficiency to 70%. By how many degrees should the temperature of the cold reservoir be decreased?

A. 101 K　　B. 104 K
C. 112 K　　D. 121 K

55. In a common base connection, $\alpha = 0.95$. The voltage drop across 2 kΩ resistance which is connected in the collector is 2 V. The base current is

A. 0.02 mA　　B. 0.03 mA
C. 0.04 mA　　D. 0.05 mA

56. A 555 timer configured to run in the astable mode oscillation is shown in figure given below. Determine the frequency of the output and the duty cycle.

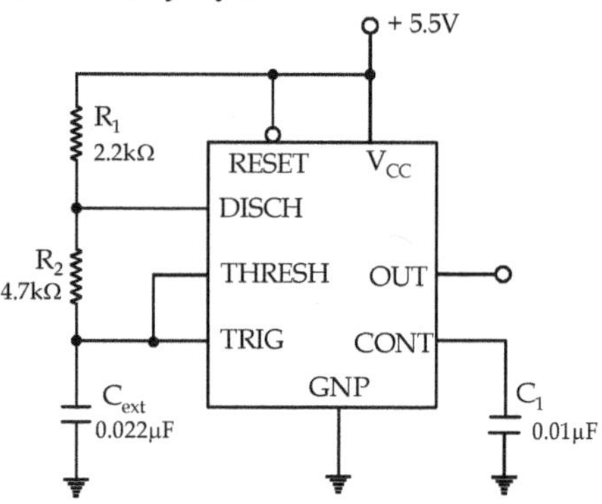

A. 59.5%　　B. 69.5%
C. 79.5%　　D. 49.5%

57. A strain gauge having a resistance 100Ω and gauge factor of 2 is connected in series with a ballast resistance of 100Ω across a 12 V, supply. Calculate the difference between the output voltage with no stress applied and a stress of 140 MN/m^2. The modulus of elasticity is 200 GN/m^2.

A. 0.39 mV　　B. 0.52 mA
C. 0.42 mV　　D. 0.62 mV

58. What is the energy, of the photon emitted by a hydrogen atom when an electron makes a transition from $n = 2$ to $n = 1$ state. Given ionization potential = 13.6 eV.

A. 16.32×10^{-19} J　　B. 15.69×10^{-18} J
C. 21.72×10^{-19} J　　D. 29.03×10^{-18} J

59. In an experiment with benzene the wavelengths of a pair of stokes and antistokes respectively. The wavelength of the corresponding infra red absorption line is

A. 2.013×10^4 Å　　B. 1.012×10^5 Å
C. 3.012×10^3 Å　　D. 4.02×10^2 Å

60. Chlorine-33 decays by position emission with a maximum energy of 4.3 MeV. The radius of the nucleus from this is

A. 2.32×10^{-15} m　　B. 4.54×10^{-15} m
C. 4.54×10^{-14} m　　D. 6.25×10^{-16} m

61. A conducting sphere of radius R, carrying charge Q, lies inside an uncharged conducting shell of radius $2R$. If they are joined by a metal wire.

A. $Q/3$ amount of charge will flow from the sphere to the shell
B. $2Q/3$ amount of charge will flow from the sphere to the shell
C. Q amount of charge will flow from the sphere to the shell
D. $k\dfrac{Q^2}{4R}$ amount of heat will be produced

62. Two capacitors of capacitances 3 μF and 6 μF are charged to a potential of 12 V each. They are now connected to each other, with the positive plate of each joined to the negative plate of the other. The potential difference across each will be

A. zero　　B. 3 V
C. 4 V　　D. 6 V

63. Determine the upper and lower trigger points for the comparator circuit in fig. given below. Assume that

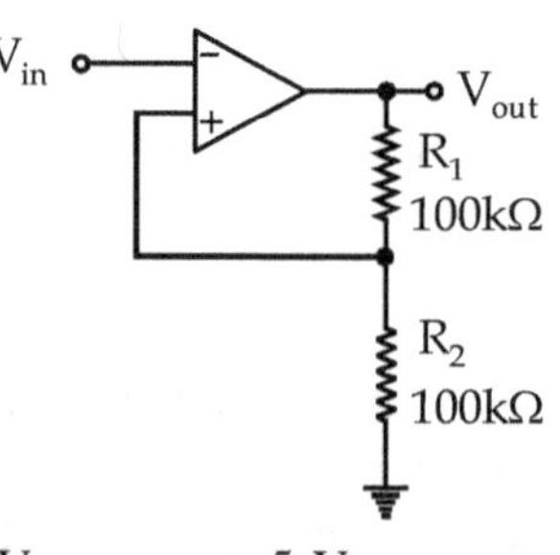

$+V_{out\,(max)} = +5$ V

and $-V_{out\,(max)} = -5$ V

A. 3.5 V, –3.5 V B. 4.5 V, –4.5 V
C. 2.5 V, –2.5 V D. 1.5 V, –1.5 V

64. The minimum number of resistors required in a 4-bit D/A network of weighted resistor type is
A. 12 B. 16
C. 13 D. 10

65. In the fig. shows a 4 : 1 MUX to be used to implement the sum S of a 1 bit full adder with inputs P & Q and the carry input C_{in}. Which of the following combinations of inputs to I_0, I_1, I_2 and I_3 of the MUX will—

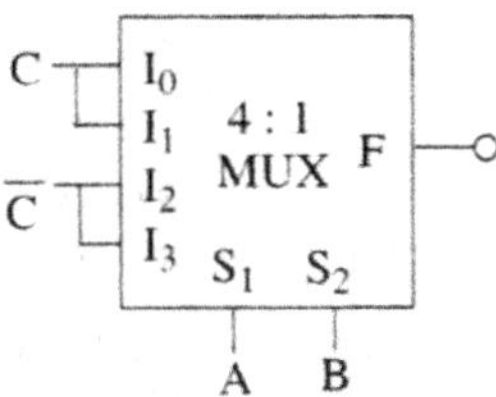

A. $I_0 = I_1 = C_{in}$; $I_2 = I_3 = \overline{C}_{in}$
B. $I_0 = I_1 = \overline{C}_{in}$; $I_2 = I_3 = C_{in}$
C. $I_0 = I_3 = C_{in}$; $I_1 = I_2 = \overline{C}_{in}$
D. $I_0 = I_3 = \overline{C}_{in}$; $I_1 = I_2 = \overline{C}_{in}$

66. Consider an 8-bit D/A converter with digital inputs $b_7 - b_0$, analog output voltage V_a, and the reference voltage V_R. Assume $V_a = FV_R$, where F is the fraction represented by the digital input code. If this D/A converter is connected as shown in Figure below:

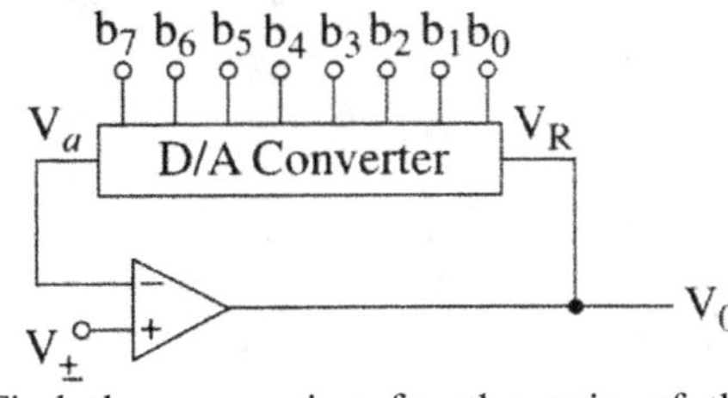

Find the expression for the gain of the OP-AMP.
A. F B. 2F
C. $\frac{1}{F}$ D. $\frac{1}{2F}$

67. The equation of states of a dilute gas at very high temperature is described by

$$\frac{PV}{k_BT} \approx 1 + \frac{B(T)}{V},$$ where V is the volume per particle and B (T) is a negative quantity. One can conclude that this is a property of—
A. A Van der Waals gas
B. An ideal Fermi gas
C. An ideal Bose gas
D. An ideal inert gas

68. Which of the following conditions should be satisfied by the temperature T of a system of N-non-interacting particles occupying a volume V, for B—E condensation to take place?

A. $T < \frac{h^2}{2\pi m k_B}\left[\frac{N}{V\Gamma(3/2)}\right]^{2/3}$

B. $T < \frac{h^2}{2\pi m k_B}\left[\frac{V}{N\Gamma(3/2)}\right]^{3/2}$

C. $T < \frac{h^2}{2\pi m k_B}\left[\frac{N}{V\Gamma(3/2)}\right]^{1/2}$

D. $T < \frac{h^2}{2\pi m k_B}\left[\frac{V}{N\Gamma(3/2)}\right]^{1/2}$

where m is the mass of each particle of the system, k_B is the Boltzmann constant, h is the Planck's constant and Γ is the well known zeta function.

69. The probability that the speed of oxygen molecule lies between 100 and 101 metre/sec. at 200°K is:
A. 2.11×10^{-5} B. 3.11×10^{-4}
C. 6.11×10^{-4} D. 9.12×10^{-4}

70. A change of 200 mV in base-emitter voltage causes a change of 100 mA in the base current. The input resistance of the transistor is
A. 3 kΩ B. 4 kΩ
C. 1 kΩ D. 2 kΩ

71. Find the relation between the true and effective values of the Q of a coil when C_d is the distributed capacitance and C is the resonance capacitance. The following are the two measurements:

$f_1 = 2$ MHz; $C_1 = 450$ pF

$f_2 = 4$ MHz; $C_2 = 90$ pF

A. 30 pF B. 50 pF

C. 20 pF D. 40 pF

72. The carbon monoxide (CO) molecule has a band length R of 0.113 nm and the masses of the ^{12}C and ^{16}O atoms are respectively 1.99×10^{-28} kg and 2.66×10^{-26} kg. The energy of the CO molecule when it is in its lowest rotational state is

A. 2.56×10^{-22} J

B. 5.67×10^{-24} J

C. 7.61×10^{-23} J

D. 3.45×10^{-21} J

73. For a charged particle in an electromagnetic field, the canonical momenta are—

A. $m\bar{v} + \frac{q^-}{c} A$ B. $\frac{1}{2}mv^2 + \frac{q^-}{c} A$

C. $m\bar{v} - \frac{q^-}{c} A$ D. $\frac{1}{2}mv^2 - \frac{q^-}{c} A$

74. A piston containing an ideal gas is originally in the state X (shown in Fig.) The gas is taken through a thermal cycle X → Y → X as shown. The work done by the gas is positive if the direction of the thermal cycle is—

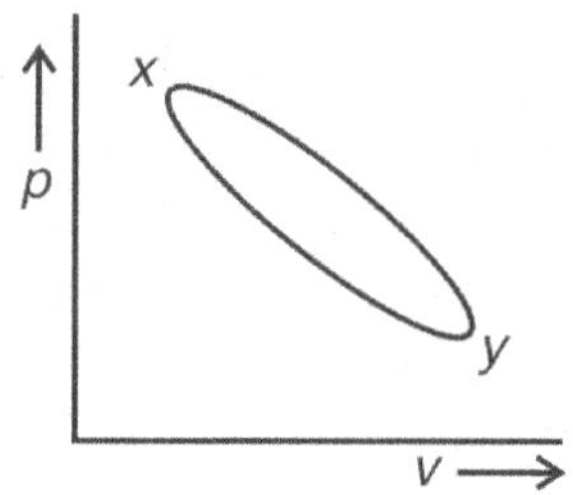

A. clockwise

B. counter clockwise

C. neither clockwise nor counter clockwise

D. clockwise from X→Y and counter clockwise from Y → X

75. Protons from an accelerator collide with hydrogen. What is the minimum energy to create antiprotons?

A. 6.6 GeV

B. 3.3 GeV

C. 2 GeV

D. 1 GeV

ANSWERS

1	2	3	4	5	6	7	8	9	10
A	B	B	A	B	C	B	C	B	A
11	12	13	14	15	16	17	18	19	20
C	B	D	C	C	B	B	B	A	A
21	22	23	24	25	26	27	28	29	30
C	D	A	D	B	C	B	D	C	A
31	32	33	34	35	36	37	38	39	40
C	D	A	C	A	C	B	D	C	D
41	42	43	44	45	46	47	48	49	50
C	C	A	B	D	D	D	C	D	A
51	52	53	54	55	56	57	58	59	60
D	C	A	C	D	A	C	A	B	B
61	62	63	64	65	66	67	68	69	70
C, D	C	C	B	C	C	A	A	C	D
71	72	73	74	75					
A	B	A	D	A					

EXPLANATORY ANSWERS

1. We have,

$$512 \text{ cm}^3 = 160 \text{ g}$$

$$64 \text{ cm}^3 = \frac{160}{512} \times 64 = 18.89 \simeq 20 \text{ g}$$

2.

Distance covered by A = MN + NO
and distance covered by B = MN + MO
∴ Distance covered by (A + B)
= MN + MO + NO = 2 MN
= 2 × 25 = 50
∴ 50 km distance is covered by A and B with the speeds of ratio 2 : 3.

$$\therefore \text{ Distance MO} = \frac{2}{2+3} \times 50 = 20 \text{ km}$$

3. Out of 100, difference in votes = (60 – 40) = 20%

∴ 20% of x = 100

$$\therefore \; x = \frac{100 \times 100}{20} = 500$$

4. Their relative speed = (40 – 20) km/hr

$$= 20 \times \frac{5}{18} = \frac{50}{9} \text{ m/s}$$

Length of the fast train

$$= \frac{50}{9} \times 5 = \frac{250}{9} \text{ m} = 27\frac{7}{9} \text{ m.}$$

5. Letter M is 13th in order of alphabetical series. So 13 (= M) × 2 (number on the opposite side) = 9 × 5 (product of numbers above and below the square) – 19 (number inside the square), *i.e.*,

$$13 \times 2 = (9 \times 5) - 19$$
$$26 = (45 - 19)$$
$$26 = 26$$

Letter B is 2nd in order, so

$$2 \times 9 = (11 \times 2) - 4$$
$$18 = 22 - 4$$
$$18 = 18$$

Similarly, letter E is 5th in order

$$5 \times ? = (3 \times 7) - 6$$
$$5 \times ? = 21 - 6$$
$$5 \times ? = 15$$
$$? = 15 \div 5 = 3.$$

6.

H		O		T		E		L		
8	+	15	+	20	+	5	+	12	=	60

No. of letters in HOTEL = 5.
So, code = 60 – 5 = 55
Clearly, forward coding sequence has been used (A = 1, B = 2 ......).
Similarly,

B		O		R		E		
2	+	15	+	18	+	5	=	40

No. of letters in BORE = 4
So, code = 40 – 4 = 36.

7. 20% of x + 30 = 32% of x – 42

⇒ 12% of x = 72

$$\Rightarrow \quad x = \frac{72 \times 100}{12} = 600$$

Pass Mark = 20% of 600 + 30 = 150

$$\text{Pass percentage} = \left(\frac{150}{600} \times 100\right)\% = 25\%.$$

8. The simplest squares are : AIKC, CKME, EMNG, IBDK, KDFM and MFHN, *i.e.*, 6 squares

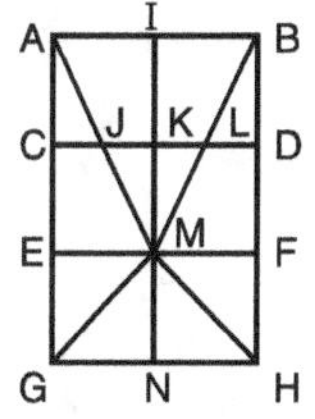

Other squares are ABFE and CDHG, *i.e.*, 2 squares.
So, the total number of squares is 6 + 2 = 8.

9. Suppose, the three sides of the triangle are a, b and c and a is the largest while c is the smallest side of the triangle.

Now, $(a + b + c) = c \times 6$

$$\Rightarrow \quad a + b = 5c$$

Again, $a^2 - b^2 = c^2$

$$\Rightarrow \quad (a + b)(a - b) = c^2$$
$$\Rightarrow \quad 5c\,(a - b) = c^2$$
$$\Rightarrow \quad a - b = \frac{c}{5} \quad [\because a + b = 5c]$$

Now, $a + b = 5c, \; a - b = \frac{c}{5}$

Since, $a = \frac{1}{2}\left(5c + \frac{c}{5}\right) = \frac{13c}{5}$

and $b = \frac{1}{2}\left(5c - \frac{c}{5}\right) = \frac{12c}{5}$

Hence, $a : b : c = \frac{13c}{5} : \frac{12c}{5} : c = 13 : 12 : 5.$

10. Area of walls = 2(8 + 6) 3 = 84 sq.m

Area of two windows and door

$= 2 \times 1\frac{1}{2} \times 1 + 2 \times 1\frac{1}{2} = 6$ sq. m

Area to be covered = 84 – 6 = 78 sq.m

So, length of paper = $\frac{78 \times 100 \text{ m}}{50} = 156$ m

So, cost= $\frac{156 \times 25}{100}$ = ₹ 39.

11. The order in which the girls are positioned is :

Rajni, Mini, Panas, Saya, Jaya.

or

Rajni, Mini, Saya, Jaya, Panas

or

Rajni, Mini, Saya, Panas, Jaya

12.

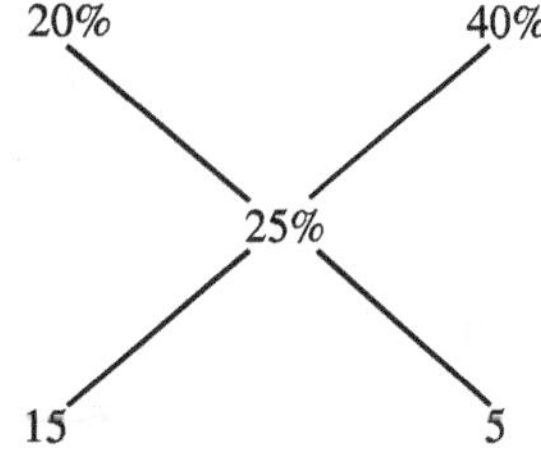

or 3 : 1

Quantity sold at 20% profit

$= \frac{3}{3+1} \times 50 = 37.5$ kgs.

Quantity sold at 40% profit

= (50 – 37.5) = 12.5 kgs.

13. $912 = 19 \times 2\,(16 + 8)$

$882 = 21 \times 2\,(7 + 14)$

$= 24 \times 2\,(6 + 12) = 864.$

14. Total time taken in 6th stroke of first = 33 × 5 = 165 seconds

Total time taken in 8th stroke of second = 22 × 7 = 154 seconds.

Hence, required interval = 165 – 154 = 11 seconds.

15.

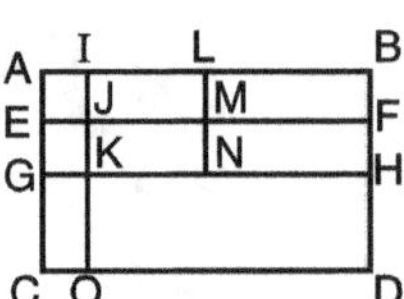

The main rectangle is ABDC, *i.e.,* 1 rectangle.

The simplest rectangles are AIJE, ILMJ, LBFM, EJKG, JMNK, MFHN, GKOC and KHDO, *i.e.,* 8 rectangles.

The rectangles which have two parts are ALME, IBFJ, EMNG, JFHK, AIKG, IKNL, LBHN, EJOC and GHDC, *i.e.,* 9 rectangles.

The rectangles which have three parts are AIOC, ABFE and EFHG, *i.e.,* 3 rectangles.

The rectangles which have four parts are ALNG and IBHK, *i.e.,* 2 rectangles.

So, the total number of rectangles

1 + 8 + 9 + 3 + 2 = 23.

16. 26% of income tax = $\frac{2}{3}$% of the net income

$\therefore$ Income tax = $\left[\frac{2}{3} \times \frac{100}{26}\right]$% of the net income

$= \frac{100}{39}$% of the net income.

Let net income = ₹ 3900

$\therefore$ Income tax = $3900 \times \frac{100}{39 \times 100}$ = ₹ 100

$\Rightarrow$ Gross income = ₹ 3900 + ₹ 100 = ₹ 4000

$\therefore$ Rate % of income tax = $\left(\frac{100}{4000} \times 100\right)\%$

$= 2\frac{1}{2}\%.$

17. Let the present ages of Namrata and Divya are 4x and 3x years respectively; then

$4x + 3x = 28 \quad \therefore \; x = 4$

Hence, their present ages are 16 and 12 years.

So, required ratio = (16 + 4) : (12 + 4)

= 20 : 16 = 5 : 4.

18. Let the three-digit number be $100x + 10y + z$, then

$x + y + z = 10$ ...(i)

$x + z = y$ ...(ii)

From equations (i) and (ii) we get, $y = 5$ and

$x + z = 5$ ...(iii)

Again,

$100z + 10y + x - (100x + 10y + z) = 99$

$\Rightarrow \quad 99z - 99x = 99$

$\therefore \qquad z - x = 1 \qquad$ ...(iv)

Solving (iii) and (iv), we get $x = 2$, $z = 3$.

Hence, number = $100 \times 2 + 10 \times 5 + 3 = 253$

19. There are 4 identical white and 4 identical black balls and we have to select 3, which can be selected in the following pattern:

white	3	2	1	–
black	–	1	2	3

i.e., in all 4 ways.

It should be noted that the ways of selecting 3 white balls from 4 white balls is not equal to $^4C_3$ since the white balls are identical, it is equal to 1. Similar is the cases for 2, 1, etc.

Now the number of ways of selecting 3 white balls = 1.

Hence, required probability = 1/4.

20. Let the total distance covered during journey = 60 km

$\frac{1}{3}$ of the distance covered during journey

$= 60 \times \frac{1}{3} = 20$ km

$\frac{1}{4}$ of the distance covered during journey

$= \frac{1}{4} \times 60 = 15$ km

$\therefore$ The distance covered during the rest of journey = 60 – (20 + 15) = 25 km

Time taken to cover 20 km at 25 km/h

$= \frac{20}{25}$ hours $= \frac{4}{5}$ hours

Time taken to cover 15 km at 30 km/h

$= \frac{15}{30}$ hours $= \frac{1}{2}$ hour

Time taken to cover 25 km at 50 km/h

$= \frac{25}{50}$ hours $= \frac{1}{2}$ hour

Total time taken $= \frac{4}{5} + \frac{1}{2} + \frac{1}{2} = \frac{9}{5}$ hours.

Hence, average speed per hour $= 60 \div \frac{9}{5}$

$= \frac{60 \times 5}{9} = \frac{100}{3}$ km/h $= 33\frac{1}{3}$ km/h.

21. As, $T = 2\pi\sqrt{\frac{2}{8}}$

or, $T^2 = 4\pi^2 \frac{L}{g}$ or $g = \frac{4\pi^2}{T^2}.L$

$$\therefore \quad \frac{\Delta g}{g} \times 100 = \frac{\Delta L}{L} \times 100 + 2 \times \frac{\Delta T}{T} \times 100$$

Now, L = 200 cm, ΔL = 1 mm = 0.1 cm,

T for 100 oscillations = 90 s, ΔT = 1 s

$$\therefore \quad \frac{\Delta g}{g} \times 100 = \frac{0.1}{20} \times 100 + 2 \times \frac{1}{90} \times 100$$

= 0.5 + 2.22 = 2.72% = 3%

22. Coefficient of performance of a refrigerator,

$$\beta = \frac{Q_2}{W} = \frac{T_2}{T_1 - T_2}$$

$$\therefore \quad Q_2 = W\frac{T_2}{T_1 - T_2}$$

But W $\rightarrow$ energy consumed by the refrigerator = 1 J, T_1 = 300 K, T_2 = 277 K

$$\therefore Q_2 = 1 \times \frac{277}{300 - 277} = \frac{277}{23} = 12 \text{ J}$$

Heat rejected by the refrigerator,

$Q_1 = W + Q_2$

$= 1 + 12 = 13$ J

23. From the fig., we see that, the flux through the entire cylinder,

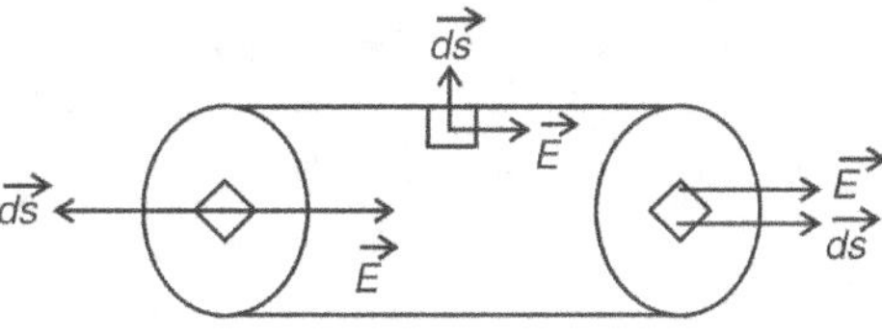

$$\phi_E = \underset{\text{left plane face}}{\int \vec{E}.\vec{ds}} + \underset{\text{right plane face}}{\int \vec{E}.\vec{ds}} + \underset{\text{curved sufrace}}{\int \vec{E}.\vec{ds}}$$

$$= \int E \cdot ds \cos 180° + \int E \cdot ds \cos 0° + \int E \cdot ds \cos 90°$$

$$= -E\int ds + E\int ds$$

$$= -E(\pi r^2) + E(\pi r^2) = 0$$

24. From fig. $V_i = 40$ V, $I_1 = 50$ mA

$\therefore$ Maximum current

$I = I_1 + I_2 = 50 + 0 = 50 \text{ mA} = 50 \times 10^{-3}\text{A}$

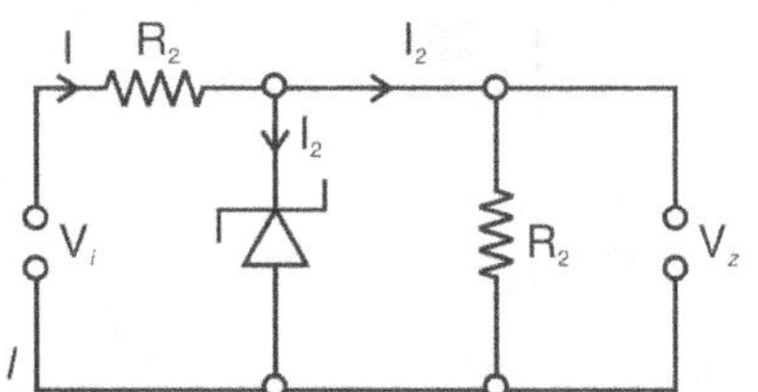

This is because maximum current flows through zener diode, so $I_2 = 0$

V_z = voltage drop across zener diode = 10 V

As, in maximum, so maximum value of R is

$$R = \frac{V_i - V_z}{I} = \frac{40-10}{50\times 10^{-3}} = 600\,\Omega$$

25. The area of triangle is

$$= \frac{1}{2}|\vec{A}\times\vec{B}|$$

Hence, $\vec{A}\times\vec{B} = \begin{vmatrix} \hat{i} & \hat{j} & \hat{k} \\ 5 & -3 & 4 \\ 0 & 1 & -1 \end{vmatrix}$

$= (3-4)\hat{i} + (0+5)\hat{j} + (5-0)\hat{k}$

$= -\hat{i} + 5\hat{j} + 5\hat{k}$

$\therefore\ |\vec{A}\times\vec{B}| = \sqrt{(-1)^2 + (5)^2 + (5)^2}$

$= \sqrt{1+25+25} = \sqrt{51}$

$\therefore$ Area of triangle $= \frac{1}{2}\sqrt{51}$

26. Maxwell's equations in free space are

curl $\bar{E} = -\mu_0 \frac{\partial \bar{H}}{\partial t}$

and curl $\bar{H} = \epsilon_0 \frac{\partial \bar{E}}{\partial t}$

and $\bar{E} = E_0 \sin(kx - \omega t)$

and $\bar{B} = B_0 \sin(kx - \omega t)$

or $\bar{H} = H_0 \sin(kx - \omega t)$

Equation (1) can be written as

$$\bar{k}\times\bar{E} = \mu_0\omega\bar{H}$$

$$k(\hat{n}\times\bar{E}) = \mu_0\omega\bar{H}$$

In term of moduli

$$k|\bar{E}| = \mu_0\omega|\bar{H}|$$

or $kE_0 = \mu_0\omega H_0$

$$E_0 k = \omega\mu_0 H_0$$

$$E_0 k = \omega B_0$$

27. $v_p = \sqrt{\frac{g\lambda}{2\pi}}$ ...(1)

Group velocity of ocean

$$v_g = v_p - \lambda\frac{dv_p}{d\lambda}$$

From eqn. (1)

$$\frac{dv_p}{d\lambda} = \frac{1}{2}\lambda^{-1/2}\sqrt{\frac{g}{2\pi}}$$

$\therefore$ $v_g = \sqrt{\frac{g\lambda}{2\pi}} - \frac{1}{2}\sqrt{\frac{g\lambda}{2\pi}}$

$$= \frac{1}{2}\sqrt{\frac{g\lambda}{2\pi}}$$

$$v_g = \frac{v_p}{2}$$

28. When $V_{in} = 0$ V, the transistor is in cut off (acts like an open switch) and

$$V_{CE} = V_{CC} = 10 \text{ V}$$

29. From the fig., we see that available energy per cycle is

$Q_1 - Q_2 = [2T_1 \times S_1 + T_1 \times S_1] - 2T_1S_1$

$= T_1S_1$

and $Q = 3T_1S_1$

$\therefore$ efficiency, $\eta = \frac{Q_1 - Q_2}{Q}$

$= \frac{T_1S_1}{3T_1S_1}$

$= \frac{1}{3}$

30. Time delay for 1-bit $= \frac{24}{8}\mu s = 3\mu s$

Clock frequency $= \frac{1}{T_P}$

$$= \frac{1}{\mu s} = \frac{10^6}{3} \text{Hz}$$

$$= 333 \text{ kHz}$$

31. 0—300 V voltmeter has an error of $\pm$ 2%

$$= 300 \times \pm\frac{2}{100}$$

$$= \pm 6 \text{ V}$$

True of 30 (range)

$$= 30 - 6 \text{ V to } 30 + 6 \text{ V}$$

$$= 24 \text{ V} - 36 \text{ V}$$

32. Following the rule

$$\Delta M_J = 0, \pm 1$$

The level of $^2D_{5/2}$ splitted as

$$\frac{5}{2}, \frac{3}{2}, \frac{1}{2}, -\frac{1}{2}, -\frac{3}{2}, -\frac{5}{2}$$

And, $^2P_{3/2}$ splitted as $\frac{3}{2}, \frac{1}{2}, -\frac{1}{2}, -\frac{3}{2}$

Total 12 transitions takes place.

33. The diamagnetism increases with the number of electrons as well as the size of the ions and atoms and is temperature independent.

34. For option (A)

Photoelectric cross-section $\propto Z^5$

So it increases with atomic number.

(B) and (D) are also true.

For (C), pair production can take place only when the photon energy exceeds $2m_0c^2$, which is the sum of the rest energies of the members of the pairs not at all energies.

35. The probability of survival (not decaying) in time t, is $e^{-\lambda t}$.

Probability of decay = $1 - e^{-\lambda t}$

36. The formula

$$p\left(\frac{\text{GeV}}{\text{C}}\right) = 0.3 \text{ B (T) R}(m)$$

Gives $\text{R} = \frac{p}{0.3\text{B}}$

$$= \frac{400}{0.3 \times 1.5}$$

$$= 880 \text{ m}$$

37. In a Kurie blot of a β-spectrum, the shape at tail and depends on the neutrino mass. Hence, option (B) is correct.

38. Given $q = ne = 1.0 \times 10^{12} \times 1.6 \times 10^{-19}$ C

$$= 1.6 \times 10^{-7} \text{ C}$$

and $\text{V} = 10 \text{ V}$

$$\therefore \quad \text{C} = \frac{q}{\text{V}} = \frac{1.6 \times 10^{-7}\text{C}}{10}$$

$$= 1.6 \times 10^{-8} \text{ F}$$

39. Forward biasing of p-n junction offers low resistance. In case of ideal p-n junction, resistance is zero.

40. The energy gap between two levels

$$(\text{E}_1 - \text{E}_2) = h\nu_0$$

or $h\nu = 0.36 \text{ ev}_0$

and zero point energy $= \frac{1}{2}h\nu$

$$= \frac{1}{2} \times 0.36 \text{ eV}$$

$$= 0.18 \text{ eV}$$

41. All minors of order 3 × 3 are zero. Since minor of order 2 is non-zero or its determinant is zero, the rank of matrix is 2.

42. We have, $\frac{\text{E}_{max}}{\text{H}_{max}} = 120\pi$

$$\Rightarrow \quad \text{H}_{max} = \frac{\text{E}_{max}}{120\pi}$$

or $\text{B}_{max} = \mu_0 \times \text{H}_{max}$

$$= 4\pi \times 10^{-7} \times 10^{-4}/120\pi$$

$$\text{B}_{max} = 3.3 \times 10^{-13} \text{ T}$$

43. We have, $\lambda = \frac{h}{\sqrt{2m\text{E}}}$

In thermal equilibrium,

$$\text{E} = k\text{T}$$

or $\lambda = \frac{h}{\sqrt{2mk\text{T}}}$

44. From the First Law of Thermodynamics,

$$d\text{Q} = d\text{V} + d\text{W}$$

In cyclic process,

$$d\text{V} = 0$$

(because initial state = final state)

$$\therefore \quad d\text{Q} = d\text{W}$$

45. r_n for hydrogen atom for Ist orbit

$$r_H = \frac{h^2 \epsilon_0}{\pi m e^2}$$

$$= \frac{(6.6 \times 10^{-34})^2 \times 8.85 \times 10^{-12}}{3.14 \times 9.1 \times 10^{-31} \times (1.6 \times 10^{-19})^2} = 0.0529 \text{ nm}$$

46. The maximum frequency

ν_{max} is given by

$$h\nu_{max} = eV$$

or

$$\nu_{max} = \frac{eV}{h}$$

47. The probability of drawing a red ball $= \frac{5}{10}$

If the ball is not replaced, the box will have a ball, so probability of drawing the red ball in next chance $= \frac{4}{9}$

Hence, the probability of drawing 2 balls

$$= \frac{5}{10} \times \frac{4}{9} = \frac{2}{9}$$

48. In complex form,

$$\vec{E} = 50\, e^{j(\omega t - \beta z)}\, \hat{a}_x (\text{V/m})$$

and since the internal impedance $\eta = 120\pi\ \Omega$ and propagation is in $+z$.

$$H = \frac{50}{120\pi} e^{j(\omega t - \beta z)} \hat{a}_y (\text{V/m})$$

Then average power

$$\rho_{av} = \frac{1}{2}\text{Re}\left(E \times H^*\right)$$

$$= \frac{1}{2}(50)\left(\frac{5}{12\pi}\right)\hat{a}_z \text{W/m}^2$$

The flow is normal to the area, and so

$$P_{avg} = \rho_{av} \times r^2$$

$$= \frac{1}{2}(50)\left(\frac{5}{12\pi}\right)(2.5)^2$$

$$= 65.1 \text{ W}$$

49. For TE_{10} mode

$m = 1, \quad n = 0$

$$f_c = \frac{1}{2\pi\sqrt{\mu_0 \epsilon_0}}\sqrt{\left(\frac{m\pi}{a}\right)^2 + \left(\frac{n\pi}{b}\right)^2}$$

Since $\quad \lambda_g = \lambda_c$

and $\quad \lambda_g \lambda_c = \lambda_0^2$

or $\quad \lambda_g = \lambda_c = \lambda_0$

$\therefore \quad f_c = f_0 = 9375$ MHz

For TE_{10} mode

$$9375 \times 10^6 = \frac{3 \times 10^8}{2\pi}\sqrt{\frac{\pi^2}{a^2}}$$

$$a = 0.016 \text{ m}$$

50. The analog output voltage V_0 is given by

$$V_0 = K(8b_3 + 4b_2 + 2b_1 + b_0)$$

For $b_3 = 1$, $b_2 = b_1 = 0$ and $b_0 = 1$; $V_0 = 4.5$V

$$\therefore \quad K = \frac{4.5}{8+1} = \frac{1}{2}$$

Therefore, the analog output voltage for the input code 0011 will be

$$V_0 = \frac{1}{2}(8 \times 0 + 4 \times 0 + 2 \times 1 + 1)$$

$$= \frac{3}{2} = 1.5$$

51. The wavelength of the second radiation is double that of the first one, $\lambda_2 = 2\lambda_1$, we can write

$$V_{s1} = \frac{hc}{e\lambda_1} - \frac{W}{e'} \quad ...(1)$$

where, W is the work function of the metal. V_{s1} is the stopping potential of the metal.

$$V_{s2} = \frac{hc}{e\lambda_2} - \frac{W}{e} = \frac{hc}{2e\lambda_1} - \frac{W}{e} \quad ...(2)$$

To obtain λ_1 we have to subtract (1) from (2) :

$$V_{s1} - V_{s2} = \frac{hc}{e\lambda_1}\left(1 - \frac{1}{2}\right) = \frac{hc}{2e\lambda_1}.$$

The wavelength thus given by

$$\lambda_1 = \frac{hc}{2e(V_{s1} - V_{s2})}$$

$$= \frac{6.6 \times 10^{-34} \text{Js} \times 3 \times 10^8 \text{ms}^{-1}}{2 \times 1.6 \times 10^{-19} \text{C} \times (3.2\text{V} - 0.8\text{V})}$$

$$= 2.6 \times 10^{-6} \text{ m}$$

52. The force between the two bodies is given by

$$F = \frac{GMm}{(a+b+c)^2}$$

where, M is the mass of planet and m that of satellite.

At equilibrium, $\dfrac{GMm}{(a+b+c)^2} = \dfrac{mv^2}{(a+b+c)}$

If P is the period, then velocity

$$\therefore \quad v = \frac{2\pi(a+b+c)}{P}$$

so $\dfrac{GMm}{(a+b+c)^2} = \dfrac{m4\pi^2(a+b+c)^2}{(a+b+c)P^2}$

or $M = \dfrac{4\pi^2(a+b+c)^3}{GP^2}$

53.

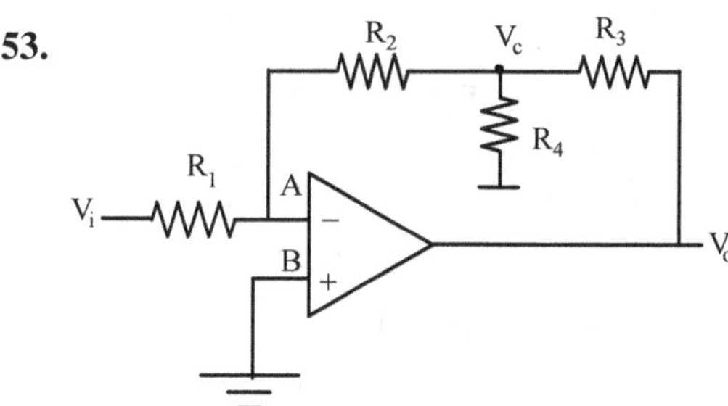

A and B are at the same potential from figure

$$\frac{V_o - V_c}{R_3} = \frac{V_c}{R_4} + \frac{V_c}{R_2}$$

or $V_c = \dfrac{V_o}{R_3} \cdot \dfrac{R_2R_3R_4}{R_2R_3 + R_3R_4 + R_4R_2}$

or $V_c = V_o \dfrac{R_2R_4}{R_2R_3 + R_3R_4 + R_4R_2}$ ...(1)

Also, $\dfrac{V_c}{R_2} + \dfrac{V_i}{R_1} = 0$

$$V_c = \frac{-R_2}{R_1} V_i \quad ...(2)$$

From equations (1) and (2), we get

$$\frac{V_o R_4}{R_2R_3 + R_3R_4 + R_4R_2} = \frac{-V_i}{R_1}$$

$$\frac{V_o}{V_i} = \frac{-1}{R_1}\left(\frac{R_2R_3 + R_3R_4 + R_4R_2}{R_4}\right)$$

$$\frac{V_o}{V_i} = \frac{-1}{R_1}\left(R_3 + R_2 + \frac{R_2R_3}{R_4}\right) \quad ...(a)$$

54. Let T be the temperature of the hot reservoir. Then

$$50 = \left(1 - \frac{273+7}{T}\right) \times 100 \text{ or } T = 560 \text{ K.}$$

Let T′ be the required temperature.
Then

$$70 = \left(1 - \frac{273+7}{T'}\right) \times 100 \text{ or } T' = 933.3 \text{ K.}$$

∴ Required rise in temperature = 933.3 – 560
= 373.3 K.

Let T″ be the required temperature of the cold reservoir.

Then $70 = \left(1 - \dfrac{T''}{560}\right) \times 100$ or $T'' = 168$ K.

∴ Require decrease in temperature
= (273 + 7) – 168 = 112 K.

55. Figure shows the required common base connection. The voltage drop across RC = (= 2 k*W*) is 2 V.

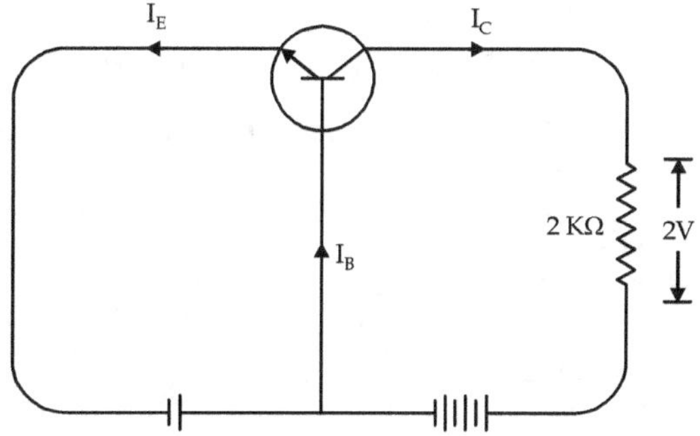

$I_C = 2$ V/2 kΩ = 1 mA

Now $\alpha = I_C / I_E$

$$\therefore \quad I_E = \frac{I_C}{\alpha} = \frac{1}{0.95} = 1.05\text{mA}$$

Using the relation,

$$I_E = I_B + I_C$$

$$\therefore \quad I_B = I_E - I_C = 1.05 - 1 = 0.05 \text{ mA}$$

56. $f_r = \dfrac{1.44}{(R_1 + 2R_2)C_{ext}}$

$= \dfrac{1.44}{(2.2k\Omega + 9.4\ k\Omega)0.022\ \mu F} = 5.64$ kHz

Duty cycle $= \left(\dfrac{R_1 + R_2}{R_1 + 2R_2}\right) \times 100$

$= \left(\dfrac{2.2\ k\Omega + 4.7\ k\Omega}{2.2\ k\Omega + 9.4\ k\Omega}\right) \times 100 = 59.5\%$

57. When no stress is applied voltage across the gauge; output voltage is

$e_0 = \dfrac{R_g}{R_b + R_g} . e_i = \dfrac{100}{100 + 100} \times 12 = 6$ V

Strain $= \dfrac{S}{E} = \left(\dfrac{140 \times 10^6}{200 \times 10^9}\right) = 0.7 \times 10^{-3}$

Change in resistance of gauge

$\Delta R_g = G_x \times R_g = 2 \times 0.7 \times 10^{-3} \times 100 = 0.014\ \Omega$

$\therefore$ Voltage across the gauge when stress is applied

$= \dfrac{100 + 0.014}{100 + 100 + 0.014} \times 12 = 6.00042$ V

Change in voltage

$- 6.00042 - 6 - 0.00042$ V $-$ 0.42 mV

58. Energy of electron in the first orbit of hydrogen atom,

$E_1 = -13.6$ eV

Energy of electron in second orbit

$E_2 = \dfrac{E_1}{n^2} = \dfrac{E_1}{4} = -\dfrac{13.6}{4} = -3.4$ eV

Energy of photon emitted $= E_2 - E_1$

$E = -3.4 + (13.6) = 10.2$ eV

$= 10.2 \times 1.6 \times 10^{-19}$ J $= 16.32 \times 10^{-19}$ J

59. We know

$v = v_0 \pm v_m$

$\therefore v_1 = v_0 + v_m$ and $v_2 = v_0 - v_m$

$\therefore\ v_1 - v_2 = 2v_m$

$\dfrac{c}{\lambda_1} - \dfrac{c}{\lambda_2}$

$= \dfrac{2c}{\lambda_m}, \lambda_m$

$= \left[\dfrac{2\lambda_1\lambda_2}{\lambda_1 - \lambda_2}\right]$

$\lambda_2 = 4554$ Å, $\lambda_1 = 4178$ Å

$\lambda_m = \dfrac{2 \times 4554 \times 4178}{4554 - 4178} = 1.012 \times 10^5$ Å.

60. The decay scheme is

$_{17}Cl^{33} \rightarrow {}_{16}S^{33} + {}_1e^r + \nu + E_\beta$

When this proton emits with a maximum energy, the neutrino energy will be zero and the daughter nucleus S^{33} will be formed in the ground state—

$\therefore\ E_\beta = \dfrac{3}{5}\dfrac{e^2 A^{2/3}}{4\pi \epsilon_0 R_0} - 180$ MeV

or $\dfrac{3}{5} \cdot \dfrac{e^2 A^{2/3}}{4\pi \epsilon_0 R_0} = 6.1 \times 1.6 \times 10^{-13}$ J

or $R_0 = \dfrac{3}{5}\dfrac{e^2 A^{2/3}}{4\pi \epsilon_0 \times 6.1 \times 1.6 \times 10^{-13}}$

$= \dfrac{3}{5}\dfrac{(1.6 \times 10^{-19})^2 (33)^{2/3} \times 109}{6.1 \times 1.6 \times 10^{-13}}$

$= 1.41 \times 10^{-15}$ m

$\therefore R = R_0 A^{2/3} = 1.41 \times 10^{-15} (33)^{1/3}$

$= 4.54 \times 10^{-15}$ m

61. The capacitances of the two are $C_1 = 4\pi\varepsilon_0 R$ and $C_2 = 4\pi\varepsilon_0(2R)$.

The initial energy, $E_i = \dfrac{Q^2}{2C_1}$.

The final energy, $E_f = \dfrac{Q^2}{2C_2}$.

The heat produced

$= E_i - E_f = \dfrac{Q^2}{2}\left[\dfrac{1}{4\pi\varepsilon_0 R} - \dfrac{1}{2 \times 4\pi\varepsilon_0 R}\right]$

$= k\dfrac{Q^2}{2R}\left[1 - \dfrac{1}{2}\right] = \dfrac{kQ^2}{4R}$

62. Charges on the two capacitors are 36 μC and 72 μC. When they are connected in opposition, the total charge on the system = (72 – 36)μC = 36 μC

This is shared between the capacitors so that they acquire the same potential difference. Let this be *V*.

(3 μF)V + (6 μF)V = 36 μC

or V = 4V

63. $$V_{UTP} = \frac{R_2}{R_1 + R_2} \times V_{out(max)}$$

$$= \frac{100}{100+100} \times 5V = 0.5 \times 5 \text{ V} = 2.5 \text{ V}$$

$$V_{LTP} = \frac{R_2}{R_1 + R_2} \times \left[-V_{out(max)}\right] = 0.5 \times -5 \text{ V}$$

$$= -2.5 \text{ V}$$

64. MSB resistance, R = 2 kΩ

LSB resistance, $R^n = 2^{n-1}$. R

As it a 4-bit weighted resistor D/A convertor, hence $n = 4$

∴ $R_n = 2^3 \times R = 8 \times 2$ kΩ $= 16$ kΩ

65. Truth Table

S_1 (P)	S_0 (Q)	C_{in}	S
0	0	0	0
0	0	1	1
0	1	0	1
0	1	1	0
1	0	0	1
1	0	1	0
1	1	0	0
1	1	1	1

Now reducing the truth table as

S_1	S_0	S	
0	0	C_{in}	I_0
0	1	$\bar{C}_{in}$	I_1
1	0	$\bar{C}_{in}$	I_2
1	1	C_{in}	I_3

Thus, $$I_0 = I_3 = C_{in}$$
$$\bar{I} = \bar{I}_2 = C_{in}$$
$$I_1 = I_2 = \bar{C}_{in}$$

66. Since the voltage at the input of the OP-AMP is 0, therefore,

$$V_I = V_a = FV_o$$

or $$V_0 = \frac{1}{F} V_I$$

or $$\text{Gain} = \frac{V_o}{V_I} = \frac{1}{F}$$

67. Van der Waal's equation

$$\left(P + \frac{a}{V^2}\right)(V - b) = RT$$

⇒ $$P = -\frac{a}{V^2} + \frac{RT}{V-b}$$

or $$PV = -\frac{a}{V} + RT$$

(since b is very small)

$$R = Nk_B$$
$$N = 1$$

∴ $$PV = -\frac{a}{V} + k_B T$$

$$PV = k_B T \left[1 - \frac{a}{k_B TV}\right]$$

$$\frac{PV}{k_B T} \approx 1 + \frac{B(T)}{V}$$

Since $$-\frac{a}{k_B T} = BT$$

68. For B – E condensation

$$\frac{Nh^3}{Vg\,(2\pi mk_B T)^{3/2}} = \sum \left(\frac{1}{l}\right)^{3/2} Z^l$$

or $$\frac{Nh^3}{Vg(2\pi mk_B T)^{3/2}} = \Gamma(3/2)$$

with $$\Gamma(3/2) = \sum_{l=1} \left(\frac{1}{l}\right)^{3/2} Z^{l/2}$$

at $T = T_0$, $Z = 1$

$$\Gamma(3/2) = \sum_{i=1}\left(\frac{1}{i}\right)^{3/2} = 2.612$$

or $$\frac{Nh^3}{Vg(2\pi mk_B T)^{3/2}} = 2.612$$

$g = 1$ for bose gas (spinless)

The region correspond to the transition region of the B–E condensation assembly in mixture of two thermodynamic phases (for $T < T_0$)

$$\frac{Nh^3}{V_g(2\pi mk_B T)^{3/2}} > \Gamma(3/2)$$

or $$\frac{Nh^3}{V\Gamma(3/2)} > (2\pi mk_B T)^{3/2}$$

or $$T < \frac{h^2}{2\pi mk_B}\left[\frac{N}{V\Gamma(3/2)}\right]^{2/3}$$

69. We know that the probability of molecule lying between v and $v + dv$ is given by

$$= 4\pi\left\{\frac{m}{2\pi kT}\right\}^{3/2} c^2 e^{-mc^2/2kT} dc.$$

From problem

$dc = 101 - 100 = 1$ met./sec.,

$k = 1.38 \times 10^{-23}$ J/K, $T = 200°K$

$$m = 32 \text{ a.m.u.} = \frac{32}{6\times10^{23}} \text{gm.} = \frac{32}{6\times10^{26}} \text{Kgm.}$$

Substituting these values in the above formula and solving, we get the probability equal to 6.11×10^{-4}.

70. Change in base-emitter voltage,

$$\Delta V_{BE} = 200 \text{ mV}$$

Change in base current,

$$\Delta I_B = 100\ \mu A$$

∴ Input resistance,

$$R_i = \frac{\Delta V_{BE}}{\Delta I_B} = \frac{200 \text{ mV}}{100\ \mu A} = 2\,k\Omega$$

71. We know that

$$Q = \frac{\omega L}{R} = \frac{1}{\omega CR}$$

Hence, the true Q

$$Q_i = \frac{1}{\omega CR}$$

The effective Q,

$$Q_e = \frac{1}{\omega(C + C_d)R}$$

$$\frac{Q_i}{Q_e} = \frac{C + C_d}{C}$$

or $$Q_i = Q_e\frac{C + C_d}{C} \qquad ...(1)$$

As $$f_2 = 2f_1$$

$$C_d = \frac{C_1 - 4C_2}{3} = \frac{450 - 4\times 90}{3} = 30 \text{ pF}$$

72. The reduced mass μ of the CO molecule is given by

$$\mu = \frac{m_1 m_2}{m_1 + m_2} = \left[\frac{1.99(2.99)}{1.99 + 2.66}\right]\times 10^{-26} \text{ kg} = 1.14 \times 10^{-26} \text{ kg}$$

And its MI is given as

$I = \mu R^2 = (1.14 \times 10^{-26}$ kg$)(1.13 \times 10^{-10}$ m$)^2$

$= 1.46 \times 10^{-46}$ kg m^2

The lowest rotational energy level corresponds to $J = 1$ and this levels into, we have

$$E_{J=r} = \frac{J(J + r)h^2}{2I} = \frac{(1.054\times10^{-34}\text{ Js})^2}{1.46\times10^{-46}\text{ kg m}^2} = 7.61\times10^{-23}\text{ J}$$

73. We have, Lagrangian for a charged particle in an em field

$$L = \frac{1}{2}mv^2 - q\phi + q\frac{\bar{v}.\bar{A}}{c}$$

The canonical moments are

$$p = \frac{\partial L}{\partial v} = m\bar{v} + \frac{q}{c}\bar{A}$$

74. For cyclic process-involving pv-work only W is the area enclosed by the path in a pv-diagram. $|a|$ is a positive area when the path corresponds to counter clockwise rotation and a negative area for clockwise rotation.

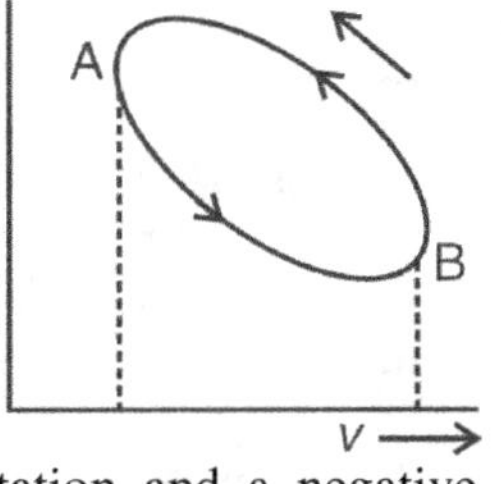

Hence, the given direction of thermal cycle is clockwise from X → Y and counter clock wise from Y → X.

75. The reaction to produce antiprotons is

$$p + p \rightarrow \bar{p} + p + p + p$$

The hydrogen can be considered to be at rest. Thus, at threshold the invariant mass squared is

$$(E + m_p)^2 - (E - m_p)^2 = (4m_p)^4$$

$$\Rightarrow \qquad E = 7m_p$$

Hence, threshold energy $= 7m_p = 6.6$ GeV

SET–6
CSIR–UGC (NET) PHYSICAL SCIENCES

PART-A

1. Consider the diagram given below:

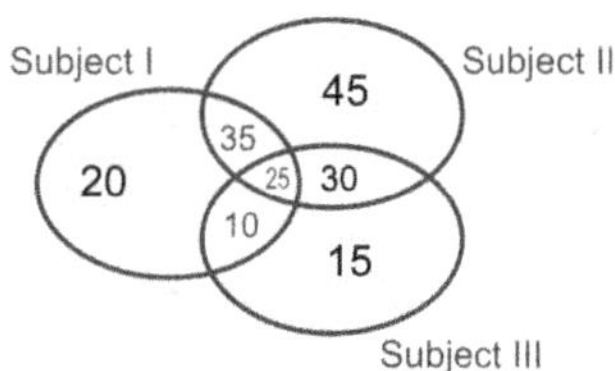

If 500 students appeared in an examination. How many students appeared at least in two subjects?

A. 120 B. 100
C. 150 D. 112

2. Ranjana remembers that her elder brother was born between 13th and 16th April while her mother remembers that she was born after 14th April before 17th April. If the statements of both are considered correct then on which date of April, she was born?

A. 14 B. 16
C. 14 or 15 D. 15

3. Nalini, her brother, her daughter and her son are tennis players and are playing game of doubles. Their positions on the court are as follows:

(i) Nalini's brother is directly across the net from her daughter.
(ii) Her daughter is diagonally across the net from the worst players sibling
(iii) The best and the worst players are on the same side of the net.

Who is the best player?

A. Nalini B. Nalini's brother
C. Nalini's daughter D. None of these

4. Which term of the progression $\sqrt{3}, \frac{1}{\sqrt{3}}, \frac{1}{3\sqrt{3}}$, ... is $\frac{1}{243\sqrt{3}}$.

A. 5th B. 7th
C. 8th D. 6th

5. John started walking towards North. After walking 50 m he turned left and walked 40 m. He then turned left and walked 20 m. He again turned left and walked 80 m. How far is he from the starting point?

A. 50 m B. 30 m
C. 70 m D. 20 m

6. In the given figure AC = AB = BC = $2r$. A circle with A as centre and radius r is drawn. Find the area of the shaded portion of the figure—

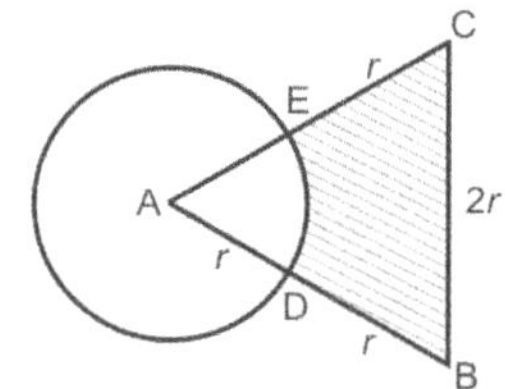

A. $\left(\sqrt{3}-\frac{\pi}{6}\right)r^2$ B. $\left(\sqrt{3+\frac{\pi}{6}}\right)r^2$

C. $\sqrt{3}r^2$ D. r^2

7. A six centimetre cube is painted green on all sides. It is cut into two centimetre cubes. How many cubes will be there with two sides painted?

A. 12 B. 8
C. 24 D. 4

8. Which of the following figs. does not represent a linear relationship between the variables X and Y?

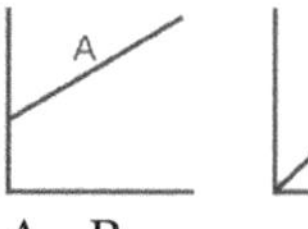

B C

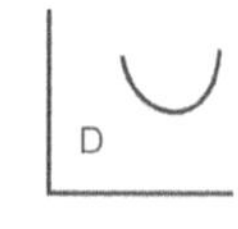

A. B B. C
C. D D. A

9. In the expression xy^2, the values of both variables x and y are decreases by 20%. By this, the value of the expression is decreased by

A. 48.8% B. 42.7%
C. 58.8% D. 38.8%

10. Two stations A and B are 110 km apart on some straightline, one trains from A at 7 AM and travels towards B at 20 km/h. Another train starts from B at 8 AM and travels towards A at a speed of 25 km/hr. At what time will they meet?
A. 9 AM B. 10 AM
C. 11 AM D. 10:30 AM

11. A monkey tries to ascend a greased pole 14 metres high. He ascends 2 metres in first minute and slips down 1 metre in the alternate minute. If he continues to ascend in this fashion, how long does he take to reach the top?
A. 25 min. B. 28 min.
C. 20 min. D. 30 min.

12. Three equal circles are so described that each circle touches the other two. If the shaded area in between the three circles is 0.64; find the radii of each of the circle—

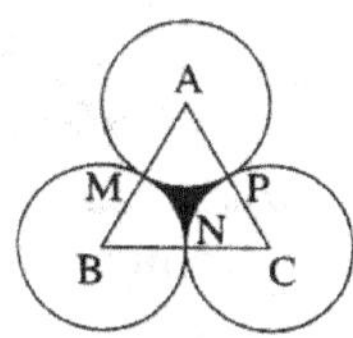

A. 1 B. 2
C. 3 D. 4

13. Anna and Panas are friends. They decide to meet between 1 pm and 2 pm on a given day. There is a condition that who ever arrive first will not wait for the other for more than 15 min. The probability that they will meet on that day is—
A. $\frac{1}{4}$ B. $\frac{1}{16}$
C. $\frac{7}{16}$ D. $\frac{9}{16}$

14. Study the following table and determine whose overall performance is best among the three.

Subject	1's Marks	2's Marks	3's Marks
Maths	30	40	35
English	60	50	45
Science	20	40	40
Soc. Sc.	40	55	40
G.K.	60	35	39
Hindi	30	20	41

A. 1
B. 2
C. 3
D. Cannot be determined

15. In a class of 65 boys, the position of Mohan is 33rd. If the last boy is given the first position, then on this basis what is the position of Mohan?
A. 32nd B. 33rd
C. 34th D. 35th

16. The ^{14}C dating method is not usually used for dating organic substances older that is 60,000 years, because—
A. Such objects rarely contain carbon
B. Such objects is accumulated ^{14}C after their formation
C. In those times there was no production of ^{14}C.
D. Most of the ^{14}C in the sample would have decayed

17. 8 persons were invited in a party. Everybody shakes hand with everybody else. What is the total number of hand shakes?
A. 28 B. 25
C. 21 D. 18

18. Pointing to a man Savita says, "He is the only son of my father's father." How is Savita related to the man?
A. Father B. Mother
C. Niece D. Granddaughter

19. In the cartesian plane, coordinates of ABC are (–2, 1), (4, 1), (2, 3) respectively. Area of triangle ABC is
A. 5 B. 6
C. 7 D. 8

20. A car is driven around a circular field at a speed of 10 km/hr during the first round, 20 km/hr during the second round and 60 km/hr in the third. What is the average speed for the three rounds journey undertaken by the car?
A. 20 km/hr B. 30 km/hr
C. 45 km/hr D. 18 km/hr

PART-B

21. If $\vec{r}$ is the position vector of any point on the surface of a cube of side L, then the surface integral $\iint_s \vec{r}.\overrightarrow{ds}$ is

A. 0 B. ∞
C. $3L^2$ D. $3L^3$

22. The eigen values of the matrix

$$A = \begin{bmatrix} \cos\theta & -\sin\theta \\ \sin\theta & \cos\theta \end{bmatrix} \text{ are}$$

A. $e^{\pm i\theta}$ B. $e^{\pm 2/\theta}$
C. $e^{\pm 3i\theta}$ D. $e^{\pm i\theta/2}$

23. Determine the values of α, β and γ when

$$\begin{vmatrix} 0 & 2\beta & \gamma \\ \alpha & \beta & -\gamma \\ \alpha & -\beta & \gamma \end{vmatrix} \text{ is orthogonal.}$$

A. $\pm\frac{1}{\sqrt{2}}, \pm\frac{1}{\sqrt{6}}, \pm\frac{1}{\sqrt{3}}$

B. $\pm\frac{1}{\sqrt{3}}, \pm\frac{1}{\sqrt{5}}, \pm\frac{1}{\sqrt{2}}$

C. $\pm\frac{1}{\sqrt{3}}, \pm\frac{1}{\sqrt{2}}, \pm\frac{1}{\sqrt{5}}$

D. $\pm\frac{1}{\sqrt{6}}, \pm\frac{1}{\sqrt{2}}, \pm\frac{1}{\sqrt{3}}$

24. The period of oscillation for compound pendulum is—

A. $2\pi\sqrt{\frac{gl}{k^2+l^2}}$ B. $2\pi\sqrt{\frac{mgl}{(k^2+l^2)}}$

C. $2\pi\sqrt{\frac{(k^2+l^2)}{gl}}$ D. $2\pi\sqrt{\frac{(k^2+l^2)}{mgl}}$

25. An inverted pendulum consists of a particle of mass m supported by a rigid massless rod of length l. The pivot 0 has a vertical motion given by z = A sin ωt, the Lagrangian of the system is

A. $\frac{1}{2}ml^2\dot{\theta}^2 + mgl\cos\theta - ml\,A\,\omega^2\sin\omega t\cos\theta$

B. $\frac{1}{2}ml^2\dot{\theta}^2 - mgl\cos\theta - ml\,A\,\omega^2\sin\omega t\cos\theta$

C. $\frac{1}{2}ml^2\dot{\theta}^2 - mgl\cos\theta + ml\,A\,\omega^2\sin\omega t\cos\theta$

D. $\frac{1}{2}ml^2\dot{\theta}^2 + mgl\cos\theta + ml\,A\,\omega^2\sin\omega t\cos\theta$

26. The volume of a mole of liquid $_2He^4$ is 27 × 10^{-6} m^3 and the mass of a $_2He^4$ atom is 6.65 × 10^{-27} kg. Assuming that liquid $_2He^4$ is an ideal boson gas with spin zero, calculate the concentration of the bosons in this volume and the Bose temperature.

A. 3.1 K B. 4.1 K
C. 5.1 K D. 2.1 K

27. Three point charges q, q and $-2q$ are located at $(0, -a, a)$, $(0, a, a)$ and $(0, 0, -a)$ respectively. The net dipole moment of this charge distribution is

A. $4qa\hat{k}$ B. $2qa\hat{k}$
C. $-4qa\hat{i}$ D. $-2qa\hat{j}$

28. The eigen function of a linear hormonic oscillator given below corresponds to energy

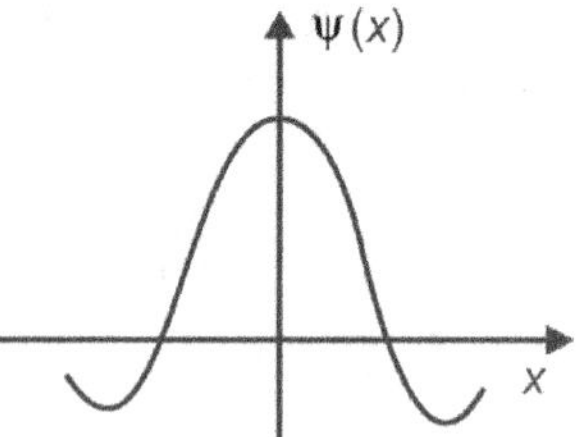

A. $\frac{5}{2}\hbar\omega$ B. $2\hbar\omega$

C. $\frac{3}{2}\hbar\omega$ D. $\frac{1}{2}\hbar\omega$

29. If the degree of freedom of a gas is n, then the ratio of C_p and C_v is

A. $1+\frac{2}{n}$
B. $1+\frac{1}{n}$
C. $1+\frac{1}{2n}$
D. $\frac{2n}{2n+1}$

30. In an experiment, on the measuring of g, using a simple pendulum, the time period was measured with an accuracy of 0.2% while the length was measured with an accuracy of 0.5%. The percentage accuracy in the value of g thus obtained is

A. 0.7%
B. 0.1%
C. 0.25%
D. 0.9%

31. Air in a cylinder is suddenly compressed by a piston, which is then maintained at the same position. After some time, the

A. pressure will increase
B. pressure remains the same
C. pressure will decrease
D. pressure may increase or decrease

32. In a photodiode, the conductivity increases when the material is exposed to light. It is found that conductivity changes only if the wavelength is less than 600 nm. What is the band gap?

A. 1.357 eV
B. 1.127 eV
C. 1.995 eV
D. 1.437 eV

33. A pair of adjacent coils has a mutual inductance of 1.5 H. If the current in one coil changes from 0 to 20A in 0.5 s, what is the change of flux linkage with the other coil?

A. 30 Wb
B. 20 Wb
C. 40 Wb
D. 50 Wb

34. A transistor is connected in CE-configuration in which collector supply is 8 V and the voltage drop across resistance R_C connected in the collector circuit is 0.5 V. The value of R_C = 800 Ω. If α = 0.96, determine the collector-emitter voltage.

A. 2.5 V
B. 4.5 V
C. 6.5 V
D. 7.5 V

35. Two events are separated by a distance of 6×10^5 km and the first event occurs 1s before the second event. The interval between the two events—

A. Is time like
B. Is light like (null)
C. Is space like
D. Cannot be determined from the information given

36. If an amplifier with gain of –1000 and feedback of β = – 0.1 had a gain change of 20% due to temperature, the change in gain of the feedback amplifier would be

A. 10%
B. 5%
C. 0.2%
D. 0.01%

37. $\phi = \frac{e^{z^2} dz}{(z-1)^2}$ where, c is the circle, | z | = z, described the counter clockwise

A. $42\pi e$
B. $1\pi e$
C. $42ie$
D. $4\pi ie$

38. The Fourier transfer in $F(e^{-t}u(t))$ is equal to $\frac{1}{j+j2\pi f}$. Therefore, $F\left[\frac{1}{1+j2\pi t}\right]$ is equal to

A. $e^{f} \cdot u(f)$
B. $e^{-f} \cdot u(f)$
C. $e^{f} \cdot u(-f)$
D. $e^{-f} \cdot u(-f)$

39. The maximum frequency of wave that can propagate with speed v through a one dimensional lattice of lattice constant a is

A. $\frac{v}{a}$
B. $\frac{v}{2a}$
C. $\frac{v}{\pi a}$
D. $\frac{2v}{\pi a}$

40. The spin and parity of ${}_4Be^9$ nucleus, as predicted by the shell model, are respectively

A. $\frac{3}{2}$ and odd
B. $\frac{1}{2}$ and odd
C. $\frac{3}{2}$ and even
D. $\frac{1}{2}$ and even

41. The period of oscillation of a simple pendulum is $T = 2\pi\sqrt{\frac{2}{g}}$. Measured value of L is 20 cm known to 1 mm accuracy and time for 100 oscillations of the pendulum is found to be 90 s using a wrist watch of 1s resolution. The accuracy in the determination of g is

A. 1%	B. 2%
C. 1.5%	D. 3%

42. The wavelength of electromagnetic waves of frequency 4×10^9 Hz in free space is
A. 0.075 m	B. 0.064 m
C. 0.045 m	D. 0.092 m

43. Half life of a radioactive materials is 4 days. After 20 days, the fraction remaining undecayed will be
A. $\frac{1}{20}$	B. $\frac{1}{8}$
C. $\frac{1}{32}$	D. $\frac{1}{16}$

44. In nuclei of $Z < 20$, the ratio of number of neutron to protons is
A. More than 1
B. Less than 1
C. Much greater than 1
D. Nearly equal to 1

45. Germanium and silicon have diamond structure for which the molecules per unit cell are equal to
A. 1	B. 2
C. 4	D. 8

PART-C

46. An electron beam of 4 keV is diffracted through Bragg's angle of 16° for the first maxima. If the energy is increased to 116 keV. The corresponding Bragg's angle of diffraction will be nearly
A. 12°	B. 16°
C. 4°	D. 8°

47. A 10-V zener diode is used to regulate the voltage across a variable load resistor. The input voltage varies between 13 V and 16 V and the load current varies between 10 and 85 mA. The minimum zener current is 15 mA. The value of series resistance R is

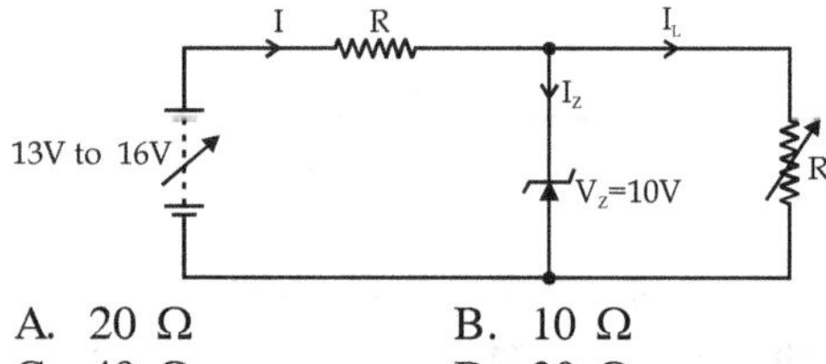

A. 20 Ω	B. 10 Ω
C. 40 Ω	D. 30 Ω

48. Calculate the exact value of emitter current in the circuit shown in the figure. Assume the transistor to be of silicon and $\beta = 100$.

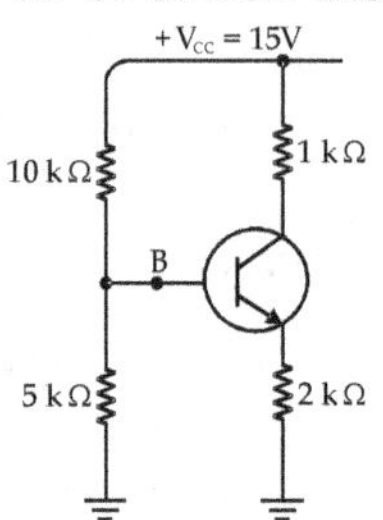

A. 1.11 mA	B. 2.11 mA
C. 3.11 mA	D. 0.11 mA

49. It is claimed that two Cs clocks, if allowed to run for 100 years, free from any disturbance, may differ by only about 0.2 s. What does this imply for the accuracy of the standard Cs clock is measuring a time-interval of 1 s?
A. 10^{-10}	B. 10^{-12}
C. 10^{-11}	D. 10^{-9}

50. A parallel plate capacitor with plate area A and plate separation d, is charged by a constant current I. Consider a plane surface of area A/2 parallel to the plates and situated symmetrically between the plates. The displacement current through this area is
A. $\frac{I}{3}$	B. I
C. $\frac{I}{2}$	D. 2I

51. Consider the differential equation $\frac{d^2x}{dt^2} + 2\frac{dx}{dt} + x = 0$. At time $t = 0$, it is given that $x = 1$ and $\frac{dx}{dt} = 0$. At $t = 1$, the value of x is given by
A. $\frac{1}{e}$	B. $\frac{2}{e}$
C. 1	D. $\frac{3}{e}$

52. A massless spring of force constant k has masses m_1 and m_2 attached to its two ends. The system rests on a horizontal table. The angular vibrational frequency ω of this system is

A. $[k/(m_1 - m_2)]^{1/2}$

B. $[k/(m_1 + m_2)]^{1/2}$

C. $[k(m_1 + m_2)/m_1m_2]^{1/2}$

D. $\left[k\left(\frac{1}{m_1}-\frac{1}{m_2}\right)\right]^{1/2}$

53. The mean free path of the particles of a gas at a temperature T_0 and pressure P_0 has a value λ_0. If the pressure is increased to 1.5 P_0 and the temperature is reduced to 0.75 T_0 the mean free path

A. Is reduced to half

B. Remains unchanged

C. Is equal to 1.125 λ_0

D. Is doubled

54. Current I_1 and I_2 flow when large forward voltage V_1 and V_2 are applied to a semiconductor diode. If $V_1 = 2V_2$, then the value of the reverse saturation current is

A. $\frac{I_1^2}{I_2}$ B. $\frac{I_1^2+I_2^2}{I_1+I_2}$

C. $\frac{I_1I_2}{I_1+I_2}$ D. $\frac{I_2^2}{I_1}$

55. The sublimation curve of solid ammonia is given by $\ln P = 23 - \frac{3750}{T}$ and the vaporization curve of the liquid ammonia is given by $\ln P = 19.5 - \frac{3050}{T}$, where P is in mm of Hg and T is in K. The temperature of the tripple point of ammonia is

A. 3750 K B. 700 K

C. 200 K D. 3050 K

56. For what values of the constant C will be the function $f(x) = Ae^{-ax}$ be an eigen function of the operator $Q = \frac{d}{dx^2} + \frac{2}{x}\frac{d}{dx} + \frac{c}{x}$?

A. $2a$ B. a

C. $3a$ D. $4a$

57. Fermi function, $f(\in) = \frac{1}{e^{(\in-\in_f)/kT}+1}$ gives the probability of occupation of electrons per energy state. Then the probability of number of electrons at absolute temperature (T = 0K), when $\in = \in_f$ is

A. 1 B. 0

C. ∞ D. $\frac{1}{2}$

58. The low frequency gain of low pass filter shown in the given fig. is

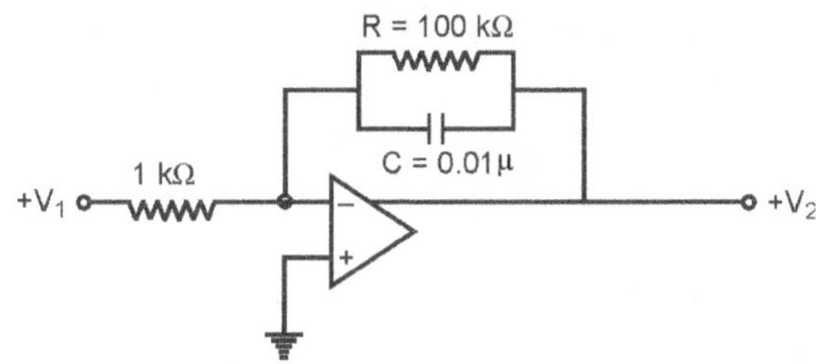

A. 10 dB B. 20 dB

C. 30 dB D. 40 dB

59. If the radiated power of AM transmitter is 10 kW. The power in the carrier for modulation index of 0.6 is nearly

A. 8.24 kW B. 8.47 kW

C. 9.26 kW D. 9.6 kW

60. If the principal quantum number and the azimuthal quantum number in the relativistic model of the atom are 3 and 1 respectively, then the magnitude of semimajor axis b in terms of the semimajor axis a is given by

A. $b = \frac{a}{3}$ B. $b = \frac{2a}{3}$

C. $b = \frac{a}{2}$ D. $b = a$

61. A vector field $\vec{F}$ is given by $\vec{F} = \sin y\hat{i} + x(1+\cos y)\hat{j}$. Find the line integral $\int_c \vec{F}\,\vec{dr}$, where c is the circular path given by $x^2 + y^2 = a^2$.

A. $\frac{\pi a^2}{2}$ B. $\frac{\pi a^2}{3}$

C. $\frac{\pi a^2}{4}$ D. πa^2

62. The wavelength of the k_α line of Ag is 0.563 Å. The radiation from the Ag target is analysed with a Bragg spectrometer using a calcite crystal (a simple cube of lattice constant 3.02945 Å). Determine the angle of reflection for the first order.

A. 3.33° B. 4.33°
C. 5.33° D. 2.33°

63. Calculate the current through 48Ω resistor in the circuit shown in fig. (*i*). Assume the diodes to be of silicon and forward resistance of each diode is 1Ω.

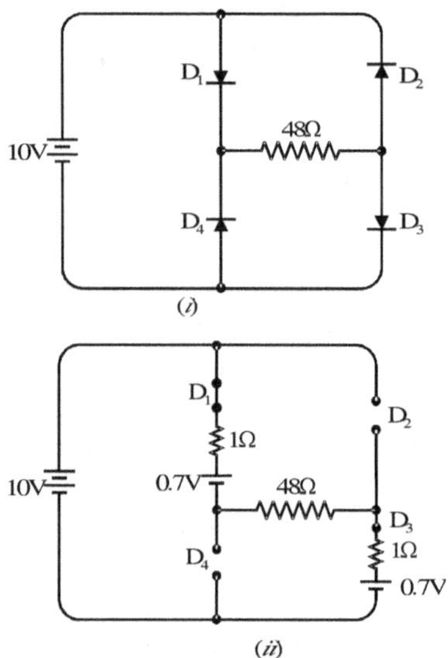

A. 172 mA B. 0.72 mA
C. 2.72 mA D. 3.72 mA

64. Determine I_D and V_{GS} for the JFET with voltage-divider bias in given figure, given that for this particular JFET the internal parameter values are such that V_D = 7 V.

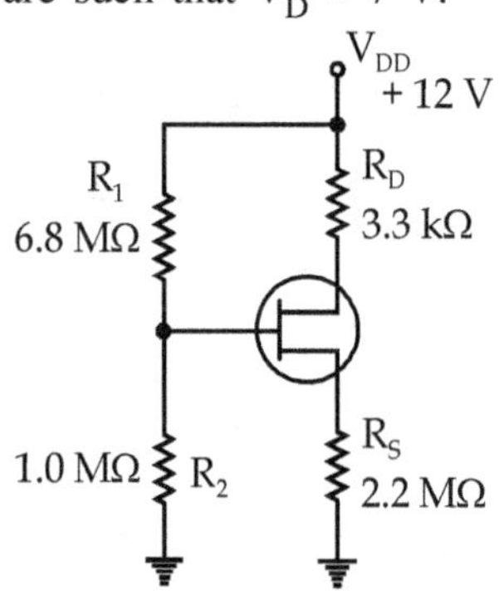

A. 1.25 mA, –1.6 V
B. 2.25 mA, –2.5 V
C. 1.52 mA, –1.8 V
D. 0.52 mA, –2.7 V

65. Obtain the Fourier transform of a rectangular pulse of duration 2 seconds and having a magnitude of 10 volts as shown.

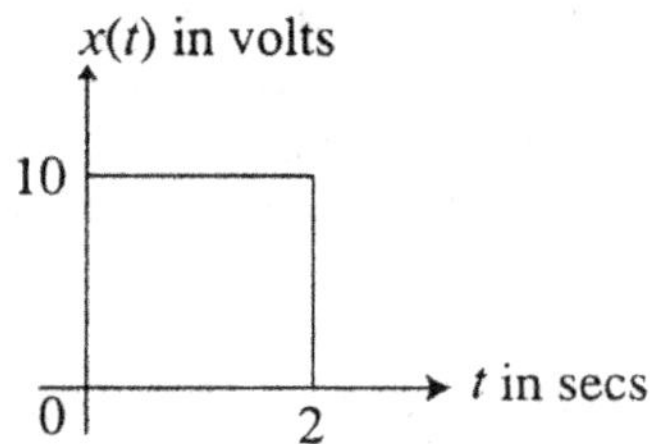

A. $10\, e^{-j\omega} \sin c(\omega)$ B. $15\, e^{-j\omega} \sin c(\omega)$
C. $25\, e^{-j\omega} \cos c(\omega)$ D. $20\, e^{-j\omega} \sin c(\omega)$

66. Rest mass energy of an electron is 0.51 MeV. A moving electron has a kinetic energy of 9.69 MeV. The ratio of the mass of the moving electron to its rest mass is

A. 19 : 1 B. 20 : 1
C. 1 : 19 D. 1 : 20

67. A 75 ohm transmission line is first short terminated. When the short is replaced by a resistive load R_L, the minima locations are not altered and the VSWR is measured to be 3. What is the value of R_L?

A. 25 ohms B. 50 ohms
C. 225 ohms D. 250 ohms

68. Efficiency for engine, following the given curve if in an isothermal expansion the gas volume increases in the same proportion

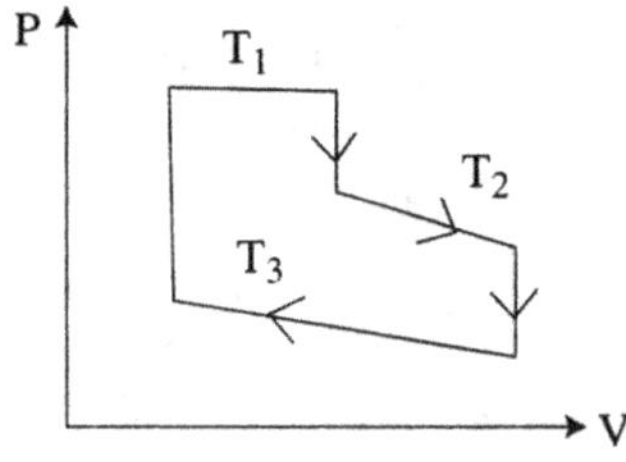

A. $1 - \frac{T_3}{T_1 + T_2}$ B. $1 - \frac{2T_3}{T_1 + T_2}$

C. $\frac{T_3}{T_1 + T_2}$ D. $\frac{2T_3}{T_1 + T_2}$

69. An Op-amp has the following input parameters : V_{OS} = 6 mV, I_{OS} = 200 *n*A and I_B = 1.5 μA. The amplifier has a gain of 10, with R_F = 100 kΩ, R_1 = 10 kΩ and R_3 = 9 kΩ.

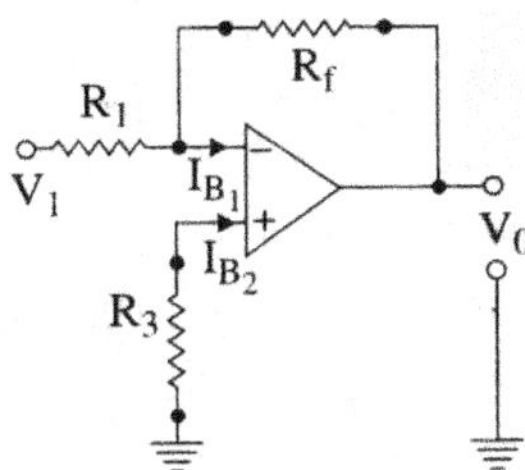

The output offset voltage is

A. 68 V B. 68 mV
C. 86 V D. 86 mV

70. Light described by the equation E = (90 V/m) [sin (6.28 × 10^{15} s^{-1}) *t* + sin(12.56 × 10^{15} s^{-1}) *t*] is incident on a metal surface. The work function of the metal is 2.0 eV. Maximum kinetic energy of the photoelectrons will be

A. 2.14 eV B. 4.28 eV
C. 6.28 eV D. 12.56 eV

71. Consider a doped semiconductor having the electron and the hole mobilities μ_n and μ_p, respectively. Its intrinsic carrier density is n_i. The hole concentration P for which the conductivity is minimum at a given temperature is

A. $n_i\sqrt{\dfrac{\mu_n}{\mu_p}}$ B. $n_h\sqrt{\dfrac{\mu_p}{\mu_n}}$

C. $n_i\sqrt{\dfrac{\mu_p}{\mu_n}}$ D. $n_h\sqrt{\dfrac{\mu_n}{\mu_p}}$

72. $^{60}_{27}Co$ is a radioactive nucleus of half-life 2 *l*n2 × 10^8 s. The activity of 10 g of $^{60}_{27}Co$ in disintegrations per second is

A. $\dfrac{1}{5}\times 10^{10}$ B. 5 × 10^{10}

C. $\dfrac{1}{5}\times 10^{14}$ D. 5 × 10^{14}

73. A parallel plate capacitive is connected to a battery and charged to a potential difference V. Another capacitor of capacitance 2 C is similarly charged to a potential difference 2 V. The charging battery is then disconnected in parallel to each other in such a way that the positive terminal of one is connected to the negative terminal of the other. The final energy of the configuration is

A. zero B. $\dfrac{3}{2}CV^2$

C. $\dfrac{25}{6}CV^2$ D. $\dfrac{9}{2}CV^2$

74. Two circular coils can be arranged in any of the three situations shown in fig. Their mutual inductance will be

(a)

(b)

(c)

A. maximum in situation (a)
B. maximum in situation (b)
C. maximum in situation (c)
D. same in all situations

75. Consider the rectangular cavity as shown in fig. If *a* < *b* < *c*, then the dominent mode is

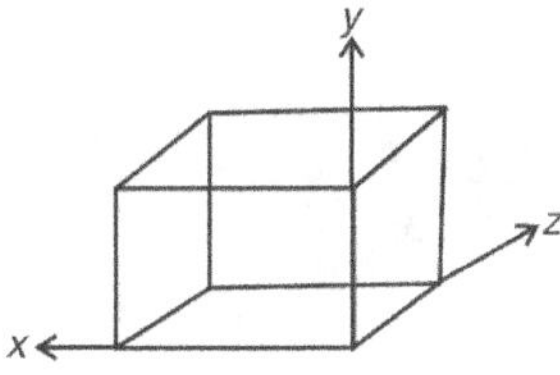

A. TE_{011} B. TM_{110}
C. TE_{101} D. TM_{101}

ANSWERS

1	2	3	4	5	6	7	8	9	10
B	D	B	B	A	A	A	C	A	B

11	12	13	14	15	16	17	18	19	20
A	B	C	C	B	D	A	A	B	D
21	22	23	24	25	26	27	28	29	30
D	A	A	C	C	A	A	A	A	D
31	32	33	34	35	36	37	38	39	40
C	C	A	D	C	C	D	C	C	A
41	42	43	44	45	46	47	48	49	50
D	A	C	D	D	C	D	B	C	C
51	52	53	54	55	56	57	58	59	60
B	C	A	D	C	A	D	D	B	A
61	62	63	64	65	66	67	68	69	70
D	C	A	C	D	B	C	B	D	C
71	72	73	74	75					
A	B	B	A	A					

EXPLANATORY ANSWERS

1. No. of students who appeared in a least two subjects

$= 35 + 30 + 10 + 25$

$= 100$

2. According to Ranjana the date of birth of her elder brother = April (14 and 15) and according to her mother the date of birth of her son = April (15 and 16).

Hence, the date of birth of Ranjana's elder brother is 15th April.

3.

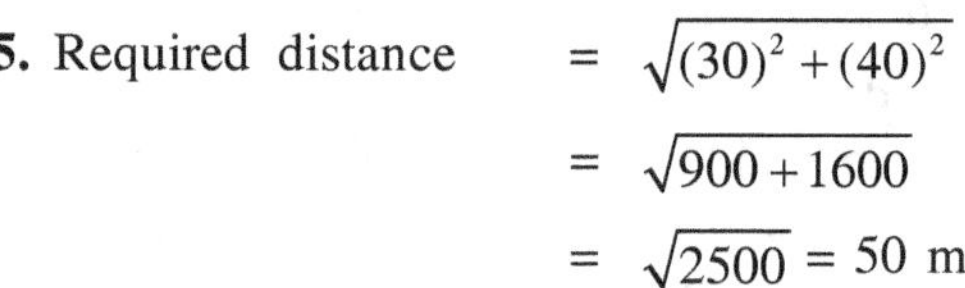

Nalini's brother (Best player)	Nalini's son (worst player)
Nalini's daughter	Nalini

4. $a = \sqrt{3}, r = \dfrac{1/\sqrt{3}}{\sqrt{3}} = \dfrac{1}{3}$

$$T_n = \frac{1}{243\sqrt{3}}$$

$$T_n = ar^{n-1}$$

$$\frac{1}{243\sqrt{3}} = \sqrt{3}\left(\frac{1}{3}\right)^{n-1}$$

$$\frac{1}{243 \times \sqrt{3} \times \sqrt{3}} = \left(\frac{1}{3}\right)^{n-1}$$

$$\left(\frac{1}{3}\right)^6 = \left(\frac{1}{3}\right)^{n-1}$$

$\Rightarrow 6 = n - 1$

$\Rightarrow n = 7$

5. Required distance $= \sqrt{(30)^2 + (40)^2}$

$= \sqrt{900 + 1600}$

$= \sqrt{2500} = 50$ m

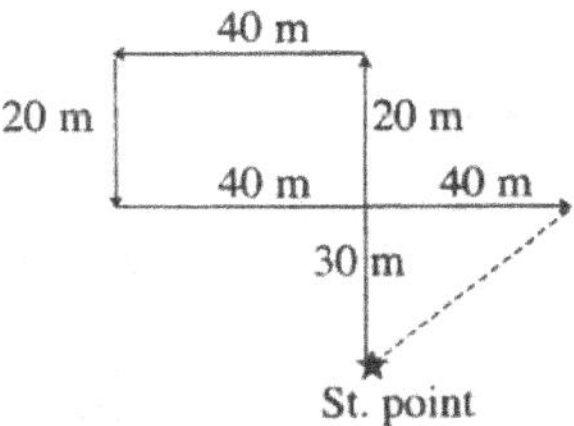

6. Area of shaded portion

= area of ΔABC – area of ΔADE

ABC being an equilateral ΔBAC = 60°

Area of ΔABC = $\sqrt{3}r^2$

Area of the sector ADE = $\dfrac{\pi r^2}{360} \times 60° = \dfrac{\pi r^2}{6}$

Shaded area = $\sqrt{3}r^2 - \dfrac{\pi r^2}{6}$

$= \left(\sqrt{3} - \dfrac{\pi}{6}\right)r^2$

7. The smaller 27 pieces of the cube will be cut in the manner that :

1. 8 pieces will be painted on 3 sides,
2. 12 pieces on 2 sides,
3. 6 pieces on 1 side, and
4. 1 piece will not have paint at all.

Diagrammatically, the explanation taking one side of the cube will be :

a	b	a
b	c	b
a	b	a

1. 'a' are the corner pieces [$4 \times 2 = 8$]
2. 'b' are the centre pieces of the cornered sides [$4 \times 3 = 12$]
3. 'c' is the centred piece [$1 \times 6 = 6$]
4. The interior blank piece will be only 1.

8. In a linear relationship, if one variable increases by a constant amount the corresponding increase in the order of the variable is also constant.

9. Decrease in expression

$$= xy^2 - \frac{80}{100} \times x\left(\frac{80}{100}y\right)^2$$

$$= xy^2 - \frac{64}{125}xy^2$$

$$= \frac{61xy^2}{125}$$

Hence, decrease per cent

$$= \frac{61xy^2}{125 \times xy^2} \times 100 = 48.8\%$$

10. Let they meet x hrs after 10 AM

Distance covered by A in x hours = $20x$ km

Distance covered by B in $(x - 1)$ hours $= 25\ (x - 1)$ km

Hence,

$20x + 25\ (x - 1) = 110$

$20x + 25x - 25 = 110$

$x = 3$

Thus, they meet at 10 AM.

11. In every 2 minutes, he is able to ascend $2 - 1 = 1$ metre. This way he ascends upto 12 metres because when he reaches at the top, he does not slip down. Thus, upto 12 metres he takes $12 \times 2 = 24$ minutes and for the last 2 metres he takes 1 minute. Therefore, he takes $24 + 1 = 25$ minutes to reach the top.

12. Let the radii of the three circles be r.

So, ABC is an equilateral triangle,

$$AB = BC = CA = 2r$$

$$\text{Area of triangle ABC} = \frac{1}{2}\text{base} \times \text{height}$$

$$= \frac{1}{2} \times 2r \times \sqrt{3}r$$

$$= \sqrt{3}r^2$$

Area of each of the circle segments AMP, BMN, CPN

$$= \text{Area of circle} \times \frac{60}{360}$$

$$= \pi r^2 \times \frac{1}{6}$$

Now, area of shaded portion

= Area of triangle ABC – area of 3 circle segments AMP, BMN and CPN

$$\text{So, shaded area} = \sqrt{3}r^2 - 3\pi r^2 \times \frac{1}{6}$$

$$= r^2\left(\sqrt{3} - \frac{\pi}{2}\right)$$

$$= r^2 \times 0.16$$

$$= 0.64 \text{ (given)}$$

$$r^2 = \frac{0.64}{0.16} = 4$$

$$r = 2$$

13.

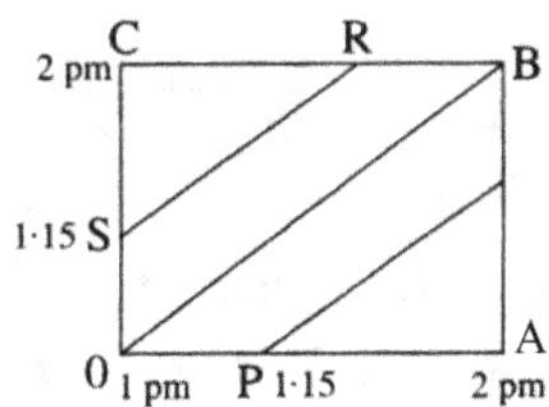

OB is the line when both Anna and Panas arrive at the same time

Total sample space = $60 \times 60 = 3600$

Favourable cases = Area of OABC –2 (Area of SRC)

$$3600 - 2\left(\frac{1}{2}\times 45\times 45\right) = 1575$$

$$\text{Probability} = \frac{1575}{3000} = \frac{7}{16}$$

14. 1, 2 and 3's mean marks are equal but
1's range is 60 – 20 = 40
2's range is 55 – 20 = 35
3's range is 45 – 35 = 10
Standard deviation will be maximum in case of 1 then comes 2 and least SD will be there in case of 3.

15. Position of Mohan on the basis of new arrangement = (65 – 33) + 1 = 33rd

16. The half-life of ^{14}C is 5700 years, because of this it is only reliable for dating objects up to 60,000 years. Objects older then this will have most ^{14}C decayed.

17. $\text{Reqd. number} = \frac{n(n-1)}{2}$

$$= \frac{8\times(8-1)}{2}$$

$$= \frac{8\times 7}{2} = 28$$

18. The only son of the father of the father of Savita is the father of Savita. So that man is the father of Savita.
Hence, Savita is the daughter of man.

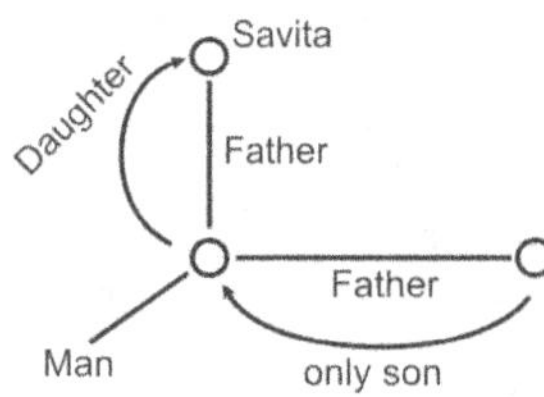

19. AB = 6 unit

Perpendicular from C on,
AB = 3 – 1 = 2 unit
∴ Area of triangle ABC

A (–2, 1)
B (4, 1)
C (2, 3)

$$= 6 \times 2 \times \frac{1}{2}$$

$$= 6 \text{ units}$$

20. Let the circumference of the circular field be S km. The speed for first round be 10 km/hr the car will take $\frac{S}{10}$ hrs to complete the first round. Similarly, it will take $\frac{S}{20}$ hrs to cover the second and $\frac{S}{60}$ hrs to cover the third round.
Total time taken to complete the three rounds

$$= \frac{S}{10} + \frac{S}{20} + \frac{S}{60} = \frac{S}{6}$$

Total distance in three rounds is 3S km.
So, average speed for three round trip

$$= \frac{3S \text{ km}}{S/6 \text{ hr}} = 18 \text{ km/hr}$$

21. Using Gauss-Divergens theorem, we have

$$\iint_S \vec{r}.\vec{ds} = \iiint_v di\text{V}\cdot\vec{r}d\text{V}$$

$$\iiint_v di\text{V}\cdot\vec{r}\,d\text{V} = \int_0^L\int_0^L\int_0^L\left(\hat{i}\frac{\partial}{\partial x} + \hat{j}\frac{\partial}{\partial y} + \hat{k}\frac{\partial}{\partial z}\right)$$

$$= \int_0^L\int_0^L\int_0^L 3\,dx\,dy\,dz\,\left(\hat{i}x + \hat{j}y + \hat{k}z\right)$$

$$= \iint_s \vec{r}.\vec{ds} = 3L^3$$

22. Characteristic equation of A is

$$|A - \lambda I| = \begin{bmatrix}\cos\theta - \lambda & -\sin\theta \\ \sin\theta & \cos\theta - \lambda\end{bmatrix} = 0$$

or $(\cos\theta - \lambda)^2 + \sin^2\theta = 0$

$\Rightarrow \lambda^2 - 2\lambda\cos\theta + 1 = 0$

Solving this, we get

$$\lambda = \frac{2\cos\theta \pm \sqrt{4\cos^2\theta - 4}}{2}$$

$$= \cos\theta \pm i\sin\theta$$

$\therefore\ \lambda = e^{\pm i\theta}$

23. Let $A = \begin{bmatrix}0 & 2\beta & \gamma \\ \alpha & \beta & -\gamma \\ \alpha & -\beta & \gamma\end{bmatrix}$

On transposing A, we have

$$A' = \begin{bmatrix}0 & \alpha & \alpha \\ 2\beta & \beta & -\beta \\ \gamma & -\gamma & \gamma\end{bmatrix}$$

If A is orthogonal,

$$\text{then } AA' = I \begin{bmatrix} 0 & 2\beta & \gamma \\ \alpha & \beta & -\gamma \\ \alpha & -\beta & \gamma \end{bmatrix} \begin{bmatrix} 0 & \alpha & \alpha \\ 2\beta & \beta & -\beta \\ \gamma & -\gamma & \gamma \end{bmatrix}$$

$$\text{or} \begin{bmatrix} 4\beta^2+\gamma^2 & 2\beta^2-\gamma^2 & -2\beta^2+\gamma^2 \\ 2\beta^2-\gamma^2 & \alpha^2+\beta^2+\gamma^2 & \alpha^2-\beta^2-\gamma^2 \\ -2\beta^2+\gamma^2 & \alpha^2-\beta^2-\gamma^2 & \alpha^2+\beta^2+\gamma^2 \end{bmatrix}$$

$$= \begin{bmatrix} 1 & 0 & 0 \\ 0 & 1 & 0 \\ 1 & 0 & 1 \end{bmatrix} = \begin{bmatrix} 1 & 0 & 0 \\ 0 & 1 & 0 \\ 0 & 0 & 1 \end{bmatrix}$$

Solving, we get

$$\left.\begin{matrix} 4\beta^2+\gamma^2=1 \\ 2\beta^2-\gamma^2=0 \end{matrix}\right\} \Rightarrow \beta = \pm\frac{1}{\sqrt{6}}, \gamma = \pm\frac{1}{\sqrt{3}}$$

But $\alpha^2+\beta^2+\gamma^2 = 1$

$$\text{as,} \quad \beta = \pm\frac{1}{\sqrt{6}}, \gamma = \pm\frac{1}{\sqrt{3}}, \alpha = \pm\frac{1}{\sqrt{2}}$$

24. For compound pendulum

$$T = \frac{2\pi}{\omega} = 2\pi\sqrt{\frac{I}{mgl}}$$

$$\text{where} \quad \omega = \sqrt{\frac{mgl}{I}}$$

If $k \to$ Radius of gyration, then

$$I = mk^2 + ml^2$$

$$\Rightarrow \quad T = 2\pi\sqrt{\frac{mk^2+ml^2}{mgl}}$$

$$\text{or} \quad T = 2\pi\sqrt{\frac{k^2+l^2}{gl}}$$

25. Kinetic energy $= \frac{1}{2}I\omega^2$

$$= \frac{1}{2}ml^2\theta^2$$

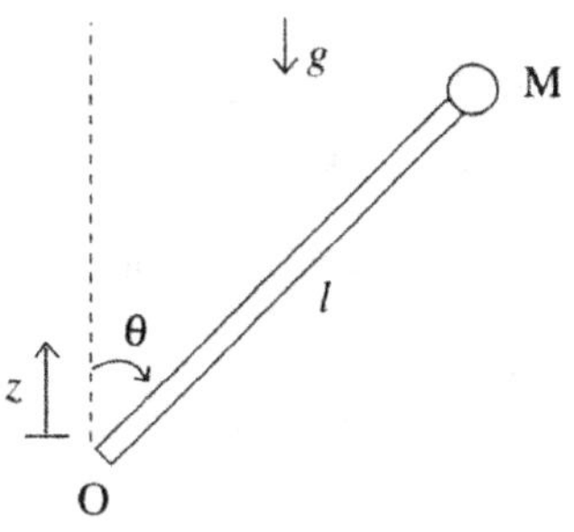

Now acceleration in vertical z-direction due to the motion of pivot

$$\ddot{z} = A\omega^2 \sin\omega t$$

Net acceleration

$$a = g - \ddot{z} = g - A\omega^2 \sin\omega t$$

Then potential energy

$$V = mal\cos\theta$$

$$= m(g - A\omega^2\sin\omega t)\, l\cos\theta$$

$$\therefore \quad L = T - V$$

$$L = \frac{1}{2}ml^2\dot{\theta}^2 - mgl\cos\theta + mlA\omega^2\sin\omega t\cos\theta$$

26. One mole of an ideal boson gas contains 6.02×10^{23} atoms. Therefore, the concentration is

$$\frac{N}{V} = \frac{6.02\times10^{23}}{27\times10^{-6}m^3} = 2.2\times10^{28}\ m^{-3}$$

Since the spin is zero,

$$g_s = 2s+1 = 1 \text{ and } m = 6.65\times10^{-27}\ kg$$

Substitute these values in

$$T_b = \frac{2\pi\hbar^2}{mk}\left(\frac{N}{2.612\times gV}\right) = \frac{3.31\hbar^2}{mk}\left(\frac{N}{V}\right)^{2/3} = 3.1\,K$$

27. Location of charge,

$$x_1 = 0\hat{i} - a\hat{j} + a\hat{k}$$

$$x_2 = 0\hat{i} + a\hat{j} + a\hat{k}$$

$$x_3 = 0\hat{i} + o\hat{j} - a\hat{k}$$

Net dipole moment,

$$= qx_1 + qx_2 + (-2q)x_3$$

$$= -qa\hat{j} + qa\hat{k} + qa\hat{j} + qa\hat{k} + 2q\hat{k}$$

$$= 4qa\hat{k}$$

28. For linear harmonic oscillator, energy

$$E = \left(n+\frac{1}{2}\right)\hbar\omega$$

For ground state, one peak, $n = 0$ and $E = \frac{1}{2}\hbar\omega$

For three peaks, $n = 2$

$$E = \left(2 + \frac{1}{2}\right)\hbar\omega$$

$$E = \frac{5}{2}\hbar\omega$$

29. Molar specific heat

$$C_v = \frac{dU}{dT} = \frac{d}{dT}\left(\frac{n}{2}RT\right) = \frac{n}{2}R$$

According to Mayer's relations

$$C_P - C_v = R$$

$$C_P = C_v + R$$

$$= \frac{n}{2}R + R = R\left(\frac{n}{2} + 1\right)$$

$$\therefore \quad \frac{C_p}{C_v} = \frac{\left(\frac{n}{2}+1\right)}{\frac{n}{2}R} = 1 + \frac{2}{n}$$

30. As, $\quad T = 2\pi\sqrt{\frac{l}{g}}$

$$\therefore \quad g = 4\pi^2 \frac{l}{T^2}$$

$$\frac{\Delta g}{g} \times 100 = \frac{\Delta l}{l} \times 100 + 2 \times \frac{\Delta T}{T} \times 100$$

$$= 0.5\% + 2 \times 0.2\%$$

$$= 0.9\%$$

31. Sudden compression increases inside temperature. After sometime, heat flows out. This decreases temperature of air. As V is constant, so pressure inside decrease ($P \propto T$).

32. As, $\quad E_g = \frac{hc}{\lambda}$

$$= \frac{6.6 \times 10^{-34} \times 3 \times 10^8}{620 \times 10^{-9}} J$$

$$= \frac{6.6 \times 3 \times 10^{-17}}{620 \times 1.6 \times 10^{-19}} eV$$

$$= 1.995 \text{ eV}$$

33. Given,

$M = 1.5$ H, $I_1 = 0A$, $I_2 = 20A$, $t = 0.5$ s

As, $\quad \varepsilon = \frac{-d\theta}{dt} = -\frac{LdI}{dt}$

$\therefore \quad d\theta = L\,dI = 1.5 \times (20 - 0)$

$= 30$ Wb

34. From fig., we see that the CE connection with various values

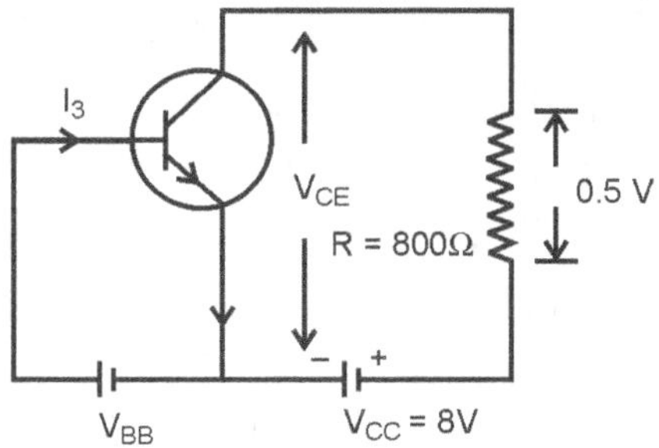

$\therefore$ CE voltage,

$$V_{CE} = V_{CC} - 0.5$$

$$= 8 - 0.5$$

$$= 7.5 \text{ V}$$

35. $\frac{r}{c} = \frac{6 \times 10^5 \text{ km/s}}{3 \times 10^8 \text{ m/s}}$

$$= \frac{6 \times 10^8 \text{ km/s}}{3 \times 10^8 \text{ m}} = 2 \text{ s}$$

event $t_2 - t_1 = 1$ s

$$\frac{r}{c} > 1$$

Hence it is a space like.

36. $A_f = \frac{A}{1 + A\beta}$

$$\frac{\partial A_f}{\partial A} = \frac{(1 + A\beta) - A\beta}{(1 + A\beta)^2} = \frac{1}{(1 + A\beta)^2}$$

$$\partial A_f = \frac{\partial A}{(1 + A\beta)^2}$$

$$\frac{\partial A_f}{A_f} = \frac{\partial A/A}{1 + A\beta}$$

$$\frac{\partial A_f}{A_f} \times 100 = \frac{200 \times 100}{1000 \times 10} = 0.2\%$$

37. Poles : $(z-1)^2 = 0$

$z = 1$ of order 2

Hence, reduce.

$$= \underset{z\to 1}{\text{Lt}} \frac{d}{d_z}\left[(z-1)^2 \frac{e^{z^2}}{(z-1)^2}\right]$$

$$\lim_{z\to 1}\left[(2z)e^{z^2}\right] = 2e$$

Integral = $2\pi i\ (2e) = 4\pi ie$

38. Using duality property of Fourier transform, we have

$g(t) \leftrightarrow G(f)$

Then $G(t) \leftrightarrow g(-f)$

Therefore, if $e^{-\eta}u(t)\frac{1}{1+j2\pi f}$

Then, $\frac{1}{1+f2\pi t} \leftrightarrow ef \cdot u(-f)$

39. The speed of longitudinal wave propagating in the lattice

$$v = \sqrt{\frac{\text{Max force on the atoms}}{\text{Mass per unit length}}}$$

$$= \sqrt{\frac{F_{max}}{\rho}}$$

From Hooke's law, $F_{max} = \beta a$

(where a is maximum displacement)

$$v = \sqrt{\frac{\beta a}{m/a}} = a\sqrt{\frac{\beta}{m}} \qquad ...(1)$$

Hence the maximum frequency υ_m of the wave which can propagate through each atomic array (or lattice) where

$$\upsilon_{max} = \frac{\omega_{max}}{2\pi}$$

$$= \frac{1}{2\pi}\times 2\sqrt{\frac{\beta}{m}}$$

$$= \frac{1}{\pi}\sqrt{\frac{\beta}{m}}$$

From equation (1)

$$\text{max freq} = \upsilon_{max} = \frac{1}{\pi}\frac{v}{a}$$

40. $_4Be^9$

Number of proton = 4

Number of neutron = 5

Unfilled state = $^1P_{3/2}$

According to shell model spin = $\frac{3}{2}$

Parity = $(-1)^L$

= $(-1)^1 = -1$

Odd parity.

41. As, $T = 2\pi\sqrt{\frac{L}{g}}$

or $T^2 = 4\pi^2 \frac{L}{g} \Rightarrow g = \frac{4\pi^2 L}{T^2}$

$$\therefore \frac{\Delta g}{g}\times 100 = \frac{\Delta L}{L}\times 100 + 2\times\frac{\Delta T}{T}\times 100$$

Now, L = 20 cm, ΔL = 1 mm, T = 0.1 cm, T for 100 oscillation = 90 s, ΔT = 1 s

$$\therefore \frac{\Delta g}{g}\times 100 = \frac{0.1}{20}\times 100 + \frac{2\times 1}{90}\times 100$$

= 0.5 + 2.22 = 2.72% = 3%

42. As, $\lambda = \frac{C}{v}$

$$= \frac{3\times 10^8}{4\times 10^9} = \frac{3}{40}\text{m}$$

= 0.075

43. We know

$$T_{1/2} = \frac{0.6931}{\lambda}$$

Since $T_{1/2}$ = 4 days

$$\lambda = \left(\frac{0.6931}{4}\right)\text{days}^{-1}$$

From $N = N_0 e^{-\lambda t}$

$$t = \frac{1}{\lambda}\log_e\frac{N_0}{N}$$

$$20 = \left(\frac{4}{0.6931}\right) \times 2.3026 \log_{10} \frac{N_0}{N}$$

or $$\log_{10} \frac{N_0}{N} = \frac{20}{4} \times \frac{0.6931}{2.3026}$$

$$\log_{10} \frac{N_0}{N} = 1.5003$$

or $$\frac{N_0}{N} = \text{antilog } (1.5003) = 31.72$$

or $$\frac{N_0}{N} \approx 32$$

or $$N = \frac{N_0}{32}$$

44. Light nuclei (Z < 20) contain approximately equal numbers of neutrons and protons, while in heavier nuclei the proportion of neutrons become progressively greater.

45. Diamond cubic structure, is a fcc structure with a basis of two atoms and in this structure each atom has 4 nearest neighbours.

∴ The total number of atoms in a unit cell is $\frac{1}{8} \times 8 + \frac{1}{2} \times 6 + 4 = 8$

46. Bragg's diffraction condition is

$$n\lambda = 2d \sin \theta \quad ...(1)$$

For $$E = 4 \text{ K eV}$$

we have $$E = h\upsilon = \frac{hc}{\lambda}$$

or $$\lambda_1 = \frac{hc}{E_1}$$

Also here $n = 1$, $\theta_1 = 16°$

$$\lambda_1 = 2d \sin 16°$$

or $$\frac{hc}{4\text{KeV}} = 2d \sin 16° \quad ..(2)$$

If E is increased to 16 KeV,

then $$\lambda_2 = \frac{hc}{16\text{ KeV}}$$

$$\frac{hc}{16\text{ KeV}} = 2d \sin \theta \quad ...(3)$$

Divide (2) by (3)

$$\frac{\frac{hc}{4\text{KeV}}}{\frac{hc}{16\text{ KeV}}} = \frac{2d \sin 16°}{2d \sin \theta}$$

or $$\frac{\sin 16°}{\sin \theta} = \frac{16}{4}$$

or $$\sin \theta = \frac{0.2867}{4}$$

$$\sin \theta = 0.0717$$

or $$\theta = \sin^{-1} (0.0717)$$
$$= 4°4'$$

or $$= 4°$$

47. The zener will conduct minimum current (*i.e.*, 15 mA) when input voltage is minimum (*i.e.*, 13 V)

$$R = \frac{E_i - E_o}{(I_Z)_{min} + (I_L)_{max}}$$

$$= \frac{(13-10)\text{V}}{(15+85)\text{mA}} = \frac{3\text{V}}{100\text{mA}} = 30\,\Omega$$

48. In order to obtain accurate value of emitter current I_E, we shall replace the bias portion of the circuit shown in figure (*i*) by its Thevenin's equivalent. Figure (*ii*) shows the desired circuit.

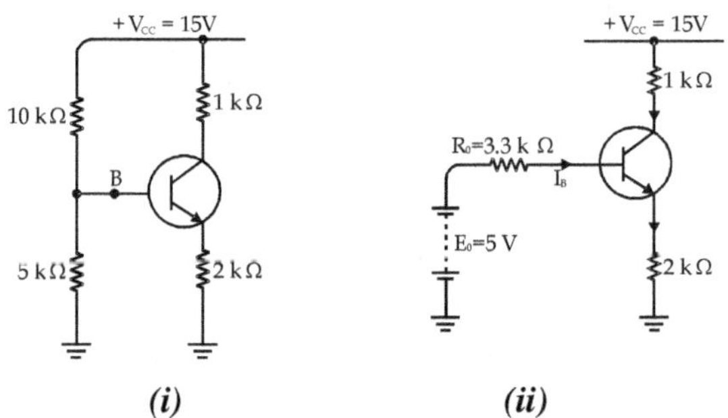

(*i*) (*ii*)

Looking from the base terminal B to the left, Thevenin's voltage E_0 is given by;

$$E_o = \frac{R_2}{R_1 + R_2} V_{CC} = \frac{5}{10+5} \times 15 = 5\text{V}$$

Again looking from the base terminal *B* to the left, Thevenin's resistance R_o is given by;

$$R_o = \frac{R_1 R_2}{R_1 + R_2} = \frac{10 \times 5}{10+5} = \frac{50}{15} = 3.3\text{k}\Omega$$

Applying Kirchhoff's voltage law to the base-emitter loop [see fig. (ii)],

$$E_o = I_B R_o + V_{BE} + I_E R_E$$

Since $I_E \simeq I_C$, therefore, $I_B = I_E/\beta$

$$E_o = \frac{I_E}{\beta}R_o + V_{BE} + I_E R_E = I_E\left(\frac{R_o}{\beta} + R_E\right) + V_{BE}$$

$$I_E = \frac{E_o - V_{BE}}{\frac{R_o}{\beta} + R_E} = \frac{5-0.7}{\frac{3.3}{100}+2}$$

(For *Si* transistor, $V_{BE} = 0.7$ V)

$$= \frac{4.3\,V}{2.033\,k\Omega} = 2.11\,mA$$

49. Given, $\Delta t = 0.02$ s

t = 100 years = 100 × 365.25 × 86,400 s

Fractional error

$$= \frac{\Delta t}{t} = \frac{0.02}{100 \times 365.25 \times 86400}$$

$= 0.63 \times 10^{-11}$

Hence, their is an accuracy of 10^{-11} part in 1s.

50. Let charge on capacitor plates at any instant be q. Then electric field between the capacitor plates will be

$$E = \frac{\sigma}{\epsilon_0} = \frac{q}{\epsilon_0 A}$$

flux through the area A/2 will be

$$\phi_E = E \cdot \frac{A}{2} = \frac{q}{\epsilon_0 A}\cdot\frac{A}{2} = \frac{q}{2\epsilon_0}$$

∴ The displacement current is

$$I_D = \epsilon_0 \frac{d\phi_E}{dt}$$

$$= \epsilon_0 \cdot \frac{I}{2\epsilon_0}\cdot\frac{dq}{dt} = \frac{I}{2}$$

51. A.E. ⇒ $D^2 + 2D + 1 = 0$

$$\text{Roots} = \frac{-2 \pm \sqrt{4-4}}{2}$$

= –1 of order 2

Solution $x = (A + Bt)\,e^{-t}$

$$\frac{dx}{dt} = Be^{-t} - (A + Bt)\,e^{-t}$$

At $t = 0$ and $\frac{dx}{dt} = 0$

$0 = B - A$ ... (i)

Also at $t = 0$, $x = 1$

∴ $1 = A$

From *(i)* $B = 1$

Solution $x = (1 + t)\,e^{-t}$

at $t = 1$, $x = (1 + 1)\,e^{-1}$

$= 2/e$

52. According to question,

m_1 —ooooo— m_2

$q_1 \rightarrow$ $q_2 \rightarrow$

The kinetic energy,

$$T = \frac{1}{2}m_1\dot{q}_1^2 + \frac{1}{2}m_2\dot{q}_2^2$$

So that the T matrix is diagonal

$$T = \begin{pmatrix} m_1 & 0 \\ 0 & m_2 \end{pmatrix} \quad ...(1)$$

The potential energy

$$V = \frac{1}{2}k(q_2 - q_1)^2$$

$$= \frac{1}{2}k(q_2^2 + q_1^2 - 2q_2q_1)$$

Hence, the V matrix has the form

$$V = \begin{pmatrix} k & -k \\ -k & k \end{pmatrix} \quad ...(2)$$

Combining these two matrices, the secular equation appears as

$$|V - \omega^2 T| = \begin{vmatrix} k - \omega^2 m_1 & -k \\ -k & k - \omega^2 m_2 \end{vmatrix} = 0$$

With solution,

⇒ $(k - \omega^2 m_1)(k - \omega^2 m_2) - k^2 = 0$

$k^2 - \omega^2 m_1 k - \omega^2 m_2 k + \omega^4 m_1 m_2 - k^2 = 0$

⇒ $m_1 k + m_2 k - \omega^2 m_1 m_2 = 0$

or $\omega^2 = \frac{k(m_1 + m_2)}{m_1 m_2}$

or $\omega = \sqrt{\left(\frac{k(m_1 + m_2)}{m_1 m_2}\right)}$

53. The mean free path

$$\lambda_1 = \frac{kT_0}{\sqrt{2}\pi\, d^2 P_0}$$

or $$\lambda_1 \propto \frac{T_0}{P_0}$$

Now $$T_0 \rightarrow 0.75\ T_0$$
$$P_0 \rightarrow 1.5\ P_0$$

$$\lambda_2 \propto \frac{0.75\ T_0}{1.5\ P_0}$$

$$\frac{\lambda_1}{\lambda_2} = \frac{T_0}{P_0} \times \frac{1.5\ P_0}{0.75\ T_0}$$

$$\frac{\lambda_1}{\lambda_2} = 2$$

or $$\lambda_2 = \frac{\lambda_1}{2}$$

54. We have $$I = I_0\, e^{eV/kT}$$

$\therefore$ $$I_1 = I_0\, e^{eV_1/kT}$$

& $$I_2 = I_0\, e^{eV_2/kT}$$

Since $$V_1 = 2V_2$$
$$I_1 = I_0\, e^{2eV_2/kT}$$

or $$= \frac{I_1}{I_2} = \frac{e^{2eV_2/kT}}{e^{eV_2/kT}} = e^{eV_2/kT}$$

or $$\frac{I_1}{I_2} = \frac{I_2}{I_0} \quad [\text{Since } I_2 = I_0 e^{eV_2/kT}]$$

or $$I_0 = \frac{I_2^2}{I_1}$$

55. At triple point temperature T_t can be found using any of the two relation and must be unique

$$19.5 - \frac{3050}{T_t} = 23 - \frac{3750}{T_c}$$

$$-\frac{3050}{T_c} + \frac{3750}{T_c} = 23 - 19.5$$

$$\frac{700}{T_c} = 3.5$$

or $$T_c = \frac{700}{3.5} = 200\ \text{K}$$

$$T_c = 200\ \text{K}$$

56. $$f(x) = Ae^{-ax}$$

Operator $$Q = \frac{d^2}{dx^2} + \frac{2}{x}\frac{d}{dx} + \frac{c}{x}$$

$$Q\, f(x) = \left(\frac{d^2}{dx^2} + \frac{2}{x}\frac{d}{dx} + \frac{c}{x}\right) Ae^{-ax}$$

$$= B \cdot e^{-ax}$$

B is the Eigen value,

$$= \left[a^2 + \frac{2}{x}(-a) + \frac{c}{x}\right] \cdot Ae^{-ax}$$

For Eigen value, x term should vanish.

$\therefore$ $$-\frac{2a}{x} + \frac{c}{x} = 0$$

or $$c = 2a$$

57. $$f(\in) = \frac{1}{e^{(\in - \in_f)/kT} + 1}$$

at, $$T = 0K$$

and $$\in = \in_f$$

$$e^{(\in - \in_f)kT} = e^0 = 1$$

Probability $$= \frac{1}{1+1} = \frac{1}{2}$$

58. For low pass filter,

$$\left|\frac{V_2}{V_1}\right| = \frac{R}{R_1} \cdot \frac{1}{RC_3 + 1}$$

$$= 100 \cdot \frac{1}{10^{-3} j + 1}$$

$\therefore$ Low pass frequency gain

$$= 20 \log \left|\frac{V_2}{V_1}\right| = 40\ \text{dB}$$

59. We know that,

$$P_t = \frac{A_c^2}{2}\left(1 + \frac{\mu^2}{2}\right) = 10\ \text{kW}$$

or $$P_c\left(1 + \frac{\mu^2}{2}\right) = 10\ \text{kW}$$

$\Rightarrow$ $$P_c = \frac{10\ \text{kW}}{1 + \frac{\mu^2}{2}} = \frac{10\ \text{kW}}{1 + 18}$$

$$= 8.47\ \text{kW}$$

60. $$\frac{b}{a} = \frac{n_\phi}{n}$$

$n_\phi \rightarrow$ Azimuthal Quantum number
$n \rightarrow$ Principal Quantum number

$$\frac{b}{a} = \frac{1}{3}$$

$$\Rightarrow \quad b = \frac{a}{3}$$

61. Given,

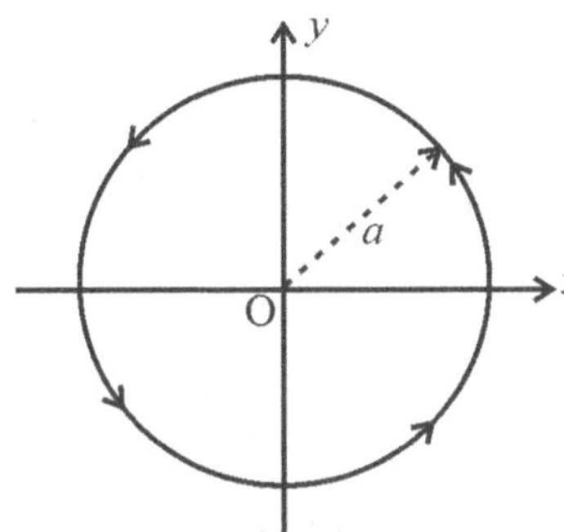

$$\vec{F} = \sin y\hat{i} + x(1+\cos y)\hat{j}$$

$$\int_C \vec{F}\cdot\vec{dr} = \int_C \left[\sin y\hat{i} + x(1+\cos y)\hat{j}\right]\cdot(\hat{i}dx + \hat{j}dy)$$

$$= \int_C \sin y dx + x(1+\cos y)dy$$

By Green's theorem,

$$= \oint_C (\phi dx + \psi dy)$$

$$= \iint_S \left(\frac{\partial\psi}{\partial x} - \frac{\partial\phi}{dy}\right) dx\,dy$$

$$\iint_S [(1+\cos y) - \cos y]\,dx\,dy$$

where s is the circular plane of radius,

$$= \iint_S dx\,dy = \text{Area of circle} = \pi a^2$$

62. For the first order (n = 1), Bragg's law gives $2d \sin\theta = \lambda$.
Here d = 3.02945 Å and λ = 0.563 Å.

Hence, $$\sin\theta = \frac{\lambda}{(2d)} = \frac{0.563}{6.0589} = 0.0929$$

Therefore, the angle of reflection is

$$\theta = \sin^{-1} 0.0929 = 5.33^\circ$$

63. Diodes D_1 and D_3 are forward biased while diodes D_2 and D_4 are reverse biased. We can therefore, consider the branches containing diodes D_2 and D_4 as "open". Replacing diodes D_1 and D_3 by their equivalent circuits and making the branches containing diodes D_2 and D_4 open, we get the circuit shown in fig. (*ii*). Note that for a silicon diode, the barrier voltage is 0.7 V.

Net circuit voltage = 10 – 0.7 – 0.7 = 8.6 V

Total circuit resistance = 1 + 48 + 1 = 50 Ω

∴ Circuit current = 8.6/50 = 0.172 A = 172 mA

64. $$I_D = \frac{V_{DD} - V_D}{R_D}$$

Since by Kirchhoff's law

$$V_D = V_{DD} - I_D R_D$$

or $$I_D = \frac{12\text{ V} - 7\text{ V}}{3.3\text{k}\Omega}$$

$$= \frac{5\text{V}}{3.3\text{k}\Omega} = 1.52 \text{ mA}$$

The gate to source voltage V_{GS} can be calculated as:

$$V_S = I_D R_S = (1.52 \text{ mA})(2.2 \text{ k}\Omega) = 3.34 \text{ V}$$

$$V_G = \left(\frac{R_2}{R_1 + R_2}\right) V_{DD} = \left(\frac{1.0\text{ M}\Omega}{7.8\text{ M}\Omega}\right) 12\text{ V} = 1.54 \text{ V}$$

$$V_{GS} = V_G - V_S = 1.54 - 3.34 \text{ V} = -1.8 \text{ V}$$

65. We know that Fourier transform is expressed as

$$F[x(t)] = X(\omega) = \int_{-\infty}^{\infty} x(t)e^{-j\omega t}dt$$

According to given figure, we may write

$$X(\omega) = \int_0^2 10.e^{-j\omega t}dt$$

$$= 10\int_0^2 e^{-j\omega t}dt = 10\left[\frac{e^{-j\omega t}}{-j\omega}\right]_0^2$$

$$= \frac{10}{-j\omega}\left[e^{-2j\omega} - 1\right]$$

or $$= \frac{10}{-j\omega}\left[\frac{e^{-j\omega}}{e^{j\omega}} - 1\right]$$

$$= \frac{10e^{-j\omega}}{-j\omega}\left[e^{j\omega} - e^{-j\omega}\right]$$

$$= \frac{20e^{-j\omega}}{\omega}\sin\omega = 20e^{-j\omega}\left[\frac{\sin\omega}{\omega}\right]$$

$$= 20\, e^{-j\omega} \sin c\,(\omega)$$

66. $E = mc^2 - m_0c^2$

$$= \frac{m_0c^2}{\sqrt{1-\frac{v^2}{c^2}}} - m_0c^2$$

$$9.69 = \frac{0.51}{\sqrt{1-\frac{v^2}{c^2}}} - 0.51$$

$\Rightarrow$ $$10.2 = \frac{0.51}{\sqrt{1-\frac{v^2}{c^2}}}$$

or $$\sqrt{1-\frac{v^2}{c^2}} = \frac{0.51}{10.2} = 0.05$$

$$m = \frac{m_0}{\sqrt{1-\frac{v^2}{c^2}}}$$

$\Rightarrow$ $$\frac{m}{m_0} = \frac{1}{0.05} = \frac{100}{5}$$

or $$\frac{m}{m_0} = \frac{20}{1}$$

67. $\text{VSWR} = \frac{1+\rho}{1-\rho} = 3$

or $$\rho = \frac{1}{2} = \frac{Z_L - Z_0}{Z_L + Z_0}$$

or $$\frac{Z_L}{Z_0} = \frac{3}{1}$$

$$Z_L = 3Z_0 = 3 \times 75 = 225\ \Omega$$

68. $V_2 = nV_1,\ V_4 = nV_3$

$Q_1 =$ Heat taken at upper term

$$= RT_1 \ln n + RT_2 \ln n$$

$$= R(T_1 + T_2) \ln n$$

Now $T_1 V_2^{\gamma-1} = T_2 V_3^{\gamma-1}$

$\Rightarrow$ $$V_3 = \left(\frac{T_1}{T_2}\right)^{1/(\gamma-1)} V_2$$

Similarly $$V_5 = \left(\frac{T_2}{T_3}\right)^{1/(\gamma-1)} V_4$$

$$V_6 = \left(\frac{T_1}{T_3}\right)^{1/(\gamma-1)} V_1$$

$Q_2 \rightarrow$ heat rejected at large temperature

$$= -RT_3 \ln \frac{V_6}{V_5}$$

$$= -RT_3 \ln \left(\frac{T_1}{T_2}\right)^{1/(1-\gamma)} \times \frac{V_1}{V_4}$$

$$= +RT_3 \ln \left(\frac{T_1}{T_2}\right)^{1/(\gamma-1)} \frac{V_2}{n^2V_3}$$

$$= RT_3 \ln\left(\frac{T_1}{T_2}\right)^{1/(\gamma-1)} \frac{1}{n^2}\left(\frac{T_1}{T_2}\right)^{1/\gamma-1}$$

$$= RT_3 \ln n$$

$\Rightarrow$ $$n = 1 - \frac{2T_3}{T_1 + T_2}$$

69. We have

$$\frac{R_fR_1}{R_f + R_1} = \frac{100\times10^3\times10\times10^3}{100\times10^3+10\times10^3} = 9000\,\Omega = 9\ \text{k}\Omega$$

$$\beta = \frac{R_1}{R_1 + R_f} = \frac{10\times10^3}{10\times10^3+100\times10^3} = \frac{1}{11}$$

Offset voltage

$$V = \frac{V_{OS}}{\beta} + I_{OS} R_f$$

$= 6 \times 10^{-3}\,(11) + 200 \times 10^{-9}\,(100 \times 10^3)$

$= 86$ mV

70. $E = (90\ \text{V/m})\ [\sin(6.28 \times 10^{15}\ \text{s}^{-1})\, t + \sin(12.56 \times 10^{15}\ \text{s}^{-1})\, t]$

ϕ_0 (W.F.) $= 2.0$ eV

$\therefore$ $K.E_{max} = ?$

The light contains two different frequencies. The one with larger frequency will cause photoelectrons with largest kinetic energy. This larger frequency is

$$v = \frac{w}{2\pi} = \frac{12.56\times10^{15}}{2\pi}$$

The maximum kinetic energy of the photoelectrons is

$$k_{max} = hv - \phi.$$

$$\Rightarrow (4.14 \times 10^{-15}\ \text{eV} - \text{s}) \times \left(\frac{12.56\times10^{15}\text{s}^{-1}}{2\pi}\right) - 2.0\ \text{eV}.$$

$$\Rightarrow \frac{4.14\times12.56}{2\pi} - 2.0\ \text{eV}$$

$$\Rightarrow \frac{4.14\times12.56}{2\times3.4} - 2.0\ \text{eV}$$

$$8.28 - 2.0\ \text{eV} = 6.28\ \text{eV}.$$

71. The total conductivity due to holes and electrons in a doped semiconductor is given by

$$\sigma = n_e e\mu_e + n_p e\mu_p$$

$$\sigma = e\left[n_e\mu_e + n_p\mu_p\right]$$

$$n_e n_h = n_i^2$$

[for an intrinsic semiconductor]

$$n_e = \frac{n_i^2}{n_p}$$

$$\sigma = e\left[\frac{n_i^2}{n_p}\mu_e + n_p\mu_p\right]$$

$$\frac{d\sigma}{dn_p} = e\frac{d}{dn_p}\left[\frac{n_i^2}{n_p}\mu_n + n_p\mu_p\right] = 0$$

$$= e\left[\frac{-n_i^2}{n_h^2}\mu_n + \mu_p\right] = 0$$

$$\mu_p = \frac{n_i^2}{n_h^2}\mu_n \Rightarrow n_h = n_i\sqrt{\frac{\mu_n}{\mu_p}}$$

72. Using formula:

$$R_0 = \frac{\ln(2)m\ N_A}{t_{1/2}M}$$

$$= \frac{\ln(2)(1.00\times10^{-6}\text{g})\left(6.022\times10^{23}\frac{\text{nuclei}}{\text{mol}}\right)}{(2\ln2\times10^{8}\text{s})\left(60\frac{\text{g}}{\text{mol}}\right)}$$

Solving the above reaction we get, 5×10^{10}.

73. Given $Q_1 = CV$, $Q_2 = 2C \times 2V = 4CV$

As the two capacitors are connected with opposite polarity, the common potential is

$$V' = \frac{Q_2 - Q_1}{C_1 + C_2} = \frac{4CV - CV}{C + 2C} = V$$

Equivalent capacitance, $C^1 = C + 2C = 3C$

Final energy of configuration is

$$U' = \frac{1}{2}CV^2 = \frac{1}{2}\times3C\times V^2 = \frac{3}{2}CV^2$$

74. In case (a) when the current flows in one coil, the other coil receives maximum flux due to maximum area intercepting the flux. Hence, mutual inductance is maximum in this case.

75.

$$f_r = \frac{v}{2}\sqrt{\left(\frac{m}{a}\right)^2 + \left(\frac{n}{p}\right)^2 + \left(\frac{p}{c}\right)^2}$$

where for TM mode to Z.

$m = 1, 2, 3, ...,\ n = 1, 2, 3, ...,\ p = 1, 2, 3, ...$

For TE made to z

$m = 1, 2, 3;\ \ n = 1, 2, 3, ...;\ p = 1, 2, 3, ...$

If $a < b < c$, then $\frac{1}{a} > \frac{1}{b} > \frac{1}{c}$.

The lowest TM mode TE_{011}, with

$$f_{r_1} = \frac{V}{2}\sqrt{\left(\frac{1}{a}\right)^2 + \left(\frac{1}{b}\right)^2}$$

The lowest TE mode is TE_{011}, with

$$f_{r_2} = \frac{v}{2}\cdot\sqrt{\left(\frac{1}{b}\right)^2 + \left(\frac{1}{c}\right)^2}$$

$$f_{r_1} > f_{r_2}$$

Hence, the dominant mode is TE_{011}.

SET–7
CSIR–UGC (NET) PHYSICAL SCIENCES

PART-A

1. A clock shows the time as 3 : 30 p.m. If the minute hand gains 2 minutes every hour, how many minutes will the clock gain by 4 a.m.?
A. 23 Minutes B. 24 Minutes
C. 25 Minutes D. 26 Minutes

2. The ratio between two numbers is 3 : 4. If each number be increased by 2, the ratio becomes 7 : 9. Find the numbers.
A. 12, 16 B. 16, 12
C. 12, 15 D. 13, 14

3. A person reached Delhi from Jaipur by his car at a speed of 60 km per hour and returned to Jaipur along the same route at a speed of 40 km per hour. What is his average speed?
A. 50 km per hour B. 45 km per hour
C. 48 km per hour D. 55.5 km per hour

4. A sum of money at compound interest amounts to thrice itself in 3 years. In how many years will it be 9 times itself?
A. 18 B. 12
C. 9 D. 6

5. A bell is rung before giving food to a dog. After doing this continuously for 10 days, which of the following is most likely to happen?
A. The dog learns to ignore the bell
B. The dog slivates on hearing the bell
C. The dog ignores food and runs towards the bell
D. The dog will not eat food without hearing the bell

6. Select the right option which can be placed at the sign of interrogation?

4	8	20
9	3	15
6	6	?

A. 24 B. 16
C. 20 D. 18

7. If the father has blood group O and the mother has blood group AB, what are the possible blood groups of their children?
A. O, AB, A B. A, B
C. A, O D. B, AB

8. The latitude and longitude of two cities A and B are as follows

	A	B
Latitude	12°N	21°N
Longitude	80°–30′ E	9°–30′ W

When the clock in city A shows 0800 hours UTC, what will be the time (UTC) in city B?
A. 0200 B. 0230
C. 0100 D. 0238

9. Match the two lists

Raw Material	Product
(*a*) Limestone	1. Porcelain
(*b*) Gypsum	2. Glass
(*c*) Silica sand	3. Plaster of Paris
(*d*) Clay	4. Cement

	(*a*)	(*b*)	(*c*)	(*d*)
A.	1	2	3	4
B.	4	3	2	1
C.	1	3	4	2
D.	4	1	3	2

10. How many different natural numbers can be formed from the digits 2, 5, 7, 9 assuming that the digits are not repeated?
A. 300 B. 325
C. 350 D. 275

For Q. No. 11: *In the following series determine the order of the letters. Then from the given options select the one which will complete the given series.*

11. B D A C F H E G ?
A. J L B. I K
C. J K D. K L

12. Virendra goes 25 km towards south from his fixed place. Then after turning to his right he goes 30 km and then again turning to his left he goes 10 km. In the end after turning to his left he goes 30 km. How far is he from his starting point?

A. 30 km B. 25 km
C. 35 km D. 40 km

13. A complete cycle of a traffic light takes 60 sec. During each cycle, the light is green for 25 sec., yellow for 5 sec., and red for 30 sec. At a randomly chosen time, the probability that the light will be not green is

A. $\frac{7}{12}$ B. $\frac{1}{12}$
C. $\frac{3}{4}$ D. $\frac{5}{12}$

14. The average of seven numbers is 30. The total of four of them is 114. The remaining three numbers are in the ratio of 1 : 2 : 3, these three numbers are

A. 14, 28, 32 B. 17, 34, 51
C. 16, 32, 48 D. 15, 30, 45

15. There are 23 steps to reach a temple. On descending from the temple Panas takes two steps in the same time. Virendra ascends one step. If they start to work simultaneously, at which step will they meet each other?

A. 10th B. 8th
C. 14th D. 6th

16. The one electron states for non-interacting electron confined in a cubic box of side a are $\in_0 < \in_1 < \in_2 < \in_3 < \in_4$. The energy of the fourth level is

A. $\frac{11\,\hbar^2\pi^2}{2\,ma^2}$ B. $\frac{10\,\hbar^2\pi^2}{2\,ma^2}$
C. $\frac{9\,\hbar^2\pi^2}{2\,ma^2}$ D. $\frac{3\,\hbar^2\pi^2}{2\,ma^2}$

17. In a certain code language DELAY is code as ABIXV. In the same code what will BXOIV stand for?

A. EARTH B. EARS
C. EARLY D. ELDER

18. 10 men can complete a work in 280 days. They started the work and after every 10 days 10 additional men were employed. In how many days the work was completed?

A. 70 days B. 88 days
C. 58 days D. 98 days

19. A, B, C, D, E, F and G are the members of a family, consisting of 4 adults and 3 childrens F and G are girls. A and D are brothers and A is a doctor. E is an engineer married to the one of the brothers and has two children. B is married to D and G is their child. Who is C?

A. G's father B. F's father
C. E's daughter D. A's son

20. The three words out of the following four words are almost same in nature and they form a group. Which one of the following does not belong to that group?

A. Wheat B. Paddy
C. Millets D. Mustard

PART-B

21. The matrix $A = \begin{bmatrix} 1 & 0 \\ 2 & 4 \end{bmatrix}$ is given. The eigen values of $4A^{-1} + 3A + 21$ are

A. 6, 15 B. 9, 12
C. 9, 15 D. 7, 15

22. A particle of mass, m, moves under the action of a central force whose potential is $V(r) = kmr^3$ $(k > 0)$, then energy for which the orbit will be a circle of radius a, about the origin is

A. $\frac{3}{2}mka^3$ B. $\frac{3}{2}mka^2$
C. $\frac{1}{2}mka$ D. $\frac{1}{2}mka^2$

23. An electron can be assumed to be uniformly charged sphere having a total charge e and radius R_0. Calculate the electrostatic energy of the electron.

A. $\frac{1}{4\pi\epsilon_0}\left(\frac{2}{5}\frac{e}{R_0^2}\right)$ B. $\frac{1}{4\pi\epsilon_0}\left(\frac{1}{5}\frac{e^2}{R_0^2}\right)$

C. $\frac{1}{4\pi\epsilon_0}\left(\frac{3}{5}\frac{e^2}{R_0}\right)$ D. $\frac{1}{4\pi\epsilon_0}\left(\frac{4}{5}\frac{e^2}{R_0}\right)$

24. A gas is enclosed in a vessel of spherical shape having a diameter of 15 cm and the diameter of a molecule is 3×10^{-10} m. Maximum number per cm^3 of the vessel if the molecules do not collide with each other.

A. 2.668×10^{12} molecules/cm^3
B. 1.668×10^{13} molecules/cm^3
C. 0.668×10^{13} molecules/cm^3
D. 3.668×10^{13} molecules/cm^3

25. Suppose the current density in the wire as shown is proportional to the distance from the axis $\overline{J} = k\overline{r}$ ($k \rightarrow$ some constant). The total current in the wire is

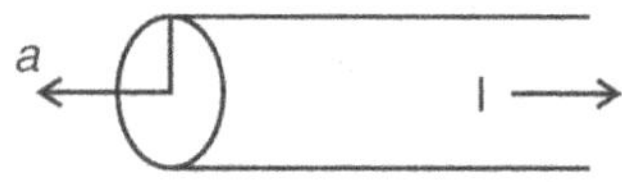

A. $\pi k a^3$ B. $\frac{2\pi k a^3}{3}$

C. $2\pi k a^3$ D. $2\pi k a^2$

26. Charges q and $-2q$ are placed at the two ends of the face diagonal of a cube and another point charge $3q$ is placed at the centre of the cube. The total electrostatics flux throughs due to the combined effect of all charges is

A. $\frac{1q}{24\epsilon_0}$ B. $\frac{7q}{24\epsilon_0}$

C. $\frac{19q}{24\epsilon_0}$ D. $\frac{11q}{24\epsilon_0}$

27. In the Barn approximation, the differential cross-section for the scattering of a particle of mass m by a delta function $V(r) = B\delta(r)$

A. $B\mu/2\pi r^2\hbar^4$ B. $B\mu^2/2\pi^2\hbar^2$

C. $B\mu^2/4\pi^2\hbar^4$ D. $B\mu^2/4\pi^2\hbar^2$

28. 100 gms of rest mass yields an amount of energy equal to

A. 10^{16} J B. 10^{18} J
C. 10^{13} J D. 10^{11} J

29. Two identical p-n junctions may be connected in series with a battery in three ways, as shown in fig.

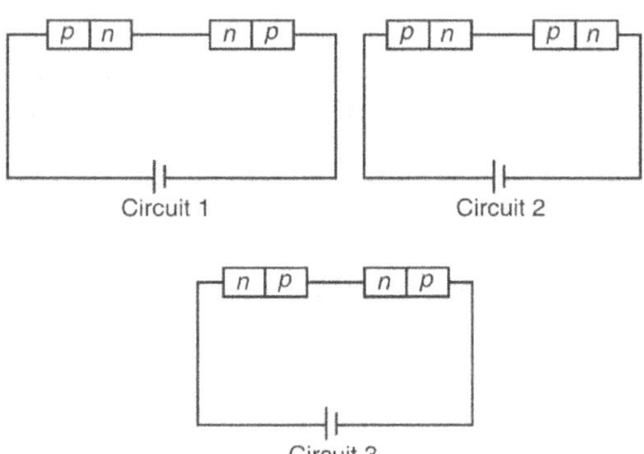

The potential drops across the two p-n Junctions are equal in

A. circuit 1 and circuit 2
B. circuit 2 and circuit 3
C. circuit 3 and circuit 1
D. circuit 1 only

30. A circular brass loop of radius a and resistance R is placed with its plane perpendicular to a magnetic field, which varies with time as $B = B_0 \sin \omega t$.

The expression for the induced current in the loop is

A. $\frac{\pi a^2 B_0 \omega \cos \omega t}{R}$ B. $\frac{2\pi a B_0 \omega \cos \omega t}{R^2}$

C. $\frac{2\pi a^2 B_0 \omega \sin \omega t}{R}$ D. $\frac{\pi a^2}{2R} B_0 \omega \sin \omega t$

31. The constant p for which $\vec{A} \times \vec{B} = \vec{C}$,

where $\vec{A} = \hat{i} + 2\hat{k}$

$\vec{B} = \hat{i} + p\hat{j} - \hat{k}$

$\vec{C} = -2\hat{i} + 3\hat{j} + \hat{k}$

is

A. 1 B. −2
C. 2 D. −1

32. The value of $\frac{d^2y}{dx^2} - 4\frac{dy}{dx} + 3y = 0$ is (where $y(0) = 0$, $y'(0) = 1$)

A. $y = \frac{1}{2}e^{2x} - \frac{1}{2}e^{-3x}$

B. $y = \frac{1}{2}e^{x} - \frac{1}{2}e^{3x}$

C. $y = -\frac{1}{2}e^{x} + \frac{1}{2}e^{3x}$

D. $y = -\frac{1}{2}e^{-x} - \frac{1}{2}e^{+3x}$

33. The mean and standard deviation of a binomial distribution are 10 and 2 respectively. The value of p is

A. 1.0 B. 0.8
C. 0.6 D. 0.4

34. In a binomial distribution, if the mean is 9 and SD is $\sqrt{6}$, the values of n and p respectively are

A. 27, $\frac{1}{3}$ B. 1, $\frac{1}{9}$
C. 36, $\frac{1}{4}$ D. 18, $\frac{1}{2}$

35. If a charged particle of mass m is accelerated through a potential difference of V volts, the de-Broglie wavelength is proportional to

A. V B. $V^{-1/2}$
C. V^2 D. $V^{1/2}$

36. The energy of free electrons in the state (1, 2, 1) in a rectangular box of sides $a = b \neq c$ is

A. $\frac{h^2}{8m}\left[\frac{5}{a^2} + \frac{1}{c^2}\right]$ B. $\frac{8m}{h^2}\left[\frac{1}{a^2} + \frac{1}{c^2}\right]$

C. $\frac{h^2}{8m}\left[\frac{3}{a^2} + \frac{1}{c^2}\right]$ D. None of these

37. The efficiency of heat engine working between heat reservoirs at temperature 327°C and 27°C respectively.

A. 25% B. 50%
C. 75% D. 100%

38. An oil bath kept at 27°C is being supplied heat at the rate of 100 Js^{-1}. Assuming the process to be quasi-static, the rate of increase of entropy of the system is approximately

A. 3.7 Jk^{-1} s^{-1} B. 3.7 Jk^{-1} s^{-2}
C. 0.33 Jk^{-1} s^{-1} D. 0.33 Jk^{-1} s^{-2}

39. For the rectifier circuit shown in fig. the sinusoidal voltage (V_1 and V_2) at the output of the transformer has a maximum value of 10 V. The load resistance R_L is 1 kΩ. If I_{av} is the average current through the resistor R_L, the circuit corresponds to a

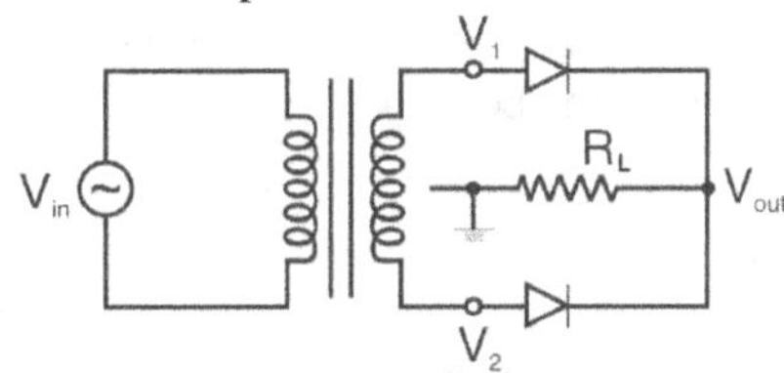

A. Half wave rectifier with $I_{av} = \frac{30}{\pi}$ mA

B. Full wave rectifier with $I_{av} = \frac{20}{\pi}$ mA

C. Full wave rectifier with $I_{av} = \frac{25}{\pi^2}$ mA

D. Half wave rectifier with $I_{av} = \frac{15}{\pi}$ mA

40. Electromagnetic waves travel in a medium at a speed of 2×10^8 ms^{-1}. The relative permeability of the medium is 1.0. The relative permittivity is

A. 3.25 B. 1.25
C. 2.25 D. 4.25

41. A coil having 500 sq loops of side 10 cm is placed normal to magnetic flux which increases at the rate A 1 T/s. The induced emf is

A. 0.1 V B. 0.5 V
C. 1 V D. 5 V

42. Yellow light is used in a single slit diffraction experiment with slit width of 0.6 mm. If yellow light is replaced by X-rays, then the observed pattern will reveal

A. that the central maximum is narrower
B. more number of fringes
C. less number of fringes
D. no-diffraction pattern

43. The angle of incidence at which reflected light is totally polarized for reflection from air to glass refractive index (μ) is
A. $\sin^{-1}\mu$ B. $\sin^{-1}(1/\mu)$
C. $\tan^{-1}(1/\mu)$ D. $\tan^{-1}(\mu)$

44. A diverging beam of light from a point sence *s* having divergence—angle α, fall symmetrically on a glass slab as shown in fig. The angles of incidence of two extreme rays are equal. If the thickness of glass slab is *t* and the refractive index μ, then the divergence angle of the emergent beam is

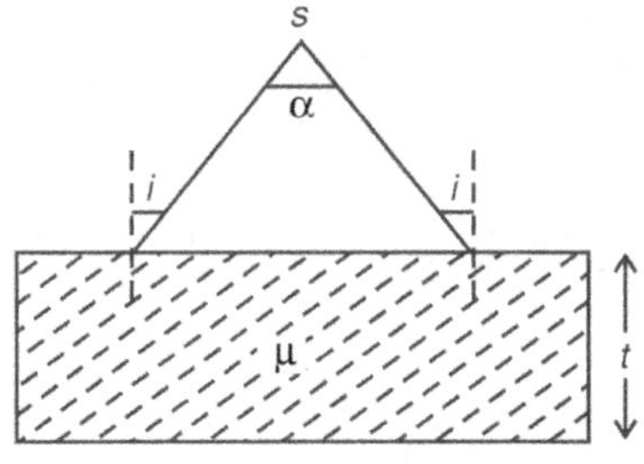

A. zero B. α
C. $\sin^{-1}(1/\mu)$ D. $2\sin^{-1}(t/\mu)$

45. When a conducting sphere is placed in a uniform field polarisibility is—the product of permittivity in free space and the volume of the sphere
A. Twice B. Thrice
C. Four times D. Equal

PART-C

46. The uncertainty in the location of a particle is equal to de-Broglie wavelength, then the uncertainty in its velocity is
A. v B. $\frac{v}{2}$
C. $2v$ D. $\frac{3}{2}v$

47. The probability of solving a problem by three students A, B, C independently are $\frac{1}{3}, \frac{1}{4}, \frac{1}{5}$. The probability that the problem will be solved as
A. $\frac{1}{60}$ B. $\frac{36}{60}$
C. $\frac{48}{60}$ D. $\frac{57}{60}$

48. An artificial satellite revolves around the earth in a circular orbit at a height H above earth's surface. Find the period of revolution of the satellite, so that the astronaut in it way be in a state of weight lessness.
A. $\frac{\pi}{R}\sqrt{\frac{(R+H)3}{g}}$ B. $\frac{2\pi}{R}\sqrt{\frac{(R+H)3}{g}}$
C. $\frac{\pi}{2R}\sqrt{\frac{(R+H)3}{g}}$ D. $2\pi\sqrt{\frac{(R+H)3}{2g}}$

49. Number of neutrons emitted per fission is 1.6 when the energy released per fission is 200 MeV. The number of neutrons emitted per second, when 20 MW power is generated will be
A. 3.9×10^{20} B. 3.9×10^{19}
C. 10^{19} D. 10^{18}

50. An a.c. supply of 230 V is applied to a half wave rectifier circuit through a transformer of turn ratio 10 : 1. The output d.c. voltage is:
A. 10.36 V B. 9.56 V
C. 13.23 V D. 15.75 V

51. A lossless, air dielectric cylindrical wave guide of inside diameter 3 cm, is operated at 14 GHz. For the TM_{11} mode propagating in $+z$ direction, the wave impedance will be (for TM_{11}) mode, $k_c a = 3.832$
A. 120 πΩ B. 185 Ω
C. 240 πΩ D. 95.25 Ω

52. The degree of degeneracy of the energy level $38\left(\frac{h^2}{8ma^2}\right)$ of the particle in a cubical potential box of side *a* is

A. 6 B. 3
C. 9 D. 12

53. A half-wave rectifier is used to supply 100 V d.c. to a load of 800 Ω. The diode has a plate resistance of 200 Ω. Find a.c. voltage required.
A. 222 V B. 425 V
C. 393 V D. 125 V

54. A photovoltaic cell produces a voltage of 0.33 V an open circuit when illuminated by 10 W/m^2 radiant incidence. When a load of 100 Ω is connected to the cell, a current of 2.2 mA is delivered at that intensity. Find the internal resistance of the cell.
A. 25 Ω B. 50 Ω
C. 70 Ω D. 30 Ω

55. A system is composed of two level atoms, the excited state 1 being 0.1 eV above the ground state, 0. Find the fraction of all atoms, which will be in state, 1 if the system is in thermal equilibrium at temperature 300 K. (Boltzmann constant = 1.38×10^{-23} J/k)
A. 42.7% B. 31.9%
C. 38.8% D. 51.4%

56. Let ΔW_i = amount of work done by a gas when compressed isothermally to volume V, ΔQ = amount of heat absorbed by the gas during the process, ΔW_a = amount of work done by the gas when expanded adiabatically to volume V; ΔE = change in internal energy of gas due to complete process. So ΔE is given by
A. $\Delta W_i + \Delta Q + \Delta W_a$
B. $\Delta Q + \Delta W_a - \Delta W_i$
C. $\Delta Q - \Delta W_i - \Delta W_a$
D. None of these

57. What should be the values of the components R_1, R_2 such that the frequency of the Wien Bridge oscillator is 300 Hz?
[Given: C = 0.01 μF and R_1 = 12 kΩ]

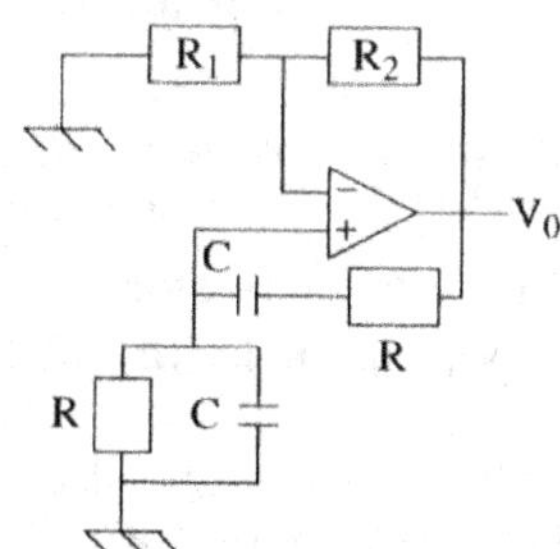

A. R = 48 kΩ and R_2 = 12 kΩ
B. R = 26 kΩ and R_2 = 24 kΩ
C. R = 530 Ω and R_2 = 1 MΩ
D. R = 53 kΩ and R_2 = 24 kΩ

58. Chlorine-33 decays by positron emission with a maximum energy of 4.3 MeV. Calculate the radius of the nucleus from this.
A. 2.54×10^{-15} m B. 4.54×10^{-15} m
C. 1.25×10^{-14} m D. 1.25×10^{-13} m

59. Find the approximate number of quanta visible light emitted as Cerenkov radiation in the frequency range corresponding to wavelengths in vacuum of λ = 4000 to 7000 A.U. given off by an electron of energy 20 MeV draversing 1 cm of lucite (μ = 1.49).
A. 170 quanta/cm B. 270 quanta/cm
C. 120 quanta/cm D. 320 quanta/cm

60. In an air filled waveguide, a TE mode operating at 6 GHz has

$$E_y = 15 \sin\left(\frac{2\pi x}{a}\right)\cos\left(\frac{\pi x}{b}\right)\sin(\omega t - 12z)\,\text{V/m}$$

The cut-off frequency is—
A. 5.973 GHz B. 3.189 GHz
C. 7.438 GHz D. 6.946 GHz

61. For a short-circuited coaxial transmission line, characteristic impedance $Z_0 = 35 + j49\Omega$, propagation constant, $r = 1.4 + 5\hat{j}$, length of line l = 0.4 m. The input impedance of short circuited line is
A. 56 + j 72 Ω B. 48 + j 64 Ω
C. 82 + j 39 Ω D. 32 + j 78 Ω

62. Find the total offset voltage for the circuit of fig. for an Op-amp with specified values of input offset voltage V_{IO} = 4 mV and input offset current I_{IO} = 150 nA.

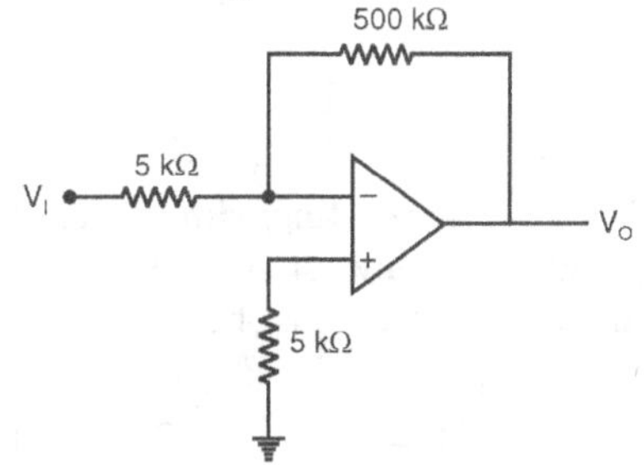

A. 255 mV B. 365 mV
C. 479 mV D. 685 mV

63. Gold has atomic weight 197 and density 19.3 gm/cc. The spacing between the atoms in solid gold is
A. 3.14 Å B. 2.57 Å
C. 4.28 Å D. 5.85 Å

64. Although mass-energy equivalence of special relativity allows conversion of a photon to an electron-positron pair such a process cannot occur in free space because
A. The mass is not conserved
B. The energy is not conserved
C. The momentum is not conserved
D. The charge is not conserved

65. Guide wavelength (λ_g), cut-off frequency (λ_C) and free-space wavelength (λ_0) of a waveguide are related as—

A. $\frac{1}{\lambda_g^2} = \frac{1}{\lambda_0^2} - \frac{1}{\lambda_C^2}$ B. $\frac{1}{\lambda_0^2} = \frac{1}{\lambda_g^2} - \frac{1}{\lambda_C^2}$

C. $\frac{1}{\lambda_C^2} = \frac{1}{\lambda_0^2} - \frac{1}{\lambda_g^2}$ D. $\frac{1}{\lambda_g^2} = \frac{1}{\lambda_0^2} - \frac{1}{\lambda_C^2}$

66. According to Maxwell's law of distribution of velocities of molecules, the most probable velocity is—
A. Less than the root mean square velocity
B. Equal to root mean square velocity
C. Equal to the mean velocity
D. Greater than the mean velocity

67. For Silver, the temp at which the electronic molar specific heat, C_{ve} and the lattice molar specific heat C_v are equal. The Debye temp. for silver is 210 K. The equality occurs at low temp., so Debye theory result can be taken as

$$C_v = \frac{12\pi^4 R}{5}\left(\frac{T}{T\alpha}\right)^3$$

A. 4.75 K B. 0
C. 1.55 K D. 2.5 K

68. A 12-bit ADC is operating with a 1 μ sec clock period and total conversion time is seen to be 14 μ secs. The ADC must be of the
A. Integrating type B. Flesh type
C. Counting type D. Successive app. type

69. A three bit DAC with resistance values R = 3 kΩ and reference voltage of 12 V is to be used with an operational amplifier of infinite gain and feedback resistance 8 kΩ. Determine the output voltage corresponding to the binary input 101.
A. – 20 V B. – 40 V
C. – 60 V D. – 10 V

70. If maximum and minimum amplitudes of an amplitude modulated waves are 10 V and 5 V respectively, the modulation index is
A. 0.44 B. 0.22
C. 0.33 D. 0.11

71. In a voltage sensitive Wheatstone, having each arm having a resistance, R, the resistance of one of the arm is changed to R + ΔR where ΔR << R. The Wheatstone bridge is supplied with an input voltage of e_i. The ouput voltage on account of unbalance is

A. $\left(\frac{\Delta R/R}{2+\Delta R/R}\right)e_i$ B. $\left(\frac{\Delta R/R}{4+\Delta R/R}\right)e_i$

C. $\left(\frac{2\Delta R/R}{4+\Delta R/R}\right)e_i$ D. $\left(\frac{\Delta R/R}{4+2\Delta R/R}\right)e_i$

72. An atom emits a photon of wavelength λ = 600 nm by transition from an excited state of life time 8 × 10^{-9} s. If Δv represents the minimum uncertainty in the frequency of the photon, the fractional width $\frac{\Delta v}{v}$ of the spectral line is of the order of
A. 10^{-4} B. 10^{-6}
C. 10^{-8} D. 10^{-10}

73. Calculate the frequency of oscillation of a hydrogen molecule if its force constant is 4.8 × 10^2 N/m and mass of hydrogen atom = 1.67 × 10^{-27} kg.
A. 2.1 × 10^{14} Hz B. 1.2 × 10^{14} Hz
C. 3.1 × 10^{14} Hz D. 4.1 × 10^{14} Hz

74. The absolute value of velocity of electrons corresponding to the point of inflexion of E-*k* diagram is
A. Maximum B. Not known
C. Minimum D. Zero

75. The decay chain of the nucleus $^{238}_{92}U$ involves eight α-decays and six β-decays. The final nucleus at the end of the process will have

A. Z = 76, A = 200

B. Z = 88, A = 206

C. Z = 84, D = 224

D. Z = 82, A = 206

ANSWERS

1	2	3	4	5	6	7	8	9	10
C	A	C	D	C	D	B	A	B	B
11	**12**	**13**	**14**	**15**	**16**	**17**	**18**	**19**	**20**
A	C	A	C	B	A	C	A	D	D
21	**22**	**23**	**24**	**25**	**26**	**27**	**28**	**29**	**30**
C	A	C	B	B	D	C	A	B	A
31	**32**	**33**	**34**	**35**	**36**	**37**	**38**	**39**	**40**
A	C	C	A	B	A	B	C	B	C
41	**42**	**43**	**44**	**45**	**46**	**47**	**48**	**49**	**50**
D	D	D	B	B	A	B	B	D	A
51	**52**	**53**	**54**	**55**	**56**	**57**	**58**	**59**	**60**
B	C	C	B	C	C	D	B	B	A
61	**62**	**63**	**64**	**65**	**66**	**67**	**68**	**69**	**70**
C	C	B	B	C	A	C	D	B	C
71	**72**	**73**	**74**	**75**					
D	B	B	A	D					

EXPLANATORY ANSWERS

1. Hours between 3:30 p.m. and 4 a.m. are — 12½ hours. Number of minutes gained will be 12½ × 2 = 25 minutes.

2. Let numbers are $3x$ and $4x$

$$\frac{3x+2}{4x+2} = \frac{7}{9}$$

$$28x + 14 = 27x + 18$$

$$x = 4$$

∴ numbers are 12 and 16.

3. Average speed $= \frac{2XY}{X+Y}$

$$= \frac{2 \times 60 \times 40}{60 + 40} = 48 \text{ kmph.}$$

4. Because $3P = P(1 + r/100)^3$

So, $3 = (1 + r/100)^3$

$3^2 = 9 = (1 + r/100)^{3\times 2}$

$= (1 + r/100)^6 = 6$ years.

5. Classical conditioning was accidentally discovered around the beginning of the 20th century by Russian physiologist Ivan Pavlov. Pavlov was studying digestive process in dogs when he discovered that the dogs salivated before they receive their food. In fact, after repeated pairing of the lab attendant and the food, the dogs started so salivate at the sight of the lab assistants. Pavlov coined this phenomenon as psychic secretions. He noted that dogs were not only responding to a biological need (hunger), but also a need developed by learning. Pavlov spent the rest of life researching why this associate learning occurred, which is now called classical conditioning.

6. $20 = 8 \times 2 + 4$, $15 = 3 \times 2 + 9$

∴ $? = 6 \times 2 + 6 = 18$.

7. Blood group AB—If you belong to the blood group AB, you have both A and B antigen on the surface of your RBCs and no A or B antibodies at all in your blood plasma.

8. For a time difference of 24 hours, difference in longitude = 360°

Longitude 80°–30' E and 9°–30' W has difference in longitude of = 80° – 30' + 9° – 30'
= 90°

the time difference = $\frac{90}{360} \times 24 = 6$

Hence, time (UTC) in city B = 8:00 + 6
= 02:00

9. Gypsum — Plaster of Paris
Porcelain — Clay
Limestone — Cement
Silica sand — Glass

10. Here, the number of the digits in forming natural no. is not restricted to 3.

Then, numbers with

5 digits = ${}^5P_5 = 5 \times 4 \times 3 \times 2 \times 1 = 120$
4 digits = ${}^5P_4 = 5 \times 4 \times 3 \times 2 \quad = 120$
3 digits = ${}^5P_3 = 5 \times 4 \times 3 \quad = 60$
2 digits = ${}^5P_2 = 5 \times 4 \quad = 20$
1 digit = ${}^5P_1 = 5 \times 1 \quad = 5$
= 325

11. The letters in the series are arranged in following order (Four letters are mixed)

A B C D is written as BDAC; and
E F G H as FHEG. Similarly,
I J K L will be JLIK.

The answer option is JL, *i.e.*, (A).

12.

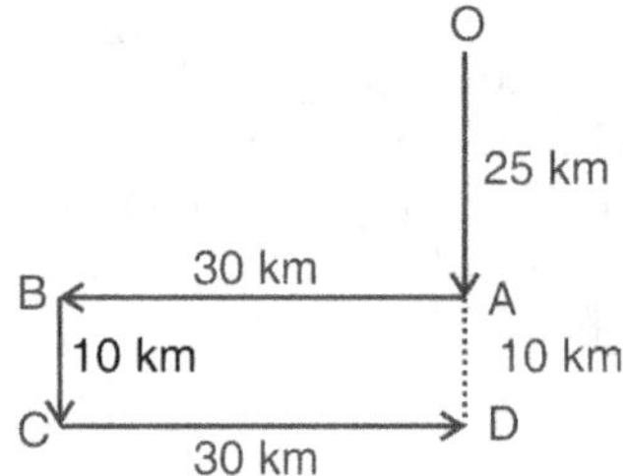

∴ Total distance = OA + AD = 25 + AD
∵ A = BC = 10 km
∴ Total distance = 25 + 10 = 35 km

13. Probability for light to be green = $\frac{25}{60} = \frac{5}{12}$

∴ Probability for light not to be green = $1 - \frac{5}{12}$
$= \frac{7}{12}$

14. Total of 7 numbers = 30 × 7 = 210
Total of 4 numbers = 114
So, total of remaining 3 numbers = 210 – 114
= 96

Then, 3 remaining numbers are $\frac{1}{6}, \frac{2}{6}, \frac{3}{6}$ of 96 or 16, 32, 48.

15. We assume that Panas and Virendra descends and ascends respectively x times.

∴ Total no. of steps = $2x + x - 1$
$23 = 3x - 1$
⇒ $x = \frac{24}{3} = 8$

They will meet at 8th step from the bottom.

16. $n_x = 3, \quad n_y = 1, \quad n_z = 1$
or $n_x = 1, \quad n_y = 3, \quad n_z = 1$
or $n_x = 1, \quad n_y = 1, \quad n_z = 3$

∴ Energy for electron confined in a cubic box

$$= \frac{\hbar^2\pi^2}{2ma^2}\left[n_x^2 + n_y^2 + n_z^2\right]$$

$$= \frac{\hbar^2\pi^2}{2ma^2}\left[3^2 + 1^2 + 1^2\right]$$

$$= \frac{11\hbar^2\pi^2}{2ma^2}$$

17. The coded letters are moved, three steps forward

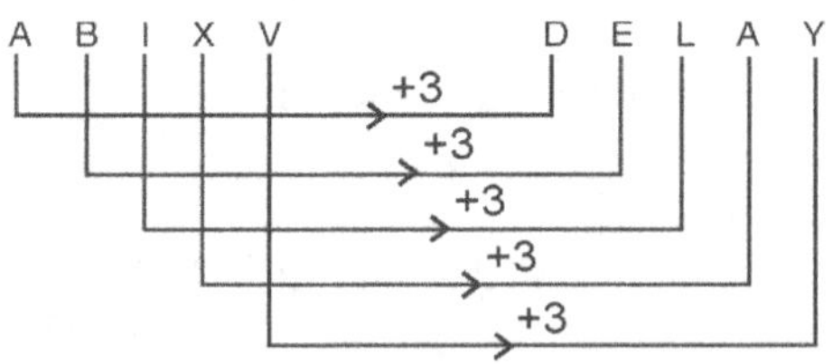

Similarly,

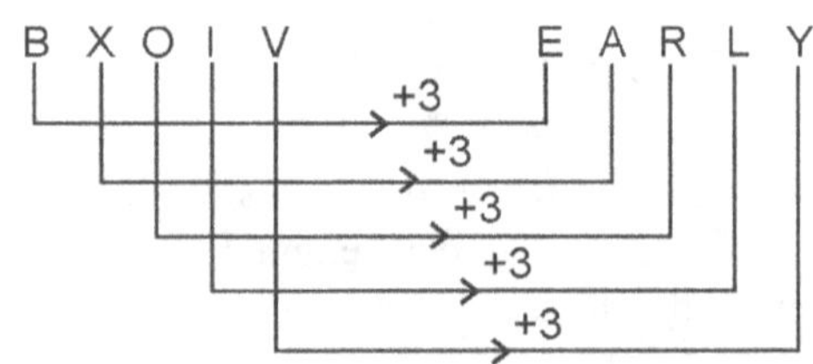

18. Work done by 10 men in first 10 days

$$= \frac{10}{280} \times \frac{10}{10} = \frac{1}{28}$$

$\therefore$ Remaining work after 10 days

$$= 1 - \frac{1}{28} = \frac{27}{28}$$

Work done by (10 + 10) men in next 10 days

$$= \frac{1}{280} \times \frac{20}{10} \times 10 = \frac{2}{28}$$

$\therefore$ Remaining work after 20 days

$$= \frac{27}{28} - \frac{2}{28} = \frac{25}{28}$$

Similarly remaining work after 30 days

$$= \frac{25}{28} - \frac{3}{28} = \frac{22}{28}$$

Remaining work after 50 days $= \frac{18}{28} - \frac{5}{28} = \frac{13}{28}$

Remaining work after 60 days $= \frac{13}{28} - \frac{6}{28} = \frac{7}{28}$

Remaining work after 70 days $= \frac{7}{28} - \frac{7}{28} = 0$

Hence, the whole work will be completed in 70 days.

19. A $\rightarrow$ Adult husband of E, Doctor
B $\rightarrow$ Wife of D adult
C $\rightarrow$ Son of A and E
D $\rightarrow$ Adult husband of B
E $\rightarrow$ Wife of A, Engineer Adult.
F $\rightarrow$ Girl and daughter of A and E.
G $\rightarrow$ Girl and daughter of B and D.

20. Mustard is oily while the rest are corns. Hence, alternative of D is different.

21. We have

$$A = \begin{bmatrix} 1 & 0 \\ 2 & 4 \end{bmatrix}$$

$$\lambda_1 = 1, 4$$

Eigen value of $A^{-1} = 1, \frac{1}{4}$

Eigen value of $A = 1, 4$

Eigen value of $1 = 1, 1$

$\therefore$ Eigen values of $4A^{-1} + 3A + 2I$ are

$$= 4(1) + 3(1) + 2(1)$$
$$= 4 + 3 + 2 = 9$$

or $\left(\frac{1}{4}\right) + 3(4) + 2(1) = 15.$

22. If the orbit is circular, then

Attractive force = Centrifugal force

$$\Rightarrow \quad f = \left(\frac{dV}{dr}\right) = \frac{mv^2}{r} \quad [V = kmr^3]$$

$$\Rightarrow \quad \frac{d}{dr}\left(kmr^3\right) = \frac{mv^2}{r}$$

$$3kr^2 = \frac{v^2}{r}$$

or $\quad v = r\sqrt{3kr}$

at $\quad r = a$

$$v|_{r=a} = a\sqrt{3ka}$$

$\therefore$ Kinetic energy $= \frac{1}{2}mv^2$

$$E = \frac{1}{2}m.a^2.3ka$$

$$E = \frac{3}{2}mka^3$$

23. We know that for free space

$$U = \int_{\text{all space}} \frac{1}{2} \epsilon_0 E^2 d\tau$$

$$i.e., \; U = \int_0^{R_0} \frac{\epsilon_0}{2} E^2_{in} \; 4\pi r^2 dr + \int_{R_0}^{\infty} \frac{\epsilon_0}{2} E^2_{out} \; 4\pi r^2 dr.$$

But

$$E_{in} = \frac{1}{4\pi \epsilon_0} \frac{e}{R_0^{\,3}} r \qquad E_{out} = \frac{1}{4\pi \epsilon_0} \frac{e}{r^2}$$

$$\therefore \; U = \int_0^{R_0} \frac{\epsilon_0}{2} \left(\frac{1}{4\pi \epsilon_0} \frac{er}{R_0^{\,3}}\right)^2$$

$$4\pi r^2 \, dr + \int_{R_0}^{\infty} \frac{\epsilon_0}{2} \left(\frac{1}{4\pi \epsilon_0} \frac{e}{r^2}\right)^2 4\pi r^2 \, dr$$

$$i.e., \; U = \frac{e^2}{8\pi \epsilon_0}\left[\int_0^{R_0} \frac{r^4}{R_0^{\,6}} dr + \int_{R_0}^{\infty} \frac{1}{r^2} dr\right]$$

$$i.e., \; U = \frac{e^2}{8\pi \epsilon_0}\left[\frac{1}{5R_0} + \frac{1}{R_0}\right] = \frac{1}{4\pi \epsilon_0}\left(\frac{3}{5}\frac{e^2}{R_0}\right)$$

24. We know that

$$\lambda = \frac{1}{(\sqrt{2})\pi d^2 n} \quad \text{or} \quad n = \frac{1}{(\sqrt{2})\pi d^2 \lambda}$$

The diameter of the vessel must be equal to the mean free path if the molecules should not have collision between thems2elves.

Therefore $\lambda = 15$ cm $= 0.15$ m

$$\therefore n = \frac{1}{(\sqrt{2}) \times 3.14 \times (3 \times 10^{-10})^2 \times 0.15}$$

$= 1.668 \times 10^{19}$ molecules/m^3

Now number of molecules per cm^3 is given by

$\frac{1.668 \times 10^{19}}{10^6} = 1.668 \times 10^{13}$ molecules/cm^3.

25. Vertical cross-section,

Current $I = \int J \cdot d\vec{s}$

$$= \int_0^a \int_0^{2\pi} (kr)(rdr\, d\phi)$$

$$= 2\pi k \int_0^a r^2 dr$$

$$= \frac{2}{3}\pi k a^3$$

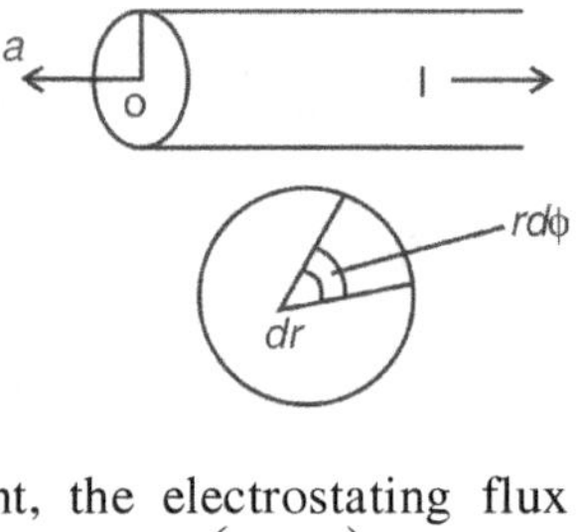

26. If only q is present, the electrostating flux passing through would be $\frac{1}{3}\left(\frac{1}{8}\frac{q}{\epsilon_0}\right) = \frac{1}{24}\frac{q}{\epsilon_0}$

Similarly, the flux due to $-2q$ is

$$= \frac{1}{3}\left(\frac{1}{8}, \frac{-2q}{\epsilon_0}\right) = \frac{1}{24}\frac{-2q}{\epsilon_0}$$

the flux due to $3q$ through the bottom force is

$$\frac{1}{6}\left(\frac{3q}{\epsilon_0}\right) \text{ or } \frac{q}{2\epsilon_0}$$

$\therefore$ the net flux due to both charges is $\frac{11q}{24\epsilon_0}$.

27. Total cross-section,

$$= 4\pi\sigma_k^B = 4\pi \times \frac{B\mu^2}{4\pi^2\hbar^4} = \frac{B\mu^2}{\pi\hbar^4}$$

Hence, differential cross-section

$$= \frac{\frac{\beta\mu^2}{\pi\hbar^4}}{4\pi} = \frac{\beta\mu^2}{4\pi^2\hbar^4}$$

28. $m = \frac{E}{c^2}$

or $E = 100 \text{ gm} \times (3 \times 10^8)^2$

$$= \frac{100}{1000} \times 9 \times 10^{16} \text{J}$$

$$= 10^{16} \text{ J}$$

29. In circuit 1, first pn junction is forward biased and second is reversed biased, their potential drop can not be equal. In circuits 2 and 3, the two p-n junctions are connected in series, they carry equal (forward or reverse) currents. Their potential drops are equal.

30. Here, $A = \pi a^2$, $\theta = 0$, so flux linked with the loop is

$$\phi = BA \cos 0° = BA$$
$$= B_0 \sin \omega t . \pi a^2$$

$$\therefore \quad |\varepsilon| = \frac{d\phi}{dt} = \frac{d}{dt}\left(B_0 \sin \omega t . \pi a^2\right)$$

$$= \pi a^2 B_0 \omega \cos\theta\, \omega t$$

$\therefore$ Induced current,

$$I = \frac{\varepsilon}{R} = \frac{\pi a^2 B_0 \omega \cos \omega t}{R}$$

31. Given $\vec{A} \times \vec{B} = \vec{C}$

Substituting their values,

$$\left(\hat{i} + 2\hat{k}\right) \times \left(\hat{i} + p\hat{j} - \hat{k}\right) = -2\hat{i} + 3\hat{j} + \hat{k}$$

or
$$\begin{vmatrix} \hat{i} & \hat{j} & \hat{k} \\ 1 & 0 & 2 \\ 1 & p & -1 \end{vmatrix} = -2\hat{i} + 3\hat{j} + \hat{k}$$

$$\hat{i}(0 - 2p) - \hat{j}(-1 - 2) + \hat{k}(p - 0) = -2\hat{i} + 3\hat{j} + \hat{k}$$

$$-2p\hat{i} + 3\hat{j} + p\hat{k} = -2\hat{i} + 3\hat{j} + \hat{k}$$

Comparing coeff. of $\hat{i}$ and $\hat{k}$, we get

$$p = 1$$

32. The AE is

$D^2 - 4D + 3 = 0$

or
$$D = \frac{4 \pm \sqrt{16 - 10}}{2} = 1, 3$$

The complementary function,

$$y = C_1e^x + C_2e^{3x}$$

Now, given conditions are

$$y = 0, \quad x = 0$$

$$0 = c_1 + c_2 \qquad ...(1)$$

$$\frac{dy}{dx} = c_1e^x + 3c_2e^{3x}$$

$$y' = 1 \text{ at } x = 0$$

$$1 = c_1 + 3c_2 \qquad ...(2)$$

Solving from eqns. (1) and (2), we get

$$c_1 = -\frac{1}{2}, \; c_2 = \frac{1}{2}$$

The complete required solution is

$$y = -\frac{1}{2}e^x + \frac{1}{2}e^{3x}$$

33. Given, $np = 10$, $npq = 2^2 = 4$

$$\Rightarrow q = \frac{4}{10} = \frac{2}{5}$$

$$\Rightarrow p = (1 - q)$$

$$= \frac{3}{5} = 0.6$$

34. Given $np = 9$ and $\sqrt{npq} = \sqrt{6}$

$$\Rightarrow npq = 6$$

$$q = \frac{6}{9} = \frac{2}{3}$$

$$p = 1 - q$$

$$= 1 - \frac{2}{3} = \frac{1}{3}$$

$$\Rightarrow np = 9$$

$$\therefore n \times \frac{1}{3} = 9$$

$$n = 27$$

35. We have, $\lambda = \dfrac{h}{\sqrt{2mE}}$

Now, if a charged particle carrying charge q is accelerated through a p.d. V volts,

$$\because E = qV$$

$$\therefore \lambda = \frac{h}{\sqrt{2mqV}}$$

If h, m and q are constant

$$\lambda \; \alpha \; \frac{1}{V^{\frac{1}{2}}} \Rightarrow \lambda \; \alpha \; V^{-1/2}$$

36. $E = \dfrac{h^2}{8m}\left[\dfrac{n_x^2}{a^2} + \dfrac{n_y^2}{b^2} + \dfrac{n_z^2}{c^2}\right]$

free state (1, 2, 1)

$\Rightarrow n_x = 1$, $n_y = 2$, $n_z = 1$ and $a = b \neq c$

$$\therefore E = \frac{h^2}{8m}\left(\frac{1^2}{a^2} + \frac{2^2}{a^2} + \frac{1^2}{c^2}\right)$$

$$= \frac{h^2}{8m}\left(\frac{5}{a^2} + \frac{1}{c^2}\right)$$

37. $T_1 = 327°C = 327 + 273 = 600$ K

and $T_2 = 27°C = 27 + 273 = 300$ K

$$\therefore \eta = \frac{T_1 - T_2}{T_1}$$

$$= \frac{600K - 300K}{600K}$$

$$= \frac{300}{600} = \frac{1}{2}$$

$$= 0.5 \text{ or } 50\%$$

38. Change in entropy $= \dfrac{d\theta}{T(\ln k)} = \dfrac{100\,J\,s^{-1}}{(273+27)k}$

$$= \frac{100}{300} Js^{-1}\,K^{-1}$$

$$= 0.33\ Js^{-1}\ K^{-1}$$

39. The maximum voltage of transformer = 10 V

Average current through R_L is

$$I_{av} = \frac{2V_m}{\pi R_L} = \frac{2 \times 10}{\pi \times 1 \times 10^3 \Omega}$$

$$= \frac{20}{\pi} \times 10^{-3} A$$

$$= \frac{20}{\pi} mA$$

40. Speed of an em wave in a medium is given by

$$v = \frac{C}{\sqrt{\mu \in}} = \frac{C}{\sqrt{\mu_r \mu_0 \in_r \in_0}} = \frac{C}{\sqrt{\mu_0 \in_0}} \cdot \frac{C}{\sqrt{\mu_r \in_r}}$$

$$\therefore \quad v^2 = \frac{c^2}{\mu_r \in_r}$$

Hence, relative permittivity,

$$\in_r = \frac{c^2}{\mu_r v^2} = \frac{\left(3\times10^8\right)^2}{1\times\left(2\times10^8\right)^2} = 2.25$$

41. Here, area A = $\left(\frac{10}{100}\right)^2 = \frac{1}{100}\text{m}^2$

$$E = NA\frac{dB}{dt}$$

$$= 500 \times \frac{1}{100} \times 1 \text{ V}$$

$$= 5 \text{ V}$$

42. For the diffraction to be pronounced, the size of the slit should be comparable to the wavelength of waves. X-rays have very small wavelength (about 1 Å) as compared to yellow light (about 6000 Å). When yellow light is replaced by X-rays, no diffraction is observed with a slit of width 0.6 mm.

43. According to Brewster's Law,

We have, $\mu = \tan i_p$

$\therefore \quad i_p = \tan^{-1}(\mu)$.

44. When a ray of light passes through a slab with parallel faces, the emergent ray is parallel to the incident ray.

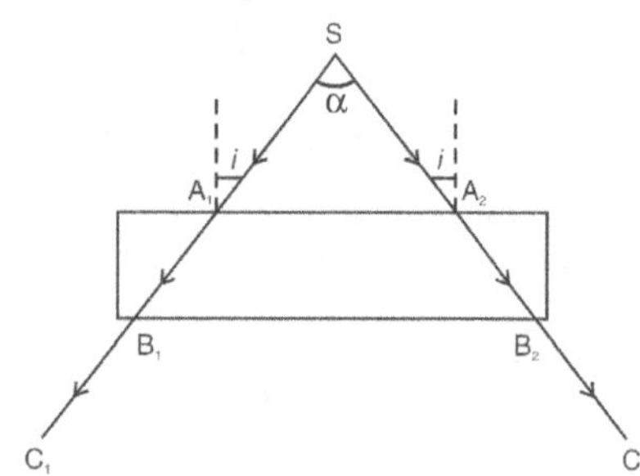

$\therefore$ $B_1C_1 \parallel SA_1$ and $B_2C_2 \parallel SA_2$

Divergence angle of emergent beam,

$\angle B_1SB_2 = \angle A_1SA_2 = \alpha$

45. $P = 4\pi \in_0 a^2 E_0$

and $P = \frac{P_o}{\text{volume}}$

$$= \frac{4\pi \in_0 a^3 E_0}{\frac{4}{3}\pi a^3}$$

$$= 3 \in_0 E_0$$

$$\therefore \quad \alpha = 4\pi \in_0 a^3$$

$$= 3 \in_0 \left(\frac{4}{3}\pi a^3\right)$$

$$= 3 \in_0 \text{ (volume of sphere)}$$

46. Δx = *de*-Broglie wavelength = $\frac{h}{mv}$

From uncertainly principle,

$$\Delta x \Delta p \sim h$$

$$\Delta p \sim \frac{h}{\Delta x} = \frac{h}{\frac{h}{mv}} = mv$$

$$\Delta p = mv \quad ...(i)$$

Now, $\quad p = mv$ or $\Delta p = m\Delta v \quad ...(ii)$

from equn *(i)* and *(ii)*, we get

$$m\Delta v = mv$$

or $\quad \Delta v = v$

47. The probability that A can solved problem = $\frac{1}{3}$.

The probability that A cannot solve the problem = $1 - \frac{1}{3}$

Similarly, the probability that = $\frac{2}{3}$

B and C cannot solve the problem is $\frac{3}{4}$ and $\frac{4}{5}$ respectively.

Hence, the probability that the problem will be solved, *i.e.*, at least one student will solve it.

$$= 1 - \frac{2}{3}\times\frac{3}{4}\times\frac{4}{5}$$

$$= 1 - \frac{2}{5} = \frac{3}{5}$$

$$= \frac{3\times12}{5\times12} = \frac{36}{60}$$

48. The stater of weightlessness will result, when the centrifugal force just balance the earth's pull. Let the radius of the earth be R and let v_0

be the speed of satellite for weightlessness, then Centripetal force = Earth's pull

i.e., $$\frac{mv_0^2}{R+H} = \frac{GMm}{(R+H)^2}$$

where, m, M are respectively mass of the particle and that of earth.

Then, $$v_0^2 = \frac{GM}{(R+H)} = \frac{gR^2}{(R+H)}$$

since, $$g = \frac{GM}{R^2}$$

$$\Rightarrow \quad v_0 = \left[\frac{gR^2}{R+H}\right]^{1/2}$$

Period of revolution for this orbit is given by

$$T_0 = \frac{2\pi(R+H)}{v_0} = \frac{2\pi}{R}\sqrt{\frac{(R+H)^3}{g}}$$

49. 200 MeV $= 200 \times 1.6 \times 10^{-13}$
$= 3.2 \times 10^{-11}$ J

Energy required = P × t
$= 20 \times 10^6 \times 1 = 2 \times 10^7$ J

No. of neutrons emitted for 3.2×10^{-11} J of energy = 1.6

∴ No. of neutrons emitted for 2×10^7 J of energy $= \frac{1.6}{3.2\times10^{-11}} \times 2\times10^7 = 10^{18}$

50. Primary to secondary turns, $\frac{N_1}{N_2} = 10$

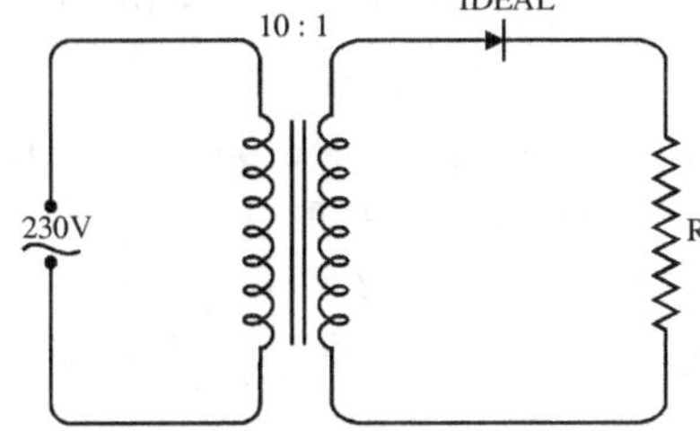

R.M.S. primary voltage = 230 V

∴ Max. primary voltage, $V_{pm} = (\sqrt{2}) \times$ r.m.s. primary voltage $= (\sqrt{2}) \times 230 = 325.3$ V

Max. secondary voltage,

$$V_{sm} = V_{pm} \times \frac{N_2}{N_1} = 325.3 \times \frac{1}{10} = 32.53 \text{ V}$$

As, $$I_{dc} = \frac{I_m}{\pi}$$

$$\therefore \quad V_{dc} = \frac{I_m}{\pi} \times R_L = \frac{V_{sm}}{\pi} = \frac{32.53}{\pi} = 10.36 \text{ V}$$

51. For TM_{11} mode,

$k_c \cdot a = 3.83$

then, $$f_c = \frac{k_c.a}{2\pi a.\sqrt{\mu \in}}, \quad \text{where } a = \text{radius}$$
$= 12.2$ GHz

Hence, Z_g (wave impedance)

$$= \eta\sqrt{1-\left(\frac{f_c}{f}\right)^2}$$

Where, $f = 14$ GHz

Then, $$Z_g = 377\sqrt{1-\left(\frac{12.2}{14}\right)^2} = 185\ \Omega$$

52. Energy for cubical box

$$E = 38\left(\frac{h^2}{8ma^2}\right)$$

$(n_x^2 + n_y^2 + n_z^2) = 38$

$n_x + n_y + n_z$ may take value.
(6, 1, 1); (1, 1, 6); (1, 6, 1) and also (2, 3, 5), (2, 5, 3), (5, 2, 3), (5, 3, 2), (3, 2, 5), (3, 5, 2)
Hence total values = 9.

53. Plate resistance, r_p = 200 W
Load resistance, R_L = 800 W
D.C. output voltage, E_{dc} = 100 V
Let V_m be the maximum value of a.c. voltage required.

Now, $$E_{dc} = I_{dc} \times R_L = \frac{V_m}{\pi(r_p + R_L)} \times R_L$$

or $$100 = \frac{V_m}{\pi(200+800)} \times 800$$

$$\therefore \quad V_m = \frac{\pi(200+800)100}{800} = 393 \text{ V}$$

Hence, a.c. voltage of maximum value of 393 V is required.

54. Let R_i = internal resistance of cell
R_L = Resistance of load

$$\therefore \quad I = \frac{E_0}{R_i + R_L}$$

$$\text{or} \quad 2.2 \times 10^{-3} = \frac{0.33}{R_i + 100}$$

or internal resistance of cell $R_i = 50\ \Omega$

55. Let the fraction be x

Energy of excited state (1) of atom = 0.1 eV

or $U_1 = 0.1 \times 1.6 \times 10^{-19}$ J

$U_1 = 1.6 \times 10^{-20}$ J

Average energy of an atom at 300 K is given by $\frac{3}{2}kT$

$$\text{or} \quad U_a = \frac{3}{2} \times 1.38 \times 10^{-23} \times 300$$

$U_a = 6.21 \times 10^{-21}$ J

$\therefore \quad xU_1 + (1 - x) \times 0 = U_a,$

$$x = \frac{U_a}{U_1} = \frac{6.21 \times 10^{21}}{1.6 \times 10^{-20}}$$

or $x = 0.388 = 38.8\%$

56.

$$dU = dQ - dW$$

$$\Rightarrow \quad \Delta V = \Delta Q - \Delta W$$

$$\Delta W = \Delta W_i + \Delta W_a$$

ΔW; work done by a gas when compressed isothermally is +ve.

Similarly ΔW_a is also a +ve quantity.

$$\Delta U = \Delta Q - (\Delta W_i + \Delta W_a)$$

$$= \Delta Q - \Delta W_i - \Delta W_a$$

57.

$C = 0.01\ \mu F$,

$f = 300$ Hz

and $R = 12\ k\Omega$ given

and for zero phase shift in Wienbridge oscillator

$$f = \frac{1}{2\pi RC}$$

$$\text{or} \quad R = \frac{1}{2\pi Cf} = \frac{1}{2\pi \times 0.01 \times 10^{-6} \times 300}$$

$= 53\ k\Omega$

Since $\frac{R_2}{R_1} = 2$

or $R_2 = 2R_1$

$= 2 \times 12\ k\Omega = 24\ k\Omega$

$\therefore \quad R_2 = 24\ k\Omega$

$R_1 = 53\ k\Omega$

58. The decay scheme is

$$_{17}C^{33} \rightarrow {}_{16}S^{33} + {}_1e^0 + \nu + E_\beta$$

When this proton emits with a maximum energy, the neutrino energy will be zero and the daughter nucleus S^{33} will be formed in the ground state

$$\therefore E_\beta = \frac{3}{5}\frac{e^2A^{2/3}}{4\pi \epsilon_0 R_0} - 1.80 \text{ MeV}$$

$$\text{or} \quad \frac{3}{5}\frac{e^2A^{2/3}}{4\pi \epsilon_0 R_0} = 6.1 \times 1.6 \times 10^{-13} \text{ joule}$$

$$\text{or } R_0 = \frac{3}{5}\frac{e^2A^{2/3}}{4\pi \epsilon_0 \times 6.1 \times 1.6 \times 10^{-13}}$$

$$= \frac{3}{5}\frac{(1.6 \times 10^{-19})^2 (33)^{2/3} \times 9 \times 10^9}{6.1 \times 1.6 \times 10^{-13}}$$

$= 1.41 \times 10^{-15}$ metre

$\therefore \quad R = R_0 A^{1/3} = 1.41 \times 10^{-15} (33)^{1/3}$

$= 4.54 \times 10^{-15}$ m.

59. Relativistic kinetic energy is given by

$E = m_0 c^2 [(1 - \beta^2)^{-1/2} - 1]$

$$\frac{1}{\sqrt{(1-\beta^2)}} - 1 = \frac{e}{m_0 c^2}$$

$$= \frac{20 \times 1.6 \times 10^{-12}}{9.109 \times 10^{-31} \times (3 \times 10^8)^2}$$

$\therefore \quad (1 - \beta^2)^{-1/2} = 40$

or, $\beta^2 = 0.9995$.

Hence the number of quanta emitted as Cerenkov radiation per metre

$$N = \frac{2\pi Z^2}{137}\left(\frac{1}{\lambda_2} - \frac{1}{\lambda_1}\right)\left(1 - \frac{1}{\beta^2\mu^2}\right)$$

$$= \frac{2 \times 3.14}{137} \times \frac{3000 \times 10^{10}}{4000 \times 7000} \times \left[1 - \frac{1}{0.9995 \times (1.49)^2}\right]$$

= 26980 quanta/metre

= 270 quanta/cm (Approx.)

60. Given, $m = 2$, $n = 1$, $\beta_P = 12$, and $f = 6$ GHz

As, $$\beta_P = \frac{\omega}{v}\sqrt{1-\left(\frac{f_C}{f}\right)^2}$$

$$12 = \frac{2\pi \times 6 \times 10^9}{3 \times 10^8}\sqrt{1-\left(\frac{f_C}{6}\right)^2}$$

$$\Rightarrow \quad f_C = 5.973 \text{ GHz}$$

61. We have,

$$Z_{in} = Z_{sc} = Z_0 \tanh rl = Z_0 \frac{\sinh rl}{\cosh rl}$$

$$rl = (1.4 + j5)(0.4) = 0.56 + j^2$$
$$\sinh rl = (1.4 + j5)(0.4) = 0.56 + j^2$$
$$\sinh rl = -0.245 + j\,1.055 \cosh rl$$
$$= -0.483 + j\,0.536$$

$$Z_{in} = \frac{(35 + j49)(-0.245 + j10.55)}{-0.483 + j\,0.536}$$

$$= 82 + j\,39\Omega$$

62. The offset due to V_{IO} is V_0 (Offset due to V_{IO})

$$= V_{IO} = \frac{R_1 + R_L}{R_1}$$

$$= (4\text{mV})\left(\frac{5\text{ k}\Omega + 500\text{ k}\Omega}{5\text{ k}\Omega}\right)$$

$$= 404 \text{ mV}$$

V_0 (offset due to I_{IO}) $= I_{IO} R_f$

$= (150$ nA$)(500$ k$\Omega)$

$= 75$ mV

Resulting in the total offset

V_0 (Total offset) $= V_0$ (Offset due to V_{IO}) $+ V_0$ (Offset due to I_{IO})

$= 404$ mV $+ 75$ mV

$= 479$ mV

63. M = 197

Density $\rho = 19.3$ gm/cc

N = Avogadro's number $= 6.02 \times 10^{23}$

Since solid gold has an fcc structure, so that the number of molecules per unit cell $= 4 = n$ (say)

By using formula

$$a^3 = \frac{nM}{\rho N} = \frac{4 \times 197}{19.3 \times 6.02 \times 10^{23}}$$

Hence $a = 5.14 \times 10^{-8}$ cm $= 5.14$ Å

So, the distance between adjacent atoms

$$d = \frac{a}{2} = \frac{5.14}{2} \text{ Å}$$

$$= 2.57 \text{ Å}$$

64. For conversation

$$h\upsilon = 2mc^2$$

But here $h\upsilon < 2mc^2$

so, energy is not conserved.

65. Guide wavelength,

$$\lambda_g = \frac{\lambda_0}{\sqrt{1-\left(\frac{f_C}{f}\right)^2}}$$

or $$\frac{1}{\lambda_0}\sqrt{1-\left(\frac{f_C}{f}\right)^2} = \frac{1}{\lambda_g}$$

$$\frac{1}{\lambda_0^2} - \frac{1}{\lambda_g^2} \times \left(\frac{f_C}{f}\right)^2 = \frac{1}{\lambda_g^2} = \frac{1}{\lambda_C^2}$$

$$\frac{1}{\lambda_0^2} - \frac{1}{\lambda_g^2} = \frac{1}{\lambda_C^2}$$

66. Maxwell's distribution of velocities law yields

Root mean square velocity,

$$v_{rms} = \sqrt{\frac{3kT}{m}}$$

Mean velocity,

$$v_{mean} = \sqrt{\frac{6kT}{\pi m}}$$

Most probable velocity,

$$v_p = \sqrt{\frac{2kT}{m}}$$

It is clear that

$$v_p < v_{rms}$$

67. $$C_{Ve} = \frac{R\pi^2 kT}{2E_{F0}}$$

$$C_V = \frac{12\,\pi^2 R}{5}\left(\frac{T}{T_d}\right)^3$$

Equating T and using $E_{F_0} = 5.5$ V $= 1.55$ K

68. For N-bit successive A/D converter, the number of clock pulses required is N-clock pulse. Thus ADC must be of the successive opp. type.

69. We know for the DAC with operational amplifier the output voltage is given by

$$V_{out} = -\frac{R_f}{R}V_{ref}$$

$$\left(S_{n-1} + \frac{S_{n-2}}{2} + \frac{S_{n-3}}{2^2} + \dots \frac{S_o}{2^{n-1}}\right)$$

For binary input 101,
$S_o = 1$, $S_1 = 0$, $S_2 = 1$ and $n = 3$

$$V_{out} = -\frac{8}{3} \times 12\left(1 + 0 \times 2^{-1} + 1 \times 2^{-2}\right)$$

$$= -40 \text{ V}$$

70. Modulation index,

$$m = \frac{V_{max} - V_{min}}{V_{max} + V_{min}}$$

Given, $V_{max} = 10$ V, $V_{min} = 5$ V

$$\therefore \quad m = \frac{10\text{V} - 5\text{V}}{10\text{V} + 5\text{V}}$$

$$= \frac{5}{15} = \frac{1}{3} = 0.33$$

71. For analysis of the bridge, we have

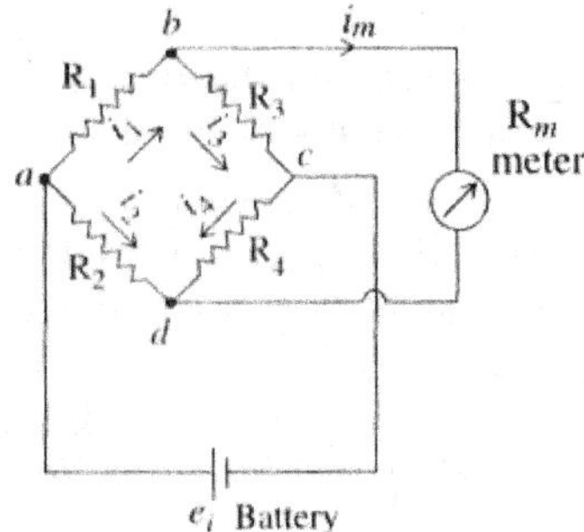

Assume that the input impedance of the meter is infinite and therefore,

$i_m = 0$

Hence, $i_1 = i_3$

and $i_2 = i_4$,

Output voltage

e_0 = Voltage across terminal b and d

$= i_1R_1 - i_2R_2$

But $\quad i_1 = \dfrac{e_i}{R_1 + R_3}$

and $\quad i_2 = \dfrac{e_i}{R_2 + R_4}$

$$\therefore \quad e_0 = \left[\frac{R_1}{R_1 + R_3} - \frac{R_2}{R_2 + R_4}\right]e_i$$

$$= \left[\frac{R_1R_4 - R_2R_3}{(R_1 + R_3)(R_2 + R_4)}\right]e_i$$

Now R_1 changes by an amount ΔR_1. This causes a change Δe_0 in the output voltage. Thus,

$$e_0 + \Delta e_0 = \left[\frac{(R_1 + \Delta R_1)R_4 - R_2R_3}{(R_1 + \Delta R_1 + R_3)(R_2 + R_4)}\right]e_i$$

$$= \left[\frac{1 + \frac{\Delta R_1}{R_1} - \frac{R_2R_3}{R_1R_4}}{\left\{1 + \left(\frac{\Delta R_1}{R_1}\right) + \frac{R_3}{R_1}\right\}\left(1 + \frac{R_2}{R_4}\right)}\right]e_i$$

In order to simplify the relationship, let us assume that initially all the resistance comprising the bridge are equal, *i.e.*,
$R_1 = R_2 = R_3 = R_4 = R$
Under these conditions

$e_0 = 0$

and $\quad \Delta e_0 = \left[\dfrac{(\Delta R/R)}{4 + 2(\Delta R/R)}\right]e_i$.

72. According to Heisenberg uncertainty principle.

$$\Delta E \cdot \Delta t \sim h \qquad \dots(1)$$

Since $\quad E = \dfrac{hc}{\lambda}$

$$\Delta E = -\frac{hc}{\lambda^2}\Delta\lambda$$

Using equation (1)

$$-\frac{hc}{\lambda^2} \cdot \Delta\lambda \cdot \Delta t \sim h \qquad \dots(2)$$

Again $\quad C = v\lambda$

$\Rightarrow \quad v\Delta\lambda + \lambda\Delta v = 0$

or $\quad v\Delta\lambda = -\lambda\Delta v$

$$\frac{\Delta\lambda}{\lambda} = -\frac{\Delta\nu}{\nu}$$

∴ Equation (2)

$$-\frac{hc}{\lambda^2}\Delta\lambda \cdot \Delta t \sim h$$

$$\Rightarrow \quad \frac{hc}{\lambda} \cdot \cdot \frac{\Delta\nu}{\nu}\Delta t \sim h$$

or

$$\frac{\Delta\nu}{\nu} \sim \frac{h}{\Delta t} \cdot \frac{\lambda}{hc}$$

$$\sim \frac{\lambda}{\Delta t . c}$$

$$\lambda = 600 \text{ nm}$$

$$\Delta t = 8 \times 10^{-9}$$

$$\Rightarrow \quad \frac{\Delta\nu}{\nu} = \frac{600 \times 10^{-9} \text{m}}{8 \times 10^{-9} \times 3 \times 10^{8}}$$

$$= \frac{1}{4} \times 10^{-6}$$

73.

$$\varpi = \frac{1}{2\pi}\sqrt{\frac{k}{\mu}}$$

For reduced mass

$$\mu = \frac{m_1 m_2}{m_1 + m_2} = \frac{m}{2}$$

$$k = 4.8 \times 10^2 \text{ N/m}$$

$$\mu = \frac{1.6 \times 10^{-27}}{2}$$

$$= 0.835 \times 10^{-27} \text{ kg}$$

$$v = \frac{1}{2\pi}\sqrt{\frac{4.8 \times 10^2}{0.835 \times 10^{-27}}}$$

$$v = 1.2 \times 10^{14} \text{ Hz}$$

74. For the band theory electron, E is not in general proportional to K^2; there the variation of E with K is shown as

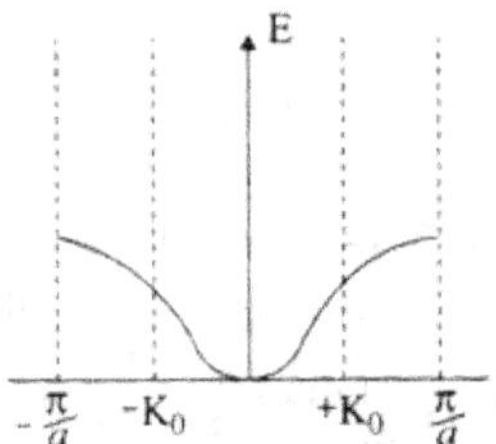

and velocity will be depicted as

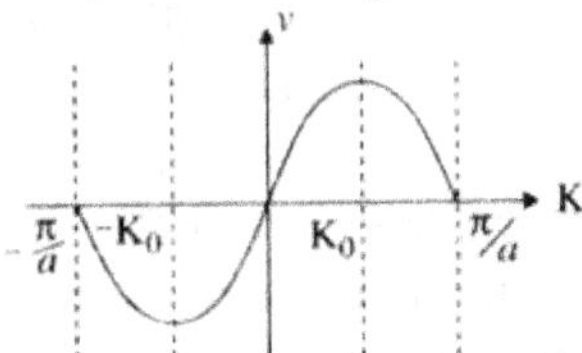

At the bottom (K = 0) of the energy band, the velocity is zero and as the value of K increases (*i.e.*, the energy E increases) the velocity increases and reaching its maximum value at $K = K_0$ where K_0 corresponds to the point of inflexion on the E-K curve.

75. For 8 α decay $\left({}^4_2\text{He}\right)$

$$A = 4 \times 8 = 32$$

$$Z = 8 \times 2 = 16$$

For 6β^- decay $\left({}^{\;0}_{-1}n\right)$

$$A = 0$$

$$Z = 6 \times -1 = -6$$

Final nucleus—

$$A = [238 - 32] = 206$$

And $Z = [92 - (16 - 6)] = 82$

SET–8

CSIR–UGC (NET) PHYSICAL SCIENCES

PART-A

1. In a row of girls, Monika is 11th from the left and Savita is 7th from the right. If they interchange their positions, then Monika becomes 15th from the left, Then-at what place will Savita be from the right.

A. 15th B. 25th
C. 11th D. 27th

2. Find the missing numbers in the bottom middle circle. (Clue: left halves of the central circles relate to the left circles and the right halves to the right circles)

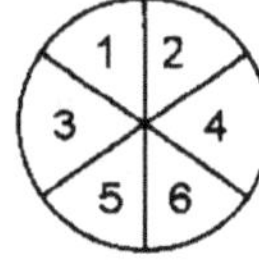
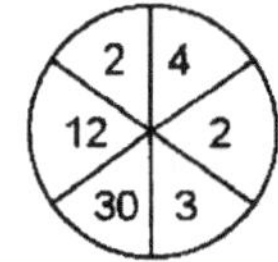
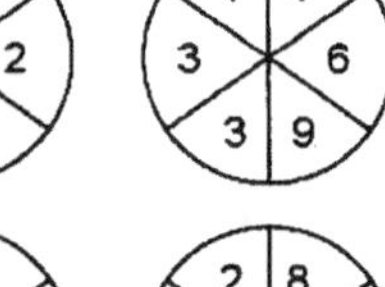

A. 10, 20 B. 15, 15
C. 21, 2 D. 6, 2

3. A bag contains 3 red, 4 white and 5 blue balls. All balls are different. Two balls are drawn at random. The probability that they are of different colours is :

A. 47/66 B. 10/33
C. 5/22 D. None of these

4. Panas walked from Mumbai to Thane on foot. Had he walked one mile/hr faster he would have reached $2\frac{1}{2}$ hrs earlier, and had he walked slower by one mile/hr, he would have taken 5 hrs. more. The distance between Mumbai and Thane is:

A. 20 miles B. 30 miles
C. 40 miles D. 60 miles

5. Three men Ram, Karan and Mohan run around an oval garden from a fixed post at the rates of 5, $5\frac{1}{7}$, $5\frac{1}{3}$ per hour. They come back to the fixed post in $3\frac{3}{4}$ hours. Find the greatest length, the race course can have.

A. $\frac{28}{5}$ km B. $\frac{5}{28}$ km
C. $\frac{11}{28}$ km D. $\frac{28}{11}$ km

6. There is a road beside a river. Two friends started from a place A, moved to a temple situated at another place B and then returned to A again. One of them moves on a cycle at a speed of 12 km/hr, while other sails on a boat at the speed of 10 km/hr. If the river flows at the speed of 4 km/hr, then which of the two friends will return to place A first?

A. Cyclist
B. Boat sailor
C. Both in same time
D. None of these

7. If two pipes function simultaneously, the reservoir will be filled in 12 hours. One pipe fills the reservoir 10 hours faster than the other. How many hours does it take the second pipe to fill the reservoir?

A. 20 hrs. B. 25 hrs.
C. 30 hrs. D. 40 hrs.

8. The average four consecutive even numbers is 27. The largest of these numbers is:

A. 30 B. 50
C. 20 D. 40

9. If the rate of income tax is 5%, the net income of a person is ₹ 17100. If the rate of income tax is 6%, how much will be the net income?

A. ₹ 15820 B. ₹ 16920
C. ₹ 17820 D. ₹ 18920

10. The owner of a cell phone shop charges his customer 32% more than the cost price. If a customer paid ₹ 6600 for the cell phone, then what was the cost price of the cell phone?

A. ₹ 5000 B. ₹ 5500
C. ₹ 5800 D. ₹ 6100

11. A and B jointly invest ₹ 2100 and ₹ 3100 respectively in a firm. A is an active partner and hence he gets 25% of the profit separately. If their business yields them total ₹ 1040 as profit, what will be the gain of each of them?

A. ₹ 415, ₹ 625 B. ₹ 575, ₹ 465
C. ₹ 515, ₹ 525 D. ₹ 560, ₹ 480

12. A started a business with an investment of ₹ 4000. B joined him after 4 months and C joined him after 5 months. At the end of year they get profit in the ratio of 3 : 4 : 7. Find the ratio of capitals invested in the business by B and C.

A. 1 : 2 B. 2 : 1
C. 3 : 2 D. 1 : 3

13. Two pipes can fill a cistern in 14 hours and 16 hours respectively. The pipes are opened simultaneously and it is found that due to leakage at the bottom, 32 minutes extra are taken for the cistern to be filled up. When the cistern is full, in what time will the leak empty it?

A. 108 hours B. 112 hours
C. 116 hours D. 120 hours

14. 10 men or 18 boys can do a piece of work in 15 days. In how many days would 25 men and 15 boys complete the same work working together?

A. $5\frac{1}{2}$ days B. $4\frac{1}{2}$ days
C. $6\frac{2}{3}$ days D. $2\frac{1}{3}$ days

15. A monkey wants to climb up a glazed pole. He climbs 12 metres in 1 minute and then he slips back 3 metres in the next minute. If the pole is 63 metre high, how long does he take to climb at the top of the pole?

A. $11\frac{1}{4}$ min B. $12\frac{1}{2}$ min
C. $12\frac{3}{4}$ min D. $14\frac{3}{4}$ min

16. A farmer took a loan at 12 per cent per annum at simple interest. After 4 years he settled the loan by paying ₹ 2442. What was the principal amount?

A. ₹ 1542 B. ₹ 1550
C. ₹ 1600 D. ₹ 1650

17. $\log_{10} \tan 1° + \log_{10} \tan 2° + \log_{10} \tan 3° + \ldots\ldots + \log_{10} \tan 89° = ?$

A. 0 B. 1
C. 2 D. 3

18. In a race of 300 metres, A beats B by 15 metres or 5 seconds. How much time does A take to complete the race?

A. 105 seconds B. 100 seconds
C. 95 seconds D. 90 seconds

19. When 60% of a number A is added to another number B, B becomes 175% of its previous value. Which one of the following is correct?

A. $A > B$ B. $B > A$
C. $A = B$ D. Data inadequate

20. A person standing on the bank of a river observes that the angle subtended by a tree on the opposite bank is 60°, when he retires 40 metres from the bank he finds the angle to be 30°. Then the breadth of the river is:

A. 40 m B. 60 m
C. 20 m D. 30 m

PART-B

21. The maximum intensity in case of interference of n identical waves each of intensity I_0, if the interference is coherent is:

A. $n^2 I_0$ B. $n I_0^2$
C. $n^2 I_0^2$ D. $\frac{n_0 I_0}{2}$

22. The binding energy per nucleon of helium nucleus is 7 MeV and that of deuteron is 1 MeV, Then:

A. deuteron nucleus is more stable
B. helium nucleus is more stable
C. both are equally stable
D. both are less stable

23. The temperature dependence of the heat conductivity of an insulating solid

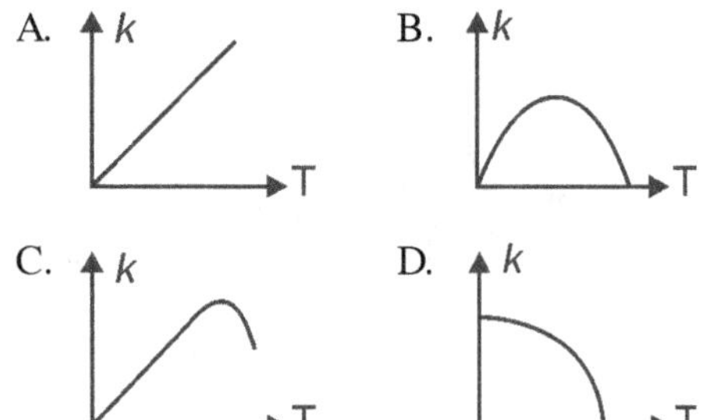

24. In the case of forward biasing of *p-n* junction, which one of the following figures correctly depicts the direction of flow of carriers?

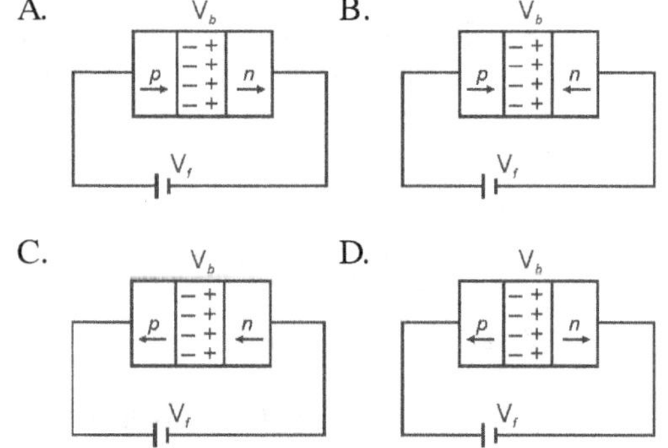

25. An 0–10 A ammeter has a guaranteed accuracy of 1 per cent of full scale deflection. The limiting error while reading 2.5 A is

A. 2% B. 5%
C. 1% D. 4%

26. Two identical capacitors, have the same capacitance C. One of them is charged to potential V_1 and the other V_2. The negative ends of the capacitors are connected together, when the positive ends are also connected, the decrease in energy of the combined system is

A. $\frac{1}{4}C(V_1^2 - V_2^2)$ B. $\frac{1}{4}C(V_1^2 + V_2^2)$

C. $\frac{1}{4}C(V_1 - V_2)^2$ D. $\frac{1}{4}C(V_1 + V_2)^2$

27. An admissible potential between the proton and the neutron in a deuteron is

A. coulom
B. harmonic oscillator
C. Finite square well
D. Infinite square well

28. The DC current gain (β) of a BJT is 50. Assuming that the emitter injection efficiency is 0.995, the base transport factor is

A. 0.985 B. 0.385
C. 0.685 D. 0.785

29. For the 555 timer circuit in astable operation, find the frequency of oscillation, if R_1 = 1K R_2 = 4.7 K and C = 10 nF.

A. 15.84 kHz B. 13.84 kHz
C. 11.84 kHz D. 17.84 kHz

30. In a Q meter, distributed capacitance of coil is measured by changing the capacitance of the tuning capacitor. The values of tuning capacitors are C_1 and C_2 for reasonant frequencies f_1 and $2f_1$ respectively. The value of distributed capacitance is

A. $\frac{C_1 - C_2}{2}$ B. $\frac{C_1 - 2C_2}{3}$

C. $\frac{C_1 - 4C_2}{3}$ D. $\frac{C_1 - 3C_2}{2}$

31. An amplifier whose bandwidth is 100 kHz has a noise power spectrum density input of 7×10^{-21} J. If the input resistance is 50 kΩ and amplifier gain 100, what is noise output voltage?

A. 0.38 mV B. 0.83 mV
C. 1.183 mV D. 11.83 mV

32. An X-ray tube operates on 30 kV. The minimum wavelength of X-ray emitted is

A. 1.2 Å B. 6.6 Å
C. 0.133 Å D. 0.4 Å

33. Metallic iron changes from bcc structure to fcc structure at 910°C with an increase in the atomic radii. The density of iron in this structural change

A. Increases B. Becomes zero
C. Remains constant D. Decreases

34. The probability of leakage of an α-particle of energy 5 MeV through a potential barrier of height 10 MeV and width 10^{-14} m
(Given $\hbar = 1.05 \times 10^{-34}$ Js, mass of α-particle $= 6.4 \times 10^{-27}$ kg)

A. 1.7×10^{-10} B. 1.7×10^{-12}
C. 1.7×10^{-8} D. 1.7×10^{-6}

35. In the muon decay $\bar{\mu} \rightarrow \bar{\beta} + \nu_{\mu} + \bar{\mu}$, the $\bar{\beta}$ is ejected with relativistic energy. If mass of μ^- meson is 206 m_e, the maximum available energy in eV for the process

A. 150 MeV B. 210 MeV
C. 105 MeV D. 100 MeV

36. It is possible to measure the impedance of a coaxial cable

A. With an ohm meter across the cable
B. By measuring the attenuation of signals through the cable
C. Making use of the reflection properties of terminations
D. None of these

37. The binding energy of ground state of positronium is a factor f times that of a hydrogen atom, f =

A. $\frac{1}{3}$ B. 3
C. $\frac{1}{2}$ D. 4

38. Two capacitors of capacitances C_1 and C_2 are connected in parallel. If a charge q is given to the assembly, the charge gets shared. The ratio of the charge on the capitance C_1 to the charge that on C_2 is

A. $\frac{C_1}{C_2}$ B. $\frac{C_2}{C_1}$
C. $C_1 C_2$ D. $\frac{1}{C_1 C_2}$

39. If the frequency of oscillating particle is n, then the frequency of oscillation of its potential energy is

A. n B. n^2
C. $2n$ D. $3n$

40. The mass a hot (120°C) air balloon of 10 m^3 volume will lift at sea level when the temperature is 20°C is closest to

A. 30 kg B. 300 kg
C. 300 g D. 3 kg

41. Given for an FET, g_m = 95 mA/Volt, total capacitance = 500 pF. For a voltage gain of –30, the bandwidth will be—

A. 100 kHz B. 3 MHz
C. 633 kHz D. 19 MHz

42. If the principal quantum number and the azimuthal quantum number in the relativistic model of the atom are 3 and –1 respectively, then the magnitude of the semi-minor axis b in terms of the semi-major axis is given by

A. $b = \frac{a}{3}$ B. $b = \frac{2a}{3}$
C. $b = \frac{a}{2}$ D. $b = a$

43. In an X-ray tube, X-rays are produced by electrons accelerated by volt. The maximum frequency of the X-rays is

A. ehV B. hV
C. $\frac{eh}{V}$ D. $\frac{eV}{h}$

44. A crystal belongs to a face centred cubic lattice with four atoms in the unit cell. The size of the crystal is 1 cm and its unit cell dimension is 1 nm. f is the scattering factor of the atom. The number of atoms in the crystal is:

A. 2×10^{21} B. 4×10^{21}
C. 2×10^{23} D. 4×10^{24}

45. The reaction $e^+ + p^- \rightarrow \nu_e + \pi^-$ forbidden because of—

A. Law of electron number conservation
B. Law of Baryon number of conservation
C. Law of momentum energy of conservation
D. Law of muon number of conservation

PART-C

46. If one interchange the spatial co-ordinate of two electron in a state of total spin

A. The wave function changes sign
B. The wave function is unchanged
C. The wave function changes to a completely different functions
D. None of these

47. The transistor amplifier is a 'grounded base' configuration *h* on the following characteristics—

A. Low input impedence
B. High current gain
C. Low output impedence
D. None of these

48. The expression for the output voltage V_0 in terms of the input voltage V_1 and V_2 in the circuit shown in the fig., assuming the operational amplifier to be ideal is

$$V_o = A_1V_1 + A_2V_2$$

The value of A_1 and A_2 would the respectively

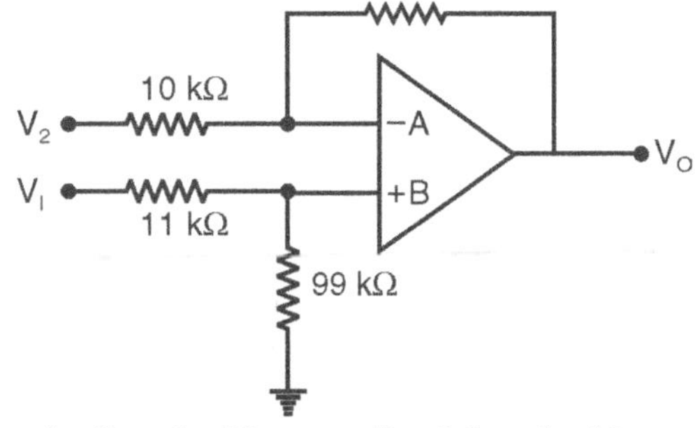

A. 9 and −10 B. 9.9 and −10
C. −9 and 10 D. −9.9 and 10

49. Out of the following unstable particles, which one has the longest half-life

A. *n* B. Ξ^{-1}
C. k^{-1} D. Σ^{-1}

50. Liquid helium-4 has a normal boiling point of 4.2 K. However, at a pressure of 1 mm of mercury, it boils at 1.2 K. Estimate the average latent heat of vapourisation of helium in this temperature range

A. 9.3 J/mol B. 93 J/mol
C. 93 kJ/mol D. 9.3 kJ/mol

51. The rotational energy levels of a diatomic molecule are

A. Continuous
B. Discrete and equispaced
C. Discrete, but not equispaced
D. Nothing can be said

52. Of the following having the same kinetic energy, which has the longest wavelength?

A. An electron B. A proton
C. A neutron D. An α-particle

53. Which of the following wave functions can be solutions of Schrodinger's equation for all values of x?

A. $\psi = A\sec x$ B. $\psi = A\tan x$
C. $\psi = Ae^{x^2}$ D. $\psi = Ae^{-x^2}$

54. It is desired to multiply the number OAH by OBH and store the result in the accumulator. The numbers are available in register B and C respectively. A part of the 8085 program for this purpose is given below

```
        MV1     A, OOH
LOOP    --------
        --------
        --------
        --------
        --------
        HLT
        END
```

The sequence of instruction to complete the program would be

A. JNZ LOOP
ADD B
DCR C

B. ADD B
JNZ LOOP
DCR C

C. DCR C
JNZ LOOP
ADD B

D. ADD B
DCR C
JNZ LOOP

55. A thermometer is calibrated 150°C to 200°C. The accuracy is specified within ± 0.25% of instrument span. What is the maximum static error?

A. $\pm$ 0.125°C B. $\pm$ 0.134°C
C. $\pm$ 0.111°C D. $\pm$ 0.102°C

56. The Bohr model gives the value for the ionization potential of Li^{2+} ion as
A. 13.6 eV B. 27.2 eV
C. 40.8 eV D. 122.4 eV

57. A crystal belongs to a face centred cubic lattice with four atoms in the unit cell. The size of the crystal is 2.7 cm and its unit cell dimension is 27 μm. *f* is the scattering factor of the atom. The number of atoms in the crystal is:
A. 2×10^9 B. 4×10^9
C. 2×10^{11} D. 4×10^{11}

58. The maximum energy of deutrons coming out of a cyclotron accelerator is 20 MeV. The maximum energy of photons that can be obtained from this accelerator is
A. 10 MeV B. 20 MeV
C. 30 MeV D. 40 MeV

59. The poisson equation Δ^2 F $g(x, y, z) = g(x, y, z)$ with a given g(x, y, z) and physical bounding condition, we have
A. More than one solution
B. One and only one solution
C. Occasionally no solution
D. Infinitely many solution

60. In the microwave spectrum of identical rigid diatomic molecules, the separation between the spectral lines is recordered to be 0.7143 cm^{-1}. The moment of inertia of the molecule in kgm^2 is
A. 2.3×10^{-36} B. 2.3×10^{-40}
C. 7.8×10^{-42} D. 7.8×10^{-46}

61. Find the directional derivative of $\vec{V}^2$, where $\vec{V} = xy^2\hat{i} + zy^2\hat{j} + xz^2\hat{k}$, at the point (2, 0, 3) in the direction of the outward normal to the sphere $x^2 + y^2 + z^2 = 14$ at the point (3, 2, 1).

A. $\frac{1404}{\sqrt{14}}$ B. $\frac{2503}{\sqrt{13}}$

C. $\frac{1204}{\sqrt{13}}$ D. $\frac{1504}{\sqrt{12}}$

62. Using Green's theorem evaluate $\int(x^2 y dx + x^2 dy)$ where c is the boundary described counter clockwise of the triangle with vertices (0, 0), (1, 0), (1, 1).

A. $\frac{1}{12}$ B. $\frac{11}{12}$

C. $\frac{7}{12}$ D. $\frac{5}{12}$

63. A bead slides on a smooth uniform circular wire of radius, a, which is rotating which a constant angular velocity, ω, about a fixed vertical diameter. Find the equation of motion of the bead.

A. $\ddot{\theta} = \omega \sin\theta\cos\theta + \frac{g}{r}\sin\theta$

B. $\ddot{\theta} = \omega \sin\theta\cos\theta + \frac{g^2}{r^2}\sin\theta$

C. $\ddot{\theta} = \omega^2 \sin\theta\cos\theta + \frac{g}{r}\sin\theta$

D. $\ddot{\theta} = \omega^2 \sin^2\theta + \frac{g}{r}\cos\theta$

64. Determine V_0 for the circuit with the input waveform as shown with $V_T = 0.7V$

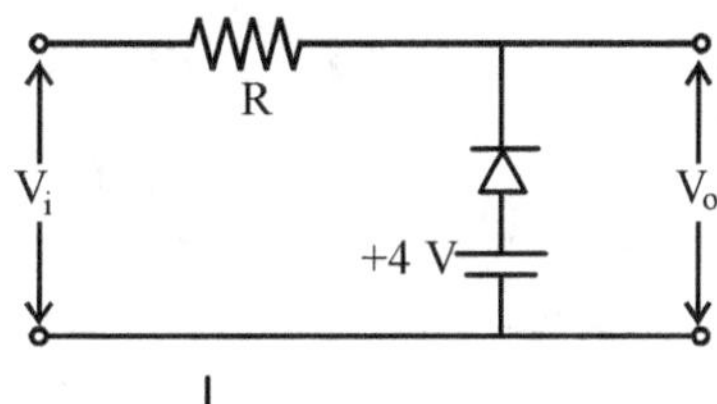

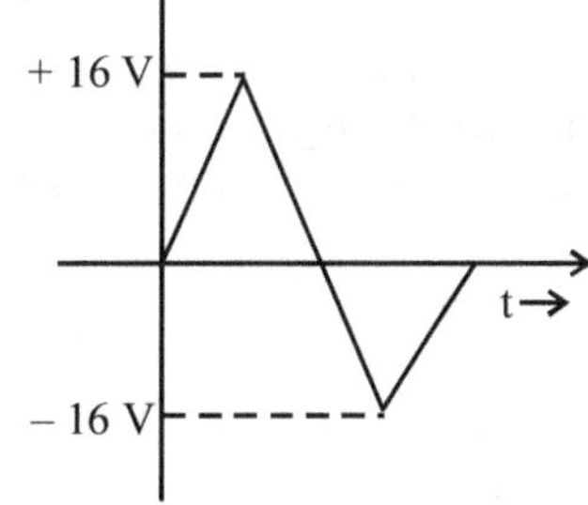

(*a*) 12 V (*b*) 12.7 V
(*c*) 3.3 V (*d*) 4.7 V

65. Fermi energy of certain metal M_1 is 5 eV. A second metal M_2 has an electron density which is 6% higher than that of M_1. Assuming that the free electron theory is valid for both the metals, the Fermi energy of M_2 is closest to
A. 5.6 eV B. 5.2 eV
C. 4.8 eV D. 4.4 eV

66. Charges Q, Q and –2Q are placed on the vartices of an equilateral triangle ABC of side length a, as shown in the figure

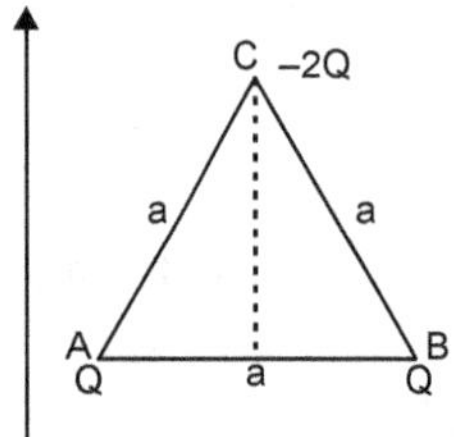

The dipole moment of this configuration of charges, irrespective of the choice of origin, is

A. $+2aQ\,\hat{i}$ B. $+\sqrt{3}aQ\,\hat{j}$

C. $-\sqrt{3}aQ\,\hat{j}$ D. 0

67. A resistance strain gauge is fastened to a steel fixture and subjected to a stress of 1000 kg/m^2. If the gauge factor is 3 and the modulus of elasticity of steel is 2×10^{10} kg/m^2, then the fractional change in resistance of the strain gauge due to the applied stress is
(**Note :** The gauge factor is defined as the ratio of the fractional change in resistance to the fractional change in length.)

A. 1.5×10^{-7} B. 3.0×10^{-7}

C. 0.16×10^{-10} D. 0.5×10^{-7}

68. A vessel has two compartments of volume V_1 and V_2 containing an ideal gas at pressure P_1 and P_2, and temperatures T_1 and T_2 respectively. If the wall separating the compartments is removed, the resulting equilibrium temperature will be

A. $\dfrac{P_1T_1 + P_2T_2}{P_1 + P_2}$

B. $\dfrac{V_1T_1 + V_2T_2}{V_1 + V_2}$

C. $\dfrac{P_1V_1 + P_2V_2}{(P_1V_1/T_1) + (P_2V_2/T_2)}$

D. $(T_1T_2)^{1/2}$

69. Consider black body radiation contained in a cavity whose walls are at temperature T. The radiation is in equilibrium with the walls of the cavity. If the temperature of the walls is increased to $2T$ and the radiation is allowed to come to equilibrium at the new temperature, the entropy of the radiation increases by a factor of

A. 2 B. 4

C. 8 D. 16

70. A given quantity of gas is taken from the state A → C reversibly, by two paths, A → C directly and A → B → C as shown in the figure below.

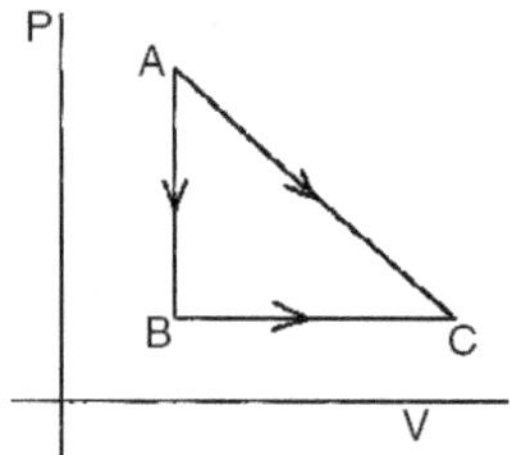

During the process A → C the work done by the gas is 100 J and the heat absorbed is 150 J. If during the process A → B → C the work done by the gas is 30 J, the heat absorbed is:

A. 20 J B. 80 J

C. 220 J D. 280 J

71. Two bodies of equal mass m are connected by a massless rigid rod of length l lying in the xy-plane with the centre of the rod at the origin. If this system is rotating about the z-axis with a frequency ω, its angular momentum is:

A. $ml^2\omega/4$ B. $ml^2\omega/2$

C. $ml^2\omega$ D. $2ml^2\omega$

72. Use Green's theorem to find
$\int (x^2 + xy)dx + (x^2 + y^2)dy$ where c is the square formed by the lines $y = \pm 1$, $x = \pm 1$.

A. 5 B. 3

C. ∞ D. 0

73. Two equal masses, joined by a rope passing over a light pulley are constrained to move on frictionless surface figure. Find the expression for the extension of the spring as a function of time. (take at $t = 0$, extension for normal length, $x = 0$)

A. $x = \frac{mg}{k}$ (1 – cos ω*t*)

B. $\frac{2mg}{k}(1+\cos\omega t)$

C. $\frac{mg}{2k}(1-\sin\omega t)$

D. $mgk(1-\cos\omega t)$

74. A photon of energy 3 keV collides elastically with an electron initially at rest. If the photon emerges at an angle of 60°C, calculate the kinetic energy of recoiling electron.

A. 8.671 eV B. 3.273 eV
C. 6.543 eV D. 1.235 eV

75. An excited state of an atom is 1.38 eV above the ground state. Calculate the number of atoms in this excited state relative to the group state at 16000 K. ($k = 1.38 \times 10^{-23}$ joule/K).

A. 0.458 B. 0.768
C. 0.368 D. 0.128

ANSWERS

1	2	3	4	5	6	7	8	9	10
C	D	A	B	B	A	C	A	B	A
11	**12**	**13**	**14**	**15**	**16**	**17**	**18**	**19**	**20**
B	A	B	B	C	D	A	C	A	C
21	**22**	**23**	**24**	**25**	**26**	**27**	**28**	**29**	**30**
A	B	B	B	D	C	C	A	B	C
31	**32**	**33**	**34**	**35**	**36**	**37**	**38**	**39**	**40**
D	D	A	C	C	C	C	A	C	D
41	**42**	**43**	**44**	**45**	**46**	**47**	**48**	**49**	**50**
C	A	D	B	B	B	C	B	A	B
51	**52**	**53**	**54**	**55**	**56**	**57**	**58**	**59**	**60**
C	A	B	D	A	D	B	A	B	D
61	**62**	**63**	**64**	**65**	**66**	**67**	**69**	**69**	**70**
A	D	C	C	B	C	A	C	C	B
71	**72**	**73**	**74**	**75**					
B	D	A	A	C					

EXPLANATORY ANSWERS

1.

11th 7th

From left → Monika Savita → From right

Monika 15th

∵ Change in position of Monika from left
= 15 – 11 = 4

∴ Same change will take place of Savita from right

∴ Position of Savita from the right
= 7 + 4 = 11th

2.

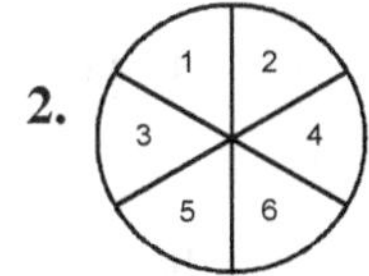

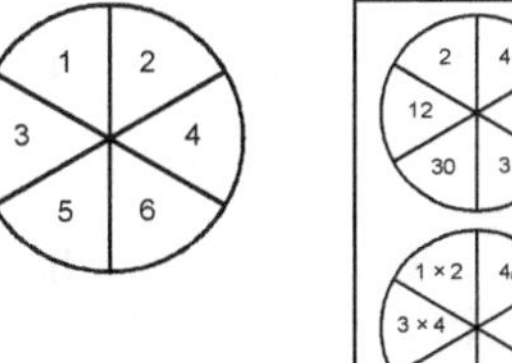

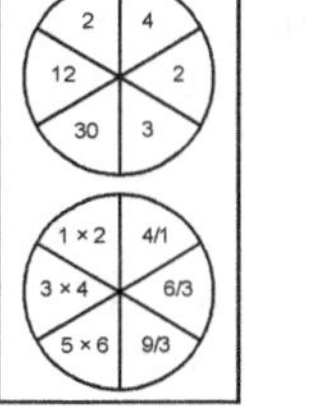

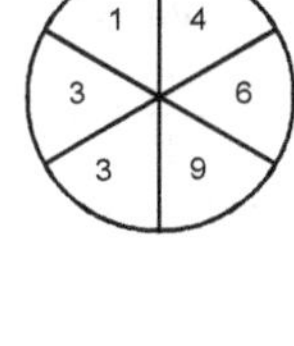

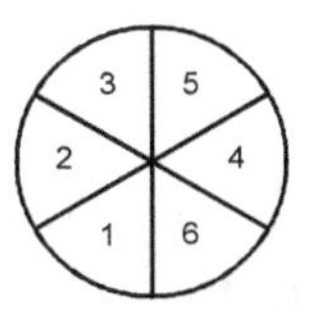

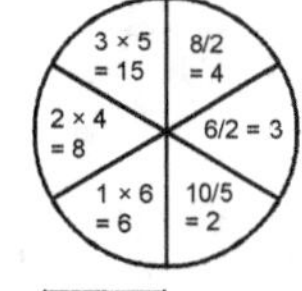

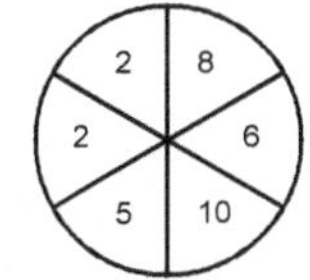

Hence answer = 6, 2.

3. We have the following pattern:

One red and one white $P_I = 3 \times 4/{}^{12}C_2$

One red and one blue $P_{II} = 3 \times 5/{}^{12}C_2$

One blue and one white $P_{III} = 4 \times 5/{}^{12}C_2$

Since all these cases are exclusive, so the required probability $= (12 + 15 + 20)/{}^{12}C_2$

$= (47 \times 2)/(12 \times 11) = 47/66.$

4. Let usual speed be x miles/hr and distance of the destination be d miles

Now, $\frac{d}{x} - \frac{d}{x+1} = \frac{5}{2} \Rightarrow d = \frac{5}{2}x(x+1)$ ...(i)

Again, $\frac{d}{x-1} - \frac{d}{x} = 5 \Rightarrow d = 5x(x-1)$ ...(ii)

From equations (i) and (ii)

$\frac{5}{2}x\,(x + 1) = 5x\,(x - 1) \Rightarrow x + 1 = 2x - 2$

$\therefore\ x = 3$ mile/hr

Now, from (*ii*), $d = 5 \times 3\,(3 - 1) = 30$ miles.

5. Total number of rounds made by Ram in $\frac{15}{4}$ hrs $= 5 \times \frac{15}{4} = \frac{75}{4}$

Total number of rounds made by Karan in $\frac{15}{4}$ hrs $= \frac{36}{7} \times \frac{15}{4} = \frac{135}{7}$

Total number of rounds made by Mohan in $\frac{15}{4}$ hrs $= \frac{16}{3} \times \frac{15}{4} = 20$

H.C.F. of $\frac{75}{4}, \frac{135}{7}$ and $20 = \frac{5}{28}$

Hence, greatest length, the race cource can have $\frac{5}{28}$ km.

6. Downstream speed = 10 + 4 = 14 km/hr.

Upstream speed = 10 – 4 = 6 km/hr.

Hence, their average speed

$$= \frac{x+x}{\frac{x}{14}+\frac{x}{6}} = \frac{2x}{5x/21} = \frac{42}{5} = 8.4 \text{ km/hr.}$$

Since, average speed of cyclist (12 km/hr) > average speed of boat sailor (8.4 km/hr).

Therefore, the cyclist will return to A first.

7. Let $(x - 10)$ and x hrs be the time taken by two pipes to fill the reservoir, then,

$$\frac{1}{x-10} + \frac{1}{x} = \frac{1}{12} \Rightarrow \frac{2x-10}{x^2-10x} = \frac{1}{12}$$

$\Rightarrow x^2 - 34x + 120 = 0$

$\Rightarrow (x - 30)\,(x - 4) = 0$

$\therefore\ x = 30$ (Taking 30 only).

Hence, second pipe will fill the reservoir in 30 hours.

8. Let us consider the four consecutive even numbers are:

$x,\ x + 2,\ x + 4,\ x + 6$

By the question,

$$\frac{x+x+2+x+4+x+6}{4} = 27$$

$4x + 12 = 27 \times 4 = 108$

$\Rightarrow 4x = 108 - 12 = 96$

$\therefore\ x = \frac{96}{4} \approx 24$

Hence, the largest number = 24 + 6 = 30

9. Gross income $= \frac{100}{95} \times 17100 =$ ₹ 18000

New net income $= \frac{94}{100} \times 18000 =$ ₹ 16920

10. Let cost price of the cell phone be ₹ x; then

$$x + \frac{32}{100} \times x = 6600 \Rightarrow \frac{132x}{100} = 6600$$

$\therefore\ x = \frac{100 \times 6600}{132} =$ ₹ 5000.

11. Separate profit for A $= \frac{1040 \times 25}{100} =$ ₹ 260

Remaining profit = ₹ (1040 – 260) = ₹ 780

Ratio of capitals of A and B

= 2100 : 3100 = 21 : 31

A's profit $= \frac{21}{52} \times 780 =$ ₹ 315

B's profit $= \frac{31}{52} \times 780 =$ ₹ 465

Total profit of A = ₹ (315 + 260) = ₹ 575.

Therefore, A and B will make profit of ₹ 575 and ₹ 46 respectively.

12. Let, B and C invest ₹ x and ₹ y respectively

∴ Ratio of their capitals = 48000 : $8x$: $7y$

But given ratio of the profits = 3 : 4 : 7

$8x : 7y = 4 : 7 \Rightarrow \frac{x}{y} = \frac{1}{2}$

Hence, $x : y = 1 : 2$.

13. In 1 hour the part filled by both the pipes

$= \frac{1}{14} + \frac{1}{16} = \frac{15}{112}$

Hence, both the pipes will fill the cistern in $\frac{112}{15}$ min.

But due to leakage, the tank will be filled in

$\frac{112}{15} + \frac{32}{60} = \frac{120}{15}$ = 8 hrs.

Since, in 1 hr. the part emptied by the leakage

$= \frac{15}{112} - \frac{1}{8} = \frac{1}{112}$

Therefore, leakage will empty the tank in 112 hrs.

14. 10 men ≡ 18 boys

25 men ≡ $\frac{18}{10} \times 25 = 45$ boys

Hence, 25 men + 15 boys = 45 + 15 = 60 boys

Now, 18 boys can do a piece of work in 15 days.

Hence, 60 boys will do a piece of work in

$\frac{15 \times 18}{60} = \frac{9}{2}$ days = $4\frac{1}{2}$ days.

15. The monkey climbs 12 metres in 1 minute and then he slips back 3 metres in the next minute

∴ The monkey climbs in the first 2 minutes = 12 – 3 = 9 metres

∴ In the first 12 minutes the monkey climbs = 9 × 6 = 54 metres

Remaining height of the pole to be covered by the monkey = 63 – 54 = 9 metres

∴ The monkey will climb the height of 9 metres in the 13th minute

∵ The monkey climbs 12 metres in 1 minute

∴ The monkey will climb 9 metres in $\frac{1}{12} \times 9$

$= \frac{3}{4}$ minute

∴ Time spent in climbing at the top of the pole = $\left(12 + \frac{3}{4}\right)$ minutes = $12\frac{3}{4}$ minutes.

16. Let principal = ₹ x, then

$$x + \frac{x \times 12 \times 4}{100} = 2442$$

$$\Rightarrow \frac{37x}{25} = 2442$$

$$\therefore \quad x = \frac{2442 \times 25}{37} = ₹\ 1650.$$

17. $\log \tan 89° = \log \cot 1°$

$= -\log \tan 1°$

∴ Given expression

$\log \tan 1° + \log \tan 2° + ... \log \tan 44°$

$+ \log \tan 45° + ... \log \tan 89°$

$= \log \tan 45°$

$= \log 1° = 0$

18. From the question it is clear that speed of B $= \frac{15}{5} = 3$ m/s

The time taken by B to cover 300 m = $\frac{300}{3}$ = 100 sec.

Hence, time taken by A to complete the race = 100 – 5 = 95 sec.

19. Here, $\frac{60}{100}$ A + B = $\frac{175}{100} \times$ B

$\Rightarrow \frac{3}{5} A + B = \frac{7}{4} B$

$\Rightarrow \frac{3}{5} A = \frac{3}{4} B$

$\therefore \frac{A}{B} = \frac{5}{4}$ Hence, A > B.

20. Let A be the position of a person on the bank of a river and OP the tree on the opposite bank and ∠OAP = 60°. When the person retires to the position B, such that

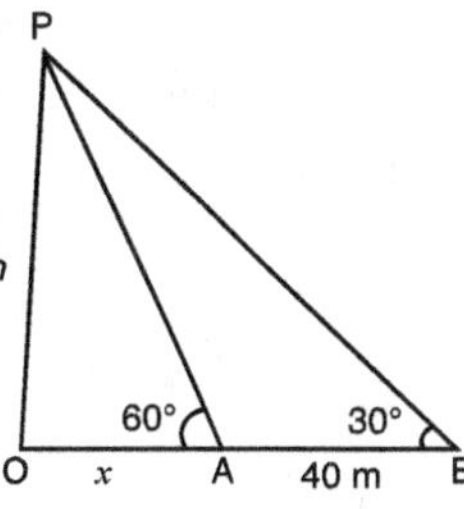

AB = 40 m, then ∠ OBP = 30°

Let OA = x m and OP = h m

In Δ OAP, OP = OA tan 60° = $x\sqrt{3}$

and in Δ OBP, OP = OB tan 30° = $(x + 40)/\sqrt{3}$

∴ $(x + 40)/\sqrt{3} = x\sqrt{3} \Rightarrow x = 20$ m.

21. When two waves of intensities I_1 and I_2 having a phase difference ϕ, interfere, the resultant intensity is given by

$$I = I_1 + I_2 + 2\sqrt{I_1 I_2}\cos\phi \quad \text{....(1)}$$

The intensity will be max, when $\phi = 0$ or $\cos\phi = 1$

$$\therefore \; I_{max} = I_1 + I_2 + 2\sqrt{I_1 I_2} = (I_1 + I_2)^2$$

In case, n identical waves each of intensity I_0, interfere,

$$I_{max} = \left(\sqrt{I_0} + \sqrt{I_0} + \sqrt{I_0} + ...n \sin\right)^2$$

$$= \left(n\sqrt{I_0}\right)^2$$

$$= n^2 I_0$$

22. The greater the binding energy per nuclear, the more stable the nucleus is, since the most energy is needed to pull a nuclear away from it.

23. Thermal conductivity of solid, k = CV, $\lambda/3$, where C is thermal capacity per unit volume V_s is velocity of sound.

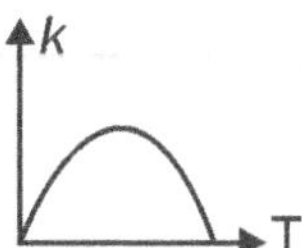

λ is mean free path of phonons kV N_s T. At the low temp, $C \propto T^3$

At high temp, $\lambda \propto \frac{1}{T}$

24. Due to forward biasing, the holes of p-region move towards n-side and electrons of n-side move towards p-side.

25. 0 – 10 A ammeter has accuracy of 1%

$$= \frac{10}{100} = 0.1$$

∴ Limiting error in reading 2.5 A is

$$= \frac{\text{Difference}}{\text{Actual reading}} \times 100$$

$$= \frac{0.1}{2.5} \times 100 = 4\%$$

26. Initial energy of combined system

$$U_1 = \frac{1}{2}CV_1^2 + \frac{1}{2}CV_2^2$$

Final common potential, $V = \frac{V_1 + V_2}{2}$

Final energy system

$$U_2 = 2 \times \frac{1}{2}C\left(\frac{V_1 + V_2}{2}\right)^2$$

Hence, loss of enegy

$$= U_1 - U_2 = \frac{1}{4}C(V_1 + V_2)^2$$

27. The nuclear poteltial that binds the deutran is a square well 27 MeV deep and width of 2.4 F.

28. Given, $\beta = 50$

$$\therefore \; \alpha = \frac{\beta}{\beta + 1} = \frac{50}{51}$$

We have, $\alpha = \beta^* \times \gamma$

where, β^* = Base transport factor

γ = emitter injection efficiency (= 0.995)

$$\therefore \quad \beta^1 = \frac{\alpha}{\lambda} = \left(\frac{50}{51}\right) . \, 0.995$$

$$= 0.9853 \simeq 0.985$$

29. The frequency of oscillation of the output wave is given by

$$f = \frac{1.44}{C(R_1 + 2R_2)}$$

$$= \frac{1.44}{10 \times 10^{-9}\left(10^3 + 2 \times 4.7 \times 10^3\right)}$$

$$= 13.84 \text{ kHz}$$

30. The value of tuning capacitor be C_1 and that of frequncy be f_1.

$$\therefore \quad f_1 = \frac{1}{2\pi\sqrt{L(C_1 + C_d)}}$$

The frequency is now increased to twice its initial value. Let the value of tuning capacitor be C_2 and that of the frequency be f_2 for the circuit to be resonanted again.

Thus, $f_2 = \frac{1}{2\pi\sqrt{L(C_2 + C_d)}}$

Now, $f_2 = 2f_1$

$$\therefore \quad \frac{1}{2\pi\sqrt{L(C_2 + C_d)}} = 2 \times \frac{1}{2\pi\sqrt{L(C_1 + C_d)}}$$

or distributed capacitance

$$C_d = \frac{C_1 - 4C_2}{3}$$

31. Power density spectrum

$S_n = kT = 7 \times 10^{-21}$

Input resistance $R = 50 \times 10^3$ W

Bandwidth $= 100 \times 10^3$ Hz

Noise voltage $E_n = 2\sqrt{kTR\Delta f}$

$$= 2 \times \sqrt{7 \times 10^{-21} \times 50 \times 10^3 \times 100 \times 10^3}$$

$= 11.83$ mV

32. $\lambda v_{max} = \frac{hc}{\lambda_{min}} = eV$

or $\lambda_{min} = \frac{hc}{eV}$

$$\lambda_{min} = \frac{(6.6 \times 10^{-34}) \times (3 \times 10^8)}{1.6 \times 10^{-19} \times V}$$

$$= \frac{12.375}{V} \times 10^{-19} \text{m}$$

Here, $V = 30$ kV

$= 30 \times 10^3$ V

$$\therefore \quad \lambda_{min} = \frac{12.375}{30 \times 10^3} \times 10^{-2} \text{ m}$$

$= 4.125 \times 10^{-11}$ m

$= 0.4$ Å

33. Since density

$$\rho = \frac{Mn}{N_A a^3}$$

or $\rho = \frac{1}{a^3}$

Density is inversely proportional to lattice parameter and hence atomic radius

⇒ Now atomic radius for bcc structure

$$r = \frac{a\sqrt{3}}{4}$$

for fcc structure

$$r = \frac{a\sqrt{2}}{4}$$

atomic radius for bcc > atomic radius for fcc. Hence, density increases.

34. Given, $E = 5$ MeV

$V_0 = 10$ MeV

$a = 10^{-14}$ m

$\hbar = 1.05 \times 10^{-34}$ Js

Probability of leakage

$$T = \frac{16E}{V_0}\left(1 - \frac{E}{V_0}\right) e^{-\left\{2\sqrt{2m(V_0 - E)}\right\}a/\hbar}$$

Now $2\sqrt{2m(V_0 - E)}\, a/\hbar$

$= 2\sqrt{2 \times 6.4 \times 10^{-27} \times (10 - 5)} \times 1.6 \times 10^{-13}$
$\times 10^{-14} / (1.05 \times 10^{-34})$

$= 19.3$

$$\therefore \quad T = \frac{16 \times 5}{10}\left(1 - \frac{5}{10}\right) e^{-19.3}$$

$= 4 \times (4.15 \times 10^{-9})$

$= 1.7 \times 10^{-8}$

35. Maximum available energy

$E = m_0 c^2$

$= 206\, m_e c^2$

$$= \frac{206 \times (9.1 \times 10^{-31})(3 \times 10^8)^2}{1.6 \times 10^{-19}} \text{eV}$$

$= 105$ MeV

36. When the impedances of the terminals of the cable match, no reflection occurs. This method may be used to measure the impedance of a coaxial cable. So (C) is correct.

37. $E_n \;\alpha\; -\frac{13.6}{n^2} = 0$

$$E_n = -\frac{\mu e^4}{2h_2 n^2}$$

$$\alpha \frac{1}{2} m_e \text{ for positronium}$$

$$\alpha\, m_e \text{ for hydrogen}$$

So, $f = \frac{E_p}{E_h}$

$= \frac{\frac{1}{2} m_e}{m_e}$

$= \frac{1}{2}$

38. For the two capacitors connected in parallel,

$V_1 = V_2$ or $\frac{C_1}{q_1} = \frac{C_2}{q_2}$

or $\frac{q_1}{q_2} = \frac{C_1}{C_2}$

39. The frequency of oscillation of PE is twice the frequency of oscillating particle.

40. The buoyancy of the balloon is equal to the difference in weight of 10^7 cm^3 of air at 293 K and at 393 K, at one atm. pressure. As

$$m_0 - m_1 = \frac{pVM}{R}\left(T_0^{-1} - T_1^{-1}\right)$$

$$= \frac{76 \times 13.6 \times 80 \times 10^7 \times 29}{8.31 \times 10^7} (293^{-1} - 393^{-1})$$

$= 3070$ g

$= 3$ kg

41. $\frac{gm}{C} = A_V \times BW$

$\frac{95 \times 10^{-3}}{500 \times 10^{-12}} = 80 \times BW$

$BW = 633$ kHz

42. $\frac{b}{a} = \frac{n\phi}{n}$

$\phi \Rightarrow$ Azimuthul Quantum number

$n \Rightarrow$ Principal Quantum number

$\frac{b}{a} = \frac{1}{3} \Rightarrow b = \frac{a}{3}$

43. The maximum frequency ν_{max} is given by

$h\,\nu_{max} = eV$

or $\nu_{max} = \frac{eV}{h}$

44. There are four atoms in cell, size of crystal is km and unit dimension is 1 nm.
Hence, the number of atoms

$= 4 \times \left(\frac{1\,\text{cm}}{1\,\text{cm}}\right)^3$

$= 4 \times (10^7)^3$

$= 4 \times 10^{21}$

45. Baryon number conservation

$0 + 1 \rightarrow 0 + 0$

$1 \rightarrow 0$

Hence, Baryon number is not conserved.

46. The state of total spin zero has eve parity, *i.e.*, spatial symmetry.
Hence, the wave function does not change when the space coordinate of the electrons are interchanged.

47. When transistor amplifier is in grounded base, configuration h has low output impedence.

48. $V_B = V_1 - \frac{V_1}{110} \times 11 = 0.9\ V_1$

$V_A = V_B = 0.9\ V_1$

Also, $\frac{V_0 - V_A}{100k} = \frac{V_A - V_2}{10k}$

$\frac{V_0 - 0.9\ V_1}{100} = \frac{0.9V_1 - V_2}{10}$

or $V_0 = 0.9V_1 + 9V_1 - 10V_2$

$V_0 = 9.9V_1 - 10V_2$

Since $V_0 = A_1V_1 + A_2V_2$

Comparing these two, we get

$A_1 = 9.9$

and $A_2 = -10$

49. Half-life in sec for

$n = 1.01 \times 10^3$ s

$\boxminus^- = 1.75 \times 10^{-10}$ s

$k^{-1} = 1.229 \times 10^{-8}$ s

$\Sigma^{-1} = 0.81 \times 10^{-10}$ s

Hence, neutron has longest half-life.

50. $\frac{dP}{dt} = \frac{L}{T(V_g - V_l)}$

$$= \frac{L}{TV_g}$$

$$PVg = RT$$

So, $$L = \frac{R \ln \frac{P}{P_o}}{\left(\frac{1}{T_o} - \frac{1}{T}\right)}$$

$$= 93 \text{ J/mol}$$

51. The rotational energy of molecule in *j*th state is

$$E_j = \frac{J(J+1)h^2}{8\pi^2 I}$$

$$= J(J + 1)B$$

where, $$B = \frac{h^2}{8\pi^2 T}$$

with $J = 0, 1, 2, 3, \ldots\ldots$

$$E_j = 0, 2B, 6B, 12B, \ldots\ldots$$

Thus, the energy levels are discrete but not equispaced.

52. Since, $$\lambda = \frac{h}{\sqrt{mI}}$$

or $$\lambda \propto \frac{1}{m\frac{I}{2}}$$

For the same KE and electron has the lowest mass 9×10^{-31} kg hence it has longest wavelength.

53. As, $\psi = A \sec x$

and $\psi = A \tan x$

are continuous and become infinite as $\frac{\pi}{2}, \frac{3\pi}{2}, \frac{5\pi}{2}, \ldots\ldots$

$\psi = Ae^{x^2}$ becomes infinite as x goes to $\pm\infty$.

Therefore, $\psi = Ae^{-x^2}$

can be the solution of Schrodinger's equation for all values of x.

54. MVI A.OOH : clear accumulator
LOOP : ADD B : Add the contents
DCR . C : Decrement C
JNZ LOOP : If C is not zero
HLT END : Jump to loop
This instruction set add to on the contents of B and accumulator to content of C times.

55. Span of thermometer = 200 °C – 150 °C = 50°C

$$\therefore \text{ Max. static error} = \pm \frac{0.25 \times 50}{100}$$

$$= \pm 0.125°C$$

56. Ionization potential for hydrogen = 13.6 eV

Since $E_n \propto Z^2$

$\therefore$ Ionization potential for Li^{++}

$$= 3^2 \times 13.6$$
$$= 9 \times 13.6$$
$$= 122.4 \text{ eV}$$

57. There are four atoms in cell, size of the crystal is 2.7 cm and unit dimension is 27 μm.

Hence, the no. of atoms.

$$= 4 \times \left(\frac{2.7}{27 \times 10^{-4}}\right)^3$$

$$= 4 \times (10^3)^3$$

$$= 4 \times 10^9$$

58. As deuteron consists of equal number of neutron and proton, the reduced mass of system.

$$\mu = \frac{M_n M_p}{M_n + M_p} = \frac{M}{2}$$

Maximum energy,

$$E = \frac{e^2 B^2 r^2}{2M}$$

For deutron, $$E_1 = \frac{e^2 B^2 r^2}{2\left(\frac{M}{I}\right)} = 20$$

Max. energy of proton,

$$= \frac{e^2 B^2 r^2}{2M} = 10 \text{ MeV}$$

59. If we consider solution that differ only by a constant as the same physically, then according to the uniqueness theorem there is only one solution under a given set of boundary conditions. Hence, the correct answer is B.

60. The separation, 2B = 0.7143

$$B = \frac{0.7143}{2}$$

$$\Rightarrow \qquad B = \frac{h}{8\pi^2 IC}$$

$$\text{or} \qquad I = \frac{h}{8\pi^2 BC}$$

$$= \frac{6.6\times10^{-27}}{8\times(3.14)^2\left(\frac{0.71432}{2}\right)(3\times10^{10})}\text{gm}^2\,\text{cm}^2$$

$= 7.8 \times 10^{-46}$ kg m^2

61. $V^2 = \bar{V}\cdot\bar{V}$

$= (xy^2i + zy^2j + xz^2k)$

$\times(xy^2i + zy^2j + xz^2k) = (x^2y^4 + z^2y^4 + x^2z^4)$

Directional derivative = ∇V^2

$$= \left(i\frac{\partial}{\partial x} + j\frac{\partial}{\partial y} + k\frac{\partial}{\partial z}\right)(x^2y^4 + z^2y^4 + x^2z^4)$$

$= (2xy^4 + 2xz^4)i$

$+ (4x^2y^2 + 4y^2z^2)j + (2y^4z + 4x^2z^3)k$

Directional derivative at (2, 0, 3)

$= (0 + 2\times2\times81)i + (0+0)j + (0 + 4\times4\times27)k$

$= 324\,i + 432\,k = 108\,(3\,i + 4\,k)$

Normal to $x^2 + y^2 + z^2 - 14 = 0$ is ∇f

$$= \left(i\frac{\partial}{\partial x} + j\frac{\partial}{\partial y} + k\frac{\partial}{\partial z}\right)(x^2 + y^2 + z^2 - 14)$$

$= (2\,xi + 2\,yj + 2\,zk)$

Normal vector at (3, 2, 1) = $6\,i + 4\,j + 2\,k$

Unit normal vector

$$= \frac{6i + 4j + 2k}{\sqrt{36+16+4}} = \frac{2(3i + 2j + k)}{2\sqrt{14}} = \frac{3i + 2j + k}{\sqrt{14}}$$

Directional derivative along the normal

$$= 108\,(3\,i + 4\,k)\cdot\frac{3i + 2j + k}{\sqrt{14}}$$

$$= \frac{108\times(9+4)}{\sqrt{14}} = \frac{1404}{\sqrt{14}}$$

62. By Green's theorem

$$\int_c(\phi\,dx + \psi\,dy) = \iint_R\left(\frac{\partial\psi}{\partial x} - \frac{\partial\phi}{\partial y}\right)dx\,dy$$

$$\int_c(x^2y\,dx + x^2dy) = \iint_R(2x - x^2)dx\,dy$$

$$= \int_0^1(2x - x^2)dx\int_0^x dy = \int_0^1(2x - x^2)dx\,[y]_0^x$$

$$= \int_0^1(2x - x^2)(x)\,dx = \int_0^1(2x^2 - x^3)\,dx = \left(\frac{2x^3}{3} - \frac{x^4}{4}\right)_0^1$$

$$= \left(\frac{2}{3} - \frac{1}{4}\right) = \frac{5}{12}$$

63. Bead at B makes an angle θ with the vertical. Angle ϕ changes as bead rotates about z-axis. Angular velocity is $\omega = \dot{\phi}$.

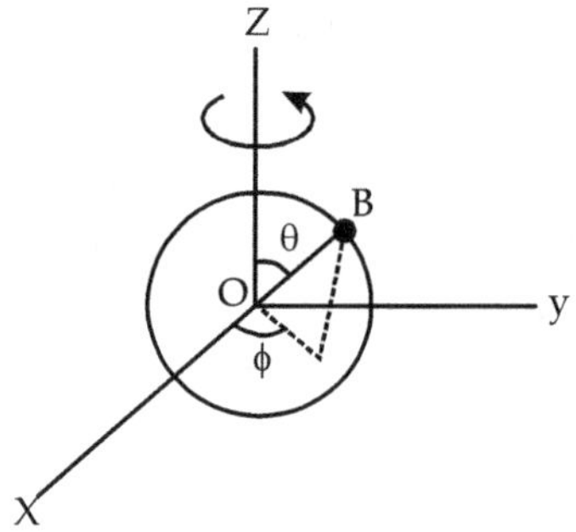

In terms of spherical coordinates

$$\text{K.E.,}\quad T = \frac{1}{2}m(\dot{r}^2 + r^2\dot{\theta}^2 + r^2\sin^2\theta\cdot\dot{\phi}^2)$$

As there is no variation in r so $\dot{r} = 0$ and $\dot{\phi} = \omega$. Then

$$T = \frac{1}{2}m(r^2\dot{\theta}^2 + r^2\omega^2\sin^2\theta)$$

and P.E., $V = mgr\cos\theta$

So that Lagrangian is

$$L = T - V = \frac{1}{2}m(r^2\dot{\theta}^2 + r^2\omega^2\sin^2\theta) - mgr\cos\theta$$

Bead slides on the wire, changing θ. Therefore there is only one variabe to be accounted as generalised coordinate

$$\frac{\partial L}{\partial\dot{\theta}} = mr^2\dot{\theta},\quad \frac{\partial L}{\partial\theta} = mr^2\omega^2\sin\theta\cos\theta + mgr\sin\theta$$

Putting in equation of motion

$$\frac{d}{dt}\left(\frac{\partial L}{\partial \dot{\theta}}\right)-\frac{\partial L}{\partial \theta}=0$$

We get

$$mr^2\ddot{\theta}-mr^2\omega^2\sin\theta\cos\theta-mgr\sin\theta=0$$

or $\ddot{\theta}=\omega^2\sin\theta\cos\theta+\frac{g}{r}\sin\theta$

which is the desired equation of motion.

64. 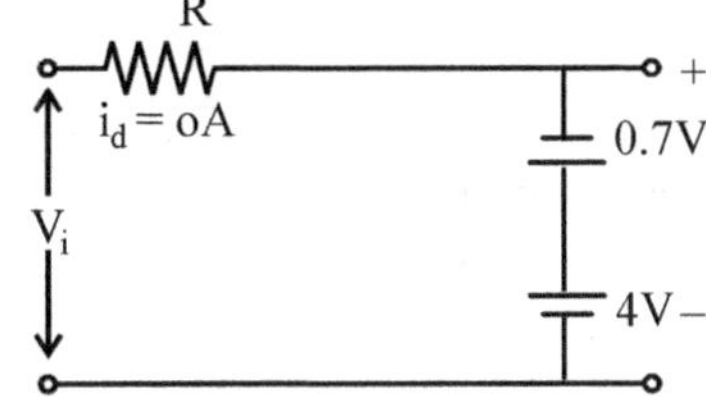

Applying Kirchhoff 's voltage law around the output loop in the clockwise direction, we find that

$$V_i + V_T - V = 0$$

and $V_i = V - V_T$

$= 4V - 0.7V$

$= 3.3V$

and $V_R = i_R.R$

$= i_d.R$

$= (0)R = 0V$

For input voltages greater than 3.3V, the diode will be an open circuit and $V_0 = V_2$.

For input voltage less than 3.3V, the diode will be in the 'ON' state ...(C)

65. $E_F=\frac{\hbar^2}{2m}\left(3\pi^2 n\right)^{2/3}$

$E_F \propto (n)^{2/3}$

For a certain metal M_1, Fermi energy is 5 eV let for metal M_2, Fermi energy is represented by E_{F_2}, and electron density represented by n_2.

$$\frac{E_{F_1}}{E_{F_2}}=\left(\frac{n_1}{n_2}\right)^{2/3}$$

According to the question

$n_2 = n_1$ + 6% of n_1

$=n_1+\frac{6n_1}{100}=\frac{106n_1}{100}$

$n_2 = 1.06n_1$

$$\frac{E_{F_1}}{E_{F_2}}=\left(\frac{n_1}{1.06n_1}\right)^{2/3}=\frac{1}{(1.06)^{2/3}}$$

$\therefore \quad E_{F_2}=E_{F_1}\times(1.06)^{2/3}=5\times\left[1+\frac{6}{100}.\frac{2}{3}\right]$

$= 5\times\left(1+\frac{1}{25}\right)=\frac{5\times 26}{25}$

$= 5.2$ eV

66. 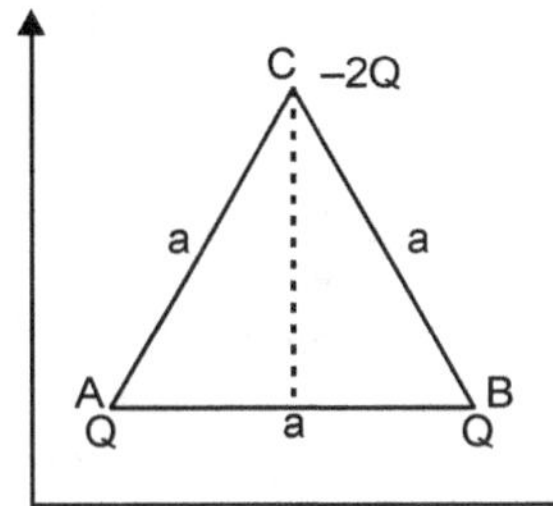

Dipole moment due to dipole AC

$$\vec{D}_{AC} = Q\cdot a\overrightarrow{CA}$$

It is along $\overrightarrow{CA}$.

Dipole moment due to dipole BC

$$\vec{D}_{BC} = Q\cdot a\overrightarrow{CB}$$

On further derivation, we get dipole moment of the configuration = $-\sqrt{3}aQ\hat{j}$

67. Gauge factor = $\frac{\text{fractional resistance change}}{\text{fractional length change}}$

And we know that

fractional length change

$$=\frac{\text{Stress}}{\text{Modulus of elasticity}}$$

fractional change in length

$$=\frac{1000}{2\times 10^{10}} = 0.5\times 10^{-7}$$

$$\text{Gauge factor} = \frac{\frac{\Delta R}{R}}{0.5\times 10^{-7}}$$

Fractional change in resistance = $3 \times 0.5 \times 10^{-7}$
$= 1.5 \times 10^{-7}$

68. No. of moles of gases in two compartments are n_1 and n_2 respectively.

From ideal gas equation,

$$P_1V_1 = n_1RT_1$$

and $$P_2V_2 = n_2RT_2$$

$$n_1 = \frac{P_1V_1}{RT_1} \text{ and } n_2 = \frac{P_2V_2}{RT_2}$$

When separating wall is removed, the equivalent temperature,

$$T = (T_1 + T_2) = \frac{P_1V_1 + P_2V_2}{(n_1 + n_2)R}$$

$$= \frac{P_1V_1 + P_2V_2}{\left(\frac{P_1V_1}{T_1} + \frac{P_2V_2}{T_2}\right)}$$

69. We know that entropy $(\Delta E) \propto (KT)^3$

where K = Constant

$$\frac{\Delta E_2}{\Delta E_1} = \frac{(2T)^3}{(T)^3}$$

$$\Delta E_2 = 8\Delta E_1$$

Hence, entropy increases by a factor of 8.

70.

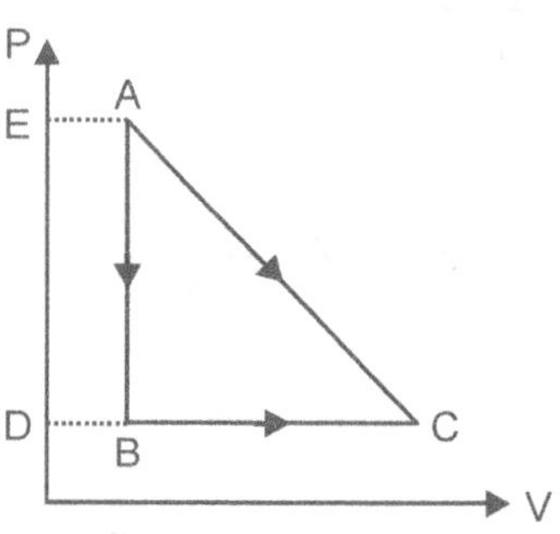

Work done by the gas in the process A → B = Area of ABDE = 30 J.

Work done by the gas in the process B → C = 0.

As there is no volume change during B → C.

So, work done from A → B → C = work done from A → B.

Work done from A → C

= Area of ACDE

= Area of ABDE + Area of ABC

100 J = 30 J + Area of ABC

Area of ABC = 100 – 30 = 70 J

So, heat absorbed during A → B → C

= 150 – 70 = 80 J.

71. The angular momentum of the rotating rod will be given by L = Iω.

Here, $$I = \frac{ml^2}{2}$$

Hence, angular momentum

$$L = \frac{ml^2}{2} \cdot \omega$$

72. $\int_C (x^2 + xy)\, dx + (x^2 + y^2)\, dy$

By Green's theorem $\oint_C (\phi\, dx + \psi\, dy)$

$$= \iint \left(\frac{\partial \psi}{\partial x} - \frac{\partial \phi}{\partial y}\right) dx\, dy$$

$$= \int_{-1}^{1}\int_{-1}^{1}\left[\frac{\partial}{\partial x}(x^2 + y^2) - \frac{\partial}{\partial y}(x^2 + xy)\right] dx\, dy$$

$$= \int_{-1}^{1}\int_{-1}^{1}(2x - x)\, dx\, dy = \int_{-1}^{1}\int_{-1}^{1} x\, dx\, dy$$

$$= \int_{-1}^{1} x\, dx \int_{-1}^{1} dy = \int_{-1}^{1} x\, dx (y)_{-1}^{1} = \int_{-1}^{1} x\, dx(1+1)$$

$$= \int_{-1}^{1} 2x\, dx = (x^2)_{-1}^{1} = 1 - 1 = 0.$$

73. Note that if spring is extended by x then by the same extent masses will be displaced. Therefore for mass at position 1 and spring system

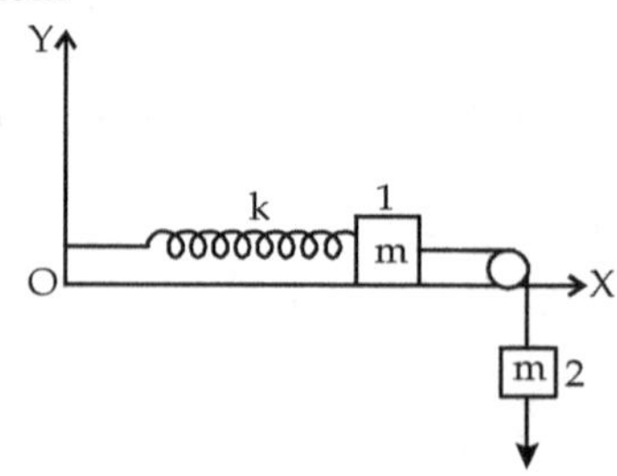

$$\text{K.E.} = \frac{1}{2}m\dot{x}^2, \quad \text{P.E.} = \frac{1}{2}kx^2$$

and for mass m at position 2,

$$\text{K.E.} = \frac{1}{2}m\dot{x}^2, \quad \text{P.E.} = -mgx$$

Therefore net Lagrangian (L = T – V)

$$\text{L} = \frac{1}{2}m\dot{x}^2 - \frac{1}{2}kx^2 + \frac{1}{2}m\dot{x}^2 + mgx$$

$$= m\dot{x}^2 - \frac{1}{2}kx^2 + mgx$$

The derivatives are

$$\frac{\partial \text{L}}{\partial \dot{x}} = 2m\dot{x}, \frac{\partial \text{L}}{\partial x} = -kx + mg$$

Putting in Lagrange's equation, we get

$$2m\ddot{x} + kx - mg = 0$$

or $$\ddot{x} + \frac{k}{2m}x - \frac{g}{2} = 0 \quad ...(1)$$

Let us put, $$\left(\frac{k}{2m}x - \frac{g}{2}\right) = \alpha \quad ...(2)$$

so that $\ddot{x} = \dfrac{2m\ddot{\alpha}}{k}$. Putting in eq. (1), we get

$$\frac{2m}{k}\ddot{\alpha} + \alpha = 0$$

$$\ddot{\alpha} + \omega^2\alpha = 0$$

where $$\omega = \sqrt{k/2m} \quad ...(3)$$

giving the solution as

$$\alpha = \text{A}\cos\omega t + \text{B}\sin\omega t \quad ...(4)$$

or from eqs. (2) and (4),

$$x = \frac{2m}{k}\left[\text{A}\cos\omega t + \text{B}\sin\omega t \frac{g}{2}\right]$$

Putting at $t = 0, x = 0$,

we get A = $-g/2$ and at $t = 0$, $\dot{x} = 0$ we get B = 0, so that final expression for extension as a function of time is

$$x = \frac{2m}{k}\left[-\frac{g}{2}\cos\omega t + \frac{g}{2}\right] = \frac{mg}{k}[1 - \cos\omega t]$$

74. From energy conservation, we have

$$h\nu + m_ec^2 = h\nu' + (K_e + m_ec^2), \quad ...(i)$$

where $h\nu$ and $h\nu'$ are the energies of the initial and scattered photons, respectively, m_ec^2 is the rest mass energy of the initial electron, $(K_e + m_ec^2)$ is the total energy of the recoiling electron, and K_e is its recoil kinetic energy. The expression for K_e can immediately be inferred from (*i*):

$$K_e = h(\nu - \nu') = hc\left(\frac{1}{\lambda} - \frac{1}{\lambda'}\right) = \frac{hc}{\lambda}\frac{\lambda' - \lambda}{\lambda'} = (h\nu)\frac{\Delta\lambda}{\lambda'}, \quad ...(ii)$$

where the wave shift $\Delta\lambda$ is given by

$$\Delta\lambda = \lambda' - \lambda = \frac{h}{m_ec}(1 - \cos\theta) = \frac{2\pi hc}{m_ec^2}(1 - \cos\theta)$$

$$= \frac{2\pi \times 197.33 \times 10^{-15}\,\text{MeV m}}{0.511\,\text{MeV}}(1 - \cos 60)$$

$$= 0.0012 \text{ nm}. \quad ...(iii)$$

Since the wavelength of the incident photon is $\lambda = 2\pi hc/(h\nu)$, we have $\lambda = 2\pi \times 197.33 \times 10^{-15}$ MeV m/(0.003 MeV) = 0.414 nm; the wavelength of the scattered photon is given by

$$\lambda' = \lambda + \Delta\lambda = 0.415 \text{ nm}. \quad ...(iv)$$

Now, subsituting the numerical values of λ' and $\Delta\lambda$ into (*ii*), we obtain the kinetic energy of the recoiling electron

$$K_e = (hv)\frac{\Delta\lambda}{\lambda'} = (3\,\text{keV}) \times \frac{0.0012\,\text{nm}}{0.4152\,\text{nm}} = 8.671\,\text{eV}.$$

75. Let E_g and E_e be the energies of ground state and excited state respectively. The probabilities of finding an atom in these states are:

$$\omega_1 = Ce^{-\beta E_g} \quad \text{and} \quad \omega_2 = Ce^{-\beta E_e},$$

where $\beta = 1/kT$

$$\frac{\omega_2}{\omega_1} = \frac{e^{-\beta E_g}}{e^{-\beta E_e}} = e^{-\beta(E_g - E_e)}$$

$$= e^{-(E_g - E_e)/kT} = \exp.[-(E_g - E_e)/kT]$$

$$= \exp.\left[-\left(\frac{1.38 \times 1.6 \times 10^{-19}}{1.38 \times 10^{-23} \times 16000}\right)\right]$$

$$= \exp.[-1] = 0.368(\because e = 2.72)$$

SET–9

CSIR–UGC (NET) PHYSICAL SCIENCES

PART-A

1. Helium and argon gases in two separate containers are at the same temperature and so have different root-mean-square (r.m.s.) velocities. The two are mixed in a third container keeping the same temperature. The r.m.s. velocity of the helium atoms in the mixture is
A. more than what it was before mixing
B. less than what it was before mixing
C. equal to what it was before mixing
D. equal to that of argon atoms in the mixture

2. In ΔABC, angle A is larger than angle C and smaller than angle B by the same amount. If angle B is 67°, angle C is
A. 67° B. 53°
C. 60° D. 57°

3. A person buys a shirt with marked price ₹ 300/- at 20% discount. In order to make a profit of 20% the person should sell the shirt for
A. ₹ 288/- B. ₹ 300/-
C. ₹ 240/- D. ₹ 360/-

4. A car is moving along a straight road. The graph below shows how the speed varies with time.

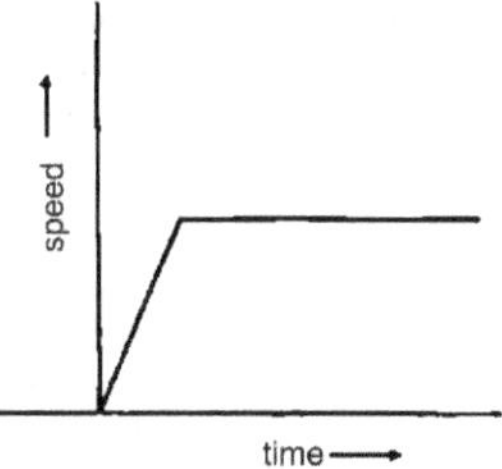

Which of the following graphs represents the distance covered by the car with time?

A.
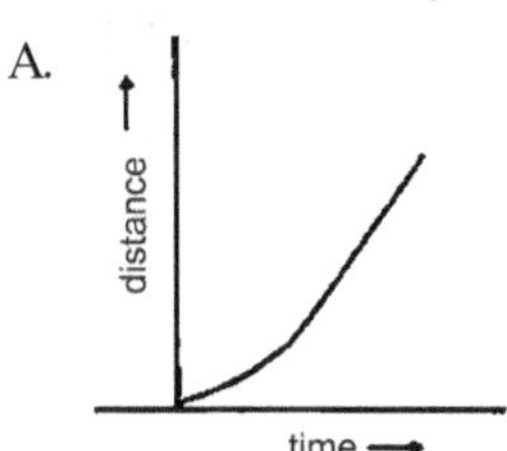

B.
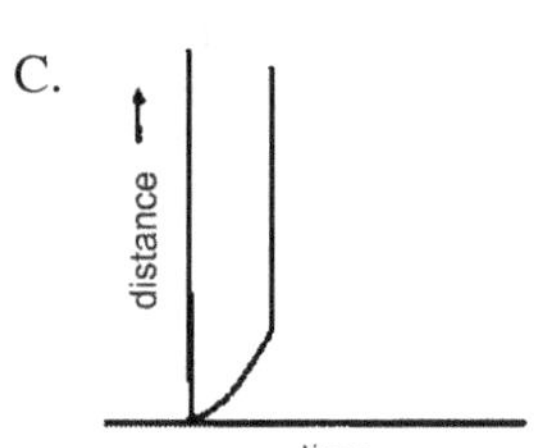

C.
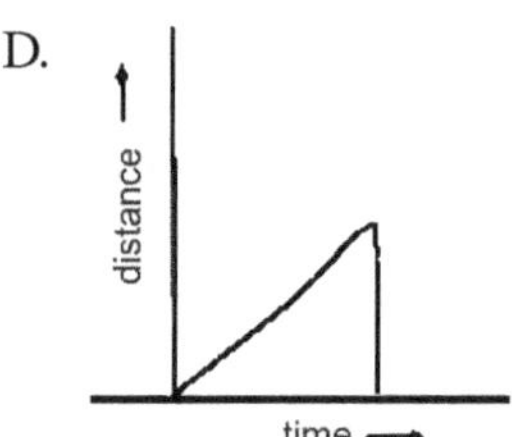

D.

distance

time

5. A man can row three quarters of a kilometre against the stream in $11\frac{1}{4}$ minutes and return in $7\frac{1}{2}$ minutes. Find the speed of the man in still water.
A. 3 km/hr B. 4 km/hr
C. 5 km/hr D. 6 km/hr

6. Twelve coupons are numbered from 1 to 12. Six coupons are selected at random one at a time with replacement. The probability that the largest number appearing on a selected coupon is less than or equal to 8, is:
A. $(2/3)^6$ B. $(7/12)^6$
C. 1/33 D. None of these

7. Seven chits are numbered 1 to 7. Four are drawn one-by-one with replacements. The probability that the least number on any selected chits is 5 is:
A. $1 - (2/7)^4$ B. $4.(2/7)^4$
C. $(3/7)^4$ D. None of these

Directions (Q. 8): *Study the following graph carefully and answer the question given below.*

Number of Building constructed, demolished and redeveloped across various cities in a year

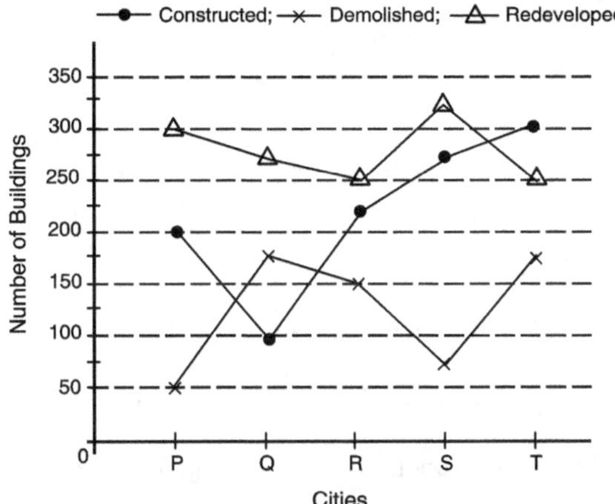

8. The total number of buildings constructed across the cities is approximately what per cent of the total number of buildings redeveloped across the cities?
A. 73 B. 74
C. 79 D. 89

9. In a certain code language, CUL WAP DIR means red little box, SUT MAD BIX means well-arranged pile, BIX FAC DIR means pile of boxes. The code for 'of' here is?
A. FAC B. SUT
C. DIR D. BIX

10. In an election, one of the two candidates gets 40% votes and loses by 100 votes. Total number of votes is:
A. 500 B. 400
C. 600 D. 1000

11. 400 persons working 9 hours a day complete $\frac{1}{4}$th of the work in 10 days. Find the number of additional persons, working 8 hours per day required to complete the remaining work in 20 days.
A. 275 B. 200
C. 225 D. 250

12. From eighty cards numbered 1 to 80, two cards are selected randomly. The probability that both the cards have the numbers divisible by 4 is given by:
A. 21/316 B. 19/316
C. 1/4 D. None of these

13. If the rate of income tax is 5%, the net income of a person is ₹ 17100. If the rate of income tax is 6%, how much will be the net income?
A. ₹ 15820 B. ₹ 16920
C. ₹ 17820 D. ₹ 18920

14. One-eighth of a number is 17.25. What will 73% of the number be?
A. 82.66 B. 96.42
C. 100.74 D. 138.00

15. How many squares are there in the figure given below?

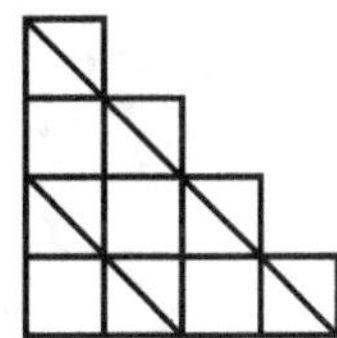

A. 10 B. 11
C. 13 D. 14

16. In how many years will a sum of ₹ 19200 placed at 10% per annum compound interest yield an interest of ₹ 4032?
A. 1½ years B. 2½ years
C. 2 years D. 3 years

17. The price of rice is reduced by 2%. How many kilograms of rice can now be bought for the money which was sufficient to buy 49 kg of rice earlier?
A. 51 kg B. 50 kg
C. 49 kg D. 48 kg

18. In a mixture of 60 litres, the ratio of milk and water is 2 : 1. If the ratio is to be 1 : 2, then the quantity of water to be further added is:
A. 60 litres B. 40 litres
B. 30 litres D. 20 litres

19. A tank is of the shape of a cuboid whose length is 7.2 m and breadth is 2.5 m. Water flows into it through a pipe whose cross-section is 5 cm × 3 cm at the rate of 10 m/s. Find the height to which water level will rise in the tank in 40 minutes.

A. 1 m B. 2 m

C. 3 m D. 4 m

20. A man travels 360 km in 4 hrs, partly by air and partly by train. If he had travelled all the way by air, he would have saved 4/5 of the time he was in train and would have arrived at his destination 2 hours early. Find the distance he travelled by air and train.

A. 80 km B. 90 km

C. 70 km D. 95 km

PART-B

21. Given that the ground state energy of the hydrogen atom is –13.6 eV, the ground state energy of postronium (which is a bound state of an electron and a positron) is

A. + 6.8 eV B. – 6.8 eV

C. – 13.6 eV D. – 27.2 eV

22. The van der Waal's equation of state for 1 mole of a gas is $\left(P+\frac{a}{V^2}\right)(V-b)=RT$

where a and b are constants. If U is the internal energy of n moles of this gas, then $\left(\frac{\partial U}{\partial V}\right)_T$ is

A. zero B. $\frac{a}{\left(\frac{V}{n-b}\right)^2}$

C. $\left(\frac{a}{nV}\right)^2$ D. $\frac{a}{(V/n)^2}$

23. Consider a Maxwellian distribution of the velocity of the molecules of an ideal gas. Let V_{mp} and V_{rms} denote the most probable velocity and the root mean square velocity, respectively. The magnitude of the ratio V_{mp} and V_{rms} is

A. 1 B. 2/3

C. $\sqrt{2/3}$ D. 3/2

24. The potential of a diatomic molecule as a function of the distance r between the atoms is given by $V(r) = -\frac{a}{r^6}+\frac{b}{r^{12}}$. The value of the potential at equilibrium separation between the atoms is

A. $-4a^2/b$ B. $-2a^2/b$

C. $-a^2/2b$ D. $-a^2/4b$

25. If the Lagrangian of a particle moving in one-dimension is given by $L=\frac{\dot{x}^2}{2x}-V(x)$, the Hamiltonian is

A. $\frac{1}{2}xp^2+V(x)$ B. $\frac{x^2}{2x}+V(x)$

C. $\frac{1}{2}x^2-V(x)$ D. $\frac{p^2}{2x}-V(x)$

26. The wave function of a particle is given by $\psi=\left(\frac{1}{\sqrt{2}}\phi_0+i\phi_1\right)$, where ϕ_0 and ϕ_1 are the normalized eigen functions with energies E_0 and E_1 corresponding to the grand state and first excited state respectively. The expectation value of the Hamiltonian in the state ψ is

A. $\frac{E_0}{2}+E_1$ B. $\frac{E_0}{2}-E_1$

C. $\frac{E_0-2E_1}{3}$ D. $\frac{E_0+2E_1}{3}$

27. The value of the integral $\int_C \frac{3z+4}{z(2z+1)}dz$, where C is the circle $|z| = 1$ is

A. $3\pi i$ B. 4

C. – 4 D. $-2\pi i$

28. The rest mass of an electron is m_0 when it moves with velocity $v = 0.6c$, then its rest mass is

A. m_0 B. $\frac{5}{4}m_0$

C. $\frac{4}{5}m_0$ D. $2m_0$

29. In figure, XY is an infinite line charge distribution P and Q are points as shown. The ratio of electric field at P and Q is

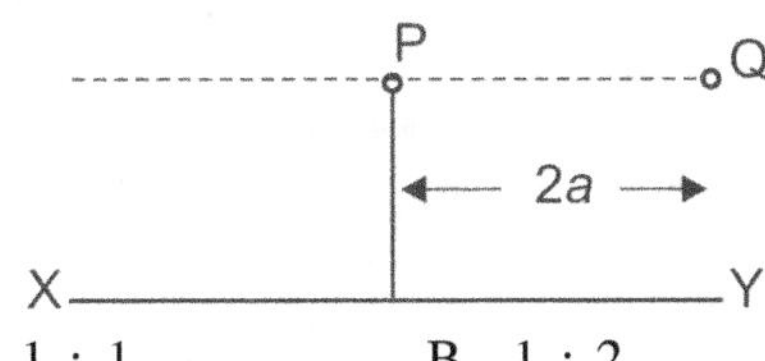

A. 1 : 1 B. 1 : 2
C. 2 : 1 D. 1 : 4

30. The electric field intensity $\vec{E}$ due to an infinite uniformly charged plane sheet at a point distance r from the sheet is related is

A. $\bar{E} \propto r$ B. $E \propto r^{-1}$
C. $E \propto r^{-2}$ D. E is independent of r

31. The rectangle of cross-sectional area A is placed in a uniform electric field. The normal to the area of the coil makes an angle of 90° with an electric field. The electric flux ϕ through the rectangle is

A. $\bar{E}$ B. $\bar{A}\cdot\bar{E}$
C. $\frac{\bar{A}\cdot\bar{E}}{\sqrt{2}}$ D. zero

32. A normally incident $\bar{E}$ field has amplitude $E_0^i = 1.0$ V/m in free space just outside of sea water in which $\epsilon_r = 80$, $\mu_r = 1$ and $\sigma = 2.5$ s/m. For a frequency of 30 MHz, at what depth will the amplitude of $\bar{E}$ be 1.0 m V/m?

A. 0.234 B. 0.125
C. 0.467 D. 0.103

33. Consider a system whose Hamiltonian H and an operator A are given by the matrices

$$H = \epsilon_0 \begin{pmatrix} 1 & -1 & 0 \\ -1 & 1 & 0 \\ 0 & 0 & -1 \end{pmatrix}, A = a \begin{pmatrix} 0 & 4 & 0 \\ 4 & 0 & 1 \\ 0 & 1 & 0 \end{pmatrix} \text{ where}$$

ϵ_0 has the dimension of energy. The uncertainty ΔA is

A. 0 B. a^2
C. $\epsilon_0 a$ D. a

34. A system consists of 10^{24} atoms and is at a temperature of 300 K. Assuming that there is no interatomic energy in the system, its total internal energy is

A. 12.4 kJ B. 12.4 J
C. 4.12 kJ D. 4.12 J

35. A dynamic RAM call which hold 5 V has to be refreshed every 20 m secs, so that stored voltage does not fall below 0.5 V. If the call has a constant discharge current of 0.1 pA, the storage capacitance of the call is

A. 4×10^{-6} B. 4×10^{-9}
C. 4×10^{-12} D. 4×10^{-15}

36. A monochromatic light of wavelength λ is incident on an isolated metallic sphere of radius a. The threshold wavelength is λ_0 which is larger than λ. Find the number of photoelectrons emitted before the emission of photoelectrons will stop

A. $n = \frac{4\pi\epsilon_0 ach}{e^2}\left(\frac{1}{\lambda^2} - \frac{1}{\lambda_0^2}\right)$

B. $n = \frac{4\pi\epsilon_0 ch}{ae^2}\left(\frac{1}{\lambda} - \frac{1}{\lambda_0}\right)$

C. $n = \frac{4\pi\epsilon_0 ach}{e^2}\left(\frac{1}{\lambda} - \frac{1}{\lambda_0}\right)$

D. $n = \frac{4\pi\epsilon_0}{hcae^2}\left(\frac{1}{\lambda^2} - \frac{1}{\lambda_0^2}\right)$

37. A memory system of size 16k bytes is required to be designed using memory chips which have 12 address lines and 4 data lines each. Then number of such chips required to designed the memory system is

A. 2 B. 4
C. 8 D. 16

38. In the given digital logic circuit, A and B form the input. The output Y is

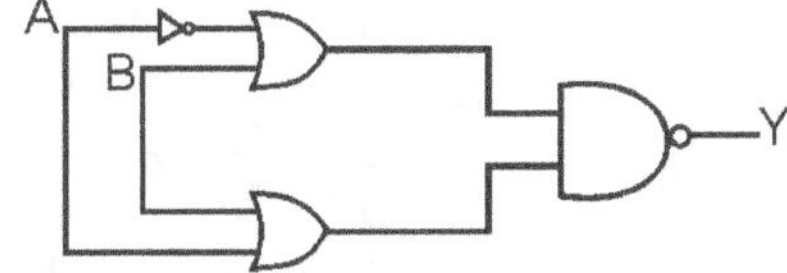

A. $Y = \bar{A}$ B. $Y = A\bar{B}$
C. $Y = A \oplus B$ D. $Y = \bar{B}$

39. A signal $m(t) = 5 \cos 2\pi\ 100t$ frequncy modulates a carrier. The resulting FM signal is $10 \cos\left[\left(2\pi\times10^5 t\right)+15\sin\left(2\pi\cdot100t\right)\right]$. The approximate bandwidth of the FM would be

A. 0.1 kHz B. 1 kHz
C. 3.2 kHz D. 100 kHz

40. The spectral terms for a certain electronic configuration are given by 3*d*, 1*d*, 3*p*, 1*p*, 5*s*, 3*s*. The term with the lowest energy is

A. 5*s* B. 3*p*
C. 3*d* D. 3*s*

41. A quark $\left(\text{mass} + \frac{m_p}{3}\right)$ is confined in a cubical box with sides of length fermions = 2×10^{-15} m. The excitation energy state in MeV is

A. 153 MeV B. 461 MeV
C. 15 MeV D. 46.1 MeV

42. The wave function in the ground state of hydrogen atom is given as

$$\psi = \left(\frac{1}{\pi a^3}\right)^{1/2} e^{-r/a}$$

The average of *r* is

A. 0 B. $\frac{3}{2}a$
C. $\frac{1}{2}a$ D. $\frac{5}{2}a$

43. The lowest energy possible for a particle in a potential box is 2 eV. The next highest energy the particle can have is

A. 4 eV B. 8 eV
C. 16 eV D. 32 eV

44. If E_1 is the energy of the lowest state of a one-dimensional potential box of length *a* and E_2 is the energy of the lowest state when the length of the box is halved, then

A. $E_2 = E_1$ B. $E_2 = 2E_1$
C. $E_2 = 3E_1$ D. $E_2 = 4E_1$

45. In an experiment, the measured values of a variables are respectively 1, 2, 3 and 4, while the probability, corresponding to them are respectively $\frac{1}{4}, \frac{1}{4}, \frac{1}{4}$ and $\frac{1}{4}$ respectively, then expectation values of x and x^2 are (respectively)

A. 2.5 and 7.5 B. 7.5 and 2.5
C. 0.5 and 0.5 D. None of these

PART-C

46. If λ_m for solar radiation is 4753Å, then the temperature of the photosphere of the sum will be

A. 6100 K B. 6100 °C
C. 61000 K D. 61000 °C

47. The gain of the amplifier shown in fig. The open loop voltage gain of the op-amp is 1,00,000

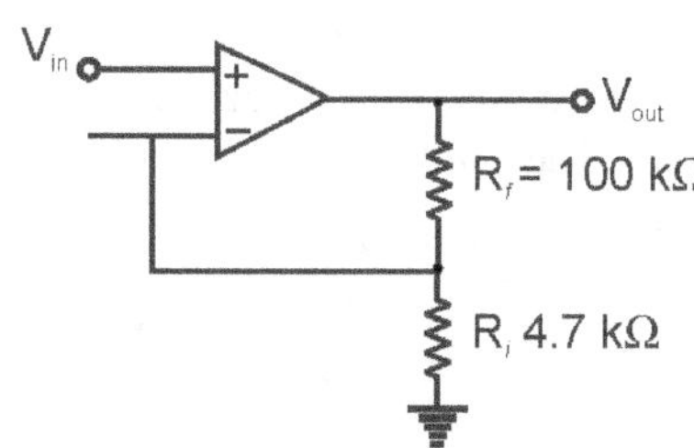

A. 20.3 B. 24.3
C. 22.3 D. 28.3

48. The output of the circuit shown in the fig. is equal to

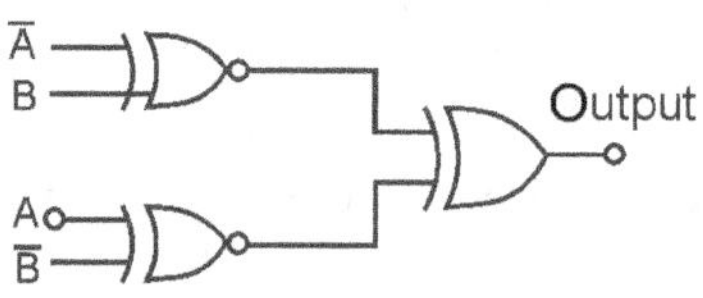

A. 0 B. 1
C. $\bar{A}B + A\bar{B}$ D. $\left(\overline{A*B}\right)*\left(\overline{A*B}\right)$

49. The angle of reflection of neutrons beam from a crystal of interplaner space 3.84 Å is 30°, the speed of neutrons will be

A. 1.03×10^6 cm/s B. 1.03×10^5 cm/s
C. 1.03×10^4 cm/s D. 1.03×10^3 cm/s

50. Magnesium crystallizes in hcp structure. If the lattice constant is 0.32 nm, the nearest neighbour distance in magnesium is

A. 0.32 nm B. 0.64 nm
C. 0.16 nm D. None of these

51. The binding energy per nucleon of helium nucleus is 7 MeV and that of deuteron is 1 MeV. Then
A. Helium nucleus is more stable
B. Deuteron nucleus is more stable
C. Both are less stable
D. Both are equally stable

52. Phonons are quantized vibrations and many aspects of these excitations can be understood in terms of simple mode counting. Estimate the number of phonon modes in 1 cm^3 of a crystalline material with an inter atomic spacing is 2Å
A. 1.25×10^{20} B. 1.25×10^{21}
C. 1.25×10^{22} D. 1.25×10^{23}

53. The angular frequency of the surface waves in a liquid is given in terms of the wave number k by $\omega = \sqrt{gk + \frac{Tk^3}{p}}$ (symbol has their usual meanings), a group velocity is given by

A. $\sqrt{\frac{8\lambda}{2\pi} + \frac{2\pi T}{p\lambda}}$ B. $\sqrt{\frac{8}{2k}}$

C. $\frac{1}{2}\sqrt{\frac{8\lambda}{2\pi}}$ D. $\frac{1}{2}\sqrt{\frac{gk}{2\pi}}$

54. The activity of a certain preparation decreases 2.5 times after 7 days, then its half-life is
A. 4 days B. 5.3 days
C. 10 days D. 18.5 days

55. The angle ϕ between [111] and $[1\bar{1}1]$ direction in a cubic crystal is
A. 30° B. 109.5°
C. 120° D. 60°

56. Proton of 1 MeV energy when meeting Rutherford scattering by nuclei of gold $z = 79$, the distance of closet approach is
A. 11.4×10^{-12} cm B. 11.4×10^{-10} cm
C. 11.4×10^{-8} cm D. 11.4×10^{-6} cm

57. The meson theory of nuclear forces assumes the virtual exchange of pions. If a nuclear emits a virtual pions of rest mass 270 Me. Calculate the range of the nuclear force.
A. 1.22 fermi B. 1.27 fermi
C. 1.33 fermi D. 1.43 fermi

58. The total energy of the electron in the nth orbit of hydrogen atom is

A. $\frac{e^2}{4\pi\varepsilon_0 r_n}$ B. $\frac{e^2}{4\pi\varepsilon_0 r_n}$

C. $\frac{e^2}{8\pi\varepsilon_0 r_n}$ D. $-\frac{e^2}{8\pi\varepsilon_0 r_n}$

59. The far infrared spectrum of H^1 Br^{79} consists of a series of lines spaced 17 cm^{-1} apart. Find the internuclear distance of H^1 Br^{79} ($h = 6.62 \times 10^{-27}$ erg-sec, $c = 3.0 \times 10^{10}$ cm sec^{-1}, $N_A = 6.023 \times 10^{23}$).
A. 1.21 Å B. 1.42 Å
C. 1.33 Å D. 0.21 Å

60. An oscillating voltage $V(t) = V_0 \cos\omega t$ is applied across a parallel plate capacitor having a plate separation d. The displacement current density through the capacitor is

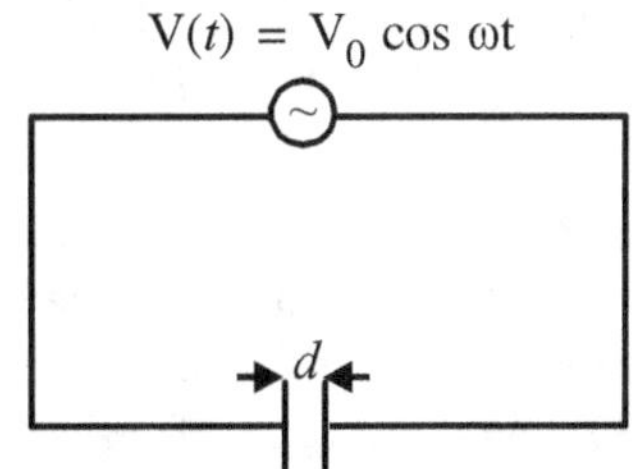

A. $\frac{\varepsilon_0 \omega V_0 \cos\omega t}{d}$ B. $\frac{\varepsilon_0 \mu_0 V_0 \cos\omega t}{d}$

C. $\frac{\varepsilon_0 \mu_0 \omega V_0 \sin\omega t}{d}$ D. $-\frac{\varepsilon_0 \omega V_0 \sin\omega t}{d}$

61. Monochromatic X-rays of wavelength 1Å are incident on a simple cubic crystal. The first order Bragg reflection from (311) plane occurs at an angle of 30° from the plane. The lattice parameter of the crystal in Å is
A. 1 B. $\sqrt{3}$

C. $\sqrt{\frac{11}{2}}$ D. $\sqrt{11}$

62. Consider the following truth table:

A	B	C	F
0	0	0	1
0	0	1	0
0	1	0	0
0	1	1	0
1	0	0	1
1	0	1	1
1	1	0	1
1	1	1	0

The logic expression for F is

A. $AB + BC + CA$

B. $\bar{A}B + A\bar{C} + \bar{B}C$

C. $\overline{C\bar{A}}\,\bar{B} + A\bar{B}$

D. $\bar{C}(A+\bar{B}) + A\bar{B}$

63. The matrix A is defined as

$$A = \begin{bmatrix} 1 & 2 & -3 \\ 0 & 3 & 2 \\ 0 & 0 & -2 \end{bmatrix}$$

Find the eigenvalues of $3A^3 + 5A^2 - 6A + 2I$.

A. 4, 110, 10 B. 5, 112, 10

C. 6, 109, 13 D. 8, 105, 12

64. The zener diode shown in figure has V_Z = 18 V. The voltage across the load stays at 18 V as long as I_Z is maintained between 200 mA and 2 A. Find the value of series resistance so that E_0 remains 18 V while input voltage E_i is free to vary between 22 V to 28 V.

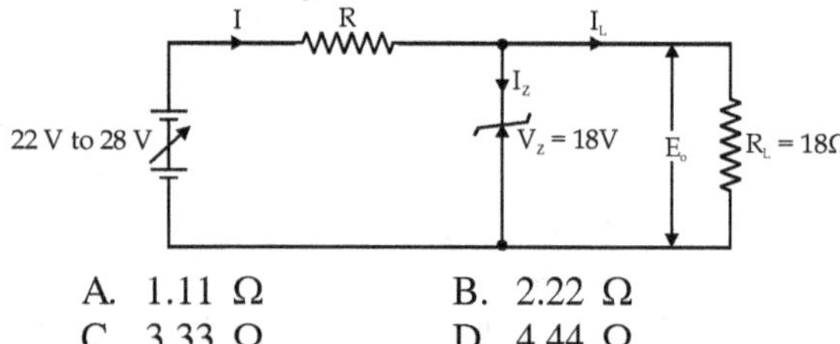

A. 1.11 Ω B. 2.22 Ω

C. 3.33 Ω D. 4.44 Ω

65. The band gap in germanium is ΔE = 0.68 eV. Assuming that the number of hole-electron pairs is proportional to $e^{-\Delta E/2kT}$ find the percentage increase in the number of charge carriers in pure germanium as the temperature is increased from 300K to 320K.

A. 117% B. 107%

C. 97% D. 127%

66. A thin massless S rod of length $2l$ has equal point massess m attached at its ends (see figure). The rod is rotating about an axis passing through its centre and making angle θ with it. The magnitude of the rate of change of its angular momentum $\left|\frac{d\bar{L}}{dt}\right|$ is

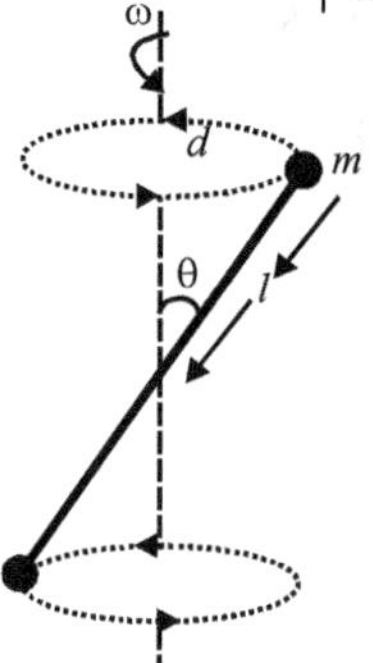

A. $2ml^2\omega^2 \sin\theta\cos\theta$ B. $2ml^2\omega^2 \sin\theta$

C. $2ml^2\omega^2 \sin^2\theta$ D. $2ml^2\omega^2 \cos^2\theta$

67. An inductor coil joined to a 6 V battery draws a steady current of 12 A. This coil is connected to a capacitor and an AC source of rms voltage 6 V in series. If the current in the circuit is in phase with the emf. Find the rms current.

A. 12 A B. 10 A

C. 8 A D. 16 A

68. A triode valve has amplification factor 21 and dynamic plate resistance 10 kΩ. This is used as an amplifier with a load of 20 kΩ. The gain factor of the amplifier is

A. 12 B. 10

C. 16 D. 14

69. In FM radio the audio signal to be transmitted ranges from 20 to 15,000 Hz. If the FM system uses a maximum modulating index β of 5.0, then find the range of frequency.

A. 15 and 25 Hz B. 15 and 45 Hz

C. 5 and 15 Hz D. 5 and 10 Hz

70. What will be Thevenin equivalent against 7 kΩ resistor in the circuit?

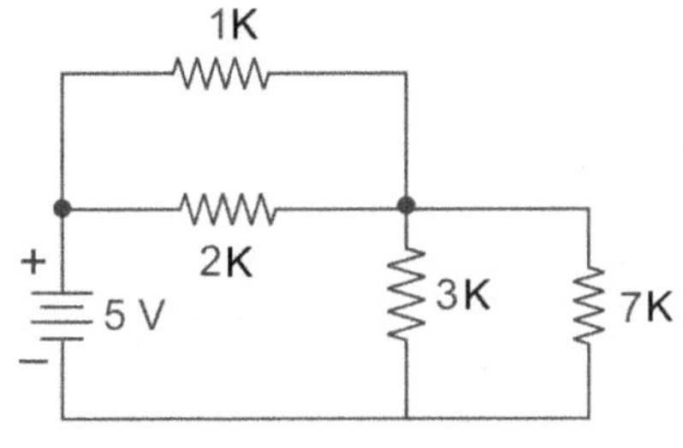

A. 3.31 V B. 4.1 V
C. 5.12 V D. 6.1 V

71. A laser beam emerging from a laser tube operating at 80 nm has a cross-sectional diameter of 2 mm. The diameter of the beam at a distance of 1 km is approximately given by
A. 10 mm B. 8 cm
C. 80 cm D. 10 m

72. The classical expression for molar electronic specific heat is 1.5 R*u*. Express its value, giving the units—
A. 12.5 JK mol^{-1} K^{-1}
B. 1250 kJ mol^{-1} K^{-1}
C. 125 kJ mol^{-1} K^{-1}
D. 12.5 kJ/K mol/K

73. The maximum energy of deuterons coming out of a cyclotron accelerator is 20 MeV. The maximum energy of protons that can be obtained from this accelerator is
A. 10 MeV B. 20 MeV
C. 30 MeV D. 40 MeV

74. Protons from an accelerator collide with hydrogen. What is the minimum energy to create anti protons?
A. 6.6 GeV B. 3.3 GeV
C. 2 GeV D. 1 GeV

75. Which particle emits the most synchrotron radiation light when bent in magnetic field?
A. Proton B. Muon
C. Electron D. Neutron

ANSWERS

1	**2**	**3**	**4**	**5**	**6**	**7**	**8**	**9**	**10**
C	D	A	A	C	A	C	C	A	A
11	**12**	**13**	**14**	**15**	**16**	**17**	**18**	**19**	**20**
A	B	B	C	C	C	B	A	B	B
21	**22**	**23**	**24**	**25**	**26**	**27**	**28**	**29**	**30**
B	D	C	C	A	D	D	B	A	D
31	**32**	**33**	**34**	**35**	**36**	**37**	**38**	**39**	**40**
D	A	D	A	D	C	C	D	C	A
41	**42**	**43**	**44**	**45**	**46**	**47**	**48**	**49**	**50**
D	B	B	D	A	A	C	A	B	A
51	**52**	**53**	**54**	**55**	**56**	**57**	**58**	**59**	**60**
A	D	C	B	B	A	D	D	B	D
61	**62**	**63**	**64**	**65**	**66**	**67**	**68**	**69**	**70**
D	D	A	C	D	A	A	D	B	B
71	**72**	**73**	**74**	**75**					
C	D	A	A	C					

EXPLANATORY ANSWERS

1. Since Root mean square (r.m.s.) velocity $=\sqrt{\frac{V^2}{2}}$.

2. Angle A is larger than angle C and smaller than angle B by the same amount means:

$$A - C = B - A$$

and since $B = 67$, then

$$A - C = 67 - A$$

$$\Rightarrow \quad 2A = 67 + C$$

$$\Rightarrow \quad A = \frac{67}{2} + \frac{C}{2}$$

Since $A + 67 + C = 180$

$\Rightarrow A = 180 - 67 - C$

$\Rightarrow \frac{67}{2} + \frac{C}{2} = 180 - 67 - C$

$\Rightarrow 67 + C = 360 - 134 - 2C$

$\Rightarrow 3C = 360 - 134 - 67$

$\Rightarrow 3C = 159$

$\therefore C = 53$

3. 100 – 20 = 80

When MP is 100 then CP = 80

When MP is 300 then CP = $\frac{80}{100} \times 300$ = ₹ 240

100 + 20 = 120

When CP 100 then SP = 120

When CP 240 then SP

= $\frac{120}{100} \times 240$ = ₹ 288.

4. Graph in option (A) represents the distance covered by the car with time.

5. Upstream speed = $\frac{3/4}{45/_{4\times60}}$ = 4 km/hr

Downstream speed = $\frac{3/4}{15/_{2\times60}}$ = 6 km/hr

$\therefore$ Speed of the man in still water

$= \frac{1}{2}(6 + 4) = 5$ km/hr.

6. Probability of a coupon selected with any number from 1 to 8 = 8/12.

In six trails: P (number from 1 to 8) = $(8/12)^6$

$P = (2/3)^6$.

7. P (5 or 6 or 7) in one draw = 3/7

$\therefore$ Probability that in each of 4 draws, the chits bear 5 or 6 or 7 = $(3/7)^4$.

8. Total number of buildings constructed across the cities

= 200 + 100 + 225 + 275 + 300 = 1100

Total number of buildings redeveloped across the cities

= 300 + 275 + 250 + 325 + 250 = 1400

Required percentage

$= \frac{1100}{1400} \times 100 = 78.57\% \approx 79\%$.

9.

CUR	WAP	DIR	.....(1)
red	little	boxes	
BIX	FAC	DIR	.....(2)
pile	of	boxes.	

So DIR = boxes

BIX	FAC	DIR	.....(2)
pile	of	boxes	
SUT	MAD	BIX	.....(3)
well	arrange	pile	

So BIX = pile

Thus of = FAC.

10. Out of 100, difference in votes = (60 – 40) = 20

20% of x = 100

$\therefore \quad x = \frac{100 \times 100}{20} = 500$.

11. Here, work done = $\frac{1}{4}$th part

$\therefore$ Remaining work = $\left(1 - \frac{1}{4}\right) = \frac{3}{4}$

We have to find the number of additional men required, hence we shall compare each other item with the number of men.

Less hours per day, more men required (Indirect proportion)

More work, more men required (Direct proportion)

More days, less men required (Indirect proportion).

Work	Days	Hours/day	Men
$\frac{1}{4}$ ↓	10 ↑	9 ↑	400 ↓
$\frac{3}{4}$	20	8	x

Since, $\frac{x}{400} = \frac{3/4}{1/4} \times \frac{10}{20} \times \frac{9}{8} = \frac{27}{16}$

$\Rightarrow x = 25 \times 27 = 675$

$\therefore$ Additional men = (675 – 400) = 275.

12. Total ways = ${}^{80}C_2$

favourable ways = ${}^{20}C_2$

$$P = \frac{{}^{20}C_2}{{}^{80}C_2} = \frac{19}{316}.$$

13. Gross income = $\frac{100}{95} \times 17100$ = ₹ 18000

New net income = $\frac{94}{100} \times 18000$ = ₹ 16920

14. The number = 8 × 17.25 = 138.00
73% of the number

$$= \frac{73}{100} \times 138 = \frac{10074}{100} = 100.74.$$

15. 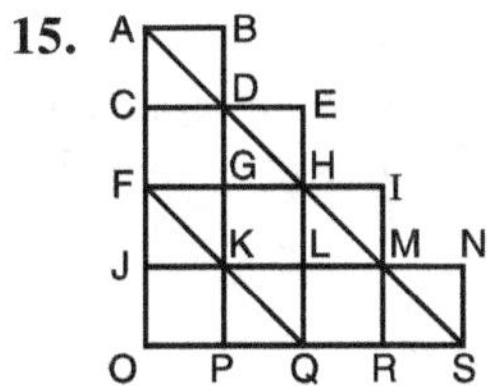

The simplest squares are : ABDC, CDGF, DEHG, FGKJ, GHLK, HIML, JKPO, KLQP, LMRQ and MNSR, *i.e.,* 10 squares.
Other squares are : CELJ, FHQO and GIRP, *i.e.,* 3 squares
So, the total number of squares is 10 + 3 = 13.

16. Amount = ₹ 19200 + ₹ 4032
= ₹ 23232

Now, $23232 = 19200\left(1+\frac{10}{100}\right)^n$

$$\Rightarrow \frac{23232}{19200} = \left(\frac{11}{10}\right)^n \Rightarrow \frac{121}{100} = \left(\frac{11}{10}\right)^n$$

$$\Rightarrow \left(\frac{11}{10}\right)^2 = \left(\frac{11}{10}\right)^n$$

∴ $n = 2$ years.

17. Let original price of the rice = ₹ 100 per kg.
Hence, reduced price of the rice = ₹ 98 per kg.
Let x kg of rice is now available for the same price, then
$x \times 98 = 100 \times 49$

$$\therefore \quad x = \frac{100 \times 49}{98} = 50 \text{ kg.}$$

18. The amount of milk = $\frac{2}{3} \times 60 = 40\ l$

The amount of water = $\frac{1}{3} \times 60 = 20\ l$

Let the $x\ l$ water required for ratio 1 : 2.

Then, $\frac{40}{20+x} = \frac{1}{2}$

$\Rightarrow 20 + x = 80 \qquad \therefore \quad x = 60\ l.$

19. Here, length of water column in 40 min
= 10 × 40 × 60 m
Since, 7.2 × 2.5 × h

$$= \frac{5}{100} \times \frac{3}{100} \times 10 \times 40 \times 60$$

$$\Rightarrow \quad h = \frac{36 \times 100}{72 \times 25} = 2 \text{ m.}$$

20. 4/5 of total time in train = 2 hours.

So, total time in train = 2 × $\frac{5}{4}$ = 5/2 hrs

So, total time spent in air = 4 – 5/2 = 3/2 hrs.
By the given hypothesis, if 360 km is covered by air, then time taken is 4 – 2 = 2 hrs.
So, when 3/2 hrs is spent in air, distance covered

$$= \frac{360}{2} \times \frac{3}{2} = 270 \text{ km}$$

So, distance covered by train
= 360 – 270 = 90 km.

21. The ground state binding energy of positronium is half of that of Hydrogen. This is so because the energy is proportional to the reduced mass and that of the positronium has a reduced mass of half that of Hydrogen.

22. $\left(P + \frac{a}{V^2}\right)(V - b) = RT$

$$P = \frac{RT}{V-b} - \frac{a}{V^2} \qquad ...(1)$$

For n moles of a gas

$$P = \frac{nRT}{V-b} - \frac{an^2}{V^2} \qquad ...(2)$$

$dU = TdS - PdV$

$$\left(\frac{\partial U}{\partial V}\right)_T = T.\left(\frac{\partial S}{\partial V}\right)_T - P$$

$$\left(\frac{\partial U}{\partial V}\right)_T = T.\left(\frac{\partial P}{\partial T}\right)_V - P$$

From equation (2)

$$\left(\frac{\partial P}{\partial T}\right)_V = \frac{nR}{(V-b)}$$

$$\left(\frac{\partial U}{\partial V}\right)_T = \frac{nRT}{(V-b)} - P = \frac{an^2}{V^2} = \frac{a}{\left(\frac{V}{n}\right)^2}$$

23. Note that $V_{rms} = 1.73\sqrt{\frac{kT}{m}}$, $v_{avg} = 1.60\sqrt{\frac{kT}{m}}$, $V_{mp} = 1.41\sqrt{\frac{kT}{m}}$ where the symbols have their usual meanings. The most probable speed V_{mp} is the speed at which the curve reaches the peak. The area under the curve is obviously the total number of molecules.

24. The general equation that represent the force between two atoms or molecules or ions is

$$\boxed{F = \frac{A}{r^M} - \frac{B}{r^N}}$$

A, B, M and N are constants; r is the *interatomic distance.*

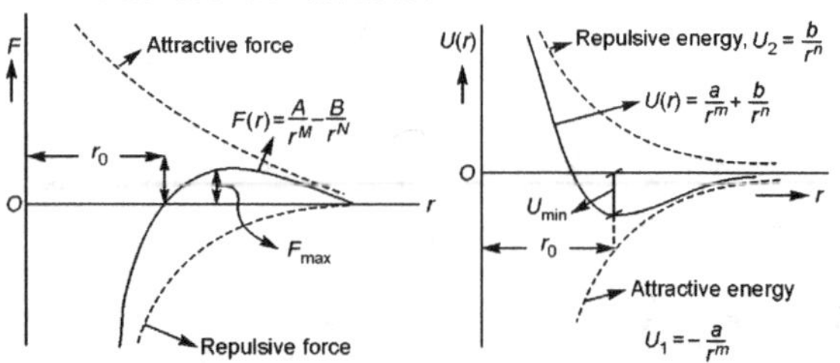

Fig. *Interatomic forces and potential energy vs distance of separation.*

From the above equation, one can arrive at the equation for the potential energy of the system:

$$i.e., \; U(r) = \int F\,dr = \left[\frac{A}{M-1}\right]\left[\frac{1}{r^{M+1}}\right] + \left[\frac{B}{N-1}\right]\left[\frac{1}{r^{N+1}}\right] + C$$

$$= -\frac{a}{r^m} + \frac{b}{r^n} + C$$

When U = 0 for $r = \infty$, C will be zero.

Thus $$\boxed{U(r) = -\frac{a}{r^m} + \frac{b}{r^n}}$$

Here a, b, m and n are different constants. The first term of the above equation refers to attraction and the second term repulsion. n is greater than m with n of the order of 9 and m = 2 for ionic structures. The forces of attraction result from interaction between outer electrons of two atoms.

The forces of repulsion are from inter-penetration of outer electronic shells. Only these forces decide the nature of bonds in solids. The *equilibrium distance* r_0 may be determined as follows:

$$\left[\frac{dU}{dr}\right]_{r=r_0} = 0 = \frac{am}{r_0^{m+1}} - \frac{bn}{r_0^{n+1}}$$

$$i.e., \quad r_0^{n-m} = \left\{\frac{nb}{ma}\right\}$$

$$r_0 = \left\{\frac{nb}{ma}\right\}^{\frac{1}{n-m}}$$

Also $$\boxed{r_0^n = r_0^m\left[\frac{nb}{ma}\right]}.$$

25. $L = \frac{\dot{x}^2}{2x} - V(x)$ (Given)

$$p = \frac{\partial L}{\partial \dot{x}}$$

$$= \frac{\dot{x}}{x}$$

$$H = \sum pq' - L$$

$$H = \frac{\dot{x}}{x}\dot{x} - \frac{\dot{x}^2}{2x} + V$$

$$= \frac{\dot{x}^2}{2x} + V(x)$$

As, $\frac{\dot{x}}{x} = p$

or $H = \frac{p^2x^2}{2x} + V(x)$

$$= \frac{p^2 x}{2} + V(x).$$

26. $\psi = \frac{1}{2}\phi_0 + i\phi_1$

The expectation value of H,

$$<H> = \frac{\langle \psi | H | \psi \rangle}{\langle \psi | \psi \rangle}$$

$$\langle \psi | \psi \rangle = \left\langle \frac{1}{\sqrt{2}}\phi_0 - i\phi_1 \,|\, \frac{1}{\sqrt{2}}\phi_0 + i\phi_1 \right\rangle$$

$$= \frac{1}{2} + 1 = \frac{3}{2}$$

$$\langle \psi | H | \psi \rangle = \left\langle \frac{1}{\sqrt{2}}\phi_0 - i\phi_1 \,|\, H \,|\, \frac{1}{\sqrt{2}}\phi_0 + i\phi_1 \right\rangle$$

$$= \frac{1}{2}E_0 - i \times iE_1$$

So, $\langle H \rangle = \frac{\frac{1}{2}E_0 + E_1}{\frac{3}{2}}$

$$= \frac{E_0 + 2E_1}{3}$$

27. Poles are $z = 0, z = -\frac{1}{2}$

circle $|z| = 1$

Both poles lies inside the

Residue at $z = 0$

$$\lim_{z \to 0} z \cdot \frac{3z+4}{z(2z+1)} = 4$$

Residue at $z = -\frac{1}{2}$

$$\lim_{z \to -\frac{1}{2}} (2z+1)\frac{3z+4}{Z(2z+1)}$$

$$= \frac{3 \times \left(-\frac{1}{2}\right) + 4}{-\frac{1}{2}} = -5$$

Total residue = 4 – 5 = –1

Integral = $-2\pi i$.

28. $m = \frac{m_0}{\sqrt{1 - \frac{v^2}{c^2}}} = \frac{m_0}{\sqrt{1 - \frac{0.36c^2}{c^2}}}$

$$= \frac{m_0}{\sqrt{0.64}} = \frac{m_0}{0.8}$$

$$= \frac{5}{4}m_0$$

29. The electric field due to an infinite line charge distribution at point P

$$\vec{E}_1 = \frac{1}{2\pi \epsilon_0} \frac{\lambda}{a}$$

and that is due to an infinite line charge distribution at point Q.

$$E_2 = \frac{1}{2\pi \epsilon_0} \cdot \frac{\lambda}{a}$$

Their ratio,

$$E_1 : E_2 = \frac{\frac{1}{2}\pi \epsilon_0 \frac{\lambda}{a}}{\frac{1}{2}\pi \epsilon_0 \cdot \frac{\lambda}{a}}$$

$$= \frac{\frac{1}{a}}{\frac{1}{a}} \quad \text{or} \quad 1 : 1.$$

30. The electric field intensity $\bar{E}$ due to an infinite uniformly charged plane sheet at a point distance r from the sheet is given by

$$\bar{E} = \frac{\sigma}{2\epsilon_0}$$

i.e., independent of r.

31. For a rectangle for cross-sectional area A is placed in a uniform electric field and the normal to the area of the coil makes an angle of 90° with electric field

Electric flux $\phi = \int \vec{E} d\vec{s}$

$$= \int E\, ds \cos 90°$$

$$\phi = 0.$$

32. Let the free space be region 1, and the sea water be region 2.

The intrinsic impedance

$$\eta_1 = \eta_0 = 120\,\pi\Omega = 377\ \Omega$$

$$\eta_2 = \sqrt{\frac{\omega\mu}{\sigma}} \angle 45° = 9.73 \angle 43.5° \Omega$$

Then the amplitude of $\vec{E}$ just inside the sea water is $E_0 t$.

$$\frac{E_0^t}{E_0^i} = \frac{2\eta_2}{\eta_1 + \eta_2}$$

or, $$E_0^t = E_0^i \cdot \frac{2\eta_2}{\eta_1 + \eta_2}$$

$$= 5.07 \times 10^{-2} \text{ V/m}$$

Now $$r = \sqrt{j\omega\mu(\sigma + j\omega \in)}$$

$$= 24.36 \angle 46.53° \text{ m}^{-1}$$

$$\propto = 24.36 \cos 46.53°$$

$$= 16.76 \text{ Np/m}$$

$\therefore$ $$1.0 = 10^{-3} = (5.07 \times 10^{-2})\, e^{-16.76z}$$

Solving z

$$z = 0.234.$$

33. Since the system, when measuring A is in the state $|\phi_2>$ the uncertainty

$$\Delta A = \sqrt{<\phi_2|A^2|\phi_2> - <\phi_2|A|\phi_2>^2}$$

where

$$<\phi_2|A|\phi_2> = a(0\,0\,1)\begin{pmatrix} 0 & 4 & 0 \\ 4 & 0 & 1 \\ 0 & 1 & 0 \end{pmatrix}\begin{pmatrix} 0 \\ 0 \\ 1 \end{pmatrix} = 0$$

$<\phi_2|A^2|\phi_2>$

$$= a^2\,(0\,0\,1)\begin{pmatrix} 0 & 4 & 0 \\ 4 & 0 & 1 \\ 0 & 1 & 0 \end{pmatrix}\begin{pmatrix} 0 & 4 & 0 \\ 4 & 0 & 1 \\ 0 & 1 & 0 \end{pmatrix}\begin{pmatrix} 0 \\ 0 \\ 1 \end{pmatrix}$$

$$= a^2$$

Thus we have $\Delta A = a$.

34. The internal energy of a system is given by

$$U = \frac{3N}{2\beta}$$

$N \rightarrow$ number of atoms and $\beta = \dfrac{1}{KT}$

$\therefore$ $$\beta = \frac{1}{1.38 \times 10^{-23} \text{JK}^{-1} \times 300\text{K}}$$

$$= 2.42 \times 10^{20} \text{ J}^{-1}$$

$\therefore$ $$U = \frac{3 \times 10^{24}}{2.42 \times 10^{20}} \text{J}$$

$$= 12.4 \text{ kJ}.$$

35. $$C = \frac{I_t}{V} = \frac{0.1 \times 10^{-12} \times 20 \times 10^{-3}}{0.5}$$

$$= 4 \times 10^{-15} \text{ F}.$$

36. As the metallic sphere is isolated, it becomes positively charged when electrons are ejected from it. There is an extra attractive force on the photoelectrons, if the potential of the sphere is related to V, the electron should have a minimum energy $\phi + eV$ to be able to come out. Thus, emission of the photoelectrons will stop when

$$\frac{hc}{\lambda} = \phi + eV \quad \text{where } \phi = \frac{hc}{\lambda_0}$$

$\therefore$ $$V = \frac{hc}{e}\left[\frac{1}{\lambda} - \frac{1}{\lambda_0}\right]$$

The charge on the sphere needed to take its potential to V is

$$Q = (4\pi\varepsilon_0 a)V$$

The number of electrons emitted is therefore,

$$n = \frac{Q}{e} = \frac{4\pi\varepsilon_0 aV}{e}$$

$$= \frac{4\pi\varepsilon_0 a hc}{e^2}\left[\frac{1}{\lambda} - \frac{1}{\lambda_0}\right]$$

37. 12 adder + 4 data lines

bit chip $= 2^{12} \times 4 = 16$ K bits/chip

Memo $= 16$ K bytes

$= 16 \text{ K} \times 8$ bits

$$\text{No. of chips} = \frac{16\text{K} \times 8}{16\text{ K}} = 8.$$

38.

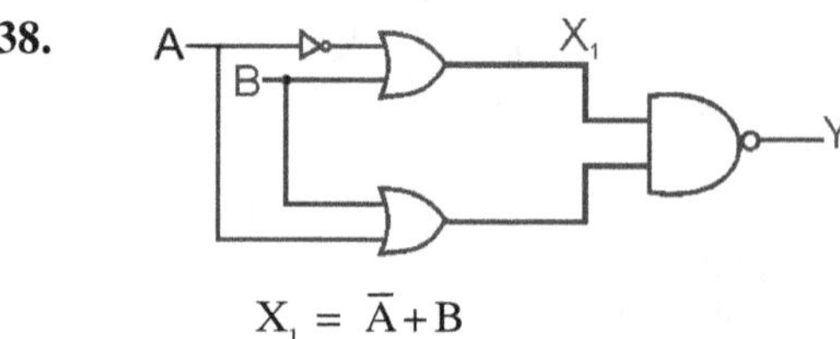

$$X_1 = \bar{A} + B$$

$$X_2 = A + B$$

$$\therefore \quad Y = \overline{(\bar{A}+B)(A+B)}$$

$$= \overline{\bar{A}A + BA + \bar{A}B + BB}$$

Since $\bar{A} \cdot A = 0$

and $\bar{B} \cdot B = 0$

$$\therefore \quad Y = \overline{O + BA + \bar{A}B + B}$$

$$= \overline{B(A+\bar{A}) + B}$$

$$= \overline{B+B}$$

$$= \bar{B}.$$

39. We know,

$$m = \frac{\delta}{f_m} = 15$$

where, $f_m = \dfrac{2\pi \times 100}{2\pi} = 100 \text{ Hz}$

$$\therefore \quad \delta = 15 \times 100 = 1500 \text{ Hz}$$

$\therefore$ Approx. bandwidth $= 2(f_m + \Delta f)$

$$= 2\,(100 + 1500)$$

$$= 3200 \text{ Hz}$$

$$= 3.2 \text{ kHz}.$$

40. s-state has lowest energy. So, $5s$ and $3s$ at lower energy level. Out of these terms : large s(spin) has lower energy

for $\quad 3s : 2s + 1 = 5$

$\quad s = 2$

$\Rightarrow \quad 3s : 2s + 1 = 3$

$\Rightarrow \quad s = 1$

So, $5s$ has the lowest energy.

41.

$$E_{n_1 n_2 n_3} = \frac{\hbar^2\pi^2}{2ma^2}\left[n_1^2 + n_2^2 + n_3^2\right]$$

$$n_i = 1, 2$$

$$E_{1,1,1} = \frac{3\hbar^2\pi^2}{2ma^2}$$

And first excited state,

$$E_{211} = \frac{6\hbar^2\pi^2}{2ma^2}$$

$$\Delta E = \frac{3}{2}\frac{\hbar^2\pi^2}{ma^2}$$

$$m = \frac{m_p}{3}$$

So, $\quad \Delta E = 46.1$ MeV.

42. Average value of r is

$$<r> = \iiint \psi^*(r)\psi dz$$

$$= \int_0^\infty \int_0^\pi \int_0^{2\pi} e^{-r/a} \frac{1}{\pi a^3} \cdot re^{-r/a} r^2 dr \; \sin\theta \, d\theta \, d\phi$$

$$= \frac{1}{\pi a^3} \cdot 4\pi \int_0^\infty r^3 e^{-2r/a} dr$$

$$= \frac{1}{a^3}\frac{3}{2}a^4 = \frac{3}{2}a$$

$$<r> = \frac{3}{2}a.$$

43.

$$E_1 = \frac{h^2}{8ma^2}$$

(lowest energy for a particle in a potential box) and

$$E_a = n^2 E_1$$

Now, $\quad n = 2$

$$E_2 = 4E_1 = 4 \times 2 \text{ eV}$$

$$= 8 \text{ eV}.$$

44. $E_2 \rightarrow$ length of box is halved lowest energy level

$$E_1 = \frac{h^2}{8ma^2}$$

$$E_2 = \frac{h^2}{8m\left(\frac{a}{2}\right)^2}$$

$$= \frac{4h^2}{8ma^2}$$

$$\therefore \quad E_2 = 4E_1$$

45. Expectation value for x,

$$<x> = \Sigma p_i x_i$$

where p_i is the probability of ith state

$$= p_1x_1 + p_2x_2 + p_3x_3 + p_4x_4$$

$$= \frac{1}{4}\times 1 + \frac{1}{4}\times 2 + \frac{1}{4}\times 3 + \frac{1}{4}\times 4 = \frac{10}{4}$$

$= 2.5$

and expectation value for x^2

$$<x> = \sum p_i x_i^2$$

$$= p_1x_1^2 + p_2x_2^2 + p_3x_3^2 + p_4x_4^2$$

$$=$$

$$\frac{1}{4}\times 1^2 + \frac{1}{4}\times 2^2 + \frac{1}{4}\times 3^2 + \frac{1}{4}\times 4^2$$

$$= \frac{30}{4} = 7.5.$$

46. From Wein's law

$$\lambda_m T = b$$

Here, $\lambda_m = 4753$ Å

$$T = \frac{b}{\lambda_m} = \frac{2.9\times 16^{-3}}{4753\times 10^{-10}}$$

$= 6100$ K.

47. This is an inverting *op-amp* configuration. Therefore, the close ∂-loop voltage gain is

$$A_{Q(N)} = 1 + \frac{R_f}{R_i}$$

$$= 1 + \frac{100\ K\Omega}{4.7\ K\Omega}$$

$= 22.3.$

48. $(A \oplus \bar{B}) + (\bar{A} \oplus B)$

$$= \overline{\left(A\bar{B} + \bar{A}\bar{B} + \bar{A}B + \bar{A}\bar{B}\right)}$$

$$= \overline{\left(A\bar{B} + \bar{A}B) + (\bar{A}B + A\bar{B}\right)}$$

$= 0.$

49. Bragg's condition,

$$2d \sin\theta = n\lambda$$

$$d = 3.84\ Å$$

$$\theta = 30°$$

$$2 \times 3.84 \sin 30° = \lambda$$

$$\lambda = 3.84\ Å$$

Then the speed A neutrons will be

$$\lambda = \frac{h}{p} = \frac{h}{mv}$$

$$v = \frac{h}{m\lambda}$$

$$= \frac{6.6\times 10^{-34}}{1.6\times 10^{-27}\times 3.84\times 10^{-8}}$$

$= 1.03 \times 10^5$ cm/s.

50. For HCP structure

The nearest neighbour distance

$$2r = a$$

Since, $a = 0.32$ nm

$\therefore$ Nearest neighbour distance is 0.32 nm.

51. The greater the binding energy per nucleon, the more stable the nucleus is since the most energy is needed to pull a nucleon away from it.

52. We have N atoms, N coupled oscillations. We therefore, have 3N normal modes

$$N = n^3$$

$$N = \frac{10^{-2}\,m}{2\times 10^{-10}\,m}$$

$= 5 \times 10^7$ N

$= 1.25 \times 10^{23}$.

53. For large wave function,

$$V_{ph} = \frac{\omega}{k}$$

$$V_g = \frac{d\omega}{dk}$$

$$= V_{ph} + h\frac{dV_{pm}}{dk}$$

$$= V_{ph} - \frac{1}{2}V_{ph}$$

$$= \frac{1}{2}V_{ph}$$

$$= \frac{1}{2}\sqrt{\frac{g\lambda}{2\pi}}.$$

54. Half-life, T

$$(2)^{-7/T} = \frac{1}{2.5}$$

$$\frac{7}{T} = \frac{\ln 2.5}{\ln 2}$$

$$T = \frac{7 \ln 2}{\ln 2.5}$$

$$= 5.3 \text{ days.}$$

55. For a cubic crystal,

$$\cos\phi = \frac{h_1h_2 + k_1k_2 + l_1l_2}{\left[\left(h_1^2 + k_1^2 + l_1^2\right)\left(h_2^2 + k_2^2 + l_2^2\right)\right]^{1/2}}$$

$$= -\frac{1}{\sqrt{9}} = -\frac{1}{3}$$

$$\phi = \cos^{-1}\left(-\frac{1}{3}\right)$$

$$= 109.5°.$$

56. The distance of closest approach is the displacement from the nucleus at which the total energy of the incident particle is only potential and given by

$$\frac{1}{2} mv^2 = \frac{Zze^2}{4\pi \epsilon_0 b}$$

or $$b = \frac{2Zze^2}{4\pi \epsilon_0 mv_0^2}$$

Given $\frac{1}{2}\ Mv_0^2 = 1 \text{ MeV}$

$$= 1.6 \times 10^{-13} \text{ J}$$

Z (for gold) = 79, z = 1, e = 1.6×10^{-19} C

$$4\pi \epsilon_0 = \frac{1}{9\times 10^{-9}}$$

$$\therefore\ b = \frac{79 \times 1 \times \left(1.6 \times 10^{-19}\right)^2 \times 10^9}{1.6 \times 10^{-13} \times 9}$$

$$= 11.4 \times 10^{14} \text{ m}$$

$$= 11.4 \times 10^{-12} \text{ cm.}$$

57. From Einstein is mass-energy relation,

$$\Delta E = \Delta\, mc^2$$

Again from the uncertainty relation,

$$\Delta E\, \Delta t = \hbar$$

We get $$\Delta t = \frac{\hbar}{\Delta E} = \frac{\hbar}{\Delta mc^2}$$

Assuming that the emitted pion travels at the speed of light, distance travelled by it during them is given by

$$r_0 = C\Delta t$$

$$= C \cdot \frac{\lambda}{\Delta\, mc^2} = \frac{\lambda}{\Delta mc}$$

$$r_0 = \frac{1.0545 \times 10^{-24} \text{ Js}}{270 \times 19.1 \times 10^{-3} \text{ kg}}$$

$$= 1.43 \text{ fermi.}$$

58. P.E. of the electron

$$= -\int_{r_n}^{\infty} F(r)\, dr$$

$$\text{P.E.} = \int_{\infty}^{r_n} \frac{Ze^2 dr}{4\pi\varepsilon_0 r_n^2}$$

$$= -\frac{Ze^2}{4\pi\varepsilon_0 r_n}$$

$$\text{K.E.} = \frac{1}{2} mv_n^2$$

Since $$\frac{mv_n^2}{r} = \frac{(Ze)e}{4\pi\varepsilon_0 r_n^2}$$

$$\therefore \quad \text{K.E.} = \frac{Ze^2}{8\pi\varepsilon_0 r_n}$$

Total energy = K.E. + P.E.

$$= \frac{Ze^2}{8\pi\varepsilon_0 r_n} - \frac{Ze^2}{4\pi\varepsilon_0 r_n}$$

$$= -\frac{Ze^2}{8\pi\varepsilon_0 r_n}$$

For hydrogen atom

$$Z = 1$$

$$\text{T.E.} = -\frac{e^2}{8\pi\varepsilon_0 r_n}.$$

59. The wave number of the lines in a pure rotational spectrum are given by

$$v = 2B\,(J + 1)$$

where J refers to the lower rotational quantum number. The separation between two successive lines corresponding to J and J + 1 is

$$\Delta v = 2B\,(J + 2) - 2B\,(J + 1) = 2B$$

Here $\Delta\nu = 17\ \text{cm}^{-1}$

$\therefore \quad 2B = 17\ \text{cm}^{-1}$

$B = 8.5\ \text{cm}^{-1}$

The moment of inertia of the molecule is

$$I = \frac{h}{8\pi^2 Bc}$$

$$= \frac{6.62 \times 10^{-27}\ \text{erg-sec}}{8 \times (3.14)^2 \times (8.5\text{cm}^{-1}) \times (3 \times 10^{10}\text{cm sec}^{-1})}$$

$= 3.29 \times 10^{-40}$ gm-cm^2

The reduced mass of $H^1\ Br^{79}$ is

$$\mu_{HBr} = \frac{(1 \times 79)/(6.023 \times 10^{23})^2}{(1+79)/(6.023 \times 10^{23})}$$

$= 1.64 \times 10^{-24}$ gm

Therefore, the internuclear distance is

$$r = \sqrt{\frac{I}{\mu}} = \sqrt{\frac{3.29 \times 10^{-40}\ \text{gm-cm}^2}{1.64 \times 10^{-24}\ \text{gm}}}$$

$= 1.42 \times 10^{-8}$ cm

$= 1.42$ Å.

60. The displacement current density is given by

$$J_d = \epsilon_0 \cdot \frac{\partial E}{\partial t}$$

Now inside a capacitor $E = \frac{V}{d} = \frac{V_0 \cos\omega t}{d}$

$$\therefore J_d = \epsilon_0 \cdot \frac{\partial (V_0 \cos\omega t)}{\partial t\, d} = \frac{-\epsilon_0\, \omega\, V_0 \sin\omega t}{d}$$

i.e., $\quad J_d = -\frac{\epsilon_0\, \omega V_0 \sin\omega t}{d}$.

61. From Bragg's law

$$2d \sin\theta = n\lambda$$

According to the question,

$n = 1$

$$d = \frac{a}{\sqrt{h^2 + k^2 + l^2}}$$

$h = 3$, $k = 1$, and $l = 1$.

$$d = \frac{a}{\sqrt{3^2 + 1^2 + 1^2}} = \frac{a}{\sqrt{11}}$$

$$\therefore \quad \frac{2.a}{\sqrt{11}} \cdot \frac{1}{2} = 1 \times 10^{-10}\ \text{m}$$

$\Rightarrow a = \sqrt{11} \times 10^{-10}$ m $= \sqrt{11}$ Å.

62. $F = \bar{A}\bar{B}\bar{C} + A\bar{B}\bar{C} + A\bar{B}C + AB\bar{C}$

$= \bar{B}\bar{C} + A\bar{B}C + AB\bar{C}$

$= \bar{B}[\bar{C} + AC] + AB\bar{C}$

$= \bar{B}\left[(\bar{C} + A)\cdot(\bar{C} + \bar{C})\right] + AB\bar{C}$

$= \bar{B}\left[(\bar{C} + A)\right] + AB\bar{C}$

$= \bar{B}\bar{C} + \bar{B}A + AB\bar{C}$

$= \bar{C}\left[\bar{B} + AB\right] + \bar{B}A$

$= \bar{C}\left[(\bar{B} + A)\cdot(\bar{B} + B)\right] + \bar{B}A$

$= \bar{B}\bar{C} + A\bar{C} + \bar{B}A = \bar{C}(A + \bar{B}) + A\bar{B}$.

63. $|A - \lambda I| = 0$

$$\begin{bmatrix} 1-\lambda & 2 & -3 \\ 0 & 3-\lambda & 2 \\ 0 & 0 & -2-\lambda \end{bmatrix} = 0$$

or $(1 - \lambda)(3 - \lambda)(-2 - \lambda) = 0$ or $\lambda = 1, 3, -2$

Eigenvalues of $A^3 = 1, 27, -8$;

Eigenvalues of $A^2 = 1, 9, 4$

Eigenvalues of $A = 1, 3, -2$;

Eigenvalues of $I = 1, 1, 1$

$\therefore$ Eigenvalues of $3A^3 + 5A^2 - 6A + 2I$

First eigenvalue $= 3(1)^2 + 5(1)^2 - 6(1) + 2 = 4$

$= 3(27) + 5(9) - 6(3) + 2(1) = 110$

$= 3(-8) + 5(4) - 6(-2) + 2(1) = 10$

Required eigenvalues are 4, 110, 10.

64. The zener current will be minimum (*i.e.*, 200 mA) when the input voltage is minimum (*i.e.*, 22V). The load current stays at constant value $I_L = V_Z/R_L = 18V/18\Omega = 1\ A = 1000$ mA

$$\therefore R = \frac{E_i - E_0}{(I_Z)_{min} + (I_L)_{max}} = \frac{(22 - 18)\text{V}}{(200 + 1000)\text{mA}}$$

$$= \frac{4\text{V}}{1200\text{mA}} = 3.33\Omega$$

65. The number of charges carriers in an intrinsic semiconductor is double the number of hole-electron pairs. If N_1 is the number of charge carriers at temperature T_1 and N_2 at T_2, we have

$N_1 = N_0\, e^{-\Delta E/2kT_1}$

$N_2 = N_0\, e^{-\Delta E/2kT_2}$

The percentage increase as the temperature is raised from T_1 to T_2 is :

$$f = \frac{N_2 - N_1}{N_1} \times 100$$

$$= \left(\frac{N_2}{N_1} - 1\right) \times 100$$

$$= 100\left[e^{\frac{\Delta E}{2k}\left(\frac{1}{T_1} - \frac{1}{T_2}\right)} - 1\right]$$

Substituting the values of ΔE, K, T_1 and T_2 for the calculation of the term

$$\frac{\Delta E}{2k}\left(\frac{1}{T_1} - \frac{1}{T_2}\right)$$

$$= \frac{0.68 \text{ eV}}{2 \times 8.62 \times 10^{-5}}\left(\frac{1}{300} - \frac{1}{320}\right)$$

$$= 0.82$$

Thus, $f = 100 \times [e^{0.82} - 1] \simeq 127\%$.

66.

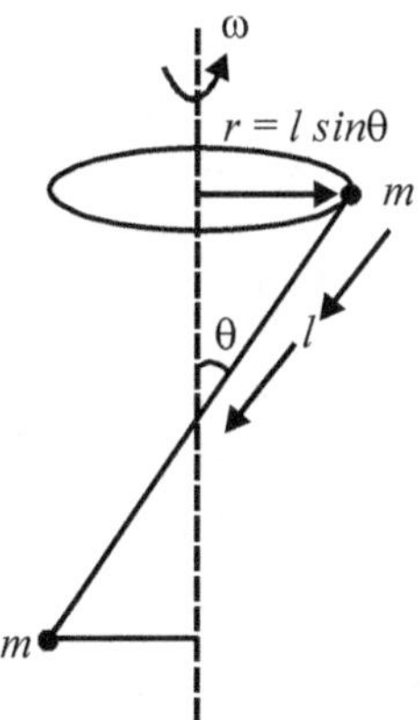

From definition

$$\bar{L} = \bar{r} \times \bar{p}$$

$$= \bar{r} \times (m\bar{v})$$

$$|\bar{L}| = l\sin\theta(m\omega l \sin\theta)$$

$$\Rightarrow \quad |\bar{L}| = m\omega l^2 \sin^2\theta$$

$$\frac{d|\bar{L}|}{dt} = m\omega l^2 . 2\sin\theta\cos\theta \frac{d\theta}{dt}$$

$$\frac{dL}{dt} = 2ml^2\omega^2 \sin\theta\cos\theta .$$

67. The resistance of the coil is $R = \frac{6V}{12A} = 0.5\Omega$

In the AC circuit, the current is in phase with the emf. This means that the net reactance of the circuit is zero. The impedance is equal to the resistance, *i.e.*, $Z = 0.5\ \Omega$.

The rms circuit $= \frac{\text{rms voltage}}{Z} = \frac{6\text{ V}}{0.5\Omega} = 12\text{A}$.

68. The gain factor of a tride valve amplifier is

$$A = \frac{\mu}{1 + \frac{r_p}{R_L}}$$

where μ is the amplitude factor, r_p is the plate resistance and R_L is the load resistance.

Thus, $A = \frac{21}{1 + \frac{10\text{ k}\Omega}{20\text{ k}\Omega}} = 14.$

69. Since the carrier is at 30 Hz and modulating frequency is 5 Hz, then the modulation index is about 3, making the peak frequency deviation of about 15 Hz. It shows that the frequency will vary between 15 and 45 Hz.

70. To find V_{th}, the voltage across the terminals, combine 1K and 2K is parallel. So, 1K || 2 K = (1K * 2K) / (1K + 2K) = 2M/3K = 667 Ω.
Using voltage divider across 3 kΩ, we get
$V_{th} = [3K / (667 + 3K)] \times 5$ V
$= 4.1$ V.

71. The semi-angle of cone of laser beam,

$$\theta = \frac{\lambda}{a} = \frac{800 \times 10^{-9}}{2 \times 10^{-3}}$$

$$= 400 \times 10^{-6}$$

Diameter of the beam 1 m away

$= 2 \times 400 \times 10^{-6} \times 10^3 = 0.8$ m

$= 80$ cm.

72. If heat is supplied to the metal, these free electrons also absorb part of the heat, and the molar electronic specific heat is obtained as

$$[C_V]_{el} = \left[\frac{dU}{dT}\right] = \frac{3}{2} k_B N_A = 1.5 R_0$$

Since $U = \frac{3}{2} N_A K_B T)$

i.e., $[C_V]_{el} = 1.5 \times 1.38 \times 10^{-23} \times 6.02 \times 10^{26}$

$= 12.5 \times 10^3$ J/K mol/K

$= 1.25$ kJ /K mol/K

73. As deutron consists of equal number of neutron and proton, the reduced mass of the system.

$$\mu = \frac{M_n M_p}{M_n + M_p} = \frac{M}{2}$$

Max. energy $E = \frac{e^2 B^2 r^2}{2\left(\frac{M}{2}\right)} = 20$

or, $\frac{e^2 B^2 r^2}{2m} = \frac{20}{2} = 10$ MeV

Max. charging of proton

$$= \frac{e^2 B^2 r^2}{2m} = 10\ MeV$$

74. The reaction to produce anti-protons is

$p + p \rightarrow \overline{p} + p + p + p$

The hydrogen can be considered to be at rest. Thus, at threshold the invariant mean squared is

$$(E + m_p) - (E^2 - m_p{}^2) = (4m_p)^4$$

$$E = 7\,m_p$$

Hence, threshold energy $= 7m_p = 6.6$ GeV

75. The synchrotron radiation is emitted when the trajectory of a charged particle is bent by a magnetic field. As the energy loss per revolution

$$\Delta E = \left(\frac{4\pi}{3}\right)\left(\frac{e^2}{4\pi \epsilon_0}\right) = \frac{1}{R}\beta^3 \gamma^4$$

where R, the radius of curvature of the trajectory, is given by

$$R = \frac{m\gamma\, \beta c}{eB}$$

Thus, for particles is same charge and *r*,

$$\Delta E \propto m^{-1}$$

SET–10
CSIR–UGC (NET) PHYSICAL SCIENCES

PART-A

1. In triangle ABC, shown in the figure, AB is perpendicular to BC. Further, BD is perpendicular to AC. If AD = 9 cm and DC = 4 cm, the length BD is

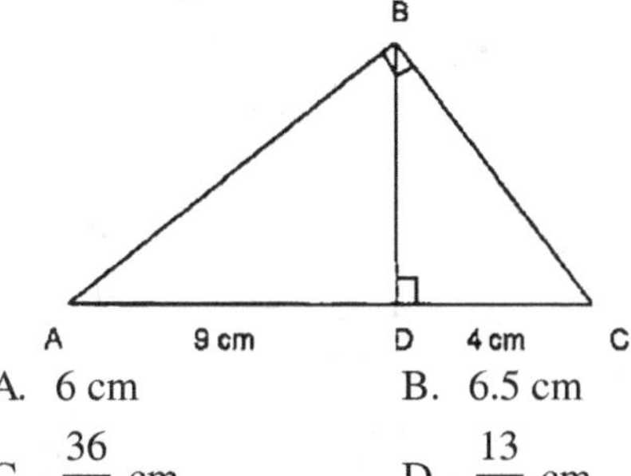

A. 6 cm B. 6.5 cm

C. $\frac{36}{13}$ cm D. $\frac{13}{36}$ cm

Directions (Q. No. 2): *Study the graph carefully to answer the questions that follow.*

Profit (in lakhs) made by three companies over the years

Profit = Income – Expenditure

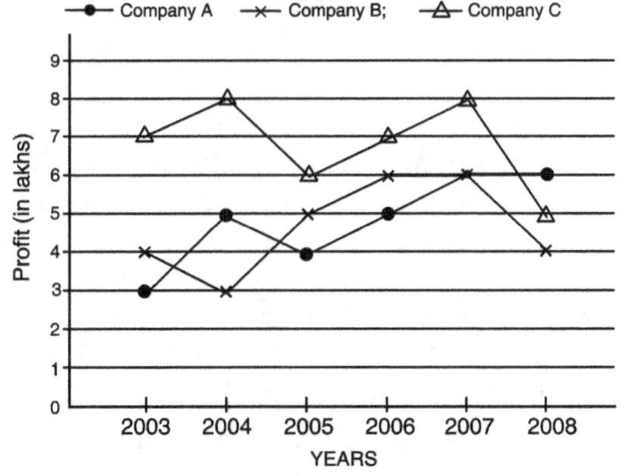

2. What is the approximate average profit made by Company A in all the years together?

A. ₹ 3,82,000 B. ₹ 3,98,000

C. ₹ 4,83,000 D. ₹ 5,12,000

3. Three sunflower plants were placed in conditions as indicated below.

Plant A : still air

Plant B : moderately turbulent air

Plant C : still air in the dark

Which of the following statements is correct?

A. Transpiration rate of plant B > that of plant A

B. Transpiration rate of plant A > that of plant B

C. Transpiration rate of plant C = that of plant A

D. Transpiration rate of plant C > that of plant A > that of plant B

4. What is the half-life of the radio isotope whose activity profile is shown below?

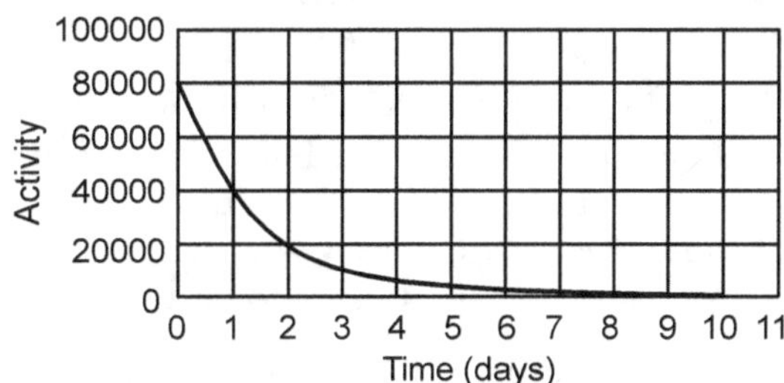

A. 1 day B. 3 days

C. 2 days D. 4 days

5. A, B and C together start a business. The amount invested by A and B are in the ratio of 4 : 3, whereas the ratio of investments of B and C is 2 : 3. If the total profit earned is ₹ 46,000, what is C's share in the profit?

A. ₹ 14000 B. ₹ 15000

C. ₹ 16000 D. ₹ 18000

6. One of the two exclusive events must occur, the chance of one is 2/3 of the other, then odds in favour of the other are :

A. 1 : 3 B. 3 : 1

C. 2 : 3 D. 3 : 2

Directions (Q.No. 7): *This question is based on the information given in the following graph.*

Rates of interest per cent per annum given by two companies 'A' and 'B' during the given years.

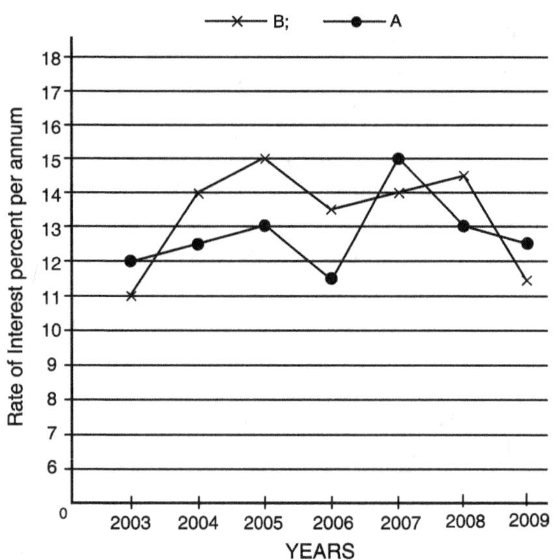

7. An amount of ₹ 20,000 was invested in Company 'B' in 2008 and after one year the entire amount alongwith interest will be reinvested in the Company A for one more year. What will be the total amount of interest accrued?

A. ₹ 5199 B. ₹ 5762.50
C. ₹ 5533.75 D. ₹ 54.25

8. The volume of a wall, 5 times as high as it is broad and 9 times as long as it is high, is 12.8 cu. metres. The breadth of the wall is:

A. 30 cm B. 40 cm
C. 22.5 cm D. 25 cm

9. A toy cube is painted orange on all sides. It is cut into 64 smaller cubes of equal size. How many smaller cubes are not painted at all?

A. 4 B. 8
C. 16 D. 20

10. The angles of elevation of the top of a vertical tower from two points, distant a and b $(a > b)$ from the base and in the same straight line with it are complementary. Then the height of the tower is:

A. $\sqrt{(ab)}$ B. $\sqrt{(a^2+b^2)}$
C. $\sqrt{(a^2-b^2)}$ D. $\sqrt{a(a-b)}$

11. A vertical pole is 75 m high. Find the angle subtended by the pole at a point 75 m away from its base.

A. 30° B. 45°
C. 60° D. 90°

12. If diameter of each of the following circles is 1 m, then area of the shaded part is:

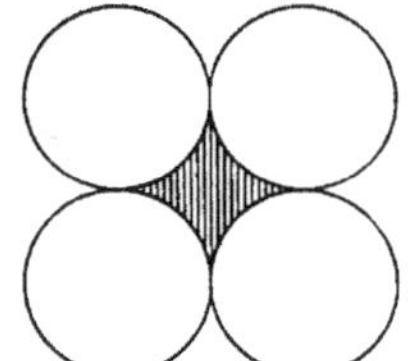

A. (1–π) square metre
B. (4–π) square metre
C. (π–1) square metre
D. (1–π/4) square metre

13. If an integer p is chosen at random in the interval $0 \leq p \leq 5$, the probability that the roots of the equation $x^2 + px + p/4 + 1/2 = 0$ are real is :

A. 4/5 B. 2/3
C. 3/5 D. None of these

14. Two events A and B have probabilities 0.25 and 0.50 respectively. The probability that both A and B occur simultaneously is 0.12. Then the probability that neither A nor B occurs is :

A. 0.13 B. 0.38
C. 0.63 D. 0.37

15. A and B jointly invest ₹ 2100 and ₹ 3100 respectively in a firm. A is an active partner and hence he gets 25% of the profit separately. If their business yields them total ₹ 1040 as profit, what will be the gain of each of them?

A. ₹ 415, ₹ 625 B. ₹ 575, ₹ 465
C. ₹ 515, ₹ 525 D. ₹ 560, ₹ 480

16. A man is observing from the top of a tower a boat speeding away from the tower. The boat makes an angle of depression of 45° with the man's eye when at a distance of 60 m from the tower. After 5 seconds, the angle of depression becomes 30°. Find the speed of the boat, assuming that it is running in still water.

A 30 km/hr B. 31.5 km/hr
C. 33 km/hr D. 34 km/hr

17. A man is known to speak truth 3 out of 4 times. He throws a dice and reports that it is a six, the probability that it is actually a six is :

A. 3/8 B. 1/5
C. 3/5 D. None of these

18. Two stations A and B are 110 km apart on a straight line. One train starts from A at 7 a.m. and travels towards B at 20 km per hour speed. Another train starts from B at 8 a.m. and travels towards A at a speed of 25 km per hour. At what time will they meet?

A. 10 a.m. B. 11 a.m.
C. 12 a.m. D. 13 a.m.

19. If the length and breadth of a rectangular field are increased, the area increases by 50%. If the increase in length was 20%, by what percentage was the breadth increased?

A. 20% B. 25%
C. 30% D. 40%

20. The cartesian coordinates of four points QRPS are (2, 4), (4, 4), (4, 1) and (0, 0) respectively. Area of the quadrilateral PQRS is—

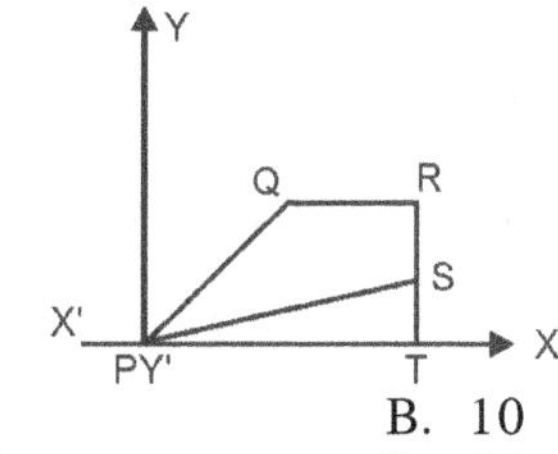

A. 9 B. 10
C. 11 D. 12

PART-B

21. Fourier series which will represents $f(x) = x \sin x$ in the inverval $-\pi < x < \pi$, then $\frac{1}{2}+\frac{1}{1.3}-\frac{1}{3.5}+\frac{1}{5.7}$.... will have value—

A. $\pi/2$ B. $\pi/4$
C. $\pi/6$ D. $\pi/8$

22. The state of a free particle is represented by a wavefunction— $\psi(x, 0) = Ne^{-x^2}/2a^2 + ik_0x$

The value of factor N is—

A. $\frac{1}{\sqrt{a\pi}}$ B. $\frac{1}{\pi^{1/2}a^{1/4}}$
C. $\frac{1}{\pi^{1/4}a^{1/2}}$ D. $\frac{1}{\pi a}$

23. Two ends of a rod are kept at 127°C and 227°C. When 2000 cal of heat flows in this rod, then the change in entropy is

A. 1 cal/K B. 20 cal/K
C. 6.9 cal/K D. 0.7 cal/K

24. A 60 V peak full wave rectified voltage is applied to a capacitor input filter. If F = 120 Hz, R_L = 10 kΩ and C = 10 μF, the ripple voltage is

A. 0.6 B. 6 mv
C. 5 V D. 2.88 V

25. The minimum number of resistors required in a 4 bit D/A network of weighted-resistor type is

A. 4 B. 8
C. 15 D. 16

26. In an experiment, on the measurement of g, using a simple pendulum, the time period was measured with an accuracy of 0.2% while the length was measured with an accuracy of 0.5%. The percentage accuracy in the value of g thus obtained:

A. 0.7% B. 0.1%
C. 0.25% D. 0.9%

27. The resistance of a thermometer is 5Ω at 30°C and 6.5Ω at 60°C. Using linear approximation, the value of resistance temperature coefficient at 45°C.

A. 0.009/°C B. 0.0087/°C
C. 0.0085/°C D. 0.01/°C

28. When an observer moves so fast that the lengths that he measures are reduced to half, his time interval measurements:

A. Be invariant B. Reduced to half
C. Becomes twice D. Reduced to 1/4th

29. Two point charges Q and – Q are located on two opposite corners of a square as shown in Fig. If the potential at the corner A is taken as 1V, then the potential at B, the centre of

the square will be

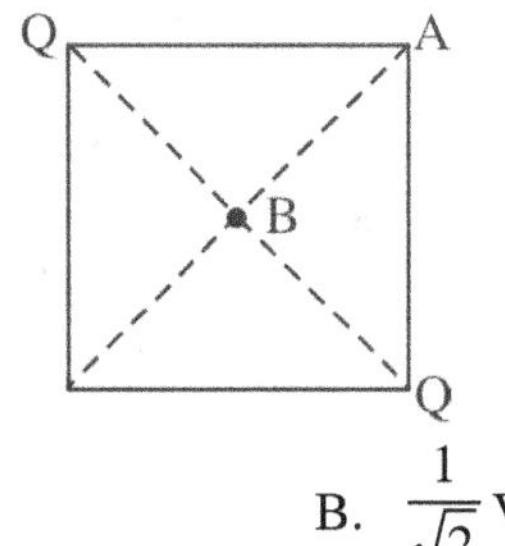

A. zero B. $\frac{1}{\sqrt{2}}$ V

C. 1 V D. $\sqrt{2}$ V

30. The explicit expression for the operator $\left(\frac{d}{dx}+x\right)^2$ is given by

A. $\frac{d^2}{dx^2}+2x\frac{d}{dx}+x^2$

B. $\frac{d^2}{dx^2}+x^2$

C. $\frac{d^2}{dx^2}+2x\frac{d}{dx}+x^2+1$

D. $\frac{d^2}{dx^2}+2x\frac{d}{dx}+x^2-1$

31. The statistical energy distribution under lying the ideal gas law is the M-B distribution. It gives the number of molecules with kinetic energies between E and E + dE as,

$$N(E)dE = \frac{2N}{\sqrt{A}(kT)^{1/2}}\sqrt{E}\,e^{-E/kT}dE$$

The average KE over the collection of N molecules

A. $\frac{3}{2}NkT$ B. $\frac{3}{2}kT$

C. $\frac{1}{2}NkT$ D. $\frac{1}{2}kT$

32. An SCR has a circuit fusing rating of 50 A^2s. The device is being used in a circuit where it could be subjected to a 100 A surge. The maximum allowable duration of such a surge

A. 5 ms B. 6 ms

C. 4 ms D. 2 ms

33. If the radius of the first orbit in hydrogen atom is 0.05 nm, the radius of the first orbit in helium atom will be

A. 0.025 nm B. 0.05 nm

C. 1 nm D. 0.5 nm

34. For a diamond structure the packing fraction is given by

A. $\frac{\pi\sqrt{3}}{8}$ B. $\frac{\pi\sqrt{3}}{4}$

C. $\frac{\pi\sqrt{3}}{2}$ D. $\frac{\pi\sqrt{3}}{16}$

35. The activity of a certain preparation decreases 2-5 times after 7 days, then its half-life is

A. 4 days B. 5.3 days

C. 10 days D. 18.5 days

36. Consider the reaction—

${}_1H + {}^{A}X \rightarrow {}^{2}H + {}^{A-1}X$. For which target nuclei ${}^{4}X$, the reaction to the strongest?

A. ${}^{39}Ca$ B. ${}^{40}Ca$

C. ${}^{41}Ca$ D. ${}^{42}Ca$

37. The mean and standard deviation of a binomial distribution are 10 and 2 respectively. The value of P is

A. 1 B. 0.8

C. 0.6 D. 0.4

38. A sample of ideal gas with initial pressure P and volume V is taken through an isothermal expansion proceed during which the change in entropy is found to be ΔS. The universal gas constant is R. Then the work done by the gas is given by

A. $\frac{P\Delta S}{n\Delta V}$ B. $\frac{PV\Delta S}{nR}$

C. PΔV D. $nR\Delta S$

39. Suppose an electron is in a state described by the wave function

$$\psi = \frac{1}{\sqrt{4\pi}}\,(e^{i\phi}\sin\theta + \cos\theta)\,g(r)$$

where $\int_0^\infty |g(r)|^2\, r^2 dr = 1$

The expansion value of L_2 is

A. 0 B. $\frac{1}{3}\hbar$

C. $\frac{2}{3}\hbar$ D. $\frac{3}{2}\hbar$

40. Steam at 100°C is mixed with 1500 grams of water at 15°C so that the final temperature of the mixture is 80°C. The mass of steam is

A. 1250 gms B. 625 gms

C. 175 gms D. 350 gms

41. If maximum and minimum amplitudes of an amplitude modulated waves are 10 V and 5 V respectively, the modulation index is

A. 2 B. 0.5

C. 3.3 D. 0.33

42. A p-type semiconductor has acceptor levels 57 meV above the valence band. Find the maximum wavelength of light which can create a hole.

A. 3.12×10^{-5} m B. 1.12×10^{-6} m

C. 2.18×10^{-5} m D. 0.18×10^{-5} m

43. A steam engine in takes 100g of steam at 100°C per minute and cools it down to 20°C. Calculate the heat rejected by the steam per minute. Latent heat of vapourisation of steam = 540 cal g^{-1}.

A. 3.2×10^4 cal B. 6.2×10^4 cal

C. 5.1×10^3 cal D. 6.9×10^2 cal

44. The electric field in an electromagnetic wave is given by E = (SONC^{-1}) sin $\omega(t - x/c)$. Find the energy contained in a cylinder of cross-section 10 cm^2 and length 50 cm along the x-axis.

A. 3.5×10^{-13} J B. 4.5×10^{-14} J

C. 5.5×10^{-12} J D. 1.5×10^{-12} J

45. Three particles of equal mass m are connected by two identical massless springs of stiffness constant k as shown in the figure:

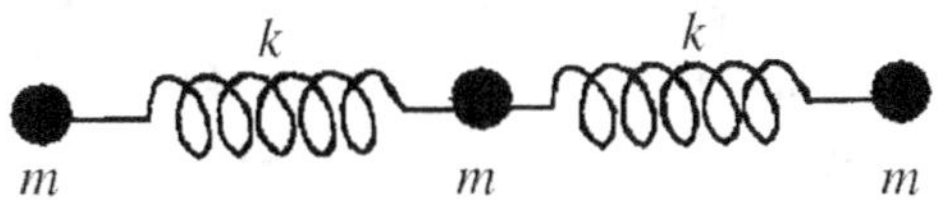

If x_1, x_2 and x_3 denote the horizontal displacements of the masses from their respective equilibrium positions, the potential energy of the system is:

A. $\frac{1}{2}k\left[x_1^2 + x_2^2 + x_3^2\right]$

B. $\frac{1}{2}k\left[x_1^2 + x_2^2 + x_3^2 - x_2(x_1 + x_3)\right]$

C. $\frac{1}{2}k\left[x_1^2 + 2x_2^2 + x_3^2 + 2x_2(x_1 + x_3)\right]$

D. $\frac{1}{2}k\left[x_1^2 + 2x_2^2 + x_3^2 - 2x_2(x_1 + x_3)\right]$

PART-C

46. A ball of radius R = 50 cm has a total charge of 36 mc which is uniformly distributed throughout the volume. What will be magnitude of electric field at 0 cm?

A. 0 B. 25

C. 50 D. 36

47. What is the entrophy change of water when 1000 gm of water are heated from 20°C to 80°C. Given that specific heat of water has a constant value 4.25/gm°C

A. 789 J/K B. 682 J/K

C. 783 J/K D. 782 J/K

48. An artificial satellite revolves about the earth at height H above the surface, the orbital period so that a man in the satellite will be in the state of weightlessness is

A. $2\pi\sqrt{\frac{R}{g}}$ B. $\frac{1}{2\pi}\sqrt{\frac{R}{g}}$

C. $2\pi\sqrt{\frac{g}{R}}$ D. $\frac{1}{2\pi}\sqrt{\frac{g}{R}}$

49. Three infinitely long wires are placed equally apart on the circumference of a circle of radius a, perpendicular to its plane. Two of the wires carry current I each, in the same direction, while the third carries current 2I along the direction opposite to the other two. The magnitude of the magnetic induction $\vec{B}$ at a distance r from the centre of the circle, for $r > a$ is

A. $-\frac{2\mu_0}{\pi}\frac{Ia}{r^2}$ B. $-\frac{2\mu_0}{\pi}\frac{I}{r}$

C. 0 D. $\frac{2\mu_0}{\pi}\frac{I}{r}$

50. If the collector current changes from 2 mA to 3 mA in a transistor when collector-emitter voltage is increased from 2 V to 10 V, what is the output resistance?

A. 1 kΩ B. 3 kΩ
C. 5 kΩ D. 8 kΩ

51. In a Bainbridge mass spectrograph singly ionized atoms of neon-20 pass into the deflection chamber with a velocity of 10^5 m/sex. If they are deflected by a magnetic field of flux density 0.08 tesla, calculate the radius of their path and where neon-22 ions would fall if they had the same initial velocity.

A. 0.125 m B. 0.456 m
C. 0.285 m D. 0.345 m

52. The mean energy for production of a free ion pair in gases by radiation is

A. Equal to the ionisation potential
B. Between 20240 eV
C. In good approximation 11.5 Z
D. None of these

53. At low E/p the drift velocity of electrons in gases V_{Dr}, follows precisely the relation $V_{Dr} \propto E/p$. This can be explained by the fact that—

A. The electrons each gains an energy $\Sigma = eE\int ds$
B. The electrons thermalize completely in inelastic encounters with gas molecules
C. The cross-section is independent of electrons velocity
D. None of these

54. A laser beam emerging from a laser tube operating at 80 nm has a cross-sectional diameter of 2 mm. The diameter of the beam at a distance of 1 km is approximately given by

A. 10 mm B. 8 cm
C. 80 cm D. 10 m

55. In the given circuit using ideal op-amps, the output voltage will be

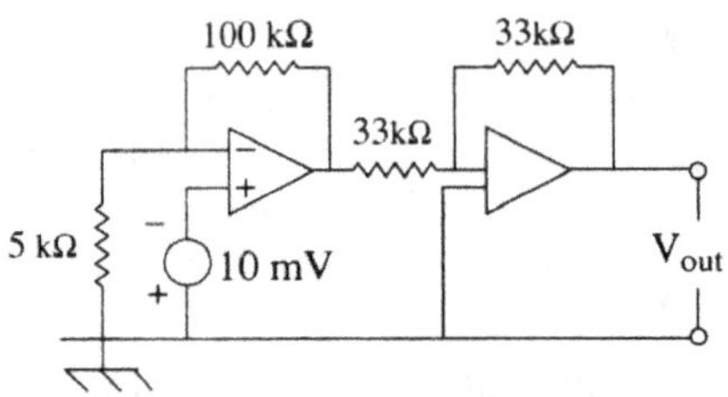

A. 200 mV B. –210 mV
C. 210 mV D. –200 mV

56. In a mass spectrometer, a single charge +ve ion is accelerated through a potential difference of 1000 volt. It then travels through a uniform magnetic field for which B = 1000 gauss and is deflected into a circular path 18.2 cm in radius. What is the speed of the ion?

A. 1.099×10^5 m/s B. 0.99×10^5 m/s
C. 2.099×10^4 m/s D. 1.239×10^4 m/s

57. The op-amp of given fig. has $I_{in(bias)} = 80$ nA, $I_{in(off)} = 20$ nA and $V_{in(off)} = 2$ mV. What is the output offset voltage?

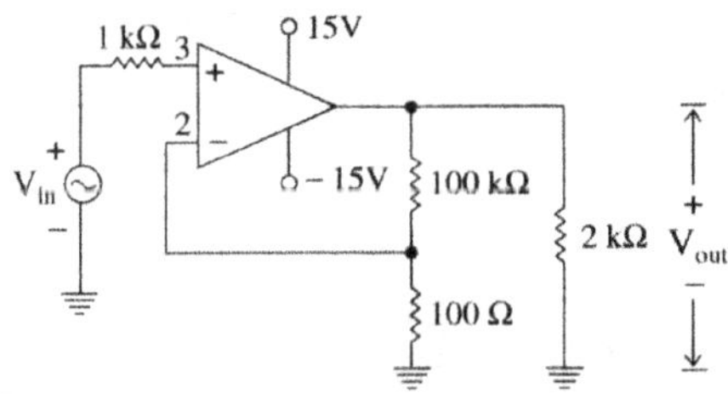

A. 0.102 V B. 0.208 V
C. 1.102 V D. 1.208 V

58. Calculate the activity of k^{40} in 100 kg. man assuming that 0.35% of the body weight is potassium. The abundance of k^{40} is 0.012%, its half life is 1.31×10^9 years.

A. 0.123 micro curie B. 1.123 micro curie
C. 0.345 micro curie D. 0.287 micro curie

59. Two of the eigenvalues of a 3 × 3 matrix, whose determinant equals 4, are –1 and +2, the third eigenvalue of the matrix is equal to

A. –2 B. –1
C. 1 D. 2

60. A metallic sphere of radius r and carrying a charge q is enclosed by a dielectric shell of thickness δ, outer radius r_2 and relative permittivity ϵ. The medium elsewhere is air. The potential $V(r)$ for $r > r_2$ is

A. $\frac{q}{4\pi\epsilon_0}\left[\frac{\epsilon r_2+\delta}{\epsilon r_2^2}+\frac{r_2-r_1}{r_2 r_1}\right]$

B. $\frac{q}{4\pi\epsilon_0}\frac{(\epsilon-1)r+r_2}{rr_2}$

C. $\frac{q}{4\pi\epsilon_0 r}$

D. $\frac{q}{4\pi\epsilon_0}\left[\frac{\epsilon r_2+\delta}{\epsilon r_2^2}+\frac{r_2-r}{r_2 r}\right]$

61. The radius R of a loop carrying a current F is doubled R $\rightarrow$ 2R while the current is halved I $\rightarrow$ I/2. The magnetic moment M of the current loop is then

A. M B. 2M
C. M/2 D. 4M

62. Given the op-amp configuration is given figure below, the value of the R_f required to produce a closed loop voltage gain of 100

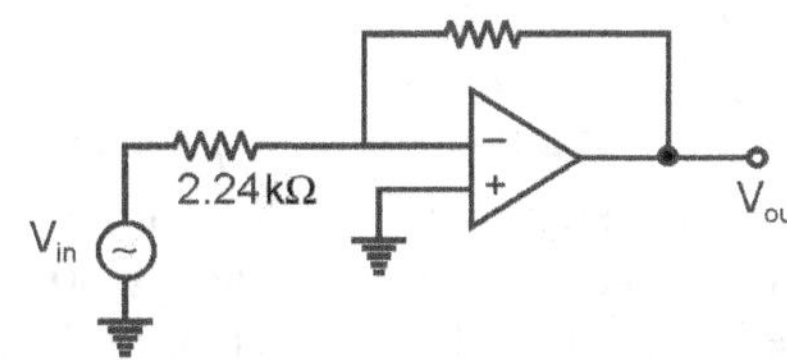

A. 480 kΩ B. 220 kΩ
C. 440 kΩ D. 110 kΩ

63. For an intrinsic semiconductor (Ge) at 300 K, $n_i = 2.4 \times 10^{19}$ m^{-3}, mobility of electron μ_n = 0.39 m^2 v^{-1}s^{-1} and mobility of holes μ_p = 0.19 m^{2}v^{-1}s^{-1}. The conductivity of sample is found to be

A. 2.42 mho/m B. 2.22 mho/m
C. 2.82 mho/m D. 1.92 mho/m

64. The maximum energy of deuterons coming out of a cyclotron accelerator is 20 MeV. The maximum energy of protons that can be obtained from this accelerator is

A. 10 MeV B. 20 MeV
C. 30 MeV D. 40 MeV

65. To go through the ionosphere an electromagnetic wave should have a frequency of at least (H_2)

A. 10 B. 10^4
C. 10^8 D. 10^9

66. The Taylor expansion of the function ln (cosh x), where x is real, about the point $x = 0$ starts with the following terms:

A. $-\frac{1}{2}x^2+\frac{1}{12}x^4+...$ B. $\frac{1}{2}x^2-\frac{1}{12}x^4+...$

C. $-\frac{1}{2}x^2+\frac{1}{6}x^4+...$ D. $\frac{1}{2}x^2+\frac{1}{6}x^4+...$

67. Bose condensation occurs in liquid He^4 kept at ambient pressure at 2.17 K. At which temperature will Bose condensation occur in He^4 in gaseous state, the density of which is 1000 times smaller than that of liquid He^4? (Assume that it is a perfect Bose gas.)

A. 2.17 mK B. 21.7 mK
C. 21.7 μK D. 2.17 μK

68. The magnetic field of the TE_{11} mode of a rectangular waveguide of dimensions $a \times b$ as shown in the figure is given by $H_z = H_0 \cos(0.3\pi x)\cos(0.4\pi y)$, where x and y are in cm.
The dimensions of the waveguide are

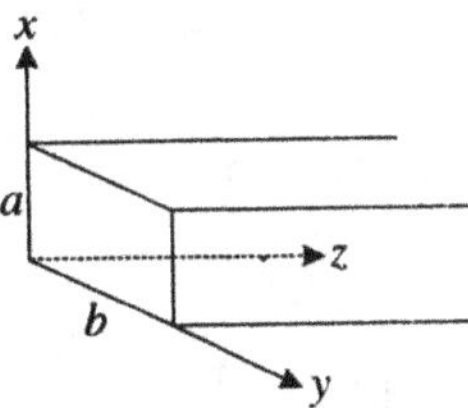

A. a = 3.33 cm, b = 2.50 cm
B. a = 0.40 cm, b = 0.30 cm
C. a = 0.80 cm, b = 0.60 cm
D. a = 1.66 cm, b = 1.25 cm

69. Consider a system of N non-interacting spins, each of which has classical magnetic moment of magnitude μ. The Hamiltonian of this system in an external magnetic field $\vec{H}$ is

$\mathcal{H} = -\sum_{i=1}^{N}\vec{\mu}_i\cdot\vec{H}$, where $\vec{\mu}_i$ is the magnetic moment of the ith spin. The magnetization per spin at temperature T is

A. $\dfrac{\mu^2 H}{k_B T}$

B. $\mu\left[\coth\hbar\left(\dfrac{\mu H}{k_B T}\right) - \dfrac{k_B T}{\mu H}\right]$

C. $\mu \sin\hbar\left(\dfrac{\mu H}{k_B T}\right)$

D. $\mu \tan\hbar\left(\dfrac{\mu H}{k_B T}\right)$

70. The spacing between the nth energy level and the next higher level in a one dimensional potential box increases by

A. $(n + 1)$ B. $(n - 1)$
C. $(2n - 1)$ D. $(2n + 1)$

71. For a spin $\frac{1}{2}$ particle, the expectation value of S_x, S_y, S_z, where S_x, S_y and S_z are spin operators is

A. $\dfrac{i\hbar^3}{8}$ B. $-\dfrac{i\hbar^3}{8}$

C. $\dfrac{i\hbar^3}{16}$ D. $-\dfrac{i\hbar^3}{16}$

72. What Boolean expression describes the output X of this arrangement?

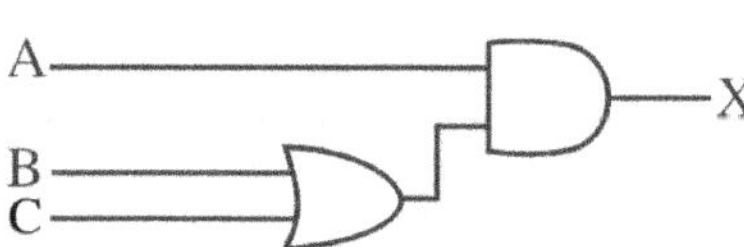

A. X = A – (B – C)
B. X = A + B + C
C. X = A · (B + C)
D. X = (A · B) – C

73. The line integral $\int_A^B \vec{F}\cdot d\vec{l}$, where

$\vec{F} = \dfrac{x}{\sqrt{x^2+y^2}}\hat{x} + \dfrac{y}{\sqrt{x^2+y^2}}\hat{y}$, along the semi-circular path as shown in the figure below is

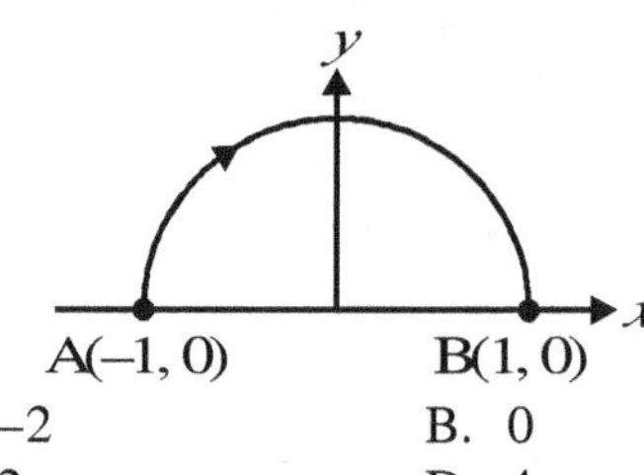

A. –2 B. 0
C. 2 D. 4

74. In the Fourier series of the periodic function (shown in the figure)

$f(x) = |\sin x|$

π 2π

$= \sum_{n=0}^{\infty}\left[\alpha_n \cos nx + \beta_n \sin nx\right]$

which of the following coefficients are non-zero?

A. α_n for odd n B. α_n for even n
C. β_n for odd n D. β_n for even n

75. A Carnot's engine whose low temperature reservoir is at 7°C has an efficiency 50%. It is desired to increase the efficiency to 70%. By how many degrees should the temperature of the hot reservoir be increased? By how many degrees should the temperature of the cold reservoir be decreased?

A. 115 K B. 112 K
C. 110 K D. 118 K

ANSWERS

1	2	3	4	5	6	7	8	9	10
A	C	A	A	D	D	B	B	B	A
11	**12**	**13**	**14**	**15**	**16**	**17**	**18**	**19**	**20**
B	D	B	D	B	B	A	A	B	B
21	**22**	**23**	**24**	**25**	**26**	**27**	**28**	**29**	**30**
B	C	B	C	A	D	B	C	C	C

31	32	33	34	35	36	37	38	39	40
B	A	A	D	B	C	C	B	C	C
41	**42**	**43**	**44**	**45**	**46**	**47**	**48**	**49**	**50**
D	C	B	C	D	A	D	A	C	D
51	**52**	**53**	**54**	**55**	**56**	**57**	**58**	**59**	**60**
C	B	C	C	D	A	B	D	A	C
61	**62**	**63**	**64**	**65**	**66**	**67**	**68**	**69**	**70**
B	B	B	A	C	B	B	A	D	D
71	**72**	**73**	**74**	**75**					
A	C	C	B	B					

EXPLANATORY ANSWERS

1. In ΔBDC,

$BD^2 = BC^2 - 16$

$BC^2 = 16 + BD^2$

In ΔABC,

$AB^2 = (13)^2 - BC^2 = 169 - 16 - BD^2$

Again In ΔABD, $BD^2 = AB^2 - 81$

$BD^2 = 169 - 16 - BD^2 - 81$

$2BD^2 = 169 - 97 = 72$

$BD^2 = 36$

$\therefore$ BD = 6 cm.

2. Average profit made by company A in all the years $= ₹\ \frac{(3+5+4+5+6+6) \text{ lakhs}}{6}$

$= ₹\frac{29 \text{ lakhs}}{6} \approx ₹\ 4.83$ lakh = ₹ 4,83,000.

3. Windy conditions results in increased transpiration rates, the increase being more pronounced at low wind speeds (breeze). High wind results in closing of stomata which may stop transpiration. When there is no breeze then the air surrounding a leaf becomes increasingly humid thus reducing rate of transpiration.

4. The term half-life is defined as the time it takes for one-half of the atoms of a radioactive material to disintegrate. Half lives for various radioisotopes can range from a few microseconds to billions of years.

5. A : B = 4 : 3 and B : C = 2 : 3

Therefore, A : B : C = 8 : 6 : 9

Hence, C's profit $= \frac{9}{23} \times 46000 = ₹\ 18000$

6. Let $P(B) = x$, $P(A) = 2x/3$

$P(A) + P(B) = x + 2x/3 = 1 \Rightarrow 5x/3 = 1$

$\Rightarrow\ x = 3/5$

$P(A) = 2/5$, $P(B) = 3/5$

Odds in favours of B $= \frac{3/5}{1-3/5} = \frac{3}{2}$.

7. Interest received in 2009 from Company B $= \frac{20000 \times 14.5 \times 1}{100} = ₹\ 2900$

Hence, their amount = 20000 + 2900 = ₹ 22900

Interest will be received in 2010 from Company A $= \frac{22900 \times 12.5 \times 1}{100} = ₹\ 2862.50$.

Hence, total amount of interests for both years = 2900 + 2862.50 = ₹ 5762.50.

8. Let, breadth = l metres.

Then, Height = 5 l metres

and length = 40 l metres

So, $l \times 5l \times 40l = 12.8$

or $l^3 = \frac{12.8}{200} = \frac{128}{2000} = \frac{64}{1000}$

So, l = 4 /10 m = (4/10 × 100) cm = 40 cm.

9. The smaller 64 pieces will be cut in the manner that :

1. 8 pieces will be painted on 3 sides,
2. 24 pieces on 2 sides.
3. 24 pieces on 1 side, and
4. 8 will not have paint at all.

Diagrammatically, the explanation taking one side of the cube will be :

a	b	b	a
b	c	c	b
b	c	c	b
a	b	b	a

1. 'a' are the corner pieces $[4 \times 2 = 8]$
2. 'b' are the centre pieces of the cornered sides $[8 \times 3 = 24]$
3. 'c' are the centre pieces $[4 \times 6 = 24]$
4. Remaining interior pieces
   $= 64 - (8 + 24 + 24)$
   $= 64 - 56 = 8.$

10. Let CD = h unit be the height of the tower and A and B be the two points on the ground, such that DA = a; DB = b; $\angle$ DAC = α and $\angle$ DBC = $90° - \alpha$.

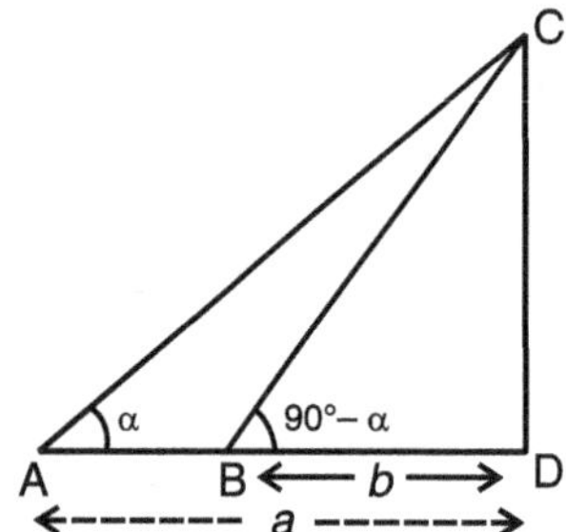

From right triangle ADC,

$$CD = h = a \tan\alpha \quad ...(i)$$

From right triangle BDC,

$$CD = h = b \tan (90° - \alpha) = b \cot \alpha \quad ...(ii)$$

Multiplying equations (i) and (ii), we get

$h^2 = a \tan \alpha \cdot b \cot \alpha$ Hence, $h = \sqrt{ab}$.

11. Let AB = 75 m be the height of pole and C is a point on the ground such that BC = 75 m.
Now, from right triangle ABC,

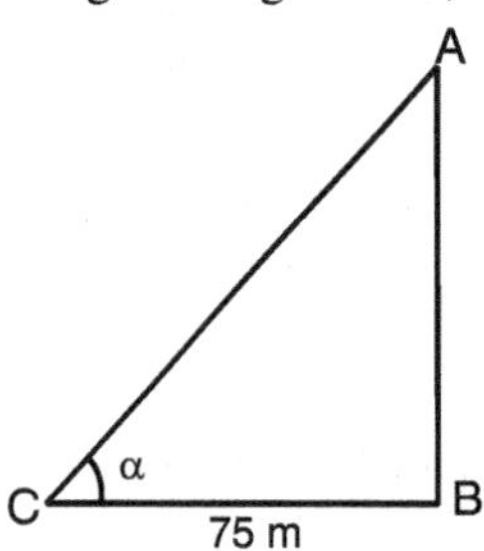

$$\tan \alpha = \frac{AB}{BC} = \frac{75}{75}$$

$\Rightarrow$ $\tan \alpha = 1$ $\therefore$ $\alpha = 45°$.

12.

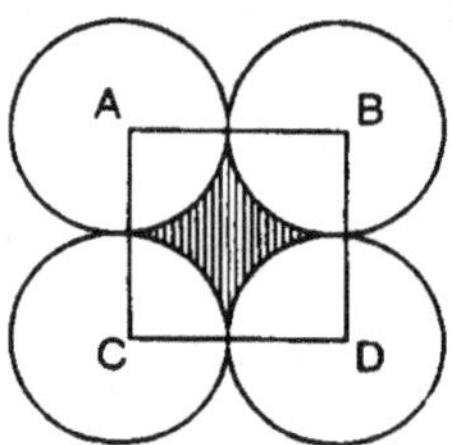

Area of square ABCD = $1^2 = 1$ square metre

And Area of the 4 sectors $= 4 \times \frac{1}{4}\pi\left(\frac{1}{2}\right)^2$

$= \pi/4$ square metre

$\therefore$ Area of the shaded part $= \left(1 - \frac{\pi}{4}\right)$ square metre.

13. Roots of the equation
$x^2 + px + p/4 + 1/2 = 0$ are real if $D = p^2 - 4(p/4 + 1/2) \geq 0$
i.e., $(p - 2)(p + 1) \geq 0$ *i.e.*, $p \leq -1$ or $p \geq 2$
In $0 \leq p \leq 5$, possible values of p are 2, 3, 4, 5
Thus, probability = 4/6 = 2/3.

14. $P(A \cup B) = P(A) + P(B) - P(A \cap B)$
$P(A \cup B) = 0.25 + 0.50 - 0.12 = 0.63$
$P(\overline{A \cup B}) = 1 - P(A \cup B) = 1 - 0.63 = 0.37.$

15. Separate profit for A $= \frac{1040 \times 25}{100} =$ ₹ 260

Remaining profit = ₹ (1040 – 260) = ₹ 780
Ratio of capitals of A and B
= 2100 : 3100 = 21 : 31

A's profit $= \frac{21}{52} \times 780 =$ ₹ 315

B's profit $= \frac{31}{52} \times 780 =$ ₹ 465

Total profit of A = ₹ (315 + 260) = ₹ 575
Therefore A and B will make profit of ₹ 575 and ₹ 465 respectively.

16. Let AB = h m be the height of the tower; C and D are the two points on the ground such that BC = 60 m; ∠ ACB = 45° and ∠ ADB = 30°. Now from right triangle ABC,

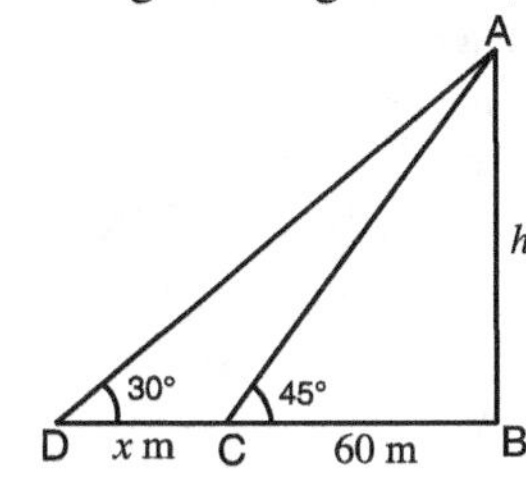

$$\tan 45° = \frac{h}{60}$$

$$\Rightarrow \quad 1 = \frac{h}{60} \qquad \therefore h = 60 \text{ m}$$

Again from right triangle ABD;

$$\tan 30° = \frac{h}{x+60}$$

$$\Rightarrow \quad \frac{1}{\sqrt{3}} = \frac{60}{x+60}$$

$$\Rightarrow x + 60 = 60\sqrt{3}$$

$$\therefore x = 60\ (1.73 - 1) = 43.8 \text{ m}$$

Hence, speed of boat = $\frac{43.8}{5}$ m/s

$$= \frac{43.8}{5} \times \frac{18}{5} \simeq 31.5 \text{ km/hr.}$$

17. Let A denotes the event that a six occurs and B the event that the man reports that it is a six. Then the probability that it is actually a six is given by

$$P(A/B) = \frac{P(A \cap B)}{P(B)}$$

Now $P(A \cap B) = \frac{1}{6} \cdot \frac{3}{4} = \frac{3}{24} = \frac{1}{8}$

$$P(B) = P(A \cap B) + P(\overline{A} \cap \overline{B})$$

$$= \frac{1}{6} \cdot \frac{3}{4} + \frac{5}{6} \cdot \frac{1}{4} = \frac{8}{24} = \frac{1}{3}$$

Hence $P(A/B) = \frac{1/8}{1/3} = \frac{3}{8}$.

18. Till 8 a.m., the train from A covers a distance of 20 km.
Now, the remaining distance 110 – 20 = 90 km is covered by the trains with relative speed = 20 + 25 = 45 km/hr.

So, they meet after = $\frac{90}{45}$ = 2 hrs

That is, at 8 + 2 = 10 a.m.

Quicker Maths (Direct formula) :

They will meet at

$$8 \text{ a.m.} + \frac{110 - (8 \text{ a.m.} - 7 \text{ a.m.})\, 20}{20 + 25}$$

$$= 8 \text{ a.m.} + 2 \text{ hr} = 10 \text{ a.m.}$$

19. Here, $20 + x + \frac{20 \times x}{100} = 50$

$$\Rightarrow x + \frac{x}{5} = 30$$

$$\Rightarrow \frac{6x}{5} = 30 \qquad \therefore x = \frac{5 \times 30}{6} = 25$$

Hence, breadth was increased by 25%.

20. Coordinates of Q and R being the same. QR is parallel to x-axis.
So, PT, being the x-axis
Now, QR = 2 units
PT = 4 units
QR ∥ PT

So, PQRT is a trapezium.

Area of quadrilateral PQRS
= Area of PQRT – area of PST

$$= \left(\frac{2+4}{2}\right) \times 4 - 4 \times \frac{1}{2} = 10.$$

21. The given function $f(x) = x \sin x$ is an even function. Hence, series will be

$$f(x) = x \sin x$$

$$= a_0 + \sum_n a_n \cos nx \qquad ...(1)$$

$$a_0 = \frac{2}{\pi} \int_0^{\pi} f(x)\, dx$$

$$= \frac{2}{\pi} \int_0^{\pi} x \sin x\, dx = 1 \qquad ...(2)$$

and $a_m = \frac{2}{\pi} \int_0^{\pi} x \sin x \cos x\, dx = \frac{2 \cos n\pi}{n^2 - 1}$ ...(3)

for $n \neq 1, n \to$ integer

If $n = 1$

$$\Rightarrow a_1 = \frac{2}{\pi}\int_0^{\pi} x \sin x \cos x \, dx = -\frac{1}{2}$$

Substituting (2), (3) and (4) in (1), we get

$f(x) = x \sin x$

$$= 1 - 2\left[-\frac{\cos x}{4} + \frac{\cos 2x}{1.3} - \frac{\cos 3x}{2.4} + \frac{\cos 4x}{3.5} + \ldots\right]$$

$\Rightarrow$ Substitute $x = \frac{\pi}{2}$

$$\Rightarrow \frac{\pi}{2}\sin\frac{\pi}{2} = 1 - 2\left[-\frac{1}{1.3} + \frac{1}{3.5} + \frac{1}{5.7} + \ldots\right]$$

Dividing each side by 2

$$\Rightarrow \frac{\pi}{4} = \frac{1}{2} + \frac{1}{1.3} - \frac{1}{3.5} + \frac{1}{5.7}\ldots\Big]$$

22. Normalization condition,

$$\int_{-\infty}^{+\infty} |\psi(x, 0)|^2 \, dx = 1$$

$$\Rightarrow |N|^2 \int_{-\infty}^{\infty}\left(e^{-x^2/2a^2} \cdot e^{-ik_0x}\right)\left(e^{-x^2/2a^2} \cdot e^{-ik_0x}\right)dx = 1$$

$$|N|^2 \int_{-\infty}^{\infty} e^{-x^2/a^2} dx = |N|^2 a\sqrt{\pi} = 1$$

$$|N| = \frac{1}{a^{1/2}\pi^{1/4}}.$$

23. Change in entropy

$$\Delta S = \frac{dQ}{dT} = \frac{2000}{500 - 400}$$

$$= \frac{2000}{100} \text{ cal/K}$$

$\Delta S = 20$ cal/K

24. Peak-to-peak ripple voltage for the capacitor input filter.

$$V_r(\text{PP}) = \left(\frac{1}{f R_L C}\right) V_P(\text{rect})$$

$$= \frac{1}{120 \times 10 \text{k}\Omega \times 10 \times \mu\text{F}} \times 60 \text{ V}$$

$$= \frac{1}{2 \times 10 \times 10^3 \times 10 \times 10^{-6}} \text{V}$$

$$= \frac{10}{2}$$

$V = 5.0$ V

25. MSB resistance,

$R = 2$ kΩ

LSB resistance, $R_n = 2^{n-1}$ R

As it a 4-bit weighted resistor D/A converter, hence

$n = 4$

26. As, $T = 2\pi\sqrt{\frac{l}{g}}$

$$\therefore \quad g = 4\pi^2 \frac{l}{T^2}$$

$$\frac{\Delta g}{g} \times 100 = \frac{\Delta l}{l} \times 100 + 2 \times \frac{\Delta T}{T} \times 100$$

$= 0.5\% + 2 \times 0.2\% \ = 0.9\%$.

27.

$\theta_1 = 30°$C

$\theta_2 = 60°$C

$\theta_0 = 45°$C

$R_1 = 5\ \Omega$

$R_2 = 6.5\ \Omega$

$$\therefore \quad R_0 = \frac{5 + 6.5}{2} = \frac{11.5}{2}$$

$\simeq 5.75\ \Omega$.

and on solving for temperature co-efficient it is found to be = 0.0087/°C.

28. $l = l_0\sqrt{1 - \frac{v^2}{c^2}}$

Now, $l = l_0$

$$\frac{1}{2}l_0 = l_0\sqrt{1 - \frac{v^2}{c^2}}$$

$$\frac{1}{4} = 1 - \frac{v^2}{c^2}$$

$$\Rightarrow \frac{v^2}{c^2} = 1 - \frac{1}{4} = \frac{3}{4}$$

Now, time period,

$$\tau = \frac{\tau_0}{\sqrt{1 - \frac{v^2}{c^2}}}$$

$$= \frac{\tau_0}{\sqrt{1-\frac{3}{4}}}$$

$$= \frac{\tau_0}{\sqrt{\frac{1}{4}}}$$

$$= 2\,\tau_0$$

Hence, time interval becomes twice.

29. Since diagonal cut orthogonally therefore, it becomes a equipotential surface. It will contain the same potential.

30. Let us consider a wave function ψ and operate at its operator.

$$\left(\frac{d}{dx}+x\right)^2 \psi = \left(\frac{d}{dx}+x\right)\left(\frac{d}{dx}+x\right)\psi$$

$$= \frac{d}{dx}\left(\frac{d\psi}{dx}+x\psi\right)+\left(\frac{xd\psi}{dx}+x\psi\right)$$

$$= \frac{d^2\psi}{dx^2}+x\frac{d\psi}{dx}+\psi+x\frac{d\psi}{dx}+x^2\psi$$

$$= \left(\frac{d^2}{dx^2}+2x\frac{d\psi}{dx}+x^2+1\right)\psi$$

or $\left(\frac{d}{dx}+x\right)^2$

$$= \left(\frac{d^2}{dx^2}+2x\frac{d}{dx}+x^2+1\right).$$

31. $\bar{E}=\frac{1}{N}\int_0^\infty E\,N(N)\,dE$

Which gives, $\bar{E}=\frac{3}{2}kT.$

32. $t_{max} = \frac{I^2+(\text{rating})}{I_s^2}$

$I_s \to$ known value of surge assume

$$t_{max} = \frac{50}{(100)^2} = 5\times10^{-3}\text{s}$$

$= 5$ ms.

33. The radius of nth permissible orbit for electron in hydrogen is given by

$$r_n = \left(\frac{\pi^2 h^2 \in_0}{\pi m Z e^2}\right) = \frac{n^2h^2 \in_o I}{\pi m Z e^2}$$

For Helium atom, Z = 2

$$\therefore\ r_{He} = \frac{n^2h^2\in_0}{2\pi m e^2} = \frac{0.05\text{ nm}}{2} = 0.025\text{ nm.}$$

34. For the diamond structure

$$r = \frac{\sqrt{3}\,a}{8}$$

$$\text{Packing fraction} = \frac{8\times\frac{4}{3}\pi\cdot r^3}{a^3}$$

$$= \frac{\frac{32\pi}{3}\cdot\left(\frac{\sqrt{3}}{8}a\right)^3}{a^3}$$

$$= \frac{\sqrt{3}}{16}\pi$$

35. Half-life T

$$(2)^{-7/T} = \frac{1}{2.5}$$

$$\frac{7}{T} = \frac{\ln 2.5}{\ln 2}$$

$$T = \frac{7\ln 2}{\ln 2.5} = 5.3\text{ days}$$

36. The reaction is strongest with the target of ^{41}Ca. In the reaction the proton combines with a neutron in ^{41}Ca to form a deuterons.The isotope ^{41}Ca has an excess neutron outside of a double full shell, which means that the BE of the last neutron is lower than those of ^{40}Ca. ^{39}Ca and so it is easier to pick up.

37. Given $np = 10$, $npq = 2^2 = 4$

$$p = \frac{4}{10} = \frac{2}{5}$$

$$p = (1-q) = \frac{2}{5}$$

$= 0.6.$

38. We know, $PV = nRT$ ...(1)

and $\Delta S = \frac{\Delta Q}{T}$

$$\therefore \quad T = \frac{\Delta Q}{\Delta S}$$

$$\Delta Q = T\Delta S$$

From equation (1), we get

$$T = \frac{PV}{nR}$$

$$\therefore \quad \Delta Q = \frac{PV\Delta S}{nR}.$$

39. $Y_{10} = \sqrt{\frac{3}{4\pi}} \cos\theta,\ Y_{1,\pm 1}$

$$= \mp\sqrt{\frac{3}{8\pi}} \sin\theta\, e^{\pm i\phi}$$

$$\psi = \sqrt{\frac{1}{3}}(-\sqrt{2})\, Y_{11} + Y_{10}\, g(r)$$

Now, expectation value of L_2

$$< L_2 > = \int \psi^{x} L_2 \psi r^2 \sin\theta\, d\theta\, d\phi\, dr$$

$$= \int \left[\sqrt{\frac{1}{3}}\left(-\sqrt{2}\, Y_{11} + Y_{10}\right)\right]$$

$$\times \hat{L}_2 \left[\sqrt{\frac{1}{3}}\left(-\sqrt{2}\right) Y_{11} + Y_{10}\right]$$

$$\times\ [g(r)]^2 r^2 dr \sin\theta\, d\theta\, d\phi.$$

$$= \frac{2}{3}\hbar \int_0^k d\theta \int_0^{2\pi} \times \frac{2}{11} d\phi = \frac{2}{3}\hbar.$$

40. Here, $m = ?$, $m_2 = 1500$ gms

$T_1 = 373$ K, $T_2 = 273 + 15 = 288$ K

$(540 + 20)\, m_1 = 1500 \times 6.5$

$\Rightarrow m_1 = 175$ gms.

41. Modulation index

$$m = \frac{V_{max} - V_{min}}{V_{max} + V_{min}}$$

Here, $\quad V_{max} = 10$ V

$V_{min} = 5$ V

$$m = \frac{10-5}{10+5} = \frac{5}{15} = \frac{1}{3}$$

$= 0.333.$

42. To create a hole, an electrons from the valence band should be given sufficient energy to go into one of the acceptor levels. Since the acceptor levels are 57 MeV above the valence band, at last 57 meV is needed to create a hole. In λ be the wavelength of light, its photon will have an energy held.

To create a hole,

$$\frac{hc}{\lambda} \geq 57 \text{ meV}$$

or, $$\lambda \leq \frac{hc}{57 \text{ meV}}$$

$$= \frac{1242 \text{ eV mm}}{57 \times 10^{-3} \text{ eV}} = 2.18 \times 10^{-5} \text{ m}.$$

43. Heat rejected during the condensation of steam in one minute

$= (100 \text{ g}) \times (540 \text{ cal g}^{-1})$

$= 5.4 \times 10^4$ cal

Heat rejected during the cooling of water

$= 100 \text{ g} \times 1 \text{ cal g}^{-1}\ {}^\circ\text{C}^{-1}\ (100^\circ\text{C} - 20^\circ\text{C})$

$= 8000$ cal

Thus, heat rejected by the engine per minutes

$= 5.4 \times 10^4 \text{ cal} + 0.8 \times 10^4$ cal

$= 6.2 \times 10^4$ cal

44. The energy density is

$$u_{av} = \frac{1}{2} \epsilon_0\, E_0^2 = \frac{1}{2} \times (8.85 \times 10^{-12} C^2 N^{-1} m^{-2}) \times (50 \text{ NC}^{-1})^2$$

$= 1.1 \times 10^{-8}$ Jm^{-3}

The volume of the cylinder is

$V = 10 \text{ cm}^2 \times 50$ cm

$= 5 \times 10^{-4}$ m^3

The energy contained in this volume is

$U = (1.1 \times 10^{-8} \text{ J m}^{-3}) \times (5 \times 10^4 \text{ m}^3)$

$= 5.5 \times 10^{-12}$ J.

45. Potential energy of the spring shown in the figure:

k k
m m m

$$= \frac{1}{2}k(x_2 - x_1)^2 + \frac{1}{2}k(x_3 - x_2)^2$$

$$= \frac{1}{2}k\left[(x_2 - x_1)^2 + (x_3 - x_2)^2\right]$$

$$= \frac{1}{2}k\left[x_1^2 + 2x_2^2 + x_3^2 - 2x_2(x_1 + x_3)\right].$$

46. According to Gauss's law

$$E(r) = \frac{Q}{4\pi \epsilon_0 r^2}$$

Also, $E(r) = \frac{pr}{(3\epsilon_0)}$

For $r = 0$

Magnitude of electric field $E(r) = 0$.

47. Suppose the process is carried out reversibly by heating the water through the baths of steadily increasing temp.
Then, change in entropy is given by

$$ds = mc\int_{T_1}^{T_2}\frac{dT}{T} = mc\left[\log_{10}\frac{T_2}{T_1}\right]$$

$$= 2.3026\, mc \log_{10}\frac{T_2}{T_1}$$

$$= 2.3026 \times 1000 \times 4.2 \times \log_{10}\frac{353}{293}$$

$$= 782 \text{ J/K}.$$

48. If orbit is circular then

Attractive force = Centrifugal force

$$\Rightarrow \frac{GMm}{(R+H)^2} = \frac{gR^2m}{(R+H)^2}$$

$$= \frac{mv_o^2}{R+H}$$

$v_o \rightarrow$ Orbital velocity

$R \rightarrow$ Radius of earth

$$\Rightarrow v_o = \frac{R}{R+H}\sqrt{[(R+H)g]} \qquad ...(1)$$

If $H << R$

$$\therefore \quad v_o = \sqrt{Rg}$$

Also orbital speed

$$v_o = \frac{2\pi(R+H)}{\tau}$$

or $$\tau = \frac{2\pi(R+H)}{v_o}$$

From equation (1),

$$\tau = 2\pi\left(\frac{R+H}{R}\right)\sqrt{\frac{R+H}{g}}$$

if $H << R$, then $\tau = 2\pi\sqrt{\frac{R}{g}}$.

49. From ampere circuital law

$$\oint \bar{B}\cdot d\bar{l} = \mu_0 I_N$$

I being the net current passing through the loop which will be

$$I_N = I + I - 2I = 0$$

$$\therefore \quad \oint \bar{B}\cdot d\bar{l} = 0$$

$$\bar{B}\cdot 2\pi r = 0$$

$$\Rightarrow \quad \bar{B} = 0.$$

50. Change in collector-emitter voltage,

$$\Delta V_{CE} = 10 - 2 = 8 \text{ V}$$

Change in collector current,

$$\Delta I_C = 3 - 2 = 1 \text{ mA}$$

Output resistance, $R_0 = \frac{\Delta V_{CE}}{\Delta I_C} = \frac{8\text{ V}}{1\text{ mA}} = 8\text{ k}\Omega.$

51. For a ion moving in a magnetic field B with velocity v along a circular path of radius R, we have a relation

$$\frac{Mv^2}{R} = Bnev \quad \Rightarrow R = \frac{Mv}{Bne}$$

For neon – 20,

$$R = \frac{20 \times 1.67 \times 10^{-27} \times 10^5}{0.08 \times 1 \times 1 \times 1.602 \times 10^{-19}} = 0.259 \text{ m}.$$

For the ions with the same velocity and charge in the same magnetic field, radius of the path followed $R \propto M$. Hence for neon-22.

$$R = \left(\frac{22}{20}\right) \times \text{Radius of the path for the neon-20}$$

$$= 0.285 \text{ m}.$$

52. The average energy needed to produce a pair of free ions is larger than the ionisation potential, as part of the energy goes to provide for the kinetic energy of the ions.

53. One electrons acquires an average velocity

$$v_{Dr} = \frac{P}{2\,me} = \frac{eE\tau}{2me}, \text{ in the electric field E,}$$

where τ is the average time-interval between two consecutive collision.

As, $$\lambda = \frac{1}{v_{Dr}} \propto \frac{1}{\sigma v_{Dr}}$$

where l is in the mean free path of the e^- in the gas and σ is the interaction cross-section, we have

$$v_{Dr} \propto \frac{E}{\sigma p} \propto \frac{E}{p}$$

If σ is independent of velocity. If σ is depend on the velocity, the relationship would be much more complicated.

54. The semi-angle of cone of laser beam,

$$\theta = \frac{\lambda}{a} = \frac{800 \times 10^{-9}}{2 \times 10^{-3}}$$
$$= 400 \times 10^{-6}$$

Diameter of the beam 1 m away

$$= 2 \times 400 \times 10^{-6} \times 10^{3}$$
$$= 0.8 \text{ m}$$
$$= 80 \text{ cm.}$$

55. $$I_1 = \frac{0-(-10)\times 10^{-3}}{5k}$$
$$= 2 \times 10^{-6} \text{ A}$$

Hence voltage V_1

$V_1 = 2 \times 10^{-6} \times 100 \times 10^{3}$

$= 200 \times 10^{-3}$ V

Since the gain of the second stage is –1,

$\therefore\ V_{OUT} = -200$ mV.

56. In passing through accelerator, the positive ion carrying a charge *ne*, acquire kinetic energy, given by the relation $\frac{1}{2}M\upsilon^2 = neV$

$$\frac{M(\upsilon)^2}{k} = Bnev$$

From these relations we have

$$v = \frac{2V}{RB} = \frac{2 \times 1000}{18.2 \times 10^{-2} \times 1000 \times 10^{-4}}$$
$$= 1.099 \times 10^{5} \text{ metre/sec}$$

57. The non-inverting input sees a Thevenin resistance of 1 kΩ and the inverting input sees a Thevenin resistance of approximately 100 Ω. We have Input bias current = 80 nA and input offset current = 20 nA.

The two possible solutions for the input bias currents are

$$I_{B_1} = 90 \text{ nA}, \quad I_{B_2} = 70 \text{ nA},$$
$$I_{B_1} = 70 \text{ nA}, \quad I_{B_2} = 90 \text{ nA}$$

The worst combination is 90 nA through the 1 kΩ and 70 nA through the 100 Ω, because this produces more output offset voltage.

The maximum input offset is

$$V_1 - V_2 = 2 \text{ mV} + (90 \text{ nA})(1 \text{ k}\Omega) - (70 \text{ nA})(100\ \Omega)$$
$$= 2 \text{ mV} + 90\ \mu\text{V} - 7\ \mu\text{V}$$
$$= 2.08 \text{ mV}$$

The desensitivity

$$1 + AB = 1 + 100{,}000\left(\frac{100}{100{,}000}\right) = 101$$

Now the closed loop output offset voltage

$$V_{OO(CL)} = \frac{100{,}000\ (2.08 \text{ mV})}{101}$$
$$= 2.06 \text{ V}$$

The means that we have lost 2.06 V of the output range because of offset voltages and currents. We can reduce the closed loop output offset voltage, by decrease the closed-loop voltage gain to 100 (done by changing feedback resistors). Then the densitivity increases to

$$1 + AB = \frac{A}{A_{CL}} = \frac{100{,}000}{100} = 1000$$

and the closed loop output offset voltage drops to approximately

$$V_{OO(CL)} = \frac{100{,}000\ (2.08 \text{ mV})}{1000}$$
$$= 0.208 \text{ V.}$$

58. Total mass of potassium in 100 kg man

$$= 100 \times 0.35 \times 10^{-2} = 0.35 \text{ kg}$$

$\therefore$ Mass of k^{40} as it is 0.012% of the total mass of potassium.

$$= 0.350 \times 0.012 \times 10^{-2}$$
$$= 4.20 \times 10^{-5} \text{ kg}$$

From Avogadro's hypothesis, kg atom of a substance consists 6.023×10^{26} atoms. Hence the number of k^{40} atoms

$$N = \frac{6.023 \times 10^{26}}{40} \times 4.2 \times 10^{-5}$$

$$= 6.32425 \times 10^{20}$$

$\therefore$ Activity of $k^{40} = \lambda N$

$$= (0.693/T)\, N$$

$$= \frac{0.693 \times 6.32425 \times 10^{20}}{1.31 \times 10^{9} \times 365 \times 24 \times 60 \times 60}$$

$= 1.061 \times 10^4$ disintegrations/sec.

$= 0.287$ micro curie.

59. The product of the eigenvalues of a matrix A is equal to the determinant of A

$$\therefore\ |A| = \lambda_1 . \lambda_2 . \lambda_3$$

$$4 = -1 \times (+2) \times (\lambda_3)$$

or $\lambda_3 = -2$.

60. Inside the metal sphere

$$E = P = D = 0$$

and $D = \in E$

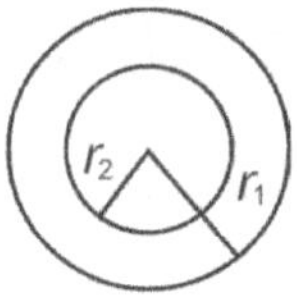

$$D = \frac{Q}{4\pi r^2}\hat{r} \text{ for all points } r > a$$

$$\therefore\quad E = \begin{cases} \dfrac{q}{4\pi \in r^2}\hat{r} & \text{for } r_1 < r < r_2 \\ \dfrac{q}{4\pi \in_0 r^2}\hat{r} & \text{for } r < r_2 \end{cases}$$

Potential at $r > r_2$

$$V = -\int E.dr = \frac{q}{4\pi \in_0 r}$$

and potential at centre

$$V = -\int_\infty^0 \bar{E}.d\bar{l}$$

$$= -\int_\infty^{r_2}\left(\frac{q}{4\pi \in_0 r^2}\right)dr$$

$$-\int_{r_2}^{r_1}\frac{q}{4\pi \in_0 r^2}dr - \int_{r_1}^{0} 0.dr$$

so for points $r > r_2$

$$V = \frac{q}{4\pi \in_0 r}.$$

61. Magnetic moment = nIA

$$M = nI\pi R^2$$

Now, $\quad I \rightarrow I/2$ and $R \rightarrow 2R$

$$M_2 = n \cdot \frac{1}{2}\pi\,(2R)^2$$

$$= 2nI\pi R^2$$

$$= 2\,M.$$

62. Knowing that $R_f = 2.2\ k\Omega$

and the absolute value of the closed loop gain is $\quad |A_{CeCi}| = 100$

R_I can be calculated as

$$|A_{CeCi}| = R_f/R_i$$

or $\quad R_f = R_i\,|A_C|$

$$= 100 \times 12.2\ k\Omega$$

$$= 220\ k\Omega.$$

63. Overall conductivity of a semiconductor containing electrons and holes given by

$$\sigma = \sigma_n + \sigma_p$$

$$= e\,(n\mu_n + p\mu_p)$$

For intrinsic semiconductor

$$n = p$$

$$\therefore\ \sigma = e \times n\,(\mu_n + \mu_p)$$

$$= 1.6 \times 10^{-19} \times 2.4 \times 10^{19}\ (0.39 + 0.19)$$

$= 2.22$ mho/m.

64. As deuteron conversion of equal number of neutron and proton, the reduced mass of system,

$$m = \frac{M_n M_p}{M_n + M_p} = \frac{M}{2}$$

Maximum energy,

$$E = \frac{e^2 B^2 r^2}{2M}$$

For deuteron,

$$E_1 = \frac{e^2B^2r^2}{2(M/2)} = 20$$

or, $$\frac{e^2B^2r^2}{2M} = \frac{20}{2} = 10 \text{ MeV}$$

Max. energy of proton

$$= \frac{e^2B^2r^2}{2M}$$

$$= 10 \text{ MeV}$$

65. To go through the ionosphere, the angular freq. ω of a wave should be greater than plasma freq.

$$\omega_p = \sqrt{\frac{Ne^2}{\epsilon_0 m}}$$

The maximum electron density of a typical layer is $N \simeq 10^{13} \text{ m}^{-3}$

For an electron, $\frac{e^2}{\epsilon_0 m} = 3 \times 10^3 \text{ m}^3 \text{ s}^{-2}$

Hence, $$\omega_p = \sqrt{3 \times 10^{16}}$$

$$= 1.7 \times 10^8 \text{ s}^{-1} \simeq 10^8 \text{ Hz}$$

66. Taylor series expansion of

$$ln\ (x) = -\sum_{K=1}^{\infty} \frac{(-1)^K(-1+x)^K}{K}$$

for $|-1 + x| < 1$

$$= \log(-1+x) - \sum_{K=1}^{\infty} \frac{(-1)^K}{K(-1+x)^K}$$

for $|-1 + x| > 1$

Based on that Taylor series of

$$ln\ (\cos hx) = \frac{x^2}{2} - \frac{x^4}{12} + \frac{x^6}{45} - \frac{17x^8}{2520}$$

$$+ \frac{31x^{10}}{14175} - \frac{691x^{12}}{935550}.$$

67. Ideal gas equation

$$\frac{P_1V_1}{T_1} = \frac{P_2V_2}{T_2}$$

or, $$\frac{T_2}{T_1} = \frac{V_2}{V_1}$$ (For $P_1 = P_2 = 1$ atm)

or, $$\frac{T_2}{T_1} = \frac{\rho_1}{\rho_2}$$

$$T_2 = \frac{1}{1000} \times T_1 = \frac{2.17}{1000} \Rightarrow 21.7 \text{ mK}$$

68. By comparing

$$H_z = H_0 \cos\left(\frac{m\pi x}{a}\right)\cos\left(\frac{n\pi y}{b}\right)$$

$$\frac{m}{a} = 0.3$$

$$\frac{n}{b} = 0.4$$

For TE_{11} mode $m = 1, n = 1$

So, $a = \frac{1}{0.3} \Rightarrow a = 3.33$

$b = \frac{1}{0.4}. \Rightarrow b = 2.5$

69. Magnetization

$$M(N, T, H) = \left\langle \sum_{i=1}^{H} \mu_i \right\rangle$$

where $\mathcal{H} = -\sum_{i=1}^{N} \bar{\mu}_i \cdot \bar{H}$

$$\langle \mathcal{H} \rangle = -H \cdot M$$

Also, $\langle \mathcal{H} \rangle = E$

So, $$M = -\frac{E}{H} \quad \text{...(1)}$$

Now, $$E = -\frac{1}{z}\frac{\partial \ln z}{\partial \beta}$$

where $$z = \sum_{\{S_i\}} e^{-\beta H} \sum_{1} \bar{\mu}_i s_i$$

$$= \sum_{\{S_i\}} \prod_{i=1}^{N} e^{-\beta H \bar{\mu}_i s_i}$$

$$= \prod_{i=1}^{N} \Sigma\, e^{-\beta H \mu_i s_i}$$

$$= (e^{\mu\beta H} + e^{-\mu\beta H})^N$$

$$= (2\cos\hbar\ \beta H \mu)^N$$

As, $$\beta = \frac{1}{k_B T}$$

So, $$E = -\frac{\partial}{\partial \beta}\left(2\cos\hbar\frac{\mu H}{kT}\right)$$

$$= -\mu H \tan \hbar \frac{\mu H}{kT}$$

So, equation (1) will give

$$M = + \mu \tan \hbar \frac{\mu H}{kT}$$

70. The energy level in a one dimensional potential box is given by

$$E_n = \frac{n^2h^2}{8ma^2}$$

lowest energy level

$$E_1 = \frac{h^2}{8ma^2}$$

and $E_n = n^2 E_1$

The spacing between the *n*th energy level and the next higher level increases as

$$(n+1)^2 E_1 - n^2 E_1$$
$$= (n^2 + 2n + 1) E_1 - n^2 E_1$$
$$= (2n+1) E_1.$$

71. $$S_x S_y S_z = \frac{\hbar\sigma_x}{2} \times \frac{\hbar\sigma_y}{2} \times \frac{\hbar\sigma_z}{2}$$

$$= \frac{\hbar^3}{8}(\sigma_x\sigma_y\sigma_z)$$

$$= \frac{\hbar^3}{8}\left[\begin{pmatrix} 0 & 1 \\ 1 & 0 \end{pmatrix}\begin{pmatrix} 0 & -i \\ i & 0 \end{pmatrix}\sigma_z\right]$$

$$= \frac{\hbar^3}{8}\left[\begin{pmatrix} i & 0 \\ 0 & -i \end{pmatrix}\sigma_z\right]$$

$$= \frac{\hbar^3}{8}(i\sigma_z \cdot \sigma_z)$$

$$= \frac{\hbar^3}{8}i$$

$$= \frac{i\hbar^3}{8}.$$

72. In the circuit, we see that there are three gates, so the Boolean expression will be

$$X = A(B + C).$$

73. $$\vec{F} = \frac{x}{\sqrt{x^2+y^2}}\hat{x} + \frac{y}{\sqrt{x^2+y^2}}\hat{y}$$

$$\int_A^B \vec{F} \cdot d\vec{l} = \int_A^B \left(\frac{x}{\sqrt{x^2+y^2}}\hat{x} + \frac{y}{\sqrt{x^2+y^2}}\hat{y}\right)(dx\,\hat{x} + dy\,\hat{y})$$

$$= \int_A^B \frac{x}{\sqrt{x^2+y^2}} dx\,\hat{x}\cdot\hat{x} + \int_A^B \frac{y}{\sqrt{x^2+y^2}} dy\,\hat{y}\cdot\hat{y}$$

since $\hat{x}\cdot\hat{x} = 1,\quad \hat{y}\cdot\hat{y} = 1$

$\hat{x}\cdot\hat{y} = 0,\quad \hat{y}\cdot\hat{x} = 0$

so, $$\int_A^B \frac{x}{\sqrt{x^2+y^2}} dx + \int_A^B \frac{y}{\sqrt{x^2+y^2}} dy$$

by figure putting limit

$$\int_{-1}^{1} \frac{x}{\sqrt{x^2+y^2}} dx + \int_0^0 \frac{y}{\sqrt{x^2+y^2}} dy$$

let $z = \sqrt{x^2+y^2}$

diff. both sides

$$dz = \frac{2x}{2\sqrt{x^2+y^2}} dx$$

$$\int_{-1}^{1} dz + \int_0^0 dz$$

$$[z]_{-1}^{1} + 0$$

$$[1 - (-1)] = 2.$$

74. The given function is $f(x) = |\sin x|$

clearly period of $f(x)$ is π

Now from Fourier formula

$$f(x) = \frac{\alpha_0}{2} + \sum_{n=1}^{\infty} \alpha_n \cos nx + \sum_{n=1}^{\infty} \beta_n \sin nx$$

Now $$\alpha_0 = \frac{1}{\pi}\int_0^{\pi} |\sin x| dx = \frac{1}{\pi}\int_0^{\pi} \sin x\, dx$$

$$= \frac{2}{\pi}. \neq 0$$

$$\alpha_n = \frac{2}{\pi}\int_0^{\pi} |\sin x| \cos n x\, dx$$

$$= \frac{2}{\pi}\int_0^{\pi} \sin x . \cos nx\, dx$$

$$= \frac{1}{\pi}\int_0^{\pi} \left[\sin(n+1)x - \sin(n-1)x\right] dx$$

$$= \frac{1}{\pi}\left[\frac{\cos[n-1]x}{n-1} - \frac{\cos(n+1)x}{n+1}\right]_0^{\pi}$$

$$= \frac{1}{\pi}\left[2\left(\frac{1}{n-1}\right) - 2\left(\frac{1}{n+1}\right)\right] \text{ if } n = \text{even}$$

$$= \frac{1}{\pi}(0-0) \text{ if } n = \text{odd};$$

$\Rightarrow \alpha_n = 0$ for n = odd.

Also $\beta_n = \frac{2}{\pi}\int_0^{\pi} f(x) \sin nx\, dx$

$$= \frac{1}{\pi}\int_0^{\pi} \left[\cos(n-1)x - \cos(n+1)x\right] dx$$

$$= \frac{1}{\pi}\left[\frac{\sin(n-1)x}{n-1} - \frac{\sin(n+1)x}{n+1}\right]_0^{\pi}$$

$$\therefore \quad \beta_n = \frac{1}{\pi}[0-0] \Rightarrow \beta_n = 0 \ \forall\ n.$$

75. Let T be the temp. of the hot reservoir.

Then, $50 = \left(1 - \frac{273+7}{T}\right) \times 100$ or $T = 560$ K

Let T' be the required temp.

Then, $70 = \left(1 - \frac{273+7}{T'}\right) \times 100$ or $T' = 933.3$ K

Let T" be the required temp. of the cold reservoir.

Then, $70 = \left(1 - \frac{T''}{560}\right) \times 100$ or T" = 168 K

$\therefore$ Required decrease in temperature

= (273 + 7) – 168 = 112 K.

YOUR SPACE

YOUR SPACE

www.ingramcontent.com/pod-product-compliance
Lightning Source LLC
Chambersburg PA
CBHW060114120726
48003CB00009B/2626
* 9 7 8 9 3 8 6 2 9 8 6 4 5 *